Alfred E. Lee's Civil War

Alfred E. Lee's Civil War

Edited by Daniel A. Masters

Columbian Arsenal Press
Perrysburg, Ohio

First Printing: 2018

ISBN: 978-1-387-30360-1

Columbian Arsenal Press
1310 Mary Lou Ct.
Perrysburg, Ohio 43551
www.columbianarsenal.com
Email: columbianarsenal@gmail.com

Dedicated to my beautiful daughters Ashley, Adeline, and Claire

~with a father's love and hopes that the nation so many gave their lives to save for our generation, will always strive to fulfill the promises of its founding for yours...

Contents

Illustrations

Introduction

Alfred Emory Lee was born February 17, 1838 in Barnesville, Belmont County, Ohio to Isaac and Esther (Zinn) Lee, the eldest brother in a family of six children. Lee grew up on a farm along the old National Road four miles west of St. Clairsville, his father becoming a successful broom maker. His education was the common school education of the time in rustic log schoolhouses, but he did attend the elite Poland Academy run by his uncle Bernard F. Lee in Poland, Mahoning County, Ohio (future President William M. McKinley also attended the Poland Academy). Captain Lee graduated with a degree in the classics at Ohio Wesleyan University on June 9, 1859 in a class of 26 students and was the 126th graduate of the university; he later graduated with M.A in 1862. He attended the Ohio State and Union Law School at Cleveland, studying law under Judge C. Hayden of New York and future Union general Mortimer D. Leggett.

Lee graduated from law school shortly after the outbreak of the Civil War and had returned to Ohio Wesleyan to further his education in the fall of 1861, but actively engaged in recruiting what became Company I, 82nd Ohio Volunteer Infantry while he was in school. He enlisted in the Union army on November 4, 1861 and was commissioned first lieutenant of the company in December, local attorney George Purdy being the company captain. Company I traveled to the regimental rendezvous at Camp Simon Kenton in Kenton, Hardin Co., Ohio in December 1861. Captain Lee's account of the next four years is told in the following pages in an extraordinary series of letters written under the nom-de-plume of "A.T. Sechand."

Following the war, Captain Lee returned to Delaware, Ohio and started practice as an attorney, marrying Emma Irwin on March 13, 1866 in Xenia, Ohio. In 1867, he was offered a commission in the regular army as a second lieutenant in the 31st U.S. Infantry, but he declined the commission as the government would not offer him a commission as a captain. In 1866, his old divisional commander Carl Schurz offered him a position on the editorial staff of the *Detroit Daily Post*, and he joined the newspaper in March 1866. By August, Captain Lee bought the *Delaware Gazette* and served as chief editor and proprietor until 1873. At that time, he assumed editorial charge of the *Ohio State Journal* in Columbus and moved to that city, serving ably in that role until his appointment as Governor Rutherford B. Hayes' private secretary in January 1876.

Politically a Republican, he was a member of the State Central Committee and served as the collector for internal revenue for a time. In 1868, he was elected to represent Delaware County in the Ohio General Assembly, and worked to pass a bill establishing the Geological Survey of Ohio. Lee also secured the establishment of the State Industrial Home for Girls, locating the home in Delaware County. Upon Governor Hayes' election to the presidency in March 1877, Captain Lee was appointed consul general to the German Empire at Frankfort-am-Main, serving overseas until November 1881 and resuming his position with the *Ohio State Journal* upon his return. Lee later purchased an interest in the *Toledo Daily Telegram*, worked as assistant writing editor on the *Cleveland Daily Herald*, and again joined the *Ohio State Journal* editorial staff in the mid-1880s. Lee served on the Columbus Board of Trade and was a trustee for the Soldiers' and Sailors' Orphans Home at Xenia, Ohio for about a year.

Captain Lee wrote extensively of his war time experiences in the 1880s and served as the Secretary of the Gettysburg Memorial Commission of Ohio from 1886-7, later writing a book about the battle. He also was active with the Grand Army of the Republic, serving as Secretary of the General Council for the 1888 national G.A.R. encampment held in Columbus, Ohio. Lee's war wound continued to trouble him for the rest of his life; he was awarded a Federal pension in July 1883. The success Lee found in war and journalism eluded him in his personal life; his marriage to Emma ended in divorce in 1893, leaving two children (Roland and Florence). The following year, Captain Lee married Ada M. (Mitchell) Granbery at Piqua, Ohio. Captain Lee moved to Redlands, California with his wife Ada and stepdaughter Miriam Granbery in the spring of 1901. In his final years, Captain Lee began to display the symptoms of general paresis, eventually being committed to the state hospital for insanity, and died August 31, 1905 in Colton, San Bernadino Co., California. He is buried at Hillside Memorial Park in Redlands, San Bernadino Co., California.

Acknowledgements

To Dr. John R. Blinn, my debt to you for advice, encouragement and support cannot be repaid- you truly are a scholar and a gentleman.

To Robert Van Dorn, thanks for your encouragement and friendship. A lifelong Civil War buff, Bob shares a deep abiding respect for preserving the story of the common soldier. Likewise to Larry Strayer; your knowledge and passion for Civil War history is truly inspirational. Thank you for your friendship and support.

To Richard Fink, I extend my heartiest thanks and appreciation for providing some incredible images that reside within this work and for generously providing feedback on the manuscript.

Special thanks to Dr. S. Eric Hill of Redlands, California, who graciously supplied research materials he gathered about Captain Lee's life in California while researching the Lee home in Redlands. Thanks also to Maria Carrillo of the Lincoln Memorial Shrine in Redlands and Mark Radeleff for providing some information about Captain Lee in California.

Thanks also to Eugene Rutigliano for providing some information regarding Alfred Lee's academic career at Ohio Wesleyan University.

I'd like to acknowledge the support, encouragement, and guidance provided along the way by Richard Baranowski, local history librarian at Way Public Library in my hometown of Perrysburg, Ohio; a gifted writer in his own right, Richard always provided encouragement and shares my deep and abiding fascination with the untold stories of American history.

My special thanks also to Hal Jespersen who created many of the maps contained herein.

In all works trying to understand and explain our nation's past, we rely on the unsung heroes of the historical societies, libraries, archives, and dedicated researchers who have labored mightily in obscurity to preserve, protect, and make available these priceless accounts of the past. My grateful acknowledgements to all of you, especially those who have contributed to the Chronicling America online newspaper database; it is an immensely valuable tool for obtaining first-hand accounts of the Civil War era.

Lastly, I'd like to thank my dear wife Amy for her constant support and encouragement.

"If there be any merit in these papers, it lies chiefly in the fact that I have written of that which I do know. It has been my humble fortune to be an eyewitness of the patriotic fortitude and gallantry of the soldiers of the Union both in the gloomy bivouac and on the weary march and on the bloody battlefield. I have seen them both when overwhelmed with disaster and when exultant with the flush of glorious victory. I have heard their wail of anguish at defeat, and listened also to their shout of triumph springing from distant hilltops and swelling along the vales and up the mountainsides in one sublime echoing peon of rejoicing. I have marked the unconquerable patriot toiling on his painful march with pale face and bleeding feet, I have hearkened to the faint echoes of his failing breath when gushing wounds have taken that heroic soul and made its last, greatest sacrifice for freedom. I have caught from feverish lips the story of long, reliefless suffering under the slow conquest of disease that could subdue the manly frame, but never provoke complaint that all was born and suffered in our country's holy cause. These are not matters of hearsay; I have seen them. And if having seen them I have been able to convey a truthful idea of the inside of army life, and of the unquenchable patriotism and devotion of our soldiers, I am content."

~ *Captain Alfred E. Lee*

Captain Alfred Emory Lee. Photographer's backmark places this image at the Whitehurst Gallery in Washington, D.C. (Richard Fink Collection)

CHAPTER ONE

In the Valley: McDowell to Port Republic

Major General Fremont assumed command of the Mountain Department on March 29, 1862 at Wheeling, West Virginia, relieving Brigadier General William S. Rosecrans.[1] The new department comprised the following territorial divisions: District of the Cumberland, containing all territory east of the Alleghenies and west of the Department of the Potomac, commanded by Brigadier General Robert C. Schenk[2]; the Cheat Mountain District, comprising all west of the Alleghenies, south of the railroad lines, north of the Valley of the Gauley, and east of the Weston and Summerville Road, commanded by Brigadier General Robert H. Milroy; the Railroad District, comprising all north and west of the railroad lines, commanded by Brigadier General Benjamin F. Kelly; the District of the Kanawha, comprising the valleys of the Kanawha and Guyandotte rivers and the mouth of the Big Sandy, commanded by Brigadier General Jacob D. Cox; and the districts of the Big Sandy Valley and Gap commanded respectively by Colonels Garfield and Carter.

Contemplating this interesting field, General Fremont laid out for himself a far-reaching and somewhat dazzling plan of operations. After collecting his forces, he proposed to move up the South Branch Valley, cross the mountains to Staunton, march thence, in conjunction with General Banks, against the Virginia and Tennessee Railroad at Salem, establish a new base at Gauley, call forward General Cox to Newberne, and then having "destroyed the connection between Knoxville and the Confederate army in eastern Virginia, and perhaps seizing some rolling stock, advance rapidly up the railroad towards Knoxville, turning the Confederate position at Cumberland Gap." After taking Knoxville, Fremont proposed to establish a "third base of operations" at Nicholasville and thus place his army "in a position to cooperate in any way in the general plan of operations for the prosecution of the war."

This ambitious and glowing scheme was approved at Washington, but with a final modification which contemplated the ultimate closing in of Fremont's columns toward Richmond rather than at Knoxville. To carry out these designs Fremont had, according to his own estimate, 19,000 effective men. To this force should be added the "German Division" about 8,000 strong under Brigadier General Louis Blenker, which was to be transferred from the Army of the Potomac and assigned to Fremont's command. General Milroy had passed the winter at Monterey- a mountain station near the headwaters of the South Branch of the Potomac- and he had with him there about 3,500 men. General Schenk's force- to which the 82nd Ohio regiment, with which the writer identified, was attached- was concentrated at Moorefield in the South Branch Valley and numbered about 3,000.

---

[1] Three articles that Captain Lee wrote for the *Magazine of American History* in 1886 form the basis of this chapter.
[2] Robert Cumming Schenk had been active in Whig and Republican politics in Ohio since the early 1840s and served four terms in Congress in that decade. A noted attorney and orator, he had served as Minister to Brazil during the Millard Fillmore administration. Schenk was a bitter enemy of John C. Fremont, so much so that he refused to render any support to Fremont's bid for the presidency in 1856. However, Schenk was noted as one of the first public men to endorse Abraham Lincoln's bid for the Republican Party's presidential nomination in 1860. Upon the outbreak of the war, Lincoln quickly made Schenk a general and the expert poker player led Ohio units at Bull Run and through the Shenandoah Valley campaign of 1862, eventually rising to divisional command.

Brigadier General Robert C. Schenk
(Library of Congress)

Blenker's division quitted its camps at Fairfax Court House for its new field of operations early in April, but was fully a month in reaching its destination. Blenker was unfamiliar with the country, became confused with his maps, and seems to have lost his way. Though the weather was very inclement, his men marched without tents or other sufficient camp equipage and were constantly exposed to snow and rain. On the 15th, the division crossed the swollen Shenandoah at Berry's Ferry in boats, one of which was swamped, drowning 60 men. To prevent further mishaps and accelerate the movement of Blenker's command, the Secretary of War directed General Rosecrans to hunt it up, take temporary charge of it and conduct it over the mountains.[3] The division was in a most wretched state of discipline and equipment. Many of the regiments were armed with old-fashioned smoothbore muskets and the whole command was deficient in necessary wagon transportation. The men suffered greatly for want of shoes, blankets, and overcoats, and also for want of food. Many were sick by reason of exposure and privation and the number increased daily. The animals in the trains were in a starved condition, and fresh horses had to be procured before the batteries could be moved from Martinsburg. The division reached Petersburg on the 9th of May, but in an exceedingly unfit condition for active service.[4]

Early in April, General Milroy, after routing a Confederate force which attacked him near Monterey, pushed across the mountains to McDowell. About the same time, General Cox, in pursuance of Fremont's orders, moved in the direction of Lewisburg and Peterstown. Concurrently with these operations, General Schenk was directed to advance toward Franklin, so as to join Milroy and cooperate with Banks in the Shenandoah Valley. Owing to the bad condition of the roads, Schenk's forces at Moorefield did not break camp until the 25th of April, on which date they moved up the South Branch to Petersburg. Here the river, swollen by rain and very swift, was found to be three feet deep at its shallowest point, making it necessary to construct a temporary footbridge for the infantry, which was done with farm wagons, ballasted down with stones. The artillery and cavalry managed to get over

---

[3] Rosecrans telegraphed the War Department that he discovered that Blenker's division had been on the march for more than a month "without tents, shelters, or knapsacks. Their clothing is worn, shoes gone, and no pay since December; not much wonder that they stole and robbed." Lamers, William M. The Edge of Glory: A Biography of General William S. Rosecrans. Baton Rouge: Louisiana State University Press, 1961, pg. 76

[4] The German soldiers of Blenker's division later formed a distinctive component of the 11th Corps. Lee's comments on the condition of Blenker's division at this early date are a prelude to his later attribution that the poor battlefield performance of the corps at Chancellorsville was the fault of these "cowardly Germans." He averred that these "men who have always made themselves notorious in the army by their thieving and straggling were not the men to depend on in the hour of danger."

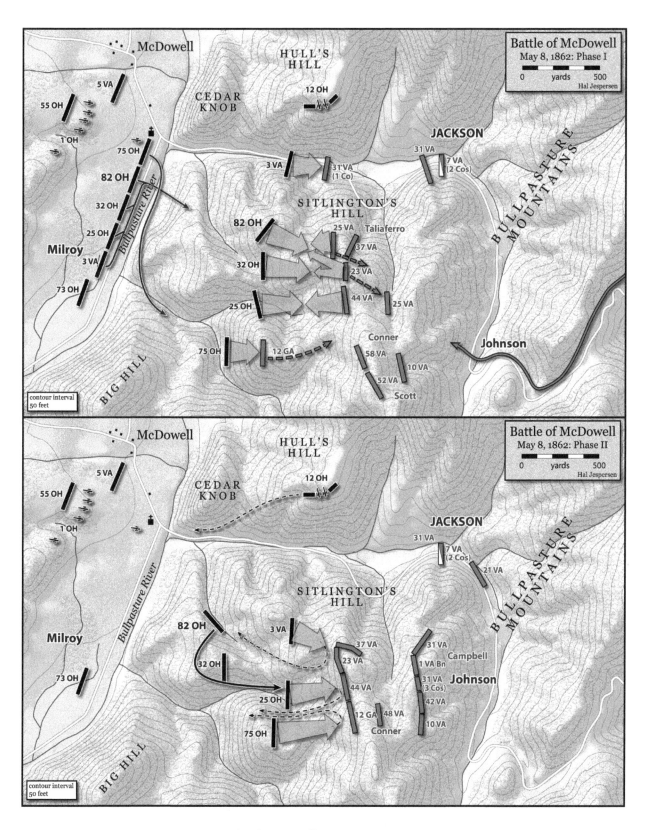

Battle of McDowell, Virginia, May 8, 1862
(Hal Jespersen, www.cwmaps.com)

by fording. The movement was resumed on the 3rd of May. Above Petersburg, the road, at best a primitive one, barely practicable for artillery and wagon trains, grew worse and worse as the column proceeded up the river, and penetrated the mountainous country from which the South Branch issues. The few people who dwelt in these elevated districts seemed to be as heartily and universally loyal as those in the lower valley had been unfriendly and rebellious, and they welcomed Schenk's soldiers with every demonstration of joy. They were generally poor, as was the soil they cultivated, and of course there were very few slaveholders among them.[5] As the column neared Franklin on May 5th, a courier arrived from Milroy with the news that Jackson, anticipating Fremont's advance, was coming over the range to meet him.

"There's work ahead, boys!" said Colonel James Cantwell of the 82nd Ohio as he rubbed his mustache in a manner peculiar to him. The brave colonel knew from his own previous experience what "work ahead" meant but there were few of his boys who, as yet, had ever heard so much as a picket shot fired at an enemy. They were quite ready for the "work" however, and rather eager for it, although the colonel's manner did indicate that he thought it was going to be in the nature of amusement. At Franklin, an old weather-beaten hamlet in a gorge of the mountains, a temporary supply depot was established and on the 7th the column pushed on, through a rough and thinly settled country, toward Staunton. On the 8th at 10 A.M., the command, having marched most of the night, arrived at McDowell, a village on the Staunton Turnpike, 34 miles southwest of Franklin. The village lies at the foot of Bull Pasture Mountain, on the upper slopes of which were descried (for the first time by Cantwell's men) the gray battalions of the Southern Confederacy. The Confederates in sight were the brigades of Edward Johnson's division which were moving into position and forming a line sheltered by rocks and trees, and fronted by clearings extending well down the mountain.

Jackson had present with him and near at hand, his own and Johnson's divisions, numbering in all about 10,000 men. Defeated March 23rd by Shields at Kernstown and then pursued by Banks up the Valley to Harrisonburg, he had been reinforced by Ewell's division from Gordonsville. Leaving that division to hold Banks in check, he had now turned to intercept and overwhelm Fremont's advance before it could arrive within reaching distance of our forces in the valley. Milroy had arrived at McDowell some days before and had thrown forward part of his force beyond Shaw's Ridge in the direction of Staunton. This force had fallen back upon the main body, which was preparing to resist Jackson's further progress. Schenk, who was the ranking officer, had brought with him about 1,300 infantry, a battalion of Connecticut cavalry, and De Beck's Ohio Battery.[6] He saw at once that our position at McDowell was not tenable, but after consultation with Milroy, he resolved to put a bold face on matters and assail the enemy. Under the cover of this attack, he proposed to get all the wagon trains well out of the way with a view to withdrawing during the night his entire force from its perilous position.

About the middle of the afternoon, the 3rd West Virginia, and the 25th, 32nd, 75th, and 82nd Ohio regiments moved to the attack, the 25th and 75th holding the right, the 32nd and 82nd the left, and the 3rd West Virginia moving by the turnpike, the center. Passing beyond the village, the 82nd crossed Bull Pasture River and ascended a steep, timbered bluff known as Hull's Ridge where there was neither road nor path. A six-pounder of Johnson's Battery was dragged up after the regiment by hand and directly opened fire with considerable effect from the summit, from whence the enemy's position, though in plain view, could not be reached with musketry. Intervening between ourselves (the 82nd Ohio) and Bull Pasture Mountain (the cleared part of which was known as Sitlington's Hill) lay a deep valley, along which the turnpike mounted the Shenandoah range. To get at our antagonists it was necessary to descend to the bottom of this valley and climb the heights on the opposite side. Colonel Cantwell, therefore, started his men on the double quick down the mountain, himself leading them on foot. The entire movement had to be

---

[5] Second Lieutenant Harvey M. Litzenberg remembered one particularly ebullient Unionist on the march from Petersburg. "Our regiment was passing a humble cottage by the roadside. There on a stile in front stood an old lady waving her handkerchief in the calm air of the evening and exclaiming as if in a transport of joy, 'God bless the Union boys! God bless the Union boys, I say!' It is needless to state that the 'Union boys' felt like an electric thrill the inspiration of that old lady's patriotism and acknowledged her compliment in their characteristic way." "From the 82nd Regiment," *Delaware Gazette*, May 23, 1862, pg. 2

[6] Battery K, 1st Ohio Volunteer Light Artillery under the command of Captain William L. De Beck.

executed in full view of the enemy, and it quickly brought us within range of his musketry. With a great shout the regiment rushed down to the turnpike and upon reaching, which the men scarcely stopped to take a breath, before they began clambering up the steep slope of Bull Pasture Mountain.

And now the crash of their Enfields began to resound through the gorge! And in spite of all the battles which have since intervened, how the bang of those muskets reverberates even yet in the living ears that heard them! The enemy's bullets, fired down the mountain, flew over us in myriads, but were not heeded.[7] The Confederate fire seemed only to add to the exhilaration and élan of our charge. Up through the slanting meadows went the blue lines with colors flying and Enfields crashing! No flinching, but forward! Some soldiers fall and lie motionless upon the grass, but there is no time to pay any attention to that! On the right, the 25th, 75th, and 32nd Ohio came up in splendid style, their muskets crashing, too. Up still go up the steady lines, until they arrive within short range of the Confederates. The action is so violent all along the front that Jackson hurries up his reserves. Our men want to go at the enemy with the bayonet and some of them even make a rush for that purpose, but are called back. It is not deemed prudent to advance the line farther against such superior odds, but the fight goes on unabated until the sun sets and darkness hides the combatants from each other.[8] Happening to look to the rear, I saw some men lying on the grass. My first impression was that they had lain down to avoid being hit. But they were motionless. The truth flashed over me- they were dead! I had scarcely noticed before that anybody had been hurt, except that a bullet had struck the musket of a man next to me, and glancing had wounded him in the wrist.

As darkness came on the firing slackened and at length ceased. The troops were then recalled. The wounded had all been carried to the rear, but there lay the dead and it seemed too bad to leave them behind. So two of us picked up one of the bodies and endeavored to bear it away with the retreating line. But we had not realized until then how fatigued we were. The slain soldier was a young German who had received a bullet full in the forehead. We laid him down gently by the stump of a tree with his face upturned to the moonlight and there we left him. A few minutes later I found myself trying to quench, in a muddy pool at the turnpike, the fever and thirst begotten of the extraordinary exertion and excitement.

"Men, remember that you are from Ohio!" had been General Schenk's admonition prior to the battle. We did not forget it. Jackson telegraphed to Richmond: "God blessed our arms with victory at

---

[7] Private George W. Sponaugle of the 25th Virginia complained that since "we were on a hill and had to shoot down at the Yankees, there was a tendency to overshoot them, while they had us between them and the skyline and we made a good mark." 'Recollections of George Sponaugle,' *Highland Recorder (Ohio)*, February 25, 1927
[8] The 82nd Ohio was primarily engaged against first the 25th Virginia of General Edward "Allegheny" Johnson's brigade, then the 23rd and 44th Virginia Infantry regiments of Brigadier General William B. Taliaferro's brigade of Jackson's division.

McDowell yesterday." He would not have coveted many such victories. His loss afterward was admitted was 72 killed and 390 wounded. Our loss was 256. The enemy did not pursue. He did not even seem to anticipate our retreat. Returning to the village, our troops halted unmolested for supper and a brief rest. Leaving their campfires burning, they then set forth, preceded by the artillery and trains, on the road toward Franklin. The wounded who could hobble along did so, and those who could not were carried in the ambulances. We marched all night, seldom stopping, and on the 10th the column arrived again at Franklin. Halting in the valley above the town, the troops, half dead with fatigue and loss of sleep, stacked their arms and laid down to rest. Suddenly a great cheer was heard in the direction of the town, and a horseman was seen galloping up the valley and swinging his hat. One regiment after another took up the cry as he passed it, and as he approached ours, we heard him shouting at the top of his voice: "The Monitor has sunk the Merrimac! Hurrah!"

We had scarcely digested this welcome information when the enemy's cavalry appeared up the valley and the troops were hurried into position covering the approaches to town. Then came more news: "General Fremont is coming with Blenker's division!" Verily we had fallen upon eventful times! The Merrimac sunk, Blenker coming, and the Confederate cavalry bearing down upon us! However, the enemy, having arrived with hearing of the racket caused by the Merrimac news, seemed to be intimidated by the thunder of the captains and the shouting. His squadrons displayed themselves very handsomely with arms glittering and banners flying, but for the time being they kept a respectful distance. A few shots from our batteries made the distance still more respectful.

Blenker's division came up according to announcement. At the same time Jackson's cavalry with infantry supports began to feel Fremont's lines and for a few hours brisk skirmishing ensued. Meanwhile the woods on the mountains took fire from the musketry, or the campfires of the combatants, and at night the contour of the peaks and ridges was outlined against the sky in flame. On the 14th Jackson withdrew his forces from Fremont's front and rapidly disappeared again beyond the Shenandoah Mountains. We were destined to renew his acquaintance, however, further along.

"For the number of men engaged, it was as hard a fought battle as has taken place since the war commenced," commented First Lieutenant Francis S. Jacobs of Company K, 82nd Ohio. "We were ordered forward on a double quick up and down a tremendous steep hill and then had to charge them up another steep hill. We arrived at the summit and pitched in. You can have a very fair idea of the manner in which our boys fought when every man went into the fight with from 35 to 50 rounds of cartridges and came out with none, even stripping the cartridges from the dead and wounded and distributing them amongst the men. A spent ball hit me in the thigh, cutting my pants and smashing my trunk key- as close as I have any desire to have them come. The balls whistled with considerable vim over our heads, where the great majority of their shots went. General Schenk says the 82nd has proven two things in the last two days: that they can march and will fight like the devil."[9] Corporal James W. Chandler reported that "after about 2 ½ hours hard fighting, we were ordered to charge bayonets and take them which seemed to be a dreadful undertaking. The charge was made by a small portion of our men, I think not exceeding 400. When we had approached within 30-40 feet of their works, they rose up and sent the balls among us like hail, killing and wounded several and smashing my cartridge box in the bargain."[10]

An unsigned article published in the May 30, 1862 issue of the *Hardin County Republican* provides some additional details regarding the 82nd Ohio's experiences at the Battle of McDowell:

The 82nd Ohio regiment, under the head of her brave and gallant Colonel James Cantwell, was ordered to double quick over a steep and rugged mountain some half mile high, and up to the top of another mountain about the same height. No sooner was the order given to advance than the entire regiment filed off in as good order as if going on dress parade, with Colonel Cantwell in the advance and Major Thomson close at his heels. Upon arriving at the top of the first mountain, the Rebels kept up a heavy fire, which they kept up while the regiment was padding down its side but

---

[9] "The 82nd in a Fight- Letter from F.S. Jacobs," *Ashland Union*, May 21, 1862, pg. 3, and "Letter from F.S. Jacobs," *Ashland Union*, May 28, 1862, pg. 3
[10] Letter from Corporal James W. Chandler, *Ashland Union*, May 28, 1862, pg. 3

fortunately wounded but one man. When the regiment arrived on the top of the first mountain, Colonel Cantwell discovered that it was a commanding position for a cannon. He at once detailed Lieutenant McConnell and the first platoon of Co. A, to return and assist in bringing forward the cannon to the position indicated.

The boys were very much exhausted when they arrived at the foot of the second mountain, and a number sunk down from pure exhaustion, but the commanding voice of the gallant old colonel as he passed from one end of the line to the other, soon revived their exhausted bodies, and the regiment moved up the mountain in good order and filed into line on the summit in front of the enemy, and opened fire. The first shot was fired by Perry Summers of Co. A. The strife between the boys for the first shot was quite animated but Perry Summers of Roundhead was the hero.[11] After this, company after company of the 82nd filed into line, the ball began in real earnest. The enemy at once opened a crossfire on the regiment which did considerable damage. For nearly four hours the battle raged, but the boys never faltered and stood their ground until they exhausted the fire of the enemy and every round of ammunition in their cartridge boxes.

The officers and men, with scarce an exception, acquitted themselves in the most gallant manner. The instances of individual bravery were numerous and excited the admiration of both the commanding generals. Old Colonel Cantwell did, beyond a question, out run all the men under his command. He was the first man on top of the mountain. He is a good runner, but he always makes the best time when *he runs toward the enemy*.[12]

Second Lieutenant Harvey M. Litzenberg of Captain Lee's own Company I wrote that "the battle in some respects was a drawn one, in others a victory for us. We attacked the enemy with an inferior force and under great disadvantages, drove him back, and maintained our position as long as we chose. True we retreated during the night, but never was march conducted in better order than was our retreat. About nine miles from McDowell, we halted and awaited the enemy, but they kept a respectful distance. That we saved General Milroy from annihilation is quite certain, to have held McDowell would only have benefited the enemy as our want of supplies would have compelled us to fall back at a time when the enemy might perhaps claim the honor of driving us."[13]

Report of Brigadier General Robert C. Schenk, commanding brigade
Headquarters, Schenk's Brigade, Mountain Department, Camp Franklin, Virginia
May 14, 1862

I have had the honor in my dispatches heretofore transmitted through you to inform the general commanding of my march with my brigade from Franklin to McDowell to the relief of Brigadier General Milroy, who, with his force, had fallen back to and concentrated at the last named place, and was threatened with attack by the combined armies of the Rebel Generals Jackson and Johnson. By leaving my baggage train under a guard in my last camp on the road 14 miles from McDowell, I was able to push forward so as to make the whole distance (34 miles) in 23 hours. I added, however, but little numerical strength to the army I was sent to relieve. My brigade, consisting of but three regiments and with several companies then on detached or other duty, brought into the field

---

[11] Private Perry Summers was later wounded July 20, 1864 at the Battle of Peach Tree Creek, Georgia and died of his wounds July 23, 1864.

[12] The O.R. gives the casualty list for the 82nd Ohio as 6 killed, 50 wounded, and 1 missing. Among the casualties was Corporal John Walker of Co. A. Wounded in the face, Walker fired off all of his ammunition, then "acted as standard bearer and when the regiment was drawn up in line of battle on the following day near Franklin, he left his bunk in the hospital to accompany the regiment. He caught cold and the result proved fatal." Walker died May 19, 1862. Overall Federal casualties totaled 259; Confederate casualties totaled 532. Historian Peter Cozzens lauded Schenk's and Milroy's generalship at McDowell. "They had accomplished their stated purpose of delaying an enemy attack and had inflicted heavy casualties in the bargain. By any reasonable calculation, McDowell was a tactical Union victory. But in a larger sense, the fruits of victory rested with the Confederates." Cozzens, Peter. Shenandoah 1862: Stonewall Jackson's Valley Campaign. Chapel Hill: University of North Carolina Press, 2008, pg. 274.

[13] "From the 82nd Regiment," *Delaware Gazette*, May 23, 1862, pg. 2 Lieutenant Litzenberg would be killed in action August 29, 1862 at the Second Battle of Bull Run.

an aggregate of only 1,300 infantry, besides De Beck's battery of the 1st Ohio Artillery and about 250 of the 1st Battalion of Connecticut Cavalry. With this help I reached General Milroy about 10 A.M. on the 8th instant. I was, to use his expression, "Just in time." I found his regiments of infantry partly in line of battle on the plain at McDowell, covering some of the various approaches from the mountain and partly disposed as skirmishers on the heights in front and his batteries in position, expecting momentarily that the enemy would attempt to descend into the valley to attack him under cover of artillery that might be brought forward to command the place from different points.

A little observation served to show at once that McDowell, as a defensive position, was entirely untenable and especially against the largely outnumbering force that was ascertained to be advancing; and if it had been otherwise, there was no choice left on account of an entire destitution of forage. I determined, therefore, to obey with as little delay as possible your orders to fall back with the force of our two brigades to this place. Such a movement, however, could not with any safety or propriety be commenced before night, nor did it seem advisable to undertake it without first ascertaining or feeling the actual strength of the Rebel force before us, and also perhaps, taking some step that would serve to check or disable him from his full power or disposition to pursue. This was effectually done by our attack of his position on the mountain in the afternoon and in the night following I was enabled to withdraw our whole little army along the road through the narrow gorge, which afforded the only egress from the valley in which McDowell was situated in the direction of Franklin. This withdrawal we effected without the loss of a man and without the loss or destruction of any article of public property, except of some stores for which General Milroy was entirely without the means of transporting.

At 3 o'clock, General Milroy having reported to me that his scouts informed him of reinforcements continually arriving to the support of the enemy, concealed among the woods on the mountain, and that they were evidently making preparations to get artillery in position for sweeping the valley, I consented to his request to be permitted to make a reconnaissance. The force detailed for this purpose consisted of portions of four regiments of infantry of Milroy's brigade (25th, 32nd, and 75th Ohio, and the 3rd West Virginia) and the 82nd Ohio of my brigade, the latter regiment gladly receiving the order to join in enterprise, although the men were exhausted with the long march from which they had just arrived with the want of food, sleep, and rest. The infantry was supported in a degree also by a 6-pounder of Johnson's battery, which General Milroy had succeeded in conveying to the top of one of the mountain ridges on his left. The movement resulted in a very sharp encounter with the Rebels, of which the details are given in the accompanying reports. To those details I refer, I will only add, by the way of a general summing up, that adding to the 1,768 of Milroy's brigade and about 500 of the 82nd Ohio, which was the number in action, the entire force we had engaged was 2,268. That these men were opposed to, I believe, not less than 5,000 of the enemy successively brought into action, besides their reserved force of some 8,000 in the rear; that the casualties on our part amounted in the aggregate to 28 killed, 80 severely wounded, 145 slightly wounded, and 3 missing, making a total of 256.

As the evening closed in and it was ascertained that, from the unexpected severity and protraction of the fight, the ammunition of some of the regiments was almost completely exhausted, I endeavored in person to get a supply of cartridges to the men and had three wagon loads taken some distance up the Staunton road for that purpose, but the only way it could reach them up the steep mountainside was to be carried by hand or in haversacks. I ordered up the road also the 5th West Virginia Infantry, Colonel Zeigler commanding, of my brigade to the relief of the other troops, if needed, and they most promptly and actively moved to the field, but it was not necessary to bring them into action. The troops that were engaged, after fighting with a coolness and order and bravery which it is impossible to excel, and after pressing back the enemy over the mountain crest and maintaining unflinchingly and under the most galling and constant fire their ground until darkness set in, were then withdrawn under the immediate order of Colonel McLean of the 75th Ohio leaving, as I believe, not a prisoner behind for the three men reported missing are supposed to be among the killed.

We took four prisoners from the enemy. His loss in killed is thought by all engaged to have exceeded ours. From prisoners since taken I have ascertained that his killed on the field was admitted to be not less than 30 and his wounded very numerous. Among the Rebels wounded I learn was General Johnson himself and at least one of his field officers. The colonel of a Virginia regiment is known to be among the slain. Too much praise cannot be awarded to General Milroy himself, to Colonel McLean of the 75th Ohio, Colonel Cantwell of the 82nd Ohio,

General Robert Schenk

"General Schenk is of about middle height, square, compact, and broad chested. His rugged features fairly indicate his strong passions and inflexible will. In military and civil life he has been the same bold, bitter, fearless fighter. He practices no concealments, displays little strategy, never shrinks from a course because it will increase the number of his enemies, strikes with a broadsword rather than thrusts with a rapier, hews his way through difficulties rather than take the trouble to turn into an equally good path that may carry him around them."

~*Whitelaw Reid*

Lieutenant Colonel Richardson of the 25th Ohio, Major Reilly 75th Ohio, Lieutenant Colonel Swinney, 32nd Ohio, Lieutenant Colonel Thompson, 3rd West Virginia Infantry, and the officers and men of their several commands for the steady gallantry and courage manifested throughout the whole affair. No veteran troops, I am sure, ever acquitted themselves with more ardor, and yet with such order and coolness as they displayed in marching and fighting up that steep mountainside in the face of a hot and incessant fire.

From McDowell, I fell back by easy marches on the 9th, 10th, and 11th to this place, the enemy cautiously pursuing. On a commanding ridge of ground 13 miles from McDowell, at the intersection of the road from that place with the turnpike to Monterey, I stopped from 8 A.M. to 2 P.M. on the 9th and made my dispositions to receive and repulse the attack of the Rebels, who appeared in our rear, but they declined the undertaking.

While awaiting the arrival of the general commanding with reinforcements at this point on the 11th, 12th, and 13th, the Rebel army having advanced to within 2 miles of our position, we were kept constantly engaged in watchful preparation for an expected assault. I had no batteries and the forces so disposed as to feel confident of repelling any attack; but we had no collision, except some skirmishing with my pickets and portions of the infantry advanced on the range of hills to my right as I confronted the enemy's approach, and which resulted only in the loss of two men-one of the 5th West Virginia on the 11th and one of the 3rd Regiment Potomac Home Brigade on the 12th. The approaches were so guarded as to prevent the enemy from getting his artillery into any commanding position, and in the night of the 13th he withdrew back along to turnpike road to the southward.
R.C. Schenk

At Franklin, Fremont's forces were soon assailed by an enemy more formidable even than Stonewall Jackson. That enemy was famine. The mountainous country around Franklin yielded almost nothing in the way of provisions and the road back to Petersburg and New Creek – the 'cracker line' as the soldiers called it- was not suited to the transportation of supplies. All the brooks and creeks along the route were destitute of bridges and greatly swollen by rain and the wagon track, edged between the rocky bed of the Potomac on the one hand and the mountain walls and precipices on the other, was almost impassable for wheels. Food and forage came forward slowly and in meager quantities. Further advance on this line was scarcely possible until the season advanced and the roads should improve. It began to look as if the army would have to go back to Petersburg or Moorefield to save itself from starvation.

Major General John C. Fremont
(Library of Congress)

Another reason, equally imperative, soon impelled a rear movement. While Fremont's wagon masters were struggling with the difficulties of the wretched cart track in the mountains, Stonewall Jackson's army was making the best use possible of the solid turnpikes of the Shenandoah Valley. After disappearing from Fremont's front at Franklin on May 14, 1862, Jackson quickly recrossed the mountain to Harrisonburg and, moving swiftly down the valley by way of New Market, pounced upon and routed a small Union force at Front Royal; and then with almost equal suddenness fell upon Banks at Winchester. Unfortunately for Banks, Shields' division, about 11,000 strong, had been sent toward Fredericksburg to join McDowell's intended advance from that point on Richmond. Banks therefore had with him less than 7,000 men wherewith to withstand Jackson's 8,000 men. After fighting stubbornly for five hours, Banks abandoned Winchester and made his way to Martinsburg, thence withdrew across the Potomac to Williamsport. Jackson pursuing captured Martinsburg, occupied Loudon Heights opposite Harper's Ferry, and took position with the main body of his army five miles nouth of Harper's Ferry at Halltown.

In this emergency, the President directed Fremont to push across the mountains to Harrisonburg "in such a way as to relieve General Banks" and ordered Shields at Fredericksburg to move rapidly back to the Shenandoah along the line of the Manassas Gap Railroad. Fremont lost no time in moving, but not in the direction indicated in his instructions. On the 25th of May- the day on which Jackson appeared before Winchester- his troops quitted Franklin for Petersburg, which place was reached by a forced march on the 26th. At Petersburg, every spare wheel was dropped and the men, throwing aside their knapsacks and taking all the ammunition and hard bread they could carry, hurried on to Moorefield. Having learned by this time that Fremont had gone back to Moorefield instead of moving eastward from Franklin, as instructed, the President telegraphed his astonishment. Fremont replied, "The reasons for my being at Moorefield are, first, the point of your order was to relieve General Banks. At the time it was issued, it was only known to me that he had been attacked at Front Royal. When my march commenced, I knew he had retreated from Winchester. Second, of the different roads to Harrisonburg, all but one, and that one leading southward, had been obstructed by the enemy and if the loss of time by taking the only open road were no consideration, it was still a simple impossibility to march in that direction. My troops were utterly out of provisions. There was nothing whatever to be found in the country except a small quantity of fresh beef, from the effects of which the troops were suffering, and in fact, all my men were only saved from starvation by taking the road to Petersburg where they found five days' rations."

This explanation being accepted, Fremont at Moorefield turned his course eastward. Colonel Cluseret of his staff led the column with a brigade of light troops consisting of the 60th Ohio, Colonel William H. Trimble, and the 8th West Virginia, Major John H. Oley.[14] The Potomac (South Branch) was crossed by fording, the men supporting themselves by a rope stretched from bank to bank while they waded waist deep through a swift current. The column then ascended the South Branch Mountain, and pushing on as fast as possible, crossed one range after another, often amid wild solitudes and by obscure and difficult roads. Rain fell much of the time and on the mountains it was chilling cold; marching all day the soldiers, exhausted, threw themselves at night on the wet ground with no other bed or covering than green pine branches and a single blanket or poncho. On one occasion a violent tempest overwhelmed them just as darkness fell. Rain and wind wrestled with each other, and the tired soldiers were lighted to bed by the storm king's torch, fitfully flaring amongst the mountain peaks. Water deluged the ground, and the night was spent for the most part sleeplessly in the cold wind and beating rain. On another occasion the writer, rolled in his gum blanket, inadvertently fell asleep beside a campfire and was conscious of nothing more until morning found him curled around a heap of drowned embers.

On the 29th upon protest of his medical director against further marching without rest, Fremont called a halt of one day at Fabius. In the ascent of the mountains hundreds of broken down men of the Blenker Division had been left along the road. Enfeebled by recent fatigue and lack of food, and by previous hardships on their march from eastern Virginia, their strength had completely failed and a rest of 24 hours was necessary. During this halt, an inspection was had of the whole command and the Blenker troops, formerly 10,000 strong, were found to number less than 6,000 fit for duty. On June 1st as the column descended Little North Mountain, its movement was quickened by the sudden outbreak of a distant cannonade. Directly an order came back for Schenk's division to hurry forward with all possible speed. The weather had all at once grown sweltering hot and a black storm cloud hung portentously over the mountains. Soon the cannonading redoubled its violence and heavy peals of thunder mingled with the detonations of the artillery. The troops, without knowing whither or for what, were rushed ahead as fast as they could go, sometimes almost upon the run. Arriving heated and breathless in the vicinity of the firing, they were thrown forward in battle array in some open fields. At the same time a heavy rain began falling, and peal after peal of terrific thunder crashed through the sky, fairly silencing the less sonorous rage of man. There had been some skirmishing in the woods in front but that, like the cannonading, seemed to be stifled by the blinding rain. The storm continued until nightfall and Schenk's troops, without becoming engaged, lay down upon their arms.

The firing which had summoned us so precipitately forward had been an exchange of compliments between Fremont's advance under Cluseret and Turner Ashby's cavalry, supported by Ewell's infantry. Cluseret had driven in Ashby's videttes early in the forenoon and some hours later made the discovery that Jackson's entire force was passing Strasburg, hurrying southward. During the storm Ashby and Ewell withdrew, followed by nightfall by Cluseret, who pushed through Strasburg and two miles beyond that place encountered Jackson's rear guard under Ashby. Although it was by that time 11 o'clock at night and very dark, Cluseret led his men to the attack and so impetuously as to throw the Confederates into confusion. He then ordered a charge, but the order was disobeyed by our cavalry, which fled disgracefully, passing over and carrying with it the artillery. But the 60th Ohio, which at that moment held the advance of the reconnoitering column, stood firm- not a man wavering- and withstood the counterattacks of the enemy.[15]

Early the next morning the main body of Fremont's army descended from the heights near Strasburg and turned its course up the valley. It was joined during the day by Bayard's cavalry and a battalion of Pennsylvania

---

[14] Colonel (later Brigadier General) Gustave Paul Cluseret was a French-born officer who came to America in 1861 to offer his services to the Federal government. Cluseret served on General Fremont's staff and later founded a newspaper with Fremont in New York.

[15] This action was fought near Middletown, Virginia between the 7th Virginia Cavalry and Cluseret's two regiments, the 60th Ohio and 8th West Virginia.

Bucktail infantry[16], leading McDowell's column, which had countermarched from Fredericksburg and had approached from the east while Fremont was coming over the mountains from the west. The President had been impatiently spurring both McDowell and Fremont by telegraph, rightly believing that a splendid opportunity was offered for uniting the forces of both generals in Jackson's rear at Strasburg. Had this been done, an army of 40,000 men would have barred the enemy's retreat, and would undoubtedly have brought his audacious expedition to a calamitous end.

But the wily raider was not to be caught napping. At Halltown, on the 29th of May, he learned that Fremont and McDowell were closing in behind him and he lost not a moment in extricating himself from his perilous position. Shields was already nearing Front Royal, only 12 miles from Strasburg, and Fremont had less than 40 miles to go to reach the same point. At Halltown, Jackson was 43 miles from Strasburg and so far as distances were concerned the chances were decidedly against his escape. Energy, skill, and audacity often outweigh adverse physical circumstances in war, and Jackson seldom displayed these qualities to better advantage than he did in this emergency. Leaving Winder's brigade and the cavalry to cover the withdrawal of his outlying detachments, he put all the rest of his command in instant movement toward Winchester, where he arrived with the bulk of his command on the 30th having marched that day 35 miles. On the same day, Shields, leading McDowell's advance, seized Front Royal but not until the Confederate detachment there, though driven off hastily, had managed to destroy a large amount of captured army stores. On the 31st, Jackson, pursuing his march from Winchester, reached Strasburg (18 miles) in advance of either of his antagonists. Banks at Williamsport had made slight show of pursuit and Shields at Front Royal had contented himself with a reconnaissance towards Winchester led by Colonel Samuel S. Carroll of the 8th Ohio. McDowell, coming up on the 31st with Ricketts' division (under Ord) hurried Shields forward, but the latter instead of moving toward Strasburg as was intended, took the road to Winchester which place Jackson had by that time quitted. Fremont had to travel a rough road and, as we have seen, did not touch the enemy's outposts until June 1. Winder, having marched 35 miles in a single day, came up by noon of the 1st and thereupon Jackson withdrew Ewell from Fremont's front and resumed his flight, taking his course up the valley along the North Fork of the Shenandoah.

Thus Jackson dexterously eluded the capture planned for him and nothing remained but to give him chase which Fremont instantly did, hoping by vigorous pursuit to compel him to turn and fight. At the same time Shields advanced up the South Fork on the eastern side of Massanutten Mountain, aiming to head off the enemy at some point farther up the valley.

A grand footrace between the three armies now began, Jackson's trying to escape, Fremont's pursuing, and Shields' endeavoring to forestall the enemy at the upper fords of the Shenandoah. Fremont spurred his command to the top of its speed. The weather was hot and sultry, and such rapid marching was exceedingly trying to soldiers who had just descended from the soft clay roads and cool atmosphere of the mountains. Hundreds fell out of the ranks exhausted, and some regiments had but a mere handful of men left with the colors. The enemy was evidently quite as much fatigued. On the 2nd over 500 prisoners fell into our hands, and some of our own men who had been taken from Banks were recovered. Confederate stragglers were picked up in the woods by the scores and the route was lined with clothing, blankets, broken ambulances, muskets, and articles of equipment left behind by the pursued. Frequently during the day the enemy's rear guard was attacked by our advance and worsted. On the 3rd the chase was continued with equal vigor, but not without hindrance, for all the water courses in the valley were greatly swollen by another excessive rainfall, and Jackson managed to destroy the bridges behind him. His cavalry broke the bridges in front of Shields also, whose hindrance by floods was more serious even than Fremont's. Our own cavalry under Bayard skirmished constantly with that of Ashby, which covered Jackson's retreat, but our infantry, notwithstanding its rapid marching, was seldom able to get forward in time take any part in these engagements.

At Mount Jackson which was reached on the 4th, the Confederate commander nimbly placed between himself and his pursuer the raging river which had overflowed its banks at that point and inundated the valley for a mile. He also destroyed the bridge, leaving to our advance the poor satisfaction of seeing his rear battalions leisurely vanishing "over the hills and far away." At the same time another heavy rain came on, drenching to the skin our

---

[16] 13th Pennsylvania Reserves Battalion under Lieutenant Colonel Thomas L. Kane

tentless soldiers. Our supply trains having fallen far behind, the haversacks of the men were empty and they were obliged to seek food by foraging. The whole country was scoured and all kinds of edibles brought in and devoured indiscriminately. Exposure to the storm, coupled with this miscellaneous diet, soon produced sickness. The foraging was generally done by stragglers, without orders or system, and as always happens in such cases, resulted in a great deal of plundering which was alike useless and inexcusable. The volunteer pillagers of General Blenker's division were on this march nicknamed "Blenkers," a term equivalent to that of "bummers" as used afterwards in the army of General Sherman. Unlike the bummers, however, the Blenkers generally carried their plunder on their own back and loaded themselves down with all manner of household stuff, much of which was not of the slightest use to them.

In the course of a day or two, the army succeeded in crossing the Shenandoah at Mount Jackson. On the 5th it reached New Market and on the 6th our cavalry advance drove the enemy's rear guard through Harrisonburg. From that place, Jackson had moved off to the southeastward, intending to cross the South Fork at Port Republic. Apprehension that he might not reach the crossing until Shields had seized it accelerated his movement. He was followed closely by our cavalry, which attacked that of Turner Ashby two miles beyond Harrisonburg but was repulsed. Our discomfited horsemen were reinforced by four companies of Kane's Rifles (Pennsylvania Bucktails) and by the 1st Pennsylvania Cavalry, led forward by General George D. Bayard. Ashby was at the same time reinforced by Stewart's brigade of infantry and a sharp engagement ensued, during which Lieutenant Colonel Kane, commanding the Bucktails, was wounded and captured. The Confederates also captured Sir Percy Wyndham, an English officer commanding the 1st New Jersey Cavalry, but they suffered a great loss in the person of General Ashby who was killed. Fremont's main army reached Harrisonburg on the 7th and early the following morning it pushed ahead again, stripped for battle. Having quit the turnpike, the column moved upon a muddy clay road which the march of Jackson's troops and trains had reduced to a wretched condition. The route traversed a somewhat broken country, upon which the abrupt headland of the Massanutten Mountain abutted a few miles to the northward. From the crest of that headland, the Confederate signal officers had observed at once the movement of Shields' army east of the Massanutten ranges and of Fremont's west of it.

At length Jackson resolved to turn and fight. South of him, and across his line of retreat, lay the Shenandoah River, in two branches, one of which was fordable and the other, too deep for fording, was spanned by a single bridge. It was currently believed in Fremont's army that Shields had seized this bridge and closed Jackson's avenue of escape. About 8:30 A.M., Fremont's advance under Cluseret, came up with and engaged the enemy near the hamlet of Cross Keys, six miles beyond Harrisonburg. Cluseret advanced about a mile, stubbornly resisted, when he encountered the main Confederate force drawn up in battle order, and covering the roads leading to the Shenandoah. General Ewell as in command of the Confederates, Jackson having gone to Port Republic with Winder's division to watch for Shields. Profiting by his knowledge of the country, Ewell had chosen his position with much skill and had posted his forces advantageously upon a ridge where they were well sheltered and flanked by timber. In front the ground was open and descended rapidly to a small creek. Trimble's brigade held Ewell's right, Elzey's his center, and Stewart's his left. Taylor's brigade, which came up about 2 P.M. from Port Republic, was held in reserve. The high ground occupied by the enemy afforded excellent position for his batteries. Fremont's formation was made upon Cluseret's Brigade[17] which had gained a good position well to the front. Stahel's brigade[18] and Bohlen's brigade[19] came in on the left and Milroy's brigade[20] and Schenk's brigade[21] came in on the right of Cluseret's. Von Steinwehr's brigade[22] acting as rear guard under Colonel Koltes was deployed as fast as it came up in support of the batteries which were skillfully posted by Lieutenant Colonel Pilsen, chief of artillery.

Fremont's effective force present on this field (his own estimate) was 10,500 men; Ewell's about the same. While the infantry was coming into position, our batteries were worked with good effect and the cannonade became

---

[17] 60th Ohio, 8th Virginia, and 39th New York-the Garibaldi Guard
[18] 8th, 41st and 45th New York, 27th Pennsylvania, Pennsylvania Bucktails, Dilger's, Buell's, and Schirmer's batteries
[19] 54th and 58th New York, 74th and 75th Pennsylvania, and Wiedrich's battery
[20] 2nd, 3rd, and 5th Virginia, 25th Ohio, and Hyman's, Johnson's, and Ewing's batteries
[21] 32nd, 55th, 73rd, 75th, and 82nd Ohio, De Beck's and Rigby''s batteries
[22] 29th, 68th, and 73rd Pennsylvania, and Dieckman's battery

"About 8 o'clock on Sunday morning we were marched to the hills overlooking Port Republic and took up a line of battle in which we remained during a heavy cannonade of some two to three hours. Orders were then received to march to the rear in the direction of the firing. Colonel Patton dispatched the 48th Virginia and ordered me to move forward to the left of the road to support a battery, strongly threatened with being charged by the enemy. Here General Ewell placed the regiment in position, ordered the front as skirmishers all the men with long range guns. We remained at this place until about 8 o'clock at night."

Lieutenant Colonel Thomas S. Garnett, 48th Virginia Infantry

violent. Fremont decided to make his principal attack upon the enemy's right and accordingly Stahel's brigade emerged from the woods and advanced up the hill in open ground against Trimble. This attack was premature. The reserves were not yet close enough to support it promptly; Von Steinwehr's brigade was still back on the road and Schenk's had not yet come into position on the right. No real assault should have been attempted until we were prepared to follow it up immediately in full strength. Stahel drove in the Confederate skirmishers and gallantly advanced to within 60 paces of their main supports, when his progress was arrested and his assaulting column staggered by a heavy musketry fire till then reserved. Two of his regiments- the 41st New York and the 27th Pennsylvania- moved to the right into the timber so that the heaviest shock fell upon the 8th and 45th New York, and particularly the 8th, which soon found itself assailed both in front and flank by a superior force. Stahel's brigade was driven back into the woods from which it had emerged, and Milroy and Cluseret, who had been making some vigorous demonstrations in the center, were given pause.

Instead of following up this success at once, the enemy addressed himself to a more deliberate movement. Schenk not having appeared yet upon our right, Ewell was able to propel the bulk of his force against our left wing and this he proceeded to do.[23] Reinforced from Taylor's brigade and by two regiments from Elzey's, Trimble struck out to the right and undertook to turn our left. At the same time his lines pressed forward in front, over the same ground from which Stahel had been driven. By this time Bohlen's brigade had made its way to the front and with the remnants of Stahel's it now joined gallantly in the action. The 58th New York under Colonel Krzyzanowski and the 74th Pennsylvania under Lieutenant Colonel Hamm moved out of the woods into the fields and resolutely encountered the advancing Confederates. Krzyzanowski ordered a charge and drove back the force confronting him. The 54th New York under Colonel Kolzay, holding Bohlen's right, crossed a morass and striking a Confederate regiment in flank, routed it. A charge made upon Buell's battery was vigorously repulsed by that battery, with the aid of the 27th Pennsylvania, and the Bucktails of Stahel's brigade. Dilger, firing grape and canister, repelled so fiercely an attempt to take his guns that the assailing force (part of Taylor's brigade) was almost annihilated. Wiedrich's battery also did excellent execution. While the enemy was thus held in check in front, the 74th Pennsylvania was forced back on the left and that flank was turned. Fremont therefore directed a general withdrawal with a view to the formation of a new line.

Let us now direct our attention to the right. Coming up from Harrisonburg, Schenk reached the scene of action at 1 P.M. Deploying his regiments, he advanced toward Milroy's right and made preparations to fall with his whole strength on Ewell's left. Ewell, in turn, dispatched Patton's brigade and portions of Elzey's and Taylor's to reinforce his line in that quarter. While

---

[23] General Jackson stated in his report: "General Ewell, having been informed by Lieutenant Hinrichs of the engineer corps who had been sent out to reconnoiter, that the enemy was moving a large column on his left, did not advance at once, but subsequently ascertaining that no attack was designed by the force referred to, he advanced, drove in the enemy's skirmishers, and when night closed, was in position on ground previously held by the enemy." Thus the Confederate commander used his forces in mass while we were using our in detail, and overwhelmed one of our wings while the other was coming into position. Evidently our attack from the left should have been reserved until Schenk had gotten up. ~Lee Note

Schenk was getting into position, his skirmishers and artillery were, at intervals, briskly engaged, and several casualties occurred. Among those who were wounded was Dr. Jacob Y. Cantwell, brother to the colonel of the 82nd Ohio and surgeon of that regiment. At a few paces from the writer, the doctor was instructing his assistants about carrying off the wounded when a bullet struck him in the leg. He did not utter a word, but smiled. Fortunately his wound did not prove fatal, and he subsequently rendered valuable service on many other battlefields. By 3 P.M. Schenk had gained favorable ground, well advanced, and was about to signal an attack with his whole command when he received an order from Fremont to withdraw and go to the support of the left wing.[24] Reluctant to relinquish his position if he thought best, but by this time the withdrawal of Milroy made it necessary to continue the movement. After retiring about half a mile Schenk halted on the right of the new line, where he remained without serious molestation until the following morning. At the same time the left wing withdrew about a mile. Some of the enemy's batteries opened upon the new position, but they were speedily silenced and the fighting ceased.

First Lieutenant Francis S. Jacobs of Co. K, 82nd Ohio relayed the following about the Battle of Cross Keys in a letter published in the July 2, 1862 issue of the *Ashland Union*:

At the Battle of Cross Keys, our brigade occupied the extreme right and the infantry portion of it was not engaged at any time. We laid in a wheat field for about 15 minutes when the Rebels got a very good range on us, and then several shells fell in pretty close proximity to us, causing us to dodge down into the wheat in a rather amusing manner, fortunately none of the shells burst. We advanced into a piece of woods and remained there until we were ordered off the field about 4 o'clock. We marched back about a half a mile to where the Rebels had first taken position and been driven from, formed in line of battle, posted our batteries, and waited for them. Pretty soon we heard a sharp hissing sound and saw a shell strike near Captain De Beck's battery; two more came in rapid succession, but by that time our battery opened its whole force on them and silenced them completely in less than five minutes.

The next morning when we got up, the bird had flown again; we started after them, the men being cheered up by the heavy cannonading we heard in front of us, supposing that Shields and his force was engaging them at Port Republic, and keeping them from crossing the bridge, and that we had bagged him certain. When we arrived there we found Jackson and his whole force across the river and the bridge burned, that Shields force only consisted of one brigade[25] and had been repulsed and badly cut up. If we had only got there an hour sooner, we might have saved the whole thing.

Report of Brigadier General Robert C. Schenk, commanding brigade

Headquarters, Schenk's Brigade, Mountain Department, Camp at Mount Jackson, Virginia
June 12, 1862

I have the honor to report the part taken by the Ohio brigade in the engagement at Cross Keys on the 8th instant. It was about 1 P.M. when I arrived near the point of the road leading to Port Republic, where the advance guard had already come upon the enemy. A staff officer, after indicating the position where my cavalry was to be left in reserve, informed me that I was to pass into the field and take position on the right, forming my line of battle and placing my batteries so as to support Brigadier General Milroy, whose brigade preceded mine in the march and was already getting into line. I was entirely without knowledge of the ground, but immediately proceeded to find the best position I could, according to these instructions, in the direction indicated.

I turned my artillery (De Beck's and Rigby's batteries) into and across the fields, supported by infantry, throwing the body of my infantry into line of battle and extending it in the rear of Milroy's brigade. As I advanced however, upon the open ridge first pointed out as probably the best on which to establish my batteries, about one-

---

[24] The 82nd Ohio was positioned near the Union right flank and was advancing towards Mill Creek opposite the Confederate 1st Maryland and 48th Virginia when Fremont's order to retire was received. The artillery exchange Lee references in his account occurred between Captain John Brockenbough's Maryland battery on the Confederate side, and De Beck's Battery K, 1st Ohio Light Artillery along with Rigby's Battery, Indiana Light Artillery.

[25] Jacobs is mistaken in this, as there were two Federal brigades engaged at Port Republic, one under Brigadier General Erastus B. Tyler and the second under Colonel Samuel S. Carroll. Despite a laudable effort by the two Federal brigades, Jackson was able to drive them back with heavy losses and secure his exit from the Valley to join with Robert E. Lee outside of Richmond a few weeks later.

fourth of a mile from the main road by which the column arrived, I discovered that I was brought into the rear of a line of woods through which Milroy was passing, also to the right. These woods at the same time concealed the enemy and character of the ground he was occupying, while they afforded no eligible protection for placing my guns so as to reach him. I became satisfied, too, from the character of the ground beyond as it now opened to us that the enemy would seek to extend the line of his forces on his left, so as, if possible, to outflank us. I hastened, therefore, to press forward to the right to anticipate any such movements and to occupy an extended ridge of higher ground half a mile farther to the south, which I found gave me a more commanding range and advanced me farther to the point, while it enabled me also to cover an early pass leading up from the enemy's position in front between the two ridges and all the open ground sloping away to the valley at the foot of the mountain, by one of which approaches the Rebels were to be expected to advance on that side. The position placed my brigade on the extreme right wing, which I occupied for the rest of the day.

To reach this point of advantage I had to cross a road in front of my first position and passing through the skirt of wood in which General Milroy had advanced, went over some wheat fields along the edge of another wood. This I accomplished without loss, though exposed to a pretty severe fire of shell from the enemy, marching my line-composed of the 73rd, 55th, and 82nd regiments of Ohio infantry, directed by flank, detaching the 73rd and 32nd Ohio to cover the artillery while moving by a more circuitous route. While effecting this, I was ordered by a messenger from the general commanding to detach Rigby's battery and send it to the relief of General Milroy. This was immediately done.

Reaching the farther position which I had selected, I found the line of woods extended still to the right and shutting in our front. An examination of these woods by companies of the 32nd and 73rd Ohio, immediately thrown forward as skirmishers, discovered the enemy concealed there in force and still endeavoring to extend himself to the left, with the evident object of turning our right, as I had expected. A few shells thrown into the woods on that side by De Beck's battery checked this movement and drove back the Rebel infantry farther to our left. The whole of the 73rd, 82nd, and 55th regiments being then deployed in the woods on my left front, formed in line of battle and slowly advanced, feeling the enemy's position and gradually being the concealed line of the Rebels to close quarters. The firing of small arms at once became brisk, especially with the 73rd Ohio, which seems to have been brought nearest the enemy's line and at this time several men were killed or wounded by the fire. It was at this point of time, too, that Dr. Cantwell, surgeon of the 82nd Ohio, fell severely wounded while he was passing along the line of his regiment carefully instructing the men detailed from each company to attend to conveying the wounded to the ambulances.

I believed that the moment for attacking and pressing the Rebels successfully on the wing had now arrived, and I brought forward the 32nd Ohio to advance also in the woods and form on the 73rd, extending thus the line to the right, and intending to order a charge which should sweep around the enemy's left flank and press him back toward our sustaining forces on the left. Never were troops in better temper for such work; but just as the 32nd Ohio was marching to the front for this purpose, leaving only the 75th Ohio in the rear to cover the battery, I received the order of the general commanding to withdraw slowly and in good order from my position and go to the relief of the left wing, composed of the brigades of Blenker's division. I felt reluctant to obey, because I was satisfied that the advantageous and promising position and condition of my brigade could not have been known at headquarters. I held my place, therefore, and sent back instantly to ascertain whether the emergency was such as to require me with all haste to retire. The order came back repeated. To prevent my being followed and harassed by the Rebels while falling back, I then began to withdraw my infantry, moving them carefully by the flank toward the left until I could uncover the enemy's line sufficiently to enable my battery to throw shot and shell into the woods. This done, I returned the 32nd Ohio to the support of the battery and commenced drawing off the whole of my force to the left along the same lines in which I had advanced them. Here, again, however, I was met by a messenger from the general commanding informing me that if I thought I could hold my ground I might remain, but stating that Milroy's brigade, my supporting force on the left had also been directed to retire, I stopped and threw the artillery again into battery at a point a few rods in the rear of the place which it had first occupied and ordered a number of rounds of quick, sharp firing into the woods occupied by the Rebels. The severe effect of this firing was discovered the next day by the number of Rebels found lying on that part of the battlefield; but while thus engaged Captain Piatt, my assistant adjutant general, ascertained for me that General Milroy, under the order he had received, was rapidly withdrawing his brigade, passing toward the left, and so I had to follow him or be left separated from all the rest of the forces. I returned however only to the ridge a half mile to the left which I had at first occupied and there remained, in pursuance of orders, encamped for the night. My other battery (Rigby's) which I understood had been very effectively engaged during the action on the left was here returned home. It was now perhaps 5:30-6 o'clock.

Late in the evening the enemy from the opposite point opened a brisk fire upon our camp and upon Hyman's battery, occupying the point of a hill at our left with what seemed to be a battery of two 6-pounders. This was probably a cover to his retreat, but he was replied to with so quick and hot a return by Hyman, Rigby, and De Beck that his fire was very soon silenced and, as afterward ascertained, both his guns dismounted. Subsequently a company of skirmishers from the 73rd Ohio had an encounter with skirmishers of the Rebels in the woods immediately in front of us, in which we had one man killed and another wounded; but otherwise we rested undisturbed until called to march in pursuit of the enemy again in the morning.

I regret to have to state that in the night a party detailed from the battalion of Connecticut cavalry (Sergeant Morehouse and four men of Company D) being sent to ascertain the position of Colonel Cluseret, commanding the advance brigade, lost their way and were captured as is supposed by the enemy pickets. The whole number of effective men of my brigade that I was enabled to action was as follows:

32nd Ohio	500
55th Ohio	525
73rd Ohio	295
75th Ohio	444
82nd Ohio	374
De Beck's Battery (6 guns)	94
Rigby's battery (5 guns)	91
Connecticut Cavalry	113

The casualties were, altogether, but four killed, seven wounded, and four missing.[26] I append in a separate report the names and commands of the killed and wounded. I cannot close this report without expressing my satisfaction with the officers and men generally of my command. Although worn down and reduced in numbers by days and weeks of constant fatigue and privation under long marches with insufficient supplies, which they have necessarily had to undergo, they were actively and cheerfully eager to meet the Rebel forces and only regretted that it could not be their fortune to encounter them for their share in more obstinate and decisive battle.

At daybreak next morning Schenk's command was called up and ordered to prepare to lead in that day's battle. In expectation of immediate action, the soldiers breakfasted hastily, examined their muskets, and replenished their ammunition. Soon after sunrise the command to advance was given and Schenk's regiments moved promptly, feeling their way through the woods. In a short time we came upon the scene of the previous day's conflict, but to our great surprise no picket was met, no shot fired, and no enemy in sight. The Confederate dead, unburied, lay scattered numerously through the woods. Among the enemy's slain I noticed as we passed along the body of a young man about 20 years of age who lay where he had fallen beside a tree. He had been instantly killed by a musket ball striking him in the forehead, and his face was illumined with a happy smile, as though death had been to him a joyous trance. In singular contrast with this in the road a little farther on was the body of an old man, also killed instantly, whose extended hands were clenched and whose features were distorted as if in a paroxysm of agony and horror. A third body, carefully deposited in the door yard of a farmhouse and covered with a blanket was that of a young Confederate officer, whose noble head and intelligent face were of a most captivating type of manly beauty. Schenk advanced over the ground which had been occupied by the enemy, prepared to encounter him at any moment and halted at the Mill Creek Church. In and around this solitary building many Confederate dead were

---

[26] The 82nd Ohio had only two men wounded this engagement: Surgeon Jacob Y. Cantwell and one enlisted man.

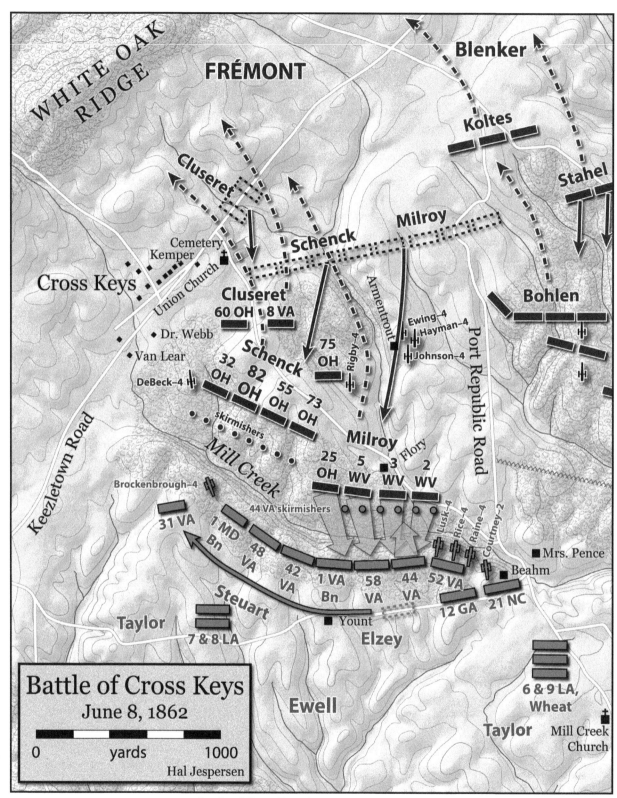

WHITE OAK RIDGE

FRÉMONT

Blenker

Koltes

Stahel

Cluseret

Milroy

Schenck

Cemetery
Kemper

Bohlen

Cross Keys

Union Church

Cluseret

60 OH   8 VA

Armentrout

Ewing–4   Hayman–4

Johnson–4

Dr. Webb

Schenck

75
OH

Rigby–4

Van Lear

32
OH

82
OH

55
OH

73
OH

DeBeck–4

skirmishers

Milroy   Flory

Mill Creek

25
OH

5
WV

3
WV

2
WV

Brockenbrough–4

44 VA skirmishers

Lusk–4

Rice–4

Raine–4

Courtney–2

Mrs. Pence

31 VA

1 MD
Bn

48
VA

42
VA

1 VA
Bn

58
VA

44
VA

52 VA

Beahm

Steuart

12 GA   21 NC

Taylor

Yount

7 & 8 LA

Elzey

Ewell

6 & 9 LA,
Wheat

Taylor

Mill Creek
Church

Keezletown Road

Port Republic Road

Battle of Cross Keys
June 8, 1862

0   yards   1000

Hal Jespersen

Battle of Cross Keys, Virginia, June 8, 1862
(Hal Jespersen, www.cwmaps.com)

lying, indicating that it had been used as a field hospital. Far ahead a column of dense smoke was seen, betokening the destruction of the Port Republic bridge and the escape of Jackson's entire army. All the fine hopes we had entertained of capturing our supple antagonist vanished immediately- vanished in smoke. But where was Shields, and what had happened to him? Let us see.

While Fremont was fighting Ewell and Dick Taylor at Cross Keys, Jackson was at Port Republic with two brigades- Winder's and Taliaferro's- looking personally after his sole avenue of retreat. His trains were yet parked on the north side of the river, and the bridgehead on the south side was held by a detachment of cavalry. Advancing up the Luray Valley, Shields' column had been detained by floods resulting from the extraordinary rainfall and also by the destruction (by Jackson's cavalry) of the principal bridges over the Shenandoah. Carroll's brigade, holding Shields' advance, was hurried forward to guard the river at Port Republic, and cut the Virginia Central Railroad at Waynesboro.

The village of Port Republic is situated in the angle formed by the junction of the North and South rivers, tributaries of the South Fork of the Shenandoah. Over the North River, which is the larger and deeper of the two streams, there was a wooden bridge connecting the town with the road leading to Harrisonburg. Across the South River there was a passable ford. The Confederate infantry with Jackson- Taliaferro's brigade of Winder's division- was encamped on the high ground north of the village about a mile from the river.

Riding ahead of his infantry, Carroll arrived on the bank of the South River opposite Port Republic about 6 o'clock on the morning of the 8th with a squadron of Virginia cavalry and four pieces of Ohio artillery. Seeing Jackson's wagon trains and beef cattle with but a small guard on the opposite side of the stream, Carroll charged and drove off the Confederate videttes at the crossing and dashed across the South River into the town. So unexpected was this attack, that two of Jackson's staff officers were captured and his wagon guards and teamsters fled in a panic. The Confederate cavalry was chased out of town, part of it escaping across the bridge and part of it in another direction. Two pieces of the Ohio artillery were then brought up and posted, one of them at the south end of the bridge. But Carroll, instead of destroying the bridge, of which he had possession for half an hour, bethought himself only as to how he should hold the town. Jackson, on the other hand, rushed for his infantry camped on the hills on the north side of the river, and with the first gun and regiment that were ready, made for the bridge on the double quick. Seeing this, our cavalry broke and fled in every direction, leaving the bridge and gun an easy prey for the charging Confederates. The other gun, posted in the town, was brought off, but in following the panic-stricken cavalry to the woods, it became entangled in the brush and was abandoned. In a few minutes the whole north bank bristled with the enemy's cannon and a shower of shot and shell rained upon our fugitive troopers and upon the infantry which was approaching to reinforce them.

Bringing off with difficulty two guns which he had posted upon an eminence to cover the bridge, Carroll retreated down the river to Lewiston- three miles- and at 2 P.M. reinforced by Tyler's brigade, sent forward to his support. Shields, with the remainder of his division, was yet at Conrad's Store, 12 miles below. Tyler and Carroll concluded that it would be hazardous while they were so far from the main body to undertake another attack with the force they had and decided to halt and observe the movements of the enemy. They did not have to wait long for interesting developments.

Having withdrawn Ewell from before Fremont, Jackson began crossing the Shenandoah at daybreak on the 9th and turned his course down the river. Upon discovering this movement, Tyler, against the judgment of Carroll who advised retreat, decided to stay where he was and fight it out. He had posted his command on high ground, with his right extending through open fields and his left resting in a dense wood east of the main road. His right wing, which was commanded by Carroll, comprised the 7th Indiana (Colonel James Gavin), 29th Ohio (Colonel Louis P. Buckley), 7th Ohio (Lieutenant Colonel William P. Creighton), 5th Ohio (Colonel Samuel H. Dunning), and the 1st West Virginia (Colonel Joseph Thoburn). On the left were the 66th Ohio under Colonel Charles Candy, commanding on that part of the field, and the 84th (Major Walter Barrett) and 110th Pennsylvania (Colonel William D. Lewis). Along the line which was so formed as to cover all the approaches from Port Republic were distributed the guns of Clarke's, Robinson's, and Huntingdon's batteries. Winder's brigade, leading Jackson's column, soon appeared on both sides of the road and drove in Tyler's skirmishers. Carroll opened at once with his artillery, firing grape and canister, and did such execution as to hold the enemy in check. Unable to either withstand or silence our guns,

Winder, reinforced by Taylor's brigade, undertook to charge and capture them. But Carroll was ready for him, and drove back his whole force in disorder. Carroll then charged in turn, and captured one gun which was taken by the 5th Ohio.

While this was going on, Jackson sent two regiments and a section of artillery under Colonel Allen around by his right flank to assail our left. With much difficulty Allen's force succeeded in breaking through the thickets, but no sooner did it appear before our lines than it was overwhelmed by a storm of musketry and canister which drove it back in confusion. Jackson then sent the bulk of Taylor's brigade to execute what Allen had failed to accomplish and after passing our flank, Taylor fell upon it so suddenly as to capture six guns. But Colonel Candy was not dismayed and with the help of the 5th and 7th Ohio sent to his assistance, he repulsed Taylor and retook the lost pieces. Unfortunately, the horses had all been killed and the guns again fell into the hands of the enemy. "Three times," says Jackson's report, "was this battery lost and won in the desperate and determined efforts to capture and recover it."[27]

Soldiers could not fight more stubbornly and bravely than did ours. But Jackson, astonished at the resistance which he met, called up nearly his whole command. Taylor was reinforced and returned to the charge. Taliaferro's brigade and some additional batteries came to the help of Winder, who rallied his broken regiments and renewed the assault. Right and left simultaneously, our troops were overwhelmed by nearly three times their number and Tyler was obliged at last to follow Carroll's advice and order a retreat. As soon as the withdrawal of our forces began, the captured guns were turned upon our rear regiments and the enemy's cavalry charged, causing for a time what seemed to be a complete rout. Colonel Carroll was directed by Tyler to cover the retreat, and with much difficulty organized a force for that purpose. The enemy pursued for five miles and captured an additional gun. He also took about 450 prisoners and 800 muskets.

Thus Jackson bore off the honors of the campaign, and made for himself an open road to Richmond, whither he was soon summoned to aid Lee in repelling McClellan. By orders from Washington, Shields was at once recalled to Luray so that McDowell might go to McClellan's assistance. Fremont was directed to withdraw to Harrisonburg and there halt, but believing that place to be untenable, he decided upon his own responsibility to proceed further down the valley.

Fremont did not finally halt, as we shall see, until he reached Middletown. At Mount Jackson, reported to the President on June 12th that he had retired thither "upon intelligence of General Shields' defeat and withdrawal towards Richmond" and asked for reinforcements, particularly Sigel's corps. On the same

---

[27] The Union guns were placed on an eminence called "The Coaling."

Port Republic

"We drove the Rebels back three times but as fast as they were driven back fresh troops filled their places. At one time a brigade of the enemy was marching toward our batteries when we opened on them with grape and canister, mowing them down by companies but their places were soon filled up."

"General Tyler seeing that we were outnumbered ordered us to retreat and I think it was a second Bull Run. We left our dead and wounded on the battlefield. Our regiment was cut all to pieces, only 270 escaping. I was taken prisoner with 12 others but while the Secesh were loading we got up and ran. They fired but missed us as we were in the woods and could not see us very plain. I could hear them behind me saying 'Halt!' and "Kill that damn Yankee," but I trusted to my legs and kept in the woods for a mile and a half and escaped without a scratch."

~ *Private John T. Coverdale, Co. C, 5th Ohio Infantry*

day he sent Colonel Charles Zagonyi, a member of his staff, a written communication to the President, making substantially the same representations and requests. On the 13th he suggested that Shields- whose position at Luray he deemed "very much exposed," should be directed to join him at Mount Jackson. He also inquired whether Sigel was under his command.

The President in different communications replied that he had ordered the halt at Harrisonburg to prevent Jackson from returning to the Upper Potomac, and to protect West Virginia against a raid, but that he acquiesced in the withdrawal to Mount Jackson; that Sigel was under Banks, and that Banks, though not subordinate to Fremont, would cooperate with him; that if Sigel and McDowell (Shields) were sent forward to Fremont, "Jackson would break through at Front Royal again;" that Jackson's game was to divert as much of our force as possible from Richmond by spreading exaggerated reports of his numbers and movements; that Jackson was "much more likely to go to Richmond than Richmond to come to him;" that "the true policy" was for Banks and Fremont, keeping within supporting distance of each other to hold both the "Front Royal line" and the "Strasburg line" and that neither Fremont nor Banks would be overwhelmed by Jackson if due diligence should be exercised.

On the 14th Fremont again telegraphed for reinforcements to hold Mount Jackson, although there appears to have been particular cause for his solicitude, except that "the enemy's pickets were ten miles this side of Harrisonburg." On the 15th, Fremont reminded the President that when he was assigned to "this command" he was informed that he should have "a corps of 35,000 men." He asked for a "fulfillment of this understanding" in order, as he says, that he may "take Staunton, hold the railroad there, go down through Lexington, seize the railroad between Lynchburg and Newberne and hold it for General Banks' troops, or destroy it, according to circumstances." He represented that "whether from Richmond or elsewhere" the forces of the enemy were certainly coming into this region; that his own force has been greatly weakened by "casualties" and that "our troops are so scattered as to be liable to attack by superior numbers."

The President on the 16th replied somewhat caustically that he was "ready to come to a fair settlement of accounts on the fulfillment of understandings," adding: "Early in March last, when I assigned you to the command of the Mountain Department, I did tell you I would give you all the force I could, and I hoped to make it reach 35,000. You at the same time told me that within a reasonable time you would seize the railroad at or east of Knoxville, Tennessee if you could. There was then in the department a force supposed to be 25,000, the exact number as well known to you as to me. After looking about two or three days, you called and distinctly told me that if I would add the Blenker division to the force already in the department, you would undertake the job. The Blenker division contained 10,000, and at the expense of great dissatisfaction to General McClellan I took it from his army and gave it to you. My promise was literally fulfilled. I have given you all I could and I have given you nearly if not quite 35,000. Now for yours. On the 23rd of May, over two months afterward, you were at Franklin, Virginia, not within 300 miles of Knoxville, nor within 80 miles of any part of the railroad east of it, and not moving anything forward, but telegraphing here that you could not move for lack of everything. Now do not misunderstand me. I do not say you have not done all you could. I presume you met unexpected difficulties; and I beg you to believe that, as surely as you have done your best, so have I. I have not the power now to fill up your corps to 35,000. I am not demanding of you to do the work of 35,000. I am only asking of you to stand cautiously on the defensive; get your force in order, and give such protection as you can to the valley of the Shenandoah and to western Virginia. Have you received the orders, and will you act upon them?" Fremont dryly responded to the telegraph: "Your dispatch of today is received. In reply to that part of it which concerns the orders sent to me, I have to say that they have been received and that, as a matter of course, I will act upon them, as I am now doing."

The retrograde march of Fremont's force from Port Republic began on the morning of June 10, in the midst of a drenching rain, which crowned the discomfort the disappointing outcome of all the hard marching and fighting of the campaign. The extraordinary exposure, fatigue, and nervous strain had by this time told fearfully upon the men, the majority of whom were yet fresh in the service, and those who were down with malignant fever or other maladies, added to the wounded in battle, more than filled all the ambulances and other disposable vehicles. The strength of many who were really not well had been sustained by the exhilaration of the pursuit of Jackson, but suddenly collapsed as soon as that stimulus was withdrawn; and thousands who were too sick to walk were nevertheless obliged to do so, or remain behind and be captured. Thus the army of stragglers that spread out through the fields and woods became nearly or quite as numerous as the army marching with the colors. The writer, who had been suffering from the prevailing malady of the camp since leaving Mount Jackson, now found himself barely able to walk even with the assistance of a fellow soldier.

Returning to Harrisonburg, the army took its course down the turnpike to New Market and thence to Mount Jackson, where a halt was called for a day or two. From Mount Jackson, the movement was continued to Strasburg and on the 24th of June the forces led by Fremont joined those under Banks and Sigel at Middletown.

CHAPTER TWO

To Slaughter Mountain and Beyond

By an order of the President dated June 26, 1862, the Army of Virginia was organized and Major General John Pope was designated as its commander. This army comprised the various forces which had been acting independently and without effective cooperation or satisfactory results under Fremont, Banks, and McDowell. It was composed of three army corps and a division of cavalry, numbering in all an effective force of 43,000 men. The troops of the Mountain Department which had been engaged in the campaign against Jackson constituted the 1st Corps, 11,500 strong under Fremont; those of the Shenandoah Department the 2nd Corps numbering on paper 14,500, but less detachments, really only 8,000 strong under Banks; and those of the Rappahannock Department, excepting the Washington garrisons, the 3rd Corps 18,500 strong under McDowell. The cavalry numbering about 5,000 horsemen, very imperfectly mounted and equipped, comprised two brigades under Generals Buford and Bayard. The Mountain Department and the Departments of the Shenandoah and Rappahannock were abolished.[28]

General Fremont, unwilling to serve under General Pope, who was his junior in rank and had been his subordinate in the West, asked to be and was immediately relieved of the command of the 1st Corps. The following correspondence is of interest in this connection:

Middletown, June 27, 1862, 12:30 P.M.

Hon. E.M. Stanton,
Secretary of War

I respectfully ask that the President will relieve me of my present command. I submit for his consideration that the position assigned me by his recent order is subordinate and inferior to those hitherto conceded me and not fairly corresponding with the rank I hold in the army. I further desire to call his attention to the fact that to remain in the subordinate command to which I am now assigned would virtually and largely reduce my rank and consideration in the service of the country. For these reasons, I earnestly request that the President will not require the order to take effect so far as I am concerned, but will consent immediately to relieve me.
J.C. Fremont, Major General, U.S. Army

War Department, June 27, 1862

Major General Fremont, Middletown:

Your telegram requesting to be relieved from duty has been received and laid before the President, who directs me to say that, Congress having by special resolution vested him with authority to assign the chief command between officers of the same grade as he might consider best for the service of the country, without regard to priority of rank, he exercised that authority in respect to the Army of Virginia, as he has done in other instances, in the manner which, in his judgment, was required for the service, and without design to detract from the "rank and consideration" of any general. General Pope was the junior in rank but of the same grade not only of yourself but also of Generals Banks and McDowell, neither of whom have considered their rank and consideration in the service of the country as a condition upon which they should withdraw from the service. The President regrets that any officer in the service should withdraw from the service of his country in any position where he is lawfully assigned by his commander-in-chief, but he cannot consistently with his sense of duty grant your request than an order made,

---

[28] The text of this chapter comprises four articles that Captain Lee wrote for the *Magazine of American History* in 1886, including "Cedar Mountain I," "Cedar Mountain II," "From Cedar Mountain to Chantilly I," and "From Cedar Mountain to Chantilly II."

according to his judgment, for the welfare of the nation, should not be required "to take effect so far as you are concerned." The obligation of duty is the same upon all officers in the service, whatever their rank, and if there be any difference it should be most readily observed by those of highest rank. Your request, therefore, to be relieved from your present command is granted. You will turn over your command and orders to the officer next highest in rank to yourself, and direct him to the department for further orders.

Edwin M. Stanton, Secretary of War

General Rufus King, commanding at Fredericksburg, was assigned to lead the 1st Corps in lieu of Fremont, but the German troops who constituted the greater part of the corps indicated a strong desire to have Major General Franz Sigel for their commander. Orders were almost immediately so changed as to gratify their wishes. General Sigel had been sent by the War Department on the 1st of June to command the troops at Harper's Ferry under Banks and after Jackson's retreat he had been advanced with a division 5,500 men to Middletown.

On the 1st of July the Army of the Potomac, beaten back by the combined forces of Lee and Jackson, withdrew to Harrison's Landing. At that time the Army of Virginia was scattered from Winchester to Fredericksburg and it became the immediate concern of General Pope, looking to the contingencies of the near future, to concentrate the whole of his forces east of the Blue Ridge. He therefore directed that Sigel's corps at Middletown should move by way of Luray and Thornton's Gap to Sperryville, and that Banks' corps should come in on the left of Sigel's, six miles farther to the east. Of McDowell's corps, the headquarters of which were at Manassas Junction, Ricketts' division was directed to take its position at Waterloo Bridge, east of Banks, and King's division was required to remain, as yet, at Falmouth. At Madison Courthouse, 25 miles south of Sigel's new position, Buford's cavalry, joined on the left by Bayard's, kept watch along the line of the Rapidan.

With a view to securing harmony and cooperation among the armies of the Union, particularly those operating in Virginia, Major General Halleck was appointed July 23, 1862 to the general command with his headquarters at Washington. To what extent this arrangement produced harmony and with what success field operations in Virginia were supervised and directed from a desk in the capital will be seen in the sequel. While the foregoing preparations were in progress, General Pope, our new commander, introduced himself to us in a series of remarkable general orders. The first of these dated from Washington July 14 ran thus:

To the officers and soldiers of the Army of Virginia:

By special assignment of the President of the United States, I have assumed command of this army. I have spent two weeks in learning your whereabouts, your condition, and your wants; in preparing you for active operations, and in placing you in positions from which you can act promptly and to the purpose. These labors are nearly completed and I am about to join you in the field. Let us understand each other. I have come to you from the West where we have always seen the backs of our enemies; from an army whose business it has been to seek the adversary and beat him when he was found; whose policy has been attack and not defense. In but one instance has the enemy been able to place our Western armies in defensive attitude. I presume that I have been called here to pursue the same system and to lead you against the enemy. It is my purpose to do so and that speedily. I am sure you long for an opportunity to win distinction you are capable of achieving. That opportunity I shall endeavor to give you. Meantime I desire you to dismiss from your minds certain phrases which I am sorry to find so much in vogue amongst you. I hear constantly of "taking strong positions and holding them" of "lines of retreat" and of "bases of supplies." Let us discard such ideas. The strongest position a soldier should desire to occupy is one from which he can most easily advance against the enemy. Let us study the probable lines of retreat of our opponents and leave our own to take care of themselves. Let us look before us, not behind. Success and glory are in the advance, disaster and shame lurk in the rear. Let us act on this understanding and it is safe to predict that your banners shall be inscribed with many a glorious deed, and that your names will be dear to your countrymen forever.

Jno. Pope, Major General commanding

Read as a sequel to the campaign of which it was the unfortunate prelude, this pronunciamento needs no exposition as a masterpiece of un-wisdom.[29] On the 18th of July, it was followed by a second order, also issued from Washington, declaring that "hereafter, as far as practicable, the troops of this command will subsist upon the country in which their operations are carried on." When supplies were taken from the inhabitants, vouchers were to be given, payable at the conclusion of the war on proof of loyalty. A third order, dated Washington July 20, proclaimed the summary and severe punishment of all bushwhackers and guerillas, with their aids and abettors. A fourth order of July 23, likewise from Washington, directed the immediate arrest of all disloyal male citizens within our reach and the expulsion beyond our lines of all such as refused to take the oath of allegiance. If any of the persons thus expelled should afterwards be found anywhere within the circuit of the Union pickets, they were to be treated as spies and any citizen detected in violating the oath of allegiance administered to him in conformity with the order, was to be shot, and suffer confiscation of property. Verily, the Secession had fallen upon hard lines so far as orders and proclamations were concerned.

Sigel's corps began its march eastward from Middletown on the 6th of July. The camps of Schurz's division were pitched the next evening near Front Royal, and the division headquarters were established at the house of a Mr. McKay, with whom the famous Confederate spy Belle Boyd, then paroled, was staying. "Belle's appearance," says one of the division staff officers "was not especially striking, except her large, black eyes which were really fine. Her face was thin, and she looked fatigued and careworn. Apparently she was about 30 years of age."[30] McKay and family were fierce secessionists, and refused to take greenbacks in pay for their hospitalities- that is to say, for meals and the privilege of sleeping on the floor. They insisted on payment in gold, but on being informed that they must accept our national paper currency or nothing, they chose the currency. On the 7th, the 1st Corps crossed the Shenandoah River by pontoon bridges and the march was resumed. The midsummer heat was intense and the troops suffered much from scarcity of water. The 1st Corps was at this time commanded by General Robert C. Schenk, in the absence of General Sigel, who had been called to Washington on business connected with the reorganization of his command, much of which, at the time Sigel took charge of it, was in an exceedingly indifferent state of discipline and equipment.[31]

---

[29] Lee was quite correct in his assessment- Pope's inflammatory rhetoric in this 'pronunciamento' was taken as a direct insult by many soldiers of the Army of the Potomac, while his subsequent general orders were interpreted by many Confederate soldiers as a declaration of war upon the civil population of Virginia. Robert E. Lee labeled Pope as a "miscreant who must be suppressed."

[30] Isabella Maria "Belle" Boyd, also known as "The Siren of the Shenandoah" was only 18 years of age in 1862 but was already notorious for her exploits in furthering the Southern cause. Boyd had been recently exchanged and was staying with relatives (the McKays) in Front Royal. She would be arrested again on July 29, 1862 and sent to Old Capitol Prison in Washington, D.C.

[31] The organization of the 1st Army Corps was at this time as follows: First Division, Brigadier General Robert C. Schenk, commanding: First Brigade General Julius Stahel; Second Brigade Colonel Nathaniel C. McLean. Second Division, Brigadier General Adolph Von Steinwehr: First Brigade Colonel John A. Koltes, Second Brigade Colonel Lloyd (afterwards Lieutenant Colonel Gustav A. Muhleck). Third Division, Brigadier General Carl Schurz: First Brigade, General Henry Bohlen (afterwards Colonel Alexander Schimmelfennig), Second Brigade Wladimir Krzyzanowski. Independent Brigade, Brigadier General Robert H. Milroy. Detached Brigade, Brigadier General A. Sanders Piatt. This brigade, though temporarily attached to the corps, never really served with it. The original intention was that the brigades of Milroy and Piatt should form a division under Milroy, but that design was not carried out. The artillery and cavalry of the corps were distributed amongst the various infantry brigades, but a cavalry brigade was afterwards organized under Colonel John Beardsley. The Blenker division of infantry was broken up, and its regiments were distributed among the divisions of Schenk, Von Steinwehr, and Schurz. The reserve artillery was commanded by Captain Louis Schirmer. ~Lee Note.

Brigadier General Robert H. Milroy
(Library of Congress)

Milroy's Independent Brigade led the column followed by Schenk's division under Colonel George Von Amsberg (45th New York); Schurz's division brought up the rear. Regardless of the excessive heat and the absence of any special occasion for haste, Milroy rushed the men along so rapidly that many suffered permanent injury from exhaustion and sunstroke. On the evening of the 10th Schurz, overtook the commands of Milroy and Von Amsberg encamped near Luray. This pretty village lies at the foot of the Blue Ridge, in the midst of a fruitful valley watered by the bright current of the Shenandoah. The war had caused, as yet, few ravages in this beautiful region. The fences were in order, the barns well filled, and the farmers undisturbed in the tillage of their land. Shields' division, which had passed through the valley some weeks before, had committed no serious depredation.

Writing at this stage of the march, a division staff officer says in his diary:

"When we marched from Luray next day, Milroy, as usual, had the advance, followed by the First Division, and then by ours. We were ready to move at the time fixed, but the First Division did not stir. An aide was therefore dispatched to Colonel Von Amsberg, inquiring the cause of the delay, and returning reporting that most of Milroy's men were yet in camp, having refused to march until they had drawn rations for the day; and that Milroy, after failing to persuade the men that rations would be brought up in wagons, had gone off with one regiment, telling the others to go to the devil, and come on when they wanted to. On that same day, while we were crossing the Blue Ridge through Thornton's Gap, I saw General Milroy in another character. There were a great many cherry trees along the line of march, and they were fairly bending with the burden of their fruit. I had occasion to ride forward during a temporary halt and found the men improving the few minutes allowed them to get as many cherries as they could. After passing through the First Division, I looked in vain for Milroy's men, although since he had the advance guard, I expected to find his men kept together. At last I saw the muskets of a regiment with knapsacks, coats, caps, and cartridge boxes lying around and here and there a soldier sleeping under the shade of a tree minus his coat, boots, and accoutrements. I asked a tall sergeant carrying the limb of a cheery tree who these men were, and he replied "Milroy's."

"And where is your general?" I asked.

"Why, don't you see him? There he is, in that cherry tree."

"And sure enough, Milroy and his staff had climbed a cherry tree and were enjoying the fruit as unconcerned as if they were at home, and no enemy at hand. The whole advance guard was picking cherries, the battery was standing in the road, and no pickets were stationed. It was fortunate that none of Stuart's cavalry happened to be around about that time. The following evening we arrived at Sperryville and after the troops were encamped, we established headquarters at the house of a secessionist named Miller. *Three days later*, the remaining regiments of Milroy's brigade arrived."[32]

In these incidents, the reader will perceive something of the nature of General Sigel's task in bringing about a proper state of discipline and military morale to his command.[33] With its headquarters at Sperryville, the 1st Corps covered with two divisions (Schenk's and Schurz's) the roads centering on the village, while Von Steinwehr's division held a post of observation at Luray, and occupied a pass over the Blue Ridge at Thornton's Gap. Milroy's brigade pitched its camps at Woodville, a pretty hamlet on the Culpeper Turnpike three miles south of Sperryville, and here, after 20 days absence caused by sickness, the writer found again his comrades of the Valley campaign.[34] On the 19th of July, a detachment comprising two infantry regiments, four guns, and some squadrons of horsemen under Colonel Gustav P. Cluseret (he of Fremont's advance guard) were thrown forward to Criglersville, five miles northwest of Madison Courthouse, to watch the enemy in that neighborhood and act as a reserve to the cavalry brigade of General Buford.

Cluseret had served over 20 years in the French army in which he had fought at Algiers, in the Crimea, and in the Austro-Italian War. Coming to this country in 1862, he received an appointment as an additional aide-de-camp and was assigned to duty with Major General Fremont, in whose command he performed the services already narrated. Cluseret was an energetic and ambitious officer, brave even to recklessness. He knew little of the English language and disdained to learn it. While he was stationed at Criglersville, he caused all the citizens of that neighborhood to be brought before him for the purpose of administering to them the oath of allegiance, as required by the orders of General Pope. In his broken English, he addressed them as follows: "All who vants to take ze oats go on zis side and who all vants not to take ze oats go on ze ozer side." The astonished Virginia farmers, hardly knowing what to make of this, thought the colonel wanted them to take back some wagon loads of oats which he had seized for the cavalry. Furious at this misapprehension, Cluseret began swearing in French and told the bewildered rustics to go to "ze devil" when a member of his staff who could speak French explained to him the mistake he had made in his pronunciation and set matters right. After that, Colonel Cluseret renounced the English language entirely. In January 1863, he was appointed brigadier general and commanded a brigade at Winchester, but during the ensuing May he resigned his commission owing to some difference with General Milroy, commanding that department, and went to New York where he became a correspondent of several French newspapers. After the war of 1870 between France and Germany, in which he participated, Cluseret took sides with the Paris Commune and was arrested and condemned to death, but escaped.

---

[32] Carl Schurz remembered that Milroy's "notions of military discipline were somewhat singular. He lived on a footing of very democratic comradeship with his men. The most extraordinary stories were told of his discussing with his subordinates what was to be done, of his permitting them to take amazing liberties with the orders to be executed. At the different headquarters of divisions and brigades of the corps, 'Old Milroy's' latest was always eagerly expected, and then circulated, frequently amplified and adorned with great freedom of invention. But he did good service and was respected and liked by all." Schurz, Carl. Reminiscences of Carl Schurz. New York: Doubleday, Page, and Company, 1917.

[33] Sigel also had the hard task of gaining respect from his new commanding officer. Pope and Sigel took a quick dislike to one another; Pope dismissed Sigel as a "nervous little German" whose military reputation rested upon questionable laurels won in the West. Sigel reciprocated, referring to Pope as "offensive, arrogant, and pompous," and claimed Pope "was affected with looseness of the brains as others with looseness of the bowels. Moreover, Pope did not manage from sound course or judgment but from mere fancy and desperation." Engle, Stephen D. Yankee Dutchman: The Life of Franz Sigel. Baton Rouge: University of Louisiana Press, 1993, pgs. 128-131, 138

[34] Lieutenant Lee was granted a 20 day leave of absence starting June 22, 1862 to recover his health. Military Service Record of Alfred E. Lee, Form 86, National Archives and Records Administration.

After passing east of the Blue Ridge, our troops were permitted to enjoy a period of rest which was most opportune. The hardships of the Valley campaign had been extreme, and the depletion of our regiments from the joint effects of sickness and the casualties of battle was enormous. Some of the newer regiments, which had gone into the campaign a thousand strong, had now not over 250 men in the ranks. Many had perished from disease and thousands were in hospitals. Fortunately our camps were pitched in a healthful and agreeable region, and the weather was propitious for the recovery of the men from their campaign ailments. I venture to reproduce here, from my diary, the following description of the surroundings of Milroy's brigade:

> July 25- Camp Dewberry is the name given by our soldiers to their encampment near Woodville. It derives its name from the Rubus Canadensis, or trailing blackberry which grows in great abundance in the unplowed fields of the neighborhood. The same lies in the midst of a gently rolling country and commands a fascinating view of the distant mountains and the intervening hills and valleys. Ranged along the western horizon, the notched outline of the Blue Ridge trends away to the northward, enveloped in a vapory shroud of delicate ever living blue. Through the long midsummer day, 'White fleecy clouds, are wandering in thick flocks along the mountains, shepherded by the slow, unwilling wind.' Their shadows creep up and down the massive slopes of the range and their silvery volumes group together and linger as if engaged in cloud gossip, or whispering their confidences to the solemn cliffs. When the sun goes down, the mountains project their lengthening shadows upon the heated camps, and as darkness gathers their giant forms are silhouetted against the star-sprinkled sky.

Camp life at Sperryville had also some interesting personal phases. Here is one taken, perhaps I should say, purloined, from the diary of a young German officer of Schurz's division:

> Whilst we were encamped near Sperryville, I made the acquaintance of a charming young lady Miss Bertha H. Captain G of an Ohio regiment introduced me, and I soon found that Miss Bertha was a perfect lady and very beautiful. Such eyes I never before beheld! Her mouth was dimpled and rosy, her teeth like pearl, her hair dark and wavy, and her figure delicately molded. She was highly accomplished, sang well, played the piano to perfection, and was called the belle of Sperryville. I must confess that the young Secesh damsel captivated me, and every afternoon found me in her delightful company. I endeavored to make myself as agreeable as I could, and Miss Bertha was particularly pleased at the little German songs I sang. She wanted to learn German and we were getting along very well, when the order to march came, and all vanished. The parting was very affectionate, and she told me if I should ever be captured, to write a few lines to her father, the Honorable Mr. H- of the Confederate Congress, and I would be well treated. I thanked her for her kindness, jumped on my horse, and never saw her again.

On the 4th of August the order was given to McClellan from Washington to withdraw his army from Harrison's Landing and transport it by water to Aquia Creek, thence to support a direct movement on Richmond. [35] Nearly at the same time the advance of General Lee's army pushed northward, drove in General Bayard's pickets, and crossed the Rapidan at several points west of the Orange and Alexandria Railroad. On the 6th of August, a broiling hot day, General Banks' corps passed Woodville going southward and for many hours the turnpike was crowded with its artillery, wagons, and dust-covered columns of infantry. On the 7th, General Pope arrived at Sigel's headquarters and made a hasty review of the troops while, as it happened, they were maneuvering in the fields near the turnpike. Pope rode on toward Culpeper Courthouse where he arrived the next morning. After quitting Sigel, he sent back the following dispatch dated August 8: "Hold your whole command in readiness to move forward at a moment's warning. The enemy is advancing."

Before receiving this, Sigel had been apprised of the enemy's designs by Cluseret who the day before (August 7) had reported from Criglersville that early on the 8th Stonewall Jackson with 25,000 men would march toward Culpeper, intending to sweep around by way of Woodville and Sperryville. Later in the day, Sigel received from Cluseret the following addressed by Colonel Ruggles, Pope's chief of staff, to General Buford and by him

---

[35] The withdrawal did not begin until some days afterward and McClellan's rear guard did not get away from Harrison's Landing until August 16, 1862. ~ Lee note.

transmitted to Cluseret: "The enemy are advancing against Bayard in force in front of this place." In forwarding this to Sigel, Cluseret endorsed these comments in French. "This dispatch seems to me to define the situation and to be in conformity with what I sent yesterday. The enemy will try to pass between Culpeper and Madison. I shall act according to what he will do, because thus far I have not decisive information."

Now at this time Buford's cavalry brigade was at Madison Courthouse and Bayard's at or near Rapidan Station. Jackson was advancing against Bayard and Sigel's position was such as to afford him an excellent opportunity, as he thought, to strike the enemy in flank. For this purpose he might march from Woodville to James City and being there joined by Buford and Cluseret, he could fall upon Jackson in the neighborhood of Calvin's Tavern. Or, at James City, he could change direction toward Culpeper, should that seem to be most expedient. Now as Pope, in directing Sigel to be ready to march, had said nothing as to the line of march, Sigel deemed it his duty to inquire what route he should take and thereby direct Pope's mind to the propriety of the flank movement and attack as just described.[36] At all events, the uncertainty which existed, as Pope himself states, as to whether the enemy was aiming toward Madison or Culpeper, made the inquiry a perfectly proper one. General Pope represents that this first inquiry of Sigel's about the road caused such delay in the movement of the 1st Corps as to render the corps unavailable in the battle on the 9th.[37]

General Pope is in error. Sigel's inquiry caused no delay whatever in the movement of his corps, nor was there any delay in the movement of that corps for which General Sigel was responsible. Sigel's dispatch inquiring what road he should take was dated, Pope says, at 6: 50 P.M. August 8. After it was written and sent, Sigel received from Pope the following dated Culpeper August 8, hour not given: "The enemy has attacked our left and is advancing on this place. Major General Pope directs, in consequence thereof, that you move your command at once to this point. You will move on the road from Sperryville to Culpeper and must encamp tonight at the point where that road crosses the Hazel River. You will continue the march tomorrow morning so as to arrive here at as early an hour as possible, unless otherwise ordered."[38] This dispatch was received by Sigel between 7 and 8 o'clock the evening of August 8. It was obeyed

General Robert H. Milroy

"General Milroy was an Indianan of gaunt appearance and was strikingly Western in character and manners. When he met an enemy, he would gallop up and down his front, fiercely shaking his fist at the 'Rebel scoundrels over there' and calling them all sorts of outrageous names. His favorite word of command was 'Pitch in, boys, pitch in!' And he would 'pitch in' at the head of his men, exposing himself with the utmost recklessness. He was a man of intense patriotism. He did not fight as one who merely likes fighting. The cause for which he was fighting- his country, the integrity of the Republic, the freedom of the slave- was constantly present in his mind."

~ *Major General Carl Schurz*

---

[36] Sigel's inquiry about the road sent Pope into a rage as there was only one road between Sperryville and Culpeper. Pope tore up Sigel's dispatch and denounced the German as "slow and stupid. He could not imagine that Sigel could be that incompetent." Engle, op. cit., pg. 132

[37] General Pope's fault-finding with Sigel, here referred to, is contained in his general report written at the close of the campaign and is quite at variance with a previous report written by him on the 13th of August in which he says, referring to the Cedar Mountain battle, "I desire publicly to express my appreciation of the prompt and skillful manner in which Generals McDowell and Sigel brought forward their respective commands and established them on the field and of their cheerful and hearty cooperation with me from beginning to end." ~ Lee note.

[38] In a later dispatch to Sigel, Pope directs: "Move your command tonight to Hazel River and march to this point early tomorrow morning." This was received by Sigel on the march and shows than an earlier movement than during the night of the 8th was not expected. ~ Lee note.

instantly. As soon as it came, it was communicated to the commanders of divisions and a few minutes later the different columns were filing out of their camps into the turnpike. Milroy's brigade led. It broke up its camps shortly after sundown, was on the road at dark, and marched all night. About an hour before midnight, the column reached Hazel River, and there, in accordance with Pope's instructions, Schenk and Schurz encamped. Milroy, with his usual impatience, desired to push on at once to Culpeper, and was allowed to do so. This continuance of the night march by Milroy was permitted all the more readily on account of the excessive heat, which in the daytime marked 100 degrees in the shade. Even at night, the atmosphere was disagreeably sultry.

Sigel was directed to proceed from Hazel River to Culpeper on the morning of the 9th "unless otherwise ordered." He was otherwise ordered. Intending to make an early start, he was ready to move at 5 o'clock when he received from Pope the following dated Culpeper Courthouse August 9: "You will please halt your command at Hazel Run. Let the men get something to eat, and lie down and rest. If it necessary for you to come forward today, word will be sent to you in time. If you are on this side of the Hazel River, you will please halt your command at the first convenient place. The major general commanding desires you to advise him when you arrive at Hazel River."

Detained by this, Sigel waited until 9 o'clock or later when he received an order to bring his corps forward at once to Culpeper. The order was immediately put into execution. The heat of the sun was again excessive and the troops moved forward amidst stifling clouds of dust. A train of 1,100 wagons followed the column. In the Valley Campaign, our wagon equipment had been insufficient and now it was redundant. The 1st Corps had to carry four wheels for every twelve men. Having put his divisions in motion at Hazel River, Sigel rode forward and at about 11 o'clock personally reported to Pope at his headquarters at Culpeper. He found the general commanding sitting in a rocking chair, smoking a cigar, and apparently in good humor. Sigel gave a full account of his movements and Pope seemed to be entirely satisfied. Nothing was said about delay, and no complaint or reproach was uttered.

Milroy, as we have seen, marched all night. He arrived at Culpeper just at sunrise, and led his troops, weary and covered with dust, into a wood east of town *where they remained all day*. Before leaving Sperryville, Sigel called up Von Steinwehr's division from Luray and directed Cluseret to move eastward from Criglersville. During the morning of the 9th these orders were in the course of execution. Banks' corps was at Culpeper, except Crawford's brigade, which had arrived there some days before, and had been thrown forward (on the 8th) to support Buford's cavalry. Rickett's division of McDowell's corps had come up from Waterloo Bridge on the 8th and had gone forward to hold an important road crossing three miles south of town. King's division of the same corps had been summoned from Falmouth, and was marching toward Culpeper via Stevensburg.

Such, in brief, was the situation of our army early on the 9th. The demonstrations against our cavalry pickets the day before had been such as to make it very uncertain whether the enemy meant to move toward Madison Courthouse or Culpeper. While in doubt on this subject, Pope had resolved to keep himself on the interior line, and concentrate his forces toward Culpeper. He was thus enabled to hold his communications with Fredericksburg and the lower fords of the Rappahannock, as he had been instructed to do. While our troops were thus concentrating the enemy was hastening to take advantage of their scattered condition. Ewell's division of Stonewall Jackson's corps, holding the advance of Lee's army, had crossed the Rapidan at Barnett's Ford on the 8th and that division, strongly reinforced, was now on the morning of the 9th driving Buford's cavalry steadily back upon its infantry reserve. That reserve, under General Crawford, had chosen its position at a point near where the Culpeper road crosses Cedar Run, just north of Cedar Mountain. This historic eminence, locally known, from the name of its proprietor as Slaughter Mountain stands alone, like a wayward straggler from the Blue Ridge range, and resembles both in its forms and its isolation Lost Mountain in Georgia. As a point d'appui, it was of great importance both to the enemy and to ourselves, and Jackson lost no time in securing possession of it. As early at 10 A.M., his advance under Ewell made its appearance before Crawford's line and opened fire from its batteries posted around the base and side of the mountain. Spurred by the sound of the firing, Jackson's old division under General Charles S. Winder was hurrying up from Robertson River to the support of Ewell. A.P. Hill's division of six heavy brigades followed Winder's. The junction of these divisions with Ewell's gave Jackson an available force on the field of little less than 25,000 men.

At 9:45 A.M., General Banks at Culpeper was directed to advance the remainder of his corps to the front. The instructions given him verbally by Colonel Lewis H. Marshall of Pope's staff and reduced to writing by Major Louis H. Pelouze, Banks' adjutant general, were as follows: "General Banks will move to the front immediately, assume command of all the forces in the front, deploy his skirmishers if the enemy approaches, and attack him immediately as soon as he approaches and be reinforced from here." Writing afterward from memory in 1864, Colonel Marshall gives the following as the phraseology of the order as he delivered it: "The general commanding directs that you move to the front and take up a strong position near the position held by General Crawford's brigade; that you will not attack the enemy unless it becomes evident that the enemy will attack you; then in order to hold the advantage of being the attacking party, you will attack with your skirmishers thrown well to the front."

It seems unaccountable that there should have been any ambiguity or misunderstanding of orders in such an emergency. The obviously proper thing to do was to hold the enemy in check until the arrival of Sigel, Ricketts, and King. Interpreting Pope's orders by the plain exigencies of the case, it can scarcely be doubted that this is what he meant, for it was not to be expected that Banks, with less than 8,000 men, should assail Jackson, in a position of his own choosing, with 25,000. But the time was not opportune for verbal or inexplicit orders, and the observation if forced upon us that upon this occasion, as upon several others during this campaign, General Pope seems to have committed or allowed too much to his staff officers. Possibly if he had rode out and personally inspected the situation at the front, instead of giving orders from Culpeper, the results might have been different.[39]

Banks' command moved promptly and rapidly. It consisted of two divisions of two brigades each. The First Division was led by Brigadier General Alpheus S. Williams, afterward so well known to the soldiers of the 20th Corps in the army of General Sherman. One of the two brigades of this division was that of General S.W. Crawford, already at the front; the other was that of General George H. Gordon. The Second Division was commanded by Brigadier General C.C. Augur, and comprised the brigades of General Henry Prince, General George S. Greene, and General John W. Geary. The march lasted until noon and so great was the heat that men fell down exhausted and even dead in the road. On reaching the field, the arriving column, by direction of Pope's chief of staff, crossed Cedar Run, and went into position on the high ground beyond that stream. North of the road Crawford's brigade with the cavalry on its flank held the right and south of the road, Geary's, Prince's, and Greene's brigades, in the order named, extended Crawford's line to the left. To the rear of Crawford, in strong position behind the run, Gordon's brigade was stationed in

Cedar Mountain

"We were steadily advanced in line into a cornfield in the face of their cannon which was pouring shell, grape, and canister into us. But it was too high. We halted after getting into a low place, then laid down. In this position we laid about an hour, while the most terrific cannonade was kept up that our regiment ever heard."

"The regiment was again moved ahead, slow but firm through the cornfield into a meadow, in which we halted under a galling fire. Dressing our lines, we opened fire. There we stood without support. There it may be said we died. We kept a good line, and were cool, collected, and determined. The casualties will show how determined we were."

~Sergeant Isaac C. Jones, Co. C, 7th Ohio Infantry

---

[39] In his testimony before the Joint Committee on the Conduct of the War in December 1864, General Banks said: "I sent to General Pope every hour, from one to two o'clock, information of what was transpiring. I did not say the enemy was in force because I did not know it; and I was a little desperate because we supposed that General Pope thought we did not want to fight. General Roberts, when he indicated the positions, said to me in a tone which it was hardly proper for one officer to use to another, "There must be no backing out this day." He said this to me from six to twelve times. I made no reply to him at all, but I felt it keenly, because I knew that my command did not want to back out; we had backed out enough. He repeated this declaration a great many times, "There must be no backing out this day." ~ Lee note.

reserve. Between our lines and the enemy lay a wide, open space, consisting of wheat, corn, and pasture fields, beyond which were dense woods in which Jackson's infantry was adroitly concealed.

These dispositions were completed by 3 P.M. While they were in progress, Ewell, gallantly but unavailingly resisted by Bayard's cavalry, pushed forward through the woods on our left until his two right brigades (Hays and Trimble) gained a commanding position high on the northern slope of Cedar Mountain. From this lofty ground some of Ewell's batteries, quickly brought into position, delivered a plunging fire, seriously annoying to that part of our line within range. Holding Ewell's left, Early drove back our cavalry until he was confronted by the infantry and artillery of Augur's division. Directly Winder's division came up on the left of Ewell's with Taliaferro's brigade south of the road, joining Early, Campbell's brigade north of the road confronting Crawford, and Ronald's (the old Stonewall Brigade) in reserve. General Winder, while making these dispositions and placing his batteries, was killed by a shell and his command devolved upon General W.B. Taliaferro.

Jackson was now waiting for A.P. Hill, whose division, as fast as it arrived, was placed to the rear and in support of Taliaferro and Ewell. As soon as all his forces were well in hand, Jackson proposed to attack. He had no expectation of being attacked himself. Banks entertained other ideas, and at 4 o'clock advanced his whole line, except Gordon's brigade, some hundreds of yards. The artillery firing, which had been going on since morning, now became violent and our batteries gave as good as they received. The friction of the skirmish lines grew more vigorous, our regiments pressed up firmly and steadily to their new positions, and thus another hour passed.

At half past 5 o'clock, while Jackson was preparing but not yet ready to spring, Banks gave the signal to attack. With a rush, Crawford's brigade crossed a wheat field and fell with all its force on Campbell's left. At the same time Geary and Prince swept forward through some cornfields and struck heavily at Campbell's right and the brigades of Early and Taliaferro. Crawford's assault was delivered with splendid momentum and carried all before it. Campbell's brigade was crushed and swept from the field, and its commander killed. Crawford's men then rushed upon Taliaferro's flank and broke that also. The Confederates, according to their own account, "fought like lions" but in vain. Assailed in front by Geary, and on the flank by Crawford, Taliaferro's brigade met the fate of Campbell's and Early's situation became critical. Ronald's brigade was too far back to render prompt assistance, and some of Early's left regiments were carried away by Taliaferro's flight. The battle had reached its crisis, and now was the time to have precipitated Gordon's brigade and Milroy's upon the enemy. Had these brigades, or Ricketts' division, or both, been brought into the fight at this moment, the tide of success would have continued in our favor, a decisive victory would have been won, and the whole course of events in Virginia would have been changed. But Gordon yet remained back of Cedar Run, Ricketts was still at his crossroad station, and Milroy was at Culpeper Courthouse.

Thomas' brigade of Hill's division came up on the right of Early, who held stubbornly to his position. Ronald's brigade broke through the woods, and struck Crawford's men just when most fagged and disorganized by their success. Supported by Thomas, Ewell threw his whole force upon Augur's division which had no reserves. To crown all, three of Hill's brigades rushed upon our right flank with Jackson himself at their head.[40] Our soldiers fought stubbornly, but the odds were greatly against them. They were driven back with heavy loss. Generals Geary and Augur were wounded, and General Prince and 400 of his men were captured.

---

[40] The presence of Jackson leading them in person seemed to produce an indescribable influence on the troops, and as he rode to and fro, amid the smoke, encouraging the men, they greeted him with resounding cheers. This was one of the few occasions when he is reported to have been mastered by excitement. He had forgotten, apparently, that he commanded the whole field and imagined himself a simple colonel leading his regiment. Everywhere in the thickest of the fire, his form was seen and his voice heard, and his exertions to rally the men were crowned with success. ~ Lee note, quoting from Cooke's Life of Jackson.

Major General Franz Sigel
(Library of Congress)

One of Crawford's finest regiments, the 10th Maine, had not joined in the assault and was now ordered by General Banks to throw itself upon the triumphant enemy. Gallantly advancing through the bloody wheat field, this regiment soon found itself alone confronting the woods filled with Confederates. Isolated and unsupported, it fought nobly until its steady lines melted away. In a few minutes, it lost 173 officers and men killed and wounded. Gordon's brigade was next summoned to the front. It should have remained where it was, and there served as a nucleus for rallying our broken regiments. But Banks peremptorily ordered it forward, and forward it went. Before it, and sweeping around its flanks, was the greater part of Hill's strong division, flushed with victory. Gordon's attack was gallant, but unavailing, and his repulse bloody. The lives sacrificed by pushing him forward at the time it was done were wasted. Gordon brought 300-400 of his men out of the fight; Crawford rode out of it alone. What was left of our forces engaged withdrew behind Cedar Run, and the battle ended. It was by this time dark. The enemy warily followed up his advantage, shelling the woods as he advanced, and thus keeping up his cannonade until midnight. Meanwhile, Ricketts' division came up about dusk and relieved a portion of Banks' thinned and exhausted regiments.

All day long, Milroy's men had been lying in the woods near Culpeper, listening to the savage uproar of artillery as it rolled louder and louder across the hills. At 4 P.M., Schenk's and Schurz's divisions arrived from Hazel River, and at 5 o'clock Sigel was ordered to move his whole command to the front. Milroy marched at once, accompanied by Sigel, and Schenk and Schurz followed after allowing their men to take a brief rest and draw rations. Our head of column soon began to encounter the rearward drifting debris of the battle. Long trains of ambulances filled with wounded were passed, and wild stories told by "demoralized" stragglers of the day's adventures and calamities. "Our regiment was all cut to pieces," said several, or "our brigade was all cut to pieces." Everything was cut to pieces. "This is all that is left of my company," said a commissioned officer as he passed me, accompanied by two or three men. "General Banks is wounded, perhaps killed," said another. "50,000 Johnnies down there!" And so on for quantity.

As Milroy's brigade neared the scene of action, the rearward tide increased and the excitement grew more intense. The cannonading was still furious, and the ignited shells, streaming and exploding against the midnight sky, presented a spectacle of savage grandeur. Riding at the head of Milroy's column, Sigel went forward, accompanied by his escort, to reconnoiter the ground just as Pegram's Battery, posted by Jackson, opened fire on the mass of Banks' stragglers and vehicles blocked in the road. A delirious panic ensued. The teamsters and stragglers broke in all directions, wagons were overturned, and two of Banks' batteries under Captain Reynolds withdrew down the road toward Milroy. Sigel directed Captain Ulric Dahlgren of his staff, to assist in posting these batteries and at the same time Milroy deployed his brigade to the front. As the panic-stricken fugitives dashed against Milroy's lines and were forbidden to go further, the shouting and swearing were prodigious.[41] At the same time Reynolds' guns, having quickly gotten into position, were making effective response to Pegram's when General Pope arrived and

---

[41] "A witness reported that Sigel was a 'wild man behind the lines' and commenced 'yelling at the straggling and retreating men' and 'generally behaving with a frenzied energy." Engle, op. cit., pg. 135

directed Sigel to cease firing, because, as Pope said, our shots were falling among Banks' men yet in the woods in front. Sigel made unavailing remonstrance and ordered the batteries to cease firing, but cautioned Milroy to be upon his guard. Directly after this the enemy's cavalry dashed out of the woods and came near capturing Pope, Sigel, and their attendants, but the reception given by Milroy's men to the Confederate troops caused them to go back as speedily as they came.

At sunrise some of the enemy's horsemen strayed into our lines, but, on discovering their mistake, turned and fled precipitately, followed by Milroy, who fired after them some ineffective pistol shots and emphatic exclamations. Milroy then advanced his lines and developed that fact that during the night Jackson had withdrawn to his original position on Cedar Mountain. Some skirmishing ensued and Sigel was disposed to attack in force, but Pope preferred to wait.

On the 11th a truce was arranged for the purpose of burying the dead and caring for the wounded who were lying exposed to the broiling sun upon the disputed ground. While engaged in this work, fatigue parties of both armies scoured the field, and frequently engaged in friendly conversations with each other. Where the severest fighting had occurred some horrible scenes were witnessed. Scores of human bodies were seen lying in different positions- some sitting and others on their knees- all enormously bloated and black as pitch from the effects of heat and thirst. Some had grown black from the heat and yet lived! One poor fellow, whose leg had been shattered by a shell, said he had not tasted a drop of water in 48 hours, yet during all that time, while suffering from the fever of his wound, he had been lying exposed to the fierce midsummer sun! Before the truce expired, King's division arrived from Falmouth and Jackson became apprehensive of being fallen upon by superior numbers and losing his connections with Lee. He therefore decamped during the night of the 11th, and withdrew beyond Robertson River.

The withdrawal of Jackson behind the Rapidan left our cavalry corps free to reoccupy the positions it had held prior to the Cedar Mountain battle, and accordingly its line of outposts was again extended from Raccoon Ford to the Blue Ridge. On the 14th of August, General Pope was joined at Culpeper Courthouse by General Reno with his own and Stevens' division of Burnside's corps, which had been called from North Carolina and had arrived by way of Newport News and Aquia Creek. These two divisions, 8,000 strong, were Pope's first reinforcement. Jackson's retrograde movement was followed up as far as Robertson River by the 1st Corps under Sigel, whose command's new position held the right, while McDowell's at Cedar Mountain held the center, Reno's at Raccoon Ford, the left, and Banks' at Culpeper the reserve of the Army of Virginia.

By this time General Lee's forces disengaged at Richmond were pushing rapidly northward. His army had been organized into two grand divisions or wings- right and left- and had an effective force variously estimated at 55-65,000 men. Its right wing under Longstreet was already at Gordonsville, ten miles south of the Rapidan, and was joined there, August 15th, by General Lee in person. The left wing (Jackson's corps) had preceded the right in this movement just a month and now held the south bank of the Rapidan River.[42] General Pope's position between the Rapidan and the Rappahannock was an indefensible one, inviting attack. His only line of railway communication extended across the enemy's line of advance, and was greatly exposed to hostile forays. Nevertheless he was disposed to hold his advanced position as long as possible in order to gain time for the withdrawal of the Army of the Potomac from the peninsula, and its approach as then intended, by way of Aquia Creek and Falmouth.

General Lee, impatient to assail Pope before he could be reinforced and hoping to catch him between the two rivers, assembled his army on the south bank of the Rapidan from Raccoon Ford to Liberty Mills, ready for a sudden push northward. His plan and orders were given to cross the Rapidan on the 18th of August, but his movement was delayed until the 20th. Meanwhile, General Pope was warned by a lucky chance of the designs

---

[42] The itinerary of General Lee's northward movement up to this time may be thus summarized; Jackson with two divisions (his own and Ewell's) was ordered to Gordonsville July 13; arrived there and established outposts on the Rapidan July 19; was joined by A.P. Hill's division July 27; advanced across the Rapidan August 8; fought at Cedar Mountain August 9; returned to the Rapidan August 11 and 12; the infantry divisions of Longstreet, Hood, and R.H. Anderson and the main body of Stuart's cavalry were ordered to Gordonsville August 13. Lee arrived there August 15 and was joined by most of the remainder of his veteran troops still at Richmond about the time McClellan disappeared from Harrison's Landing. ~ Lee note

against him. A cavalry expedition which he had sent out on the 16th toward Louisa Courthouse captured on the person of General J.E.B. Stuart's adjutant general an autograph letter of Lee's dated Gordonsville August 15th betraying his purposes. Pope lost no time in profiting by this information, and gave orders for the immediate withdrawal of his army behind the Rappahannock, the line of which he was instructed to defend. The wagon trains were first put into motion, and preceded the troops, those of Reno moving by way of Stevensburg to Kelly's Ford, and those of Banks and McDowell crossing the Rappahannock at the point where that river is intersected by the Orange and Alexandria Railroad. Sigel, having occupied the most westerly position, was ordered to move by way of Culpeper and Jefferson and cross the Rappahannock at White Sulphur Springs. By these routes the different columns, screened by the cavalry, withdrew rapidly to their new defensive position.

From the beginning of this retrograde movement until its end at the close of the campaign, the enormous baggage and supply trains accompanying the army were a troublesome encumbrance. To dispose of and protect them without hindrance to the rapid and intricate movements and the troops required much skill and forecast. Unfortunately our regiments had not yet learned how to get along with a minimum allowance of baggage, or no baggage at all, and the proportion of wheels carried was much greater than was customary later in the war. Sigel's movement from Robertson River began on the 17th and during the whole of the following night Milroy's brigade, which followed the 1st Corps trains, waited for them to get on the road. Time and again during the night the brigade quitted its bivouacs, expecting to begin its march, but it had to return to its camp fires and smother its impatience. There seemed to be no end to the sluggish caravan, and the sun was already up when the column got fairly into motion.

At noon we reached the Cedar Mountain battlefield and at dusk marched once more through the sullenly secession town of Culpeper. The movement continued far into night, and resumed early the following morning. The weather was still fiercely hot. At evening on the 19th, Sigel's corps reached Warrenton, Sulphur Springs, and there crossed the Rappahannock. Next morning, by Pope's order, it reversed its course and moved down the left bank of the river until it joined the right of McDowell's corps which, in turn, connected with the forces of Reno, who had crossed the day before at Kelly's Ford. The entire body of cavalry was sent to the right of Sigel to watch the enemy's movements and picket the line of the Rappahannock, which in its upper part, is but an inconsiderable stream, offering no serious obstacle to the advance of an army.

Thus General Pope nimbly escaped from the trap laid for him, much to the chagrin no doubt of the Confederate commander, who was prompt, however, to follow up our movements and early on the 20th attacked and drove in our pickets. The position of our army was now a strong one, as against front attack and the enemy, not being able to force a passage of the river without great loss, contented himself with heavy skirmishing and artillery dueling through the 20th. By nightfall, the bulk of Lee's force had been brought up from the Rapidan and confronted Pope's new position from his extreme left at Kelly's Ford to a point beyond his extreme right, which rested about three miles above Rappahannock Station.

It was now manifest that unless Pope should be largely reinforced, or should withdraw from the line of the Rappahannock, he could not prevent the enemy from turning his right by way of Sulphur Springs and marching on Warrenton, from whence a good turnpike leads directly to Washington. Obviously intending a movement of this kind, Lee's column pushed steadily on up the west bank of the river. Pope, it should be borne in mind, was still under orders to keep himself in close communication with Fredericksburg, from whence the Army of the Potomac was expected to approach after landing at Aquia Creek. These instructions were coupled with positive assurances that all necessary help would be given for carrying them into execution, as witness the following dispatched to Pope on the 18th by General Halleck at Washington: "I fully approve your movement. I hope to push Burnside's forces to near Barnett's Ford by tomorrow night, to assist you in holding that pass. Stand firm on the line of the Rappahannock till I can help you. Fight hard, and aid will soon come." And this, on the 21st: "I have telegraphed General Burnside to know at what hour he can reinforce Reno. Am waiting his answer. Every effort must be made to hold the Rappahannock. Large forces will be in tomorrow." And later on the same day: "I have just sent General Burnside's reply. General Cox's forces are coming in from Parkersburg, and will be here tomorrow or next day. Dispute every inch of ground and fight like the devil until we can reinforce you. Forty-eight hours more and we can make you strong enough. Don't yield an inch if you can help it."

Freeman's Ford

"They began to flank us on the right and left with the intention of surrounding us, marching right up in front with their flags flying. We stood as long as we possibly could, and then fell back into the woods and so fast that we came near forgetting to stop. We rallied again, loaded, marched forward, and fired. This time I was hit across the head and fell; I gathered myself up and was then struck across the kneecap which came near knocking it off. The colonel ordered me to be taken to the rear. I gave the flag to a brave little corporal on my right as I left. As I was leaving the field, General Bohlen was shot within 30 feet of me and his horse came near running over the boys that were helping me from the field."

~ Color Sergeant William Kirkwood, Co. C, 61st Ohio Infantry

These instructions and promises of Halleck, of course, implied and anticipated the speedy arrival of the Army of the Potomac. The order for the withdrawal of that army from the Peninsula was given on the 4th of August. It was directed to proceed to Fortress Monroe, and thence by transports up the Chesapeake Bay and the Potomac River to Aquia Creek Landing. After much hesitation, General McClellan began embarking his forces at Harrison's Landing as if intending to carry his whole command- sick, cavalry, and all- from that point by water. Impelled from Washington, he marched the bulk of his forces by land to Fortress Monroe, but the last of his army did not get away from Harrison's Landing until August 16. Meanwhile, as early as the 13th, Lee had started Longstreet's corps by rail to Gordonsville. Thus the enemy had ample time and opportunity to make his concentration in front of Pope, for the moment the Army of the Potomac set out for Fortress Monroe, it was completely "put out of the fight." During the period of its transit northward from the James River and to the front, lasting from 10-15 days, its military potentiality ceased to exist. Moreover, by taking a roundabout course on transports, instead of marching directly north overland as Sherman afterward did through the Carolinas (instead of embarking his army, as requested, at Savannah), the troops became separated from their wagon transportation and were obliged to go to the front scantily supplied with food and ammunition.

General Pope's estimate of his effective force at this time, after allowing for losses by fighting and sickness, is 40,000 men. Probably it did not exceed 45,000 including Reno's two divisions. Most of our troops were constantly in motion or under fire and owing to their perpetual changes of position were imperfectly fed. It was very difficult to keep the supply trains within reach and yet out of the way of the shifting columns. The troops, therefore, often went hungry simply because the quartermasters could not follow or find them. Along the river, the skirmish firing was incessant, and from the heights on the opposite banks the batteries hammered each other with unflagging persistency.

On the 20th, Pope was confronted from Kelly's Ford northward by Longstreet and farther up, toward Beverly Ford, by Jackson. The railway crossing at Rappahannock Station was still in our possession with a tete-du-pont on the south bank of the Rappahannock held by a brigade. On the 21st, the enemy extended his left still farther northward, his infantry and artillery often moving in plain view of ours on the hills skirting the west bank of the river. Nevertheless a strong show of force continued to be made in front of our own left in the vicinity of Rappahannock Station.

On the 22nd, Jackson, holding the Confederate left, moved up the west bank of the river as far as Warrenton Sulphur Springs, and there threw one of his brigades (Early's) which advanced to a position behind Great Run. Sigel, holding our right with the 1st Corps, made a corresponding movement along the east bank and at Freeman's Ford sent across the 74th Pennsylvania, Colonel Alexander Schimmelfennig, to reconnoiter. Part of Sigel's artillery, including Buell's, Dilger's, and Wiedrich's batteries, had meanwhile been hotly engaged at Freeman's Ford, and Captain Frank Buell, a valuable officer of the 1st West Virginia Artillery, had been killed. The river was, at this point, about 250 yards wide and waist deep. Having gained the west bank by fording, Schimmelfennig captured some wagons and stragglers and discovered a Confederate force marching parallel to the river with its flank and wagon trains exposed. Reporting these facts, he asked for reinforcements and accordingly General Bohlen led over his two remaining regiments- the 8th West Virginia and the 61st Ohio. General Schurz, commanding the division, and Captains Spraul and Fritz Tiedemann of his staff accompanied the movement. Sigel deemed this a good opportunity to cut Lee's army in two[43] and was about to follow Schurz with the entire 1st Corps when he found that the river was rising and that his pontoon train- the only one in the army- had been ordered away by General McDowell.

Bohlen attacked vigorously and at first successfully, but he was soon fiercely assailed, in turn, by Trimble's heavy brigade, covering Jackson's rear, and by Hood, who was commanding Longstreet's advance. Under the impetus of this counterattack, the 8th West Virginia broke in disorder, but the 74th Pennsylvania and the 61st Ohio (the latter led with conspicuous gallantry by Lieutenant Colonel McGroarty) held their ground stubbornly and with beating drums and loud cheers renewed the fight. It was not possible, however, for such an unequal contest to last long, nor was it prudent that so small a force as Bohlen's should longer remain detached from the main body, especially as a heavy rain was falling and rapidly increasing the depth of the river. Our troops, therefore, withdrew fighting to the ford. Covered by our batteries and by the musketry fire of Milroy's and McLean's brigades, the entire reconnoitering party recrossed to the east bank, though not without some casualties by drowning. During the movement back to the river and while bravely rallying and directing his men, Brigadier General Henry Bohlen, an officer of rare ability and accomplishments, fell from his horse mortally wounded. His body was recovered after the fight under a flag of truce. Our loss in the affair was about 200 in killed and wounded.[44]

Sigel was now very anxious, as he had reason to be, about his exposed right flank, and expressed his apprehensions to Pope who (at 6:30 P.M. on August 22nd) telegraphed from Rappahannock Station to Halleck: "Everything indicates clearly to me that the enemy's movement will be upon Warrenton by way of Sulphur Springs. If I could know with anything like certainty by what time to expect troops that are starting from Alexandria, I could act more understandingly. I have not heard of the arrival of any of the forces from Fredericksburg at the fords below, though I have withdrawn nearly the whole of Reno's forces from Kelly's Ford. I cannot move against Sulphur Springs just now without exposing my rear to the heavy force in front of me and having my communication with the forces coming up the Rappahannock intercepted, and most likely the railroad destroyed. I think it is altogether well to bring Franklin's force to Alexandria. Lee made his headquarters at Culpeper last night. He has the whole of his army in front of me. Its numbers you can estimate as well as myself. As soon as his plans are fully developed, I shall be ready to act."

Three hours later Pope telegraphed again to Halleck: "Reports from our forces near Sulphur Springs just in. Enemy was crossing the river today at Sulphur Springs and on the road from Warrenton to Sperryville. He is still in heavy force at Rappahannock Ford, and above, and my rear is entirely exposed if I move toward Sulphur Springs or Warrenton. I must do one of two things- either fall back and meet Heintzelman behind Cedar Run or cross the Rappahannock with my whole force and assail the enemy's flank and rear. I must do one or the other at daylight. Which shall it be? I incline to the latter, but don't wish to interfere with your plans." To this came the following response dated August 22, 11 P.M. "I think the latter of your two propositions best. I also think you had better stop

---

[43] That Sigel did not misjudge the situation and his opportunity appears from the report of General Trimble, commanding the Confederate force attacked who says "As General Ewell's division was five or six miles in advance and General Longstreet's division the same distance in the rear, I deemed it most prudent to hold my brigade on the defensive and endeavor to protect the trains." ~ Lee note.

[44] General Trimble conveys the impression in his report that our loss was much greater. He says: "Our men pursued them closely, and slaughtered great numbers as they waded the river or climbed up the opposite bank. The water was literally covered with dead and wounded." Trimble further says: "The battle lasted two hours, during which time we drove the enemy one mile." This certainly does not speak badly of the resistance made by Bohlen's little force, for General Hood, who reinforced Trimble, says in his report, "On my arrival, the Texas brigade being placed on Trimble's right and Colonel Law's on the left, the attack was made at once, General Trimble leading off in the center." Three brigades against three regiments. ~ Lee note.

Heintzelman's corps[45] and the troops of Sturgis and Cox (the latter coming from the Kanawha Valley and the former from Alexandria) as they arrive tomorrow at Warrenton Junction, instead of taking them to Bealton."

From these dispatches it will be seen that Pope, reassured from Washington, clung to his expectations of immediate reinforcement and that Halleck, encouraging and himself cherishing this illusion, still inculcated the idea that the Army of Virginia must hold, at all hazards, the line of the Rappahannock. Pope therefore, upon receiving Halleck's answer, resolved to mass his entire force, re-cross the river by bridges and fords at Rappahannock Station and Kelly's Ford below, and fall with all his strength upon the flank and rear of the enemy. The chances for success of this venture were exceedingly few, and its result would probably have been to place both the Rappahannock River and Lee's army between ours and Washington. Fortunately, it was never attempted. During the night, a heavy rainstorm set in which caused a rise of six or eight feet in the river, sweeping away the bridges and drowning the fords. The intended movement was thus rendered impracticable, and at the same time a formidable barrier was interposed to the advance of the enemy.

During this same night of the 22nd, while Pope was preparing to fall upon the rear of Lee's army, a demonstration was made in our own rear by General J.E.B. Stuart with a Confederate force of 1,500 cavalry and two guns. Passing our right flank by way of Waterloo Bridge and Warrenton, Stuart, in the midst of a furious rainstorm and pitch darkness, surprised Pope's headquarters train at Catlett's Station, destroyed a few wagons, and set fire to the railway bridge over Cedar Run. Fortunately, the rain put out the fire and saved the bridge. At the time of this raid, most of the wagons of Pope's army were at or near Catlett's and were under guard of not less than 1,500 infantry and five companies of cavalry. The shameful negligence of this guard in allowing itself to be surprised needs no comment, and the fact that such a raid as Stuart's was possible tells its own story of the illusive expectation that McClellan's army would by this time be near enough to protect our line of communications.

Having been thwarted for the time being in his intended movement to the left, Pope now, as was more prudent, directed his attention to his right. Sigel, convinced that the enemy had outflanked us near the Sulphur Springs crossing, proposed to withdraw his corps to Beverly Ford or Bealton with a view to concentrating the army in that vicinity. Adopting just the reverse course, Pope directed Sigel on August 23rd at 7:15 A.M. to march upon Sulphur Springs, attack and beat whatever opposing force he might encounter and push along the river to Waterloo Bridge. Banks' corps was ordered to support Sigel's in this movement, and McDowell's corps, augmented by the Pennsylvania

On the Field
with
General Sigel

A veteran of Sigel's corps wrote that listening to Sigel direct an artillery battery in the midst of action was sometimes laughable, as the General shouted at his men with his thick Germanic brogue "Come out here my prave Dutchmen mit your duck-ass pattery clear to de night where I shows you and get ready to give de tam Rebels fits. Pless my hearts, man you shoots wild! There coes another no hit, donder and blitzen you break my hearts! Lower de mount, now give it ein, that's it my prave boys!"

~ *Charles Boyce*

---

[45] Heintzelman's corps of two divisions (Hooker and Kearny) from the Army of the Potomac. Pope estimated the strength of this corps at about 10,000 men. It did not join Pope until August 25. ~ Lee note.

Reserves under General John F. Reynolds[46], moved on Warrenton, whither Pope, first ordering that the bridge be destroyed and the works abandoned at Rappahannock Station, directed his own course.

During the afternoon of the 23rd, McDowell's advance, accompanied by Pope, occupied Warrenton, which place Stuart's cavalry had quit a few hours before. Sigel did not get along so smoothly. Late in the afternoon of his advance, held as usual by the impetuous Milroy, came upon Early's brigade in the vicinity of Great Run Creek, and a sharp action ensued, lasting until after dark. During the night the Confederates withdrew across the bridge, burning it. Next morning Sigel crossed Great Run and with his entire corps drawn up in line of battle, moved toward Sulphur Springs. No enemy was discovered for Early, who had been as he thought in a position of great peril, had decamped and re-crossed the Rappahannock. However, as our lines moved down the slope toward the springs, a heavy fire was opened upon them from the Confederate batteries which had been posted all along the west bank of the river. Milroy, who was leading, discovered the enemy in strong force holding the bridge near the springs and made dispositions to attack. Sigel, having learned what his frantic subordinate was about, was much vexed, and sent him a peremptory order to "let the bridge alone" and push on toward Waterloo as he had been instructed to do. Milroy, somewhat crest-fallen, obeyed and arrived at Waterloo late in the afternoon.[47]

Buford's cavalry, which had preceded us, had attempted to burn the Waterloo Bridge and failed. Something therefore was left for the impetuous Milroy to do which was worthy of his rash and adventurous temper. A strong Confederate force held the high ground on the west bank of the river and their sharpshooters made it exceedingly interesting for anyone attempting to approach the bridge from our side. However, Milroy's marksmen were tolerably expert in this business and they soon made it exceedingly interesting for the Confederates. In the 82nd Ohio regiment were many hardy deer hunters and pioneers who were very skillful with the rifle, and to that regiment under Colonel James Cantwell was confided the perilous duty of setting the bridge on fire. Supported by a furious fusillade of musketry and artillery, some platoons of picked men from the 82nd Ohio dashed forward to the river, followed by fatigue parties carrying bundles of combustible matter. Amidst a wild tumult of arms, the bridge was reached and in a twinkling fired. A column of smoke and flame and the cheers of our troops, announced the success of this brave exploit. The destruction of the bridge took place during the afternoon of the 25th.[48]

During the night of the 24th, our army was situated as follows: Sigel's corps extended along the river from Waterloo toward Sulphur Springs; Reno's near Sulphur Springs; Reynolds' division at Warrenton; Ricketts' division four miles east of Waterloo on the Warrenton road; and King's division between Sulphur Springs and Warrenton. These dispositions were modified by an order of General Pope's, issued early on the 25th, having in view the formation of a new line of battle extending from Warrenton to Kelly's Ford via Bealton. In the meantime, Sigel's situation on the river had become one which caused him great anxiety and the contradictory and confusing instructions given him aggravated his uneasiness. During the night of the 24th he received an order to move to Fayetteville, so as to take his position on the new line of battle, but on the morning of the 25th he was directed by General Roberts, Pope's chief of staff, to hold Waterloo Bridge at all hazards. With this latter order, the assurance was given to Sigel that he would be supported by McDowell and Buford on the right and by Banks and Reno on the left. Soon after these instructions and assurances were given, the enemy made a strong demonstration at Waterloo Bridge and vicinity as though he meant to force a crossing. Sigel was alarmed and, looking around for the supports promised him, found they were wanting. Confronted by an enemy twice his strength, he stood isolated and alone. He discovered that the enemy's cavalry had crossed the river on both of his flanks, while before him were 28 regiments of Confederate infantry with six batteries of artillery and considerable cavalry. At the same time, he observed the movement of a large body of the enemy toward his right. Sigel reported to Pope that he believed the enemy to be

---

[46] This division of three brigades numbering 2,500 men arrived from Aquia Creek on August 23rd and was the first reinforcement received by General Pope from the Army of the Potomac. ~ Lee note.

[47] While at Waterloo, Lieutenant Lee was assigned command of the brigade ammunition train.

[48] First Lieutenant Francis S. Jacobs of Company K recalled that "two men from each company were detailed under the charge of Sergeant Conrad Lue of Co. B to burn the bridge; and right under the fire of the enemy and in full view, they did it and before we left, the smoke rolled up in clouds. While Corporal Smith was blowing the fire, a bullet whistled through scattering the fire in all directions." *Ashland Union,* September 17, 1862, pg. 3

advancing upon him in force, and received no response. Then came from McDowell (at that time commanding the right wing) a dispatch directed partly to Banks inquiring as to his (Banks') corps and partly to Sigel directing him to move to Fayetteville. Now, to withdraw in the presence of a formidable foe in broad daylight is a perilous undertaking. Sigel therefore decided to remain where he was until nightfall and then march to Fayetteville, although he did not consider this last a wise thing to do. Meanwhile, a detachment of cavalry which he had sent to Sulphur Springs under Colonel Beardsley routed the enemy there and either by its own cannonade or by that which it provoked, set fire to that village.

At nightfall, just as Sigel was about to set out for Fayetteville as instructed, he received an order to march to Warrenton. This latter order he put into execution at once. Cautiously, the 1st Corps withdrew from the river and then marched nearly all night. About 3 o'clock in the morning the head of the column was approaching Warrenton when Sigel, to his great consternation, was overtaken by an order to force a passage at Waterloo Bridge (which had been burned) and see what was in front of him! This order had been issued by Pope the evening before. Let us trace its history and the reasons which had prompted it.

Up to this time our army had baffled all attempts of the enemy to pass the line of the Rappahannock. As late as the afternoon of the 24th, General Pope had not abandoned the idea of holding that line, for he then telegraphed Halleck his intention of sending a considerable part of his force back to Rappahannock Station. But a crisis was at hand requiring that other plans should be considered. Longstreet's corps, having arrived from below, made its appearance before Waterloo and relieved Jackson, who adroitly withdrew westward toward Jefferson. These, in part, were the movements which had alarmed Sigel. Next day (August 25), our signal corps, from its stations on the high points along the Rappahannock, observed the mysterious departure from the head of Lee's column. A large detachment of the enemy, comprising 36 regiments of infantry, with the usual proportion of artillery and cavalry, was seen moving off to the northward and then inclining to the east in the direction of Salem. For hours the signals reported movements of this strange detachment, until, at length, it disappeared beyond the farthest range of vision. What did it mean? When General Pope, apprehending that the enemy intended turning his right, suddenly reversed his purpose of re-crossing the Rappahannock by the left, and moved his entire army toward Warrenton, he evidently expected serious resistance in that quarter. But this expectation was not realized. The Confederate force (Early's brigade) which had crossed the river at Sulphur Springs had been easily compelled to re-cross to the west bank, and now that this supposed flanking movement was thwarted and appeared to be a feint, what could be the purpose of this new expedition?

General Banks, watching it through the eyes of his signal officer, and perhaps with the memory of Winchester fresh in his mind, reported to Pope on August 25th and 11:25 A.M. as follows: "It seems to me apparent that the enemy is threatening or moving upon the valley of the Shenandoah via Front Royal with designs on the Potomac- possibly beyond." And so Pope at Warrenton Junction sent to Sigel at 9:30 P.M. August 25 the following ill-tempered and ill-timed dispatch already referred to: "You will force the passage of the river at Waterloo Bridge tomorrow morning at daylight and see what is in front of you. I do not believe there is any enemy in force there, but I do believe that the whole of their army has marched west and northwest. I am not satisfied with your reports or your operations of today, and expect to hear tomorrow early something more satisfactory concerning the enemy."

At the same hour Pope dispatched to General McDowell: "I believe that the whole force of the enemy has marched for the Shenandoah by way of Luray and Front Royal. The column which has marched today towards Gaines' Crossroads has turned north and when last seen was passing under the east base of Buck Mountain toward Salem and Rectortown. I desire you, as early as possible in the morning, holding Reynolds in reserve at Warrenton or vicinity, to make a reconnaissance with your whole corps and ascertain what is beyond the river at Sulphur Springs." Inasmuch as Sigel had already quit the river, as repeatedly ordered to do, and his troops were much fatigued with their all night march, these reconnaissances were made by King's division and Buford's cavalry, under the direction of General McDowell. They developed the enemy's main force still at Waterloo Bridge and Sulphur Springs, where General Sigel had truthfully reported it to be. The belief that Lee's whole army had marched off to the Shenandoah Valley was therefore a delusion. But how about the northward moving detachment? Where did that go?

The mysterious column was Stonewall Jackson's. Shot like an arrow from Lee's extended line, it swept northward as if aiming, as Generals Pope and Banks believed, for Front Royal, the Potomac, and "possibly beyond," but really making for a widely different destination. Its movement is thus graphically described by John Esten Cooke of J.E.B. Stuart's staff:

> The famous foot cavalry were now called upon to put forth their utmost strength. A long and exhausting march was before them; every moment was precious; Thoroughfare Gap must be reached before the enemy arrived and the ordinary rules of marching must be changed. So though recognizing the maxim, that wherever two men can place their feet an army can move, Jackson pushed on beneath the shadow of the Blue Ridge, "across open fields," declares one of his men, "by strange country roads, by a little town in Fauquier called Orleans, on and on, as if he would never cease." The troops were not permitted to pause for an instant; weary, footsore, almost without food, they were still marched steadily forward and at night, worn out but gay, hungry but full of enthusiasm, they bivouacked near the town of Salem on the Manassas Gap railroad.

> Reaching Salem at midnight, the troops were again in motion at daylight and passing crowds all welcoming, cheering, staring with blank amazement at the sight of the Confederate troops in that region, pressed on through the plains of Thoroughfare Gap. The mountain gorge was undefended, the enemy had been headed off and passing rapidly between the frowning ramparts with their belts of dusky pines, Jackson, with his army hungry and exhausted but resolute as ever, descended like a hawk upon Manassas.

Let the reader keep in his mind this description of Jackson's celerity and energy as a companion piece to other descriptions, soon to be given, of the manner in which some of our own soldiers were led. Cooke proceeds:

> General Stuart was on the right flank of the Confederate column with a cordon of pickets and network of scouting parties, scouring the whole region and to penetrate Stuart's chain of videttes in any important movement was next to impossible. Had General Pope felt convinced that the force advancing to assail his rear was not a body of cavalry only, but an army corps under a commander so active and dangerous as Jackson, his operations on the Rappahannock would doubtless have terminated two days sooner. Thoroughfare Gap would have been defended and the conditions under which the great battles at Manassas were fought would have been changed.

General Pope had valuable hints of what was going on, but he failed to realize their significance. Moreover, the delusion into which he had been led that the Army of the Potomac was rushing to his assistance induced him to believe that the line upon which his army was supposed to be approaching was sufficiently secure against disturbance. Still, it is hard to understand why Thoroughfare Gap was left wholly unwatched, not to say undefended. Cooke's narrative continues:

> Thoroughfare Gap was passed; the open country lay before Jackson, and at Gainesville General Stuart came up with his cavalry and took position on the right flank. It was important to strike the Federal communications immediately, and attack Manassas if possible before General Pope received intelligence of the advance upon his rear; and with this end in view, Jackson hurried forward to Bristoe, a station on the Orange and Alexandria Railroad, four miles from Manassas, which was reached and a small guard captured after sunset on the 26th. As Stuart approached this place, the sound of cars was heard from the direction of Warrenton and a train was soon seen approaching rapidly. Colonel Munford of the 2nd Virginia Cavalry, fired into it but did not succeed in stopping it. It continued its way and reached Manassas in safety.[49] Others trains were coming from the same direction however and, dividing his force, General Ewell took possession of two points on the railroad, which was obstructed by logs placed on the track. The trains came on without suspicion and the result in this case was more satisfactory.

The position which Jackson had thus gained, though perilous, gave him every opportunity for mischief, and proceeded to make the most of it. Without a moment's delay he started a detachment down the railroad and broke it

---

[49] This train did not stop even at Manassas, but rushed on full speed and crashed into a southbound train loaded with soldiers, which was standing on the track at Bull Run Bridge. Three soldiers were killed and several wounded by the collision. ~ Lee Note.

up at Kettle Run, only six miles east of Warrenton Junction. At the same instant another detachment, under Stuart, moved up the railroad intending to seize Manassas Junction, where several million dollars' worth of army supplies was at the time accumulated. In spite of the darkness of the night and the weariness of his men, who had marched all day, Stuart made good time, and before midnight (August 26) reached the Junction, where he surprised and captured the garrison and made himself master of everything within reach. Cooke thus enumerates the spoils seized by the raiders: eight pieces of artillery, 72 horses with equipment, 300 prisoners, 200 Negroes, 200 new tents, 175 additional horses exclusive of artillery horses, ten locomotives, two railroad trains of enormous size heavily loaded with stores, 50,000 lbs of bacon, 1,000 barrels of beef, 20,000 barrels of pork, several thousand barrels of flour, and a large quantity of forage. The hungry Confederates helped themselves to everything they could eat or wear, and destroyed the rest, including the public buildings.

At Centreville, eight miles east of the Junction, was Brigadier General George W. Taylor's New Jersey brigade which had been sent forward from Alexandria. Learning of the surprise and rout at Manassas, this brigade pushed forward and at 7 o'clock in the morning drove in the Confederate skirmishers posted in the hills skirting Bull Run. Taylor then pushed on and was permitted to approach within easy range of the fortifications around the Junction where the enemy's infantry and cavalry awaited him in silence. Suddenly the artillery opened upon him from the breastworks and his line was driven to the shelter of a neighboring ridge. Here Taylor was assailed by infantry but made a gallant resistance, but he was obliged to fall back and re-cross Bull Run. His attack was hopeless from the beginning, for Jackson had by this time come up from Bristoe and had with him two Confederate divisions. In this affair General Taylor was mortally wounded. The way now being open eastward, Stuart's cavalry went raiding at will in that direction, down the railroad, which was broken up as far east at Burke's Station within 15 miles of Alexandria. Such was the first stage of Jackson's daring raid. It cost us dearly, but it was worth to us every cent it cost provided only we could promptly and fully avail ourselves of the opportunities it gave us. But of that further along.

In a military sense, Jackson's exploit seems an impossible one, and it certainly would have been impossible had all the precautions which General Pope says he had provided against it been carried to fulfillment. But in one important particular he was not as vigilant as he should have been. While thinking of his left and vainly extending his hand in that direction to grasp that of McClellan, a hand by the way which he was never able to seize in this campaign[50], he set too little store by Sigel's warnings of what was going on upon his right. He, therefore, left the gateways of the Bull Run Mountains open. For this he was responsible.

On the other hand, as early as the 22nd, he tells us he had instructed General Sturgis, commanding at Alexandria, to see personally that strong detachments were posted along the railroad from Manassas Junction to Catlett's Station. He had furthermore sent orders to the commandant of the Junction to retain there, as a garrison, the first division that should come from Alexandria and to push forward all his cavalry toward Thoroughfare Gap. He had also requested General Halleck to push Franklin's corps with all possible speed to Gainesville, where, he says, he had reason to expect confidently, from assurances given him, that Franklin would arrive during the afternoon of the 26th. Such are General Pope's claims.

But no detachments adequately strong were posted along the railroad; no division reached Manassas, and no cavalry was thrown forward to Thoroughfare Gap. As for Franklin, he did not reach Alexandria until the afternoon of the 26th and did not get as far forward as Centreville even until this campaign was virtually over. Reynolds' division, 2,500 strong, came up as we have seen on the 23rd. On the 25th, Heintzelman's corps reported to Pope at Warrenton Junction, and on the 26th Fitz John Porter's[51] at Bealton. These three commands, numbering in all about 22,500 effective men (General Pope says 20,500) constitute the whole of the reinforcements which the Army

---

[50] On July 4th, General Pope had written to McClellan a full statement of his forces, situation, and plans and made cordial proffers of cooperation. McClellan replied that he would not fall back from his position at Harrison's Landing "unless absolutely forced to do so." ~Lee note.

[51] Porter's corps (5th) including Piatt's brigade was about 12,000 strong. It contained most of the regular troops and was thoroughly officered and equipped. ~ Lee note.

of Virginia received from the Army of the Potomac. They were, indeed, the only troops from McClellan's veteran army of 90,000 which took any efficient part in this campaign.

General Pope thus states, with substantial correctness, the condition of his army at this time:

> From the 18th of August until the morning of the 27th, the troops under my command had been continually marching and fighting night and day, and during the whole of that time there was scarcely an interval of an hour without the roar of artillery. The men had had but little sleep, were greatly worn down with fatigue, had but little time to get proper food or eat it, had been engaged in constant battles and skirmishes, and had performed services laborious, dangerous, and excessive beyond any previous experience in this country. As was to be expected under such circumstances, the numbers of the army under my command had been greatly reduced by death, by wounds, by sickness, and by fatigue, so that on the morning of the 27th of August I estimated my whole effective force (and I think the estimate was large) as follows: Sigel's corps, 9,000; Banks corps, 5,000; McDowell's corps including Reynolds' division, 15,500; Reno's corps, 7,000; the corps of Heintzelman and Porter (the freshest by far in that army), about 18,000 men; making in all 54,500 men. Our cavalry numbered on paper about 4,000, but their horses were completely broken down, and there were not 500 men all told, capable of doing such service as should be expected from cavalry. The corps of Heintzelman had reached Warrenton Junction, but without wagons, without artillery, and with only 40 rounds of ammunition to the man, and without even horses for the general field officers. The corps of Porter had also reached Warrenton Junction with a very small supply of provisions, and but 40 rounds of ammunition for each man.

This is no exaggerated picture of the services our army had performed, and of its condition at the moment when Jackson swooped down upon its supply depot and line of communications. The bulk of Lee's army was still in front of us at Waterloo; a cavalry detachment sent out on the morning of the 26th to reconnoiter toward Thoroughfare Gap had not yet reported, and Pope was still unadvised and unsuspecting as to what was taking place in his rear. But during the afternoon of the 26th he discovered symptoms of something wrong in that direction, and sent by a staff officer the following order to General Heintzelman at Warrenton Junction: "The Major General commanding the Army of Virginia directs me to request you to put a regiment on a train of cars, and send it down immediately to Manassas to ascertain what has occurred, repair the telegraph wires, and protect the railroad there until further orders." At midnight of the 26th, Pope instructed McDowell as follows: "General Sigel reports the enemy rear guard at Orleans tonight with his main force encamped at White Plains. You will please ascertain very early in the morning whether this is so, and have the whole of your command in readiness to march. You had better ascertain tonight if you possibly can. Our communications have been interrupted by the enemy's cavalry near Manassas. Whether his whole force, or the larger part of it, has gone round is a question which we must settle instantly, and no portion of his force must march opposite to us tonight without our knowing it. I telegraphed you an hour ago what dispositions I had made, supposing the advance through Thoroughfare Gap to be a column of not more than 10-15,000 men. If his whole force, or the larger part of it, has gone, we must know it at once."

Such was the state of General Pope's information at midnight of the 26th. Very soon after that hour, he realized more clearly, though still not fully, what the enemy was doing, and he acted upon the information as we shall see, with promptness and energy. Twenty-four hours earlier, he had decided to mass his army between Warrenton and Gainesville and there deliver battle. This determination and the disposition of his forces which it had prompted, prepared him well for the unforeseen emergency now to be met.

On Wednesday morning August 27th, General Pope put his entire army in motion toward Gainesville and Manassas. Sigel and Reynolds, followed by King and Ricketts, all under McDowell, moved in the order named, directly on Gainesville, and Heintzelman and Reno, instructed to support McDowell if need be, marched from Catlett's Station toward Greenwich. Porter was directed remain at Warrenton Junction until relieved by Banks, now coming up from Fayetteville, and then to push forward toward Greenwich and Gainesville to assist in the operations in that quarter. Banks was charged with the duty of covering the march of the railroad and wagon trains, and on reconstructing the railroad bridges destroyed by Jackson, so as to bring the cars locomotives through, if possible, to Manassas. All the army trains were sent toward Warrenton Junction, with instructions to follow Hooker's division of Heintzelman's corps, advancing along the railroad to Manassas Junction. Bayard, with three regiments of cavalry, joined Sigel on the evening of the 27th, but did not remain with him, while Buford with most of Sigel's cavalry and a few pieces of artillery, was sent out to reconnoiter in the direction of Chester Gap. By these movements, if continued, the bulk of Pope's army would be brought directly between Lee and Jackson. Gainesville, near which McDowell and Sigel were expected to be during the evening of the 27th, lies at the intersection of the Warrenton Turnpike with the Manassas Gap Railroad, and midway between Thoroughfare Gap and Manassas Junction. It was therefore upon the direct line of Lee's approach and of Jackson's retreat. Lee's army, it will be borne in mind, was yet west of the Bull Run Mountains and Longstreet's corps leading it could not possibly reach Gainesville before the 29th. Until then, Jackson would be obliged to take care of himself as best he might.

About 3 o'clock Wednesday afternoon of the 27th as Hooker approached Bristoe Station, he encountered Ewell's division, which Jackson had left behind to retard our movement toward Manassas. Hooker attacked at once and with such vigor that the enemy's line were broken and his positions carried. The fighting began about four miles west of the station and continued until dark, by which time Ewell had been driven back as far as Bristoe with a loss of 300 men. Leaving his dead, many of his wounded, and much baggage on the field, Ewell withdrew across Broad Run, first burning the railroad bridge which spanned that stream. Hooker, having only five rounds of ammunition per man left, was unable to prevent this and during the night Ewell, without further molestation, rejoined Jackson at Manassas. The encounter with Ewell had a most exhilarating effect upon our army, not only because it was a skillfully managed and successful battle on our part, but especially because, in developing the whereabouts of the enemy, it disclosed a strong probability that the bulk of our forces, coming up from Warrenton, would interpose directly between Jackson and Lee. There was scarcely a soldier in the ranks who did not understand this, and perceive that Jackson was in a perilous predicament, and that his capture, "bag and baggage," which had been one of the standing jests of the camp, was in a fair way to become a reality.

General Pope arrived upon the field at sunset, and concluded at once that he had Jackson's whole force in front of him. He therefore became apprehensive that the enemy would pass around our right, and fall upon our immense wagon trains coming up from Warrenton Junction, or turn and crush Hooker, who had but one division, and that nearly out of ammunition. He therefore issued immediately the following order dated Bristoe Station, August 27, 6:30 P.M. to General Porter at Warrenton Junction: "The Major General commanding directs that you start at 1 o'clock tonight and come forward with your whole corps, or such part of it as is with you, so as to be here by daylight tomorrow morning. Hooker has had a very severe action with the enemy, with the loss of about 300 killed and wounded. The enemy has been driven back, but is retiring along the railroad. We must drive him from Manassas, and clear the country between that place and Gainesville, where McDowell is. If Morrell has not joined you, send him word to push forward immediately; also send word to Banks to move forward with all speed to take your place at Warrenton Junction. It is necessary, on all accounts, that you should be here by daylight. I send an officer with this dispatch who will conduct you to this place. Be sure to send word to Banks, who is on the road from Fayetteville, probably in the direction of Bealton. Say to Banks also that he had best run back the railroad trains to this side of Cedar Run. If he is not with you, write him to that effect."

Two and a half hours later (9 P.M.) Pope sent the following to General Kearny: "At the very earliest dawn of day, push forward with your command with all speed to this place (Bristoe Station). You cannot be more than three or four miles distant. Jackson, A.P. Hill, and Ewell are in front of us. Hooker had a severe fight with them today. McDowell marches upon Manassas Junction from Gainesville tomorrow at daybreak; Reno upon the same place at the same hour. I want you here at daybreak, dawn if possible, and we shall bag the whole crowd. Be prompt and expeditious, and never mind wagon trains or roads until this affair is over. Lieutenant Brooks will deliver you this communication. He has one for General Reno and one for General McDowell. Please have these dispatches sent forward instantly by a trusty staff officer, who will be sure to deliver them without fail, and make him bring back a receipt to you before daylight. Use the cavalry I send you to escort your staff officer to McDowell and Reno."

The dispatch (dated at the same hour as the foregoing) which General Kearny was requested to forward to McDowell (supposed to be at Gainesville, but really at Buckland Mills) was as follows: "At daylight tomorrow morning march rapidly on Manassas Junction with your whole force, resting your right on the Manassas Gap Railroad, throwing your left well to the east. Jackson, Ewell, and A.P. Hill are between Gainesville and Manassas Junction. We had a severe fight with them today, driving them back several miles along the railroad. If you will march promptly and rapidly at the earliest dawn of day upon Manassas Junction, we shall bag the whole crowd. I have directed Reno to march from Greenwich at the same hour on Manassas Junction and Kearny, who is in his rear, to march on Bristoe at daybreak. Be expeditious, and the day is our own."

These orders were based upon the assumption that Jackson, Ewell, and A.P. Hill were between Manassas Junction and Gainesville, and that the next day would find them still in that position. In this General Pope was mistaken. With McDowell, Sigel, and Reynolds at or near Gainesville, and Heintzelman, Porter, and Banks coming up from Greenwich and Catlett's Station, Jackson had no mind to stay at Manassas Junction. He was yet there, it is true, at 9 P.M. on the 27th. He had with him his own and A.P. Hill's divisions, and Ewell's was hastening up from Bristoe to join him. But before daylight his whole force had decamped from Manassas, Ewell's and Hill's divisions going toward Centreville, and Taliaferro's (Jackson's own) toward Sudley Springs.

It was therefore a mistake to call McDowell in the direction of Manassas. His proper course was that toward Haymarket or Centreville. To call him to Manassas was to take him away from his vital strategic position between Lee and Jackson, and open the way for the Confederate armies to unite. It would have been more discreet for General Pope to reserve his orders for McDowell until he knew more of the enemy's whereabouts and intentions. But the propriety of calling up Porter and Banks was manifest. There was no mistake in that. There was also justification, at least, for summoning Reno and Kearny from Greenwich. All this remains true, no matter in what direction Jackson had gone or intended to go. General Pope saw the enemy before him, knew that their retreat by the left was intercepted, and apprehended that Jackson would mass his forces and throw them upon our right flank, which was in no condition to withstand such a shock. It seemed, therefore, but the part of prudence to strengthen that flank. At any rate, whatever the enemy might do, Reno at Manassas Junction and Porter with Kearny at Bristoe could not be far out of place. They would be at hand to fight if Jackson should make a stand, or to pursue him toward Gainesville, Centreville, or Dudley Springs, as the case might be, should he run away. So much for the orders. Let us see how they were executed.

General Pope enjoined haste, as it was proper to do. The crisis of the campaign had arrived, and had brought with it a great opportunity. Minutes were precious, and whatever was done must be done quickly. As for orders, they must be given and changed to suit the varying exigencies of the moment. The all-important thing was to do what the moment seemed to require and do it energetically. As for General Kearny, he never needed any second prompting to be "prompt and expeditious." He was promptness and expedition itself. Obeying implicitly the order given him, he marched at daylight, and arrived at Bristoe at 8 A.M. Equally prompt, Reno, at dawn, put his command in motion for Manassas. General Porter, we have seen, was explicitly ordered to move at one o'clock in the night, so as to reach Bristoe at daylight. This order General Porter failed to comply with: of this there is no question. He did not move at one o'clock, nor did he reach Bristoe at daylight, nor (with his corps) until five or six hours after daylight. And now, as the time at which he actually did move, the importance of his movement, and the impediments alleged to have detained him, have been matters of prolonged dispute, it is proper to refer to them with some particularity.

On the morning when Sigel's corps left Warrenton (August 27), the officer having charge of Milroy's ammunition train moved the train, according to usage and instructions, following the troops to which it belonged. A short distance east of Warrenton General Sigel, in person, ordered the train to leave the column, saying there would be a battle that day and that no wagons of any kind should encumber the column. The officer therefore parked his train beside the road until the troops had passed, and then conducted it back to Warrenton and thence, under cavalry escort, to Warrenton Junction, where he encountered the mass of wagon and railway trains which were being conducted to Manassas by General Banks. At sundown, he encamped with his teams and infantry train guard near Catlett's Station. About 8 o'clock next morning, he arrived at Catlett's, and there encountered the troops and trains of General Fitz John Porter, moving leisurely, and completely filling the road contiguous to the railway. Finding his progress obstructed and being in haste to overtake his corps, the officer rode out from Catlett's in search of another road. He had not gone more than a mile east of the station when he struck an excellent road leading toward Bristoe, entirely clear of troops or wagons. Moving his trains by this route (the teams going much of the time on the trot) he again encountered Porter's column about 11 A.M. at a point where the two roads met a little south of Bristoe. Porter's troops were then halting and although the heat was oppressive, they did not have the appearance of men who had marched rapidly. Being unable to go forward, the officer waited until the column started, and then followed one of the brigades. Half an hour later, the troops moved out of the road into the fields, saying they were going to encamp. The officer then pursued his way to Bristoe Station, where he gave his men and teams an hour's rest. He then pursued his march to the ford over Broad Run, near the scene of Hooker's encounter with Ewell, and although he was detained for an hour or more by a jam of wagons at the ford, he reached Manassas Junction before sundown and that same evening encamped within a short distance of Milroy's brigade, some miles west of the junction.[52]

These simple facts, not important in themselves, yet important in their relations, dispose of all the petty questions about the road and its obstruction. Between Catlett's and Bristoe, there were, as we see, two parallel roads, at least one of which was in excellent condition and unobstructed. The wagon trains were not in motion during the night, but were parked under guard in the woods and fields so that the troops were really much less hindered by wagons at night than in daytime. As for the darkness, which is said to have been a hindrance, it did not embarrass Ewell, Hill, or Taliaferro, all of whom were in movement during the night, and in spite of the great fatigue of their troops, were turning both time and darkness to good account. The distance which General Porter was required to make between one o'clock and daylight was nine miles. During that same four hours, Ewell and Hill marched an equal or greater distance without any particular difficulty.

Much has been said to disparage the importance of this march to Bristoe. Kearny and Reno did not stop or assume to judge whether or not the march was important. They marched. It should also be borne in mind that at the time Pope gave the order, he feared that Jackson would fall, with all his force, on Hooker who was nearly out of ammunition. Had Jackson done that, history would have been cleared of any controversy as to whether General Porter should have marched promptly or not. Nor was the obligation to do so lessened by the enemy's disappearance from Bristoe during the night of the 27th for General Porter should, at any rate, have been on hand at daylight to pursue Jackson to say nothing of the reinforcement of Hooker. It has been said that our battle with Jackson should have been fought on the 28th instead of the 29th; but how could this be unless our troops should move up promptly to the encounter? Jackson was moving most of the night of the 27th, and the only way to overtake him was to push him with energy something like his own.

General Pope seems to have remained in Bristoe on the morning of the 28th until about 11 o'clock. He was probably waiting for Porter's corps to arrive. Undoubtedly, he was more or less held back in his advance on Manassas by Porter's delay. Thus near half a day was lost when moments were of the utmost value. It may be added, upon Pope's testimony, that General Porter insisted when his corps arrived at Bristoe that it should be allowed to stop there and rest. General Pope then rode on to Manassas Junction, and arrived there about noon. He there inferred from what he learned that Jackson had personally just quit the place and that his forces had gone off toward Centreville. Appearances certainly indicated that, and it was General Pope's misfortune to be governed in this instance by appearances instead of obtaining more exact information. In justice to him it should be said that he had but little cavalry available for scouting and reconnaissance. What he had was so broken down as to be able to travel little faster than the infantry, and the bulk of his mounted force which could render any service was at this time absent with Buford and Bayard exploring the country in the direction of Lee's approach.

---

[52] The "officer" mentioned is none other than Lieutenant Alfred E. Lee.

Major General John Pope
(Library of Congress)

Two of Jackson's divisions (Hill's and Ewell's) had gone toward Centreville and this fact led General Pope to believe that Jackson's entire force was retreating in that direction. The truth was that, during the night, Taliaferro's division quit the Junction, and at daybreak arrived upon the old Bull Run battlefield near Sudley Springs; that Hill's division, marching at one o'clock in the morning, proceeded to Centreville and at 10 A.M. on the 28th turned down from the Warrenton Pike toward the Stone Bridge; that Ewell, going from the Junction toward Centreville at the dawn of the 28th crossed Bull Run at Blackburn's Ford, recrossed at the Stone Bridge, and during the day halted near the Matthews House near the Warrenton Pike; and that by the time Pope reached the Junction, Jackson had most of his command with him at or near Sudley Springs. These movements, so far as directed toward Centreville, quite misled Pope, and Stuart's cavalry raid down the railroad toward Alexandria augmented his deception. He therefore sent orders to Hooker to push for Centreville, and dispatched Kearny and Reno in the same direction. He also sent a message to Porter to come forward at once to Manassas Junction.[53] Late in the afternoon, Kearny drove the enemy's rear guard (a regiment of cavalry) out of Centreville. Reno and Hooker, following Kearny, encamped, the one on the east and the other on the west side of Bull Run. General Pope made his headquarters for the night at Blackburn's Ford. Such were the operations of the right wing up to sundown on the 28th. They left Jackson in a position, extending from Sudley Springs westward, north of the Warrenton pike with his cavalry pickets watching us south of the pike, and one of his brigades (Bradley T. Johnson's) thrown westward on the pike to Groveton. Let us now turn to the operations of the left wing.

On the 27th, marching from Warrenton, Sigel sent ahead Milroy's brigade to seize the bridge over Broad Run at Buckland Mills. Milroy found the bridge afire but saved it, drove off the Confederate detachment which was guarding it, and pushed on to Gainesville where he captured 150 of Jackson's stragglers and at 9 P.M. encamped for the night. Schurz and Schenk, following Milroy, took positions behind him in the order named. Sigel was thoroughly impressed with the idea that the enemy in force was not far distant, and held about one third of his troops under arms all night. Milroy kept his whole command on the qui vive.

Thus the 1st Corps lay, during the night of the 27th, on the Warrenton Turnpike, with its head of column at Gainesville, and its reserve (Von Steinwehr's brigade) at Buckland Mills, where General Sigel was joined in the course of the evening by McDowell who, by that time, had learned the result of Buford's reconnaissance made during the day. Buford had marched to Salem, where he discovered Longstreet approaching, and learned that Jackson had passed through Salem the day before and gone on through Thoroughfare Gap. Having resisted Longstreet sufficiently to compel him to form a line of battle and cause him an hour's detention, Buford moved toward White Plains, and then back to Warrenton, picking up on the way many stragglers from Jackson's command.

---

[53] General Pope so testifies and his testimony is corroborated by Colonel Strother (then serving on Pope's staff) who says in his published diary: "Just as we neared the smoking ruins of the Junction, I was sent back with a message to Generals Porter, Hooker, and Heintzelman ordering them to move their commands on Manassas without delay. I found Porter at Bristoe, and delivered the message. I afterward found Generals Heintzelman and Hooker with their officers." From this it appears that General Porter received the order first. ~ Lee note.

Sigel had acquired similar information as to the enemy. From his own scouting parties he had learned during the day that Jackson had passed through Thoroughfare Gap to Manassas, and that Longstreet was following him by way of Salem and White Plains. He therefore proposed to McDowell, in dispatches sent early in the afternoon from Buckland Mills, that they should rapidly concentrate their joint forces at Gainesville and press forward against the enemy. General McDowell, when he arrived at Buckland Mills in the evening, suggested a movement to Salem, but Sigel was disinclined to this, believing that it would lead to a division of our forces and enable Longstreet and Jackson to unite. Whether influenced or not by these suggestions, General McDowell prepared an order dated 11:30 P.M. directing that General Sigel's corps should be concentrated near Haymarket and Gainesville; that a division of the 3rd Corps (McDowell's) should be left at Buckland Mills to operate against the flanks of the enemy, or march to Haymarket as might be expedient; that King's and Ricketts' divisions should march to Gainesville, starting at two o'clock in the morning "to attack the enemy's position in the direction of Manassas;" and that the attack should be supported on the right by General Heintzelman then at Greenwich. These dispositions were excellent and had they been allowed to stand, the campaign would have turned out far differently than it did.

At Haymarket and Gainesville, Sigel was just in the right place and could move eastward against Jackson or go back and hold Thoroughfare Gap, as occasion might require. He would also have a short road to the Hopewell and Aldie gaps should Longstreet or Jackson try to break through there.[54] But General McDowell had scarcely sent out his instructions when he received Pope's 9 P.M. order, directing him to march with his whole force on Manassas Junction. That order, the parent of so much mischief, came just in time to stop the concentration of the left wing between Lee and Jackson and to re-open the avenues of approach to each other. When it arrived, General McDowell was making arrangement to send Sigel's corps and Ricketts' division up to Thoroughfare Gap, and had he been allowed to execute his plans, he would have undoubtedly held Lee's whole army back for a day at least. But it was not in calling McDowell eastward that harm was done so much as in giving him the wrong course. Obviously he should have been directed upon Centreville, and not upon Manassas. During the morning of the 28th two of Jackson's divisions were yet east of Bull Run, moving down the Warrenton pike from Centreville. Now Gainesville, Centreville, and Manassas Junction mark the apexes of a triangle, of which the turnpike from Gainesville to Centreville may be considered the base. Moving along this base line, McDowell would strike Jackson full in front, but moving toward Manassas he was inclining too far to the right, and giving Jackson a free road.

Nevertheless, General McDowell applied himself at once to putting Pope's orders into execution. Sigel was directed to move toward Manassas Junction with "his right resting on the Manassas railroad," Reynolds following by the turnpike on Sigel's left, King following Reynolds, and Ricketts following King, all in echelon. Ricketts was enjoined to be constantly on the lookout for an attack from the direction of Thoroughfare Gap and to turn and resist such an attack if made. General McDowell complains in his report that Sigel's movement was too slow, that he took the wrong route, and that his column was too much encumbered with wagons. It is difficult to understand how this last could have been so, for we have seen that, while marching from Warrenton, Sigel ordered even ammunition wagons out of his column. He sent all his baggage trains to Catlett's, as Pope had instructed, and from Buckland Mills he sent back an officer to conduct his supply train to Manassas. Possibly some wagons not carrying ammunition followed his troops, but if so, it was without the knowledge and against the orders of General Sigel.

There was no detention of the 1st Corps on the morning of the 28th caused by wagons, but there was some detention of it arising from other causes. In the first place, the order to march to Manassas Junction was not delivered to Sigel until 2:45 A.M., the messenger bearing it having roved about with it in the dark for two hours. In the next place, Sigel's column extended from Gainesville back to Buckland Mills, a distance of four miles, his divisions having been separated so as to be placed where they could get water which was very scarce in that region. Now as Sigel believed the enemy to be in front of him, he deemed it prudent to close up his column before calling in the detachments which Milroy had thrown out at Gainesville, or putting his head of column (Milroy's brigade) in motion. Nevertheless, Sigel was at Gainesville by 6 o'clock, having personally hurried up his divisions as he passed along the road.

---

[54] Thoroughfare Gap is five miles, Buckland Mills four miles, and Haymarket and Groveton each three and a half miles from Gainesville. ~ Lee note.

McDowell's instructions were that Sigel should "march with his whole corps on Manassas Junction, his right resting on the Manassas railroad." Sigel seems to have understood this to mean that he should march to the Junction, his right halting on the Manassas railroad. He therefore sought the shortest route to the Junction, which was a road parallel with and a little south of the railroad. This was a variation from McDowell's instructions, but it was not important, so far as compliance with orders was concerned. If we were going to Manassas, the shortest route was best. In the movement now making, King's division extended farthest to the left, and Sigel's corps farthest to the right. Between was Reynolds' division, which before turning southward toward Manassas, found itself confronted by a hostile battery posted on a hill near the pike. This battery, being properly attended to, disappeared and the march was resumed.[55] General Sigel halted when he heard the firing, suspecting that Jackson was in the neighborhood and it would have been well had General McDowell shared that suspicion, as he does not seem to have done. It required a more vigorous blow to wake everybody up to the fact that the enemy (the very one we were seeking) was not far off.

The march continued without interruption for two or three miles father when at 2 o'clock, Sigel's scouting parties reported that they had seen Confederate infantry, cavalry, and artillery, accompanied by a wagon train. One of the parties had been attacked. Major Franz Kappner, Sigel's chief engineer, observed this hostile force for half an hour, moving on the road from Haymarket to Groveton. Lieutenant Burchard, as assistant engineer, was with Kappner and reported what he had seen to General McDowell. Major Heintz, also of the 1st Corps staff, reported to Sigel that he had discovered a large wagon train on the Warrenton Pike, and believed it might be captured if attacked by a strong force of cavalry. Later, Heintz sent word that the enemy had opened fire with four pieces of artillery. "General Von Steinwehr," he added, "intends to attack the enemy's flank with the brigade and is preparing for the advance. I shall follow with the cavalry on his right." These various reports convinced Sigel that the Confederates had quit Manassas and were concentrating on the old Bull Run battlefield. Before him their pickets were scattered through the timber for the distance of a mile. Behind these, near the Warrenton-Centreville Pike, was Bradley T. Johnson's brigade, supported as yet only by cavalry. The moment was opportune for making an attack, and Sigel began putting his corps in line of battle. At the same time, he reported the situation to McDowell and quick and peremptory order came back to him to proceed to Manassas. "I reluctantly obeyed this order," says Sigel "and marched off from the right, and was within two and a half miles from Manassas when our cavalry reported that Manassas was evacuated by the enemy and that General Kearny was in possession of that point." The "phlegmatic German" had been going slow, it is true. Pity that he had not gone slower- pity that he went at all in the direction he was required to take.

In the course of the forenoon, stirring news came from Thoroughfare Gap. Colonel Percy Wyndham was there with the 1st New Jersey Cavalry, accompanied by Captain Leski of McDowell's staff. "The enemy is advancing through the pass," reported Leski. "Colonel Wyndham will halt there as long as he can and asks to be reinforced." McDowell acted promptly and wisely. "Send a brigade and a battery to assist Colonel Wyndham and follow them up by your whole division," was his immediate command to General Ricketts. Ricketts' division, being yet on the road between New Baltimore and Gainesville, was moving rapidly by way of Haymarket where it dropped its knapsacks, reached the Gap about 3 P.M. and there met Colonel Wyndham's skirmishers retiring before the enemy already in possession. Pressing forward, Ricketts met with severe resistance and was unable to seize the pass, but held his ground until dark and then, finding that the enemy had turned his position by way of Hopewell Gap, he withdrew and took a position for the night between Haymarket and Gainesville.

At Bethlehem Church, where Sigel learned that Manassas was evacuated, he halted and being sure that the enemy was somewhere between Centreville and Gainesville, he reported his situation directly to Pope, who ordered him to push on to Centreville. Sigel then asked permission to go by way of New Market and this being granted, he turned his column up the Sudley Springs road and proceeded. Milroy, who had, as usual, rushed ahead and had arrived within a mile of Manassas, marched across the country and resumed his place in the advance. He was joined by McLean's brigade of Schenk's division and in connection with that brigade soon struck the enemy's cavalry and

---

[55] The hostile detachment may have belonged to Stuart's cavalry, or to Johnson's brigade which Jackson had thrown out toward Groveton as already mentioned. Its artillery firing killed three and wounded four of our men. ~Lee Note.

pushed through the woods, skirmishing as he advanced and keeping his artillery in action. Learning that Centreville had been abandoned by the enemy, Sigel drew Schurz's division (which had gone toward Bull Run) with the rest of his troops to the support of McLean and Milroy.

Let us now go back to McDowell. Between 3 and 4 o'clock in the afternoon he received two dispatches from Pope, in one of which he was directed to move to Gum Springs[56] to intercept Jackson and in the other to march to Centreville. Complying with this last command, Reynolds' division (spurred by Sigel's firing) shifted north toward Centreville Pike, which King's division had quit but a short time before and at 5:30 P.M. proceeded to follow King. In the first of the dispatches just mentioned Pope referred to McDowell's superior knowledge of the country, and asked him for a full expression of his views. McDowell, therefore, most imprudently and unfortunately, rode off to Manassas to confer personally with Pope, and thus separated from his command at a most critical juncture as we shall now see. Not finding Pope, who had left Manassas for Centreville, McDowell turned back to rejoin his division but darkness coming on he lost his way and was obliged to spend the night with troops of Sigel's corps.

Having regained the Warrenton pike, King's division tranquilly took its course toward Centreville. Hatch's brigade led, and the brigades of Doubleday, Gibbon, and Patrick followed in the order named. This movement fell under the eye of Jackson, who had by this time brought his whole force into line between Groveton and Sudley Springs. Seeing our troops at Manassas flying off toward Centreville, he believed, he says, that Pope's army was in full retreat and he prepared himself to strike it in flank. He was, therefore, lurking near with Ewell's and Taliaferro's divisions while King was passing along the pike.

A soldier of King's division (partly quoting from his diary) thus describes what took place:

About 6 P.M. with unloaded muskets, marching to the charming music of our bands and unconscious of the bloody reception awaiting us, we started on the turnpike for Centreville. Suddenly, the stillness of the summer evening was broken by six shots fired in quick succession right into our regiment (6th Wisconsin) from a battery not 500 yards away. Surprise is no name for our astonishment. The reverberation had scarcely died away when the old colonel's[57] voice was heard "Halt! Front! Load at will, load!" The men fairly jumped to their work and the ramrods were jingling lively when whack! Whack! Whack! The Rebel cannon fired again, almost it seemed, in our faces."

The commander of the brigade was General John Gibbon; let his official report continue the story. "I had not information of an infantry force in that position. I therefore supposed this was one of the enemy's cavalry batteries and ordered the 2nd Wisconsin to face to the left." There you have it; the 2nd Wisconsin ordered to attack 32 regiments! The writer well remembers the sagacious wag of the head with which General Gibbon informed us that we should be delayed a 'few minutes while the 2nd Wisconsin captured that squad.' He would doubtless justify his action in ordering that attack by General McDowell's belief that there was 'nothing but cavalry" in our way to Centreville. He says in his report "I sent repeated and earnest requests to division headquarters for assistance. Two of General Doubleday's regiments finally got into line." Six regiments and yet Jackson says in his report that 'the enemy maintained his ground with obstinate determination.' Taliaferro describes it as "one of the most terrific conflicts that can be conceived." He adds that "for two hours and a half, without an instant's cessation of the most deadly discharges of musketry, round shot, and shell, both lines stood unmoved, neither advancing, and neither broken or yielding, until at last about 9 o'clock at night, the enemy slowly and sullenly fell back and yielded the field to our victorious troops." If 3,000 men, well handled, could wrest such tributes to their valor, what might have been accomplished by McDowell's whole command? Gibbon's brigade, having proved itself on this bloody field as superior to the famous 'Stonewall' men of Jackson, it was forever afterward called the Iron Brigade.

---

[56] Pope seems to have believed when he wrote this dispatch that Jackson was retreating toward the Aldie Gap. In his next dispatch, however, he said the enemy was reported in force east of Bull Run. ~ Lee Note.
[57] Colonel Lysander Cutler of the 6th Wisconsin Volunteer Infantry was severely wounded through the leg in this action fought on August 28, 1862 which became known as the Battle of Groveton.

Groveton

"A little before sunset on the 28th, our brigade was marching on the Centreville road when we were fired upon by a Rebel battery. Not expecting to find much force with it, we started to take it and found ourselves attacked by four brigades of the enemy. We were in for it, and fought until 9 o'clock. Our men fought like tigers. They were charged upon by the enemy repeatedly, but never quailed but stood calmly until they were close upon us, and then they would mow them down in heaps. The 6th stood in ranks as steadily as they would in a dress parade. When a man was wounded or killed, he was carried to the rear and cared for, and the rest fought on. Most of the fight was in the dark and we stood our ground until we silenced the fire of the enemy, and then spent the night in gathering up the dead and wounded. Just before the close of the action I got shot through the thigh, just grazing the bone. My horse was soon after shot and my spare horse wounded."

~ *Colonel Lysander Cutler, 6th Wisconsin Infantry*

Says General Rufus King: "It was near 9 o'clock before the firing ceased. Then came the question what next to be done? The enemy in greatly superior force barred the way by which the division was marching (as if our only object in life that night was to reach Centreville). The only alternative was to deflect to the right to join the bulk of Pope's army at Manassas. Pope's army was not at Manassas, but 'deflect' we did, stumbling along at three miles per hour after our terrible fight through the darkness, in which it was impossible for Porter to march to our help." The account I am quoting concludes "It is impossible to restrain a feeling of indignation when I think of our dead comrades left unburied in the dark shadows of Gibbon's woods. Of the dead heroes who warred against Troy, Homer says "Their bones unburied on the bending shore, Devouring dogs and hungry vultures tore." Our tale is sadder than that, for the hogs were found to have mutilated the bodies of these brave men thus left in our midnight retreat."

This sanguinary conflict took place about a mile west of Groveton. Our losses attest to its fury. Only Gibbon's brigade and two regiments of Doubleday's were engaged. Gibbon had 2,300 men of whom he lost 782 in killed, wounded, and missing. Our total loss was about 1,000. On the Confederate side, Generals Taliaferro and Ewell were severely wounded, the latter losing a leg. Taliaferro and Jackson represent that our troops were obliged to quit the field. This is a mistake. They held their ground until 1 o'clock in the morning, and then withdrew voluntarily.

Observing King's battle from the Robinson House, Sigel pushed forward Schenk and Reynolds on the left to support him. This closed the operations of the 1st Corps for the day. Its lines rested on the heights fronting Young's Branch, and covered the turnpike back to the Stone Bridge. The officer conducting Milroy's ammunition train, to whom reference has been made, saw the smoke of King's conflict from one of the forts at Manassas Junction. He also heard the sound of the cannon calling with mighty voice to our forces far and near. The sights that met the eye added to the impressiveness of this sonorous summons. All around the Junction was a scene of appalling wreck. Upon the railway track, locomotives battered with cannon shot were standing and the smoky remains of hundreds of freight cars were strewn. In every direction boxes, barrels, cans, hard bread, sabers, muskets, blankets, tents, and ammunition were scattered over the ground. Great piles of bacon and cured beef were still burning, and solitary blackened chimneys and heaps of ashes were all that remained of our well-stored magazines. This, while 30,000 troops had been detained at Alexandria, ostensibly for supplies, and Pope's army, marching and fighting day and night, was obliged to go hungry!

About 9 o'clock in the evening information of King's engagement reached Pope at his headquarters near the Bull Run crossing, north of Manassas. The news was a revelation to his mind, and believing Jackson to be now entrapped, he sent orders repeatedly during the night to Generals McDowell and King[58] to hold their ground and prevent the retreat of the enemy west. To General Kearny, near Centreville, he sent at 9:50 P.M. the following: "General McDowell has intercepted the retreat of the enemy and is

---

[58] For reasons disclosed in the narrative, these orders failed to reach either King or McDowell. ~ Lee Note.

now in his front, Sigel on the right of McDowell. Unless he can escape by by-paths leading to the north tonight, he must be captured. I desire you to move forward at 1 o'clock tonight even if you have to carry with you no more than 2,000 men, though I trust you will carry the larger part of your division. Pursue the turnpike from Centreville to Warrenton. The enemy is not more than 3 ½ miles from you. Seize any of the people of the town to guide you. Advance cautiously and drive the enemy's pickets tonight, and at early dawn attack him vigorously. Hooker shall be close behind you. Extend your right well toward the north and push forward your right wing well in the attack. Be sure to march not later than one, with all the men you can take."

With the same emphasis Pope ordered Heintzelman to push forward Hooker's division at 3 A.M. following Kearny. To General Porter, he sent the following dated 3 A.M. August 29: "Sigel is immediately on the right of McDowell. Kearny and Hooker march to attack the enemy's rear at early dawn. Major General Pope directs you to move upon Centreville at the first dawn of day with your whole command, leaving your trains to follow. It is very important that you should be here at a very early hour in the morning. A severe engagement is likely to take place and your presence is necessary."

It was expected that this order would find Porter at Manassas. Colonel Strother, who was the bearer of it, says, "I found no troops at Manassas and it was broad daylight when I reached Porter's quarters at Bristoe. Entering his tent, I found the handsome general lying on his cot, covered with a blanket of imitation leopard skin. At his request, I lit a candle and read the message then handed it to him. While he coolly read it over, I noted the time which marked 5:20 precisely. He then proceeded to dress himself and continued to question me in regard to the location of the different commands and the general situation. Meanwhile, headquarters breakfast had been served and I sat down with the staff officers to partake. General Porter, who was busy writing dispatches on the corner of the same table, looked up and asked "How do you spell chaos?' I spelled the word by letter. Completing his dispatch, he folded and asked if any of us had letters we wished to send to Washington. He remarked that he had daily communication with Washington."[59]

We have seen that at 1 o'clock in the morning, King's division relinquished the position it had so bravely held and marched off toward Manassas. Ricketts, learning that King should withdraw, put his division in motion for Bristoe Station. Reynolds, although aware of King's movement, kept firmly to his place. Toward daylight Pope learned with consternation of King's retreat. He was greatly disappointed, but addressed himself with energy and decision to the new situation of affairs. Jackson had taken his position on rolling ground in the neighborhood of Groveton, a hamlet on the Warrenton turnpike, six miles west of Centreville. With his left in Sudley Springs and his right a little south of the pike, his front was covered by an unfinished railroad grade- part excavation, part embankment- extending from Gainesville toward Leesburg. In front of him was Sigel, who was ordered to attack him vigorously at daybreak, supported by Reynolds. Porter, who had come up at last to Manassas, and was proceeding towards Centreville was directed by Pope as follows: "Push forward with your corps and King's division, which you will take with you, upon Gainesville. I am following the enemy down the Warrenton turnpike. Be expeditious, or we will lose much." Heintzelman and Reno, already instructed to move forward rapidly from the neighborhood of Centreville, were not the men to need any additional spur. It was expected that, in the early forenoon, they would establish connection with Sigel on the left and join in the general assault.

Soon after issuing these orders, General Pope received from McDowell a note, dated Manassas Junction, requesting that King's division should not be taken from him. Thereupon Pope issued from Centreville (about 9

[59] General Porter's animus toward Pope at this time is further disclosed by the following quotes. Porter to Burnside August 27: "Everything here is sixes and sevens, and I find I am to take care of myself in every respect. Our line of communication has taken care of itself in compliance with orders." Porter to Burnside from Warrenton Junction August 27: "We are working now to get behind Bull Run and I presume will be there in a few days if strategy doesn't use us up. The strategy is magnificent, the tactics in inverse proportion. I wish Sumner was at Washington, and up near the Monocacy with good batteries. I do not doubt the enemy have large amounts of supplies provided for them, and I believe they have a contempt for this Army of Virginia. I wish myself away from it, with all our old Army of the Potomac, and so do our companions." Porter to Burnside, August 28: "All that talk about bagging Jackson was bosh. That enormous gap, Manassas, was left open and the enemy jumped through." Porter to McClellan, September 1: "This week is the crisis of our fate." ~ Lee note.

A.M. on August 29) the following joint order to McDowell and Porter: "You will please move forward with your joint commands towards Gainesville. I sent General Porter written orders to that effect an hour and a half ago. Heintzelman, Sigel, and Reno are moving on the Warrenton turnpike, and must now be not far from Gainesville. I desire that, as soon as communication is established between this force and your own, the whole command shall halt. It may be necessary to fall back behind Bull Run at Centreville tonight. I presume it will be so on account of supplies. I have sent no orders of any description to Ricketts, and none to interfere in any way with the movements of McDowell's troops, except what I sent by his aide-de-camp last night, which were, to hold his position on the Warrenton pike until the troops from here should fall upon the enemy's flank and rear. I do not even know Ricketts' position, as I had not been able to find out where General McDowell was until a late hour this morning. General McDowell will take immediate steps to communicate with General Ricketts, and instruct him to rejoin the other divisions of the corps as soon as practicable. If any considerable advantages are to be gained by departing from this order, it will not be strictly carried out. One thing must be had in view- that the troops must occupy a position from which they can reach Bull Run tonight or by morning. The indications are that the whole force of the enemy is moving in this direction, at a pace that will bring them here by tomorrow night or next day. My own headquarters will be for the present with Heintzelman's corps or at this place." Such were the orders. Let us next attend to their execution.

Colonel James Cantwell, 82nd Ohio (Richard Fink Collection)

CHAPTER THREE

Second Bull Run

The morning of the 29th of August found Sigel's corps standing alone before Stonewall Jackson's entire force. Of the rest of the army only Reynolds' division was within supporting distance. McDowell and his other two divisions had gone astray and Pope with two other divisions had been decoyed away toward Centreville. The 1st Corps had become the nucleus upon which Pope's army should rally.[60]

The order that Sigel should attack vigorously at dawn was punctually obeyed and as soon as it was fairly light, the thunder of his cannon rolled across the hills. Men and officers had neither time for breakfast nor much to eat. The supply wagons with which our columns are said to have been encumbered we had not seen for many days. Scarcely a vehicle carrying provisions was anywhere near, and our supplies at Manassas had been destroyed. The men of the 1st Corps had lain down and arisen with empty stomachs. In that condition they marched into the fight. To make matters worse, there seemed to be little prospect that supplies would come forward. In response to his urgent request that food and forage might be sent out from Alexandria, General Pope had received the following addressed under the date of August 29 8P.M. to the "Commanding officer at Centreville" and signed by General Franklin commanding the 6th Corps: "I have been instructed by General McClellan to inform you that he will have all available wagons at Alexandria loaded with rations for your troops and all the cars also, as soon as you will send a cavalry escort to Alexandria as a guard to the train." General Pope justly remarks that "such a letter when we were fighting the enemy and Alexandria swarming with troops needs no comment" and adds "it was not until I received this letter than I began to feel discouraged and nearly hopeless of any successful issue to the operations with which I was charged."

The condition of our cavalry from which a railway train guard was required as a condition to forwarding supplies is thus described in General Pope's official report. "Our cavalry at Centreville was completely broken down, no horses whatever having reached us to remount it. Generals Buford and Bayard, commanding the whole of the cavalry force of the army, reported to me that there were not five horses to the company that could be forced to trot." During the march of the 28th, General Sigel had with him but 150 horsemen and most of his reconnoitering had to be done by his own staff officers.

Schurz's light division of six regiments held the right of Sigel's line. It was deployed on the north side of the turnpike, parallel with the Sudley Springs road. Schimmelfennig held Schurz's right, and Krzyzanowski's with Captain Romer's battery, his left. Milroy with his independent brigade and one battery held the center. To the left of Milroy and south of the pike was Schenk's division- first Stahel's brigade and then McLean's. Beyond Schenk was General Reynolds who had brought up his division during the night and thrown forward one brigade (George G. Meade's) towards Jackson's right flank. The Confederate line was about two miles in length. On the left was A.P. Hill's division with four batteries; in the center was Ewell's division under Lawton; and on the right was Jackson's own division (Starke commanding) with five batteries. Jackson's aggregate force present on the field must have been little short of 25,000 men; our own, including Reynolds division, was not above 12,000. Such was the disparity of numbers when Sigel, with the formation described, moved to the attack.

Milroy led off in developing the enemy's position. "Fall in boys, we're going to whip them before breakfast," he shouted as he galloped about among his regiments, already thoroughly aroused by the cannonade. Throwing away their coffee, just brought to them from the rear, the men fell into their places and the independent brigade moved forward. It had not proceeded more than 500 yards when the enemy's skirmishers opened fire upon it from the woods in front. Milroy was about to make a dash into the woods when Sigel checked him in order that the

---

[60] The text of this chapter comprises two articles that Captain Lee wrote for the *Magazine of American History* in 1886, including "From Cedar Mountain to Chantilly III," and "From Cedar Mountain to Chantilly IV."

proper connections might first be established. After a brief pause, the whole line moved forward. Milroy took possession of a hill in front of the Stone House, and Schenk and Schurz kept abreast right and left, driving the enemy before them. Pressing steadily on from point to point, Sigel's whole command soon became engaged in a violent infantry and artillery contest. Schurz advanced a mile and Schenk two miles. Milroy was impatient to outstrip both. Pushing two of his regiments (the 82nd Ohio under Colonel Cantwell and the 5th West Virginia Colonel Zeigler) into a strip of dense timber, he made ready to charge a Confederate battery with the other two. He had no supports and had lost connections both right and left. During the advance Schurz's division had shifted a little to the right and Schenk's to the left, leaving the independent brigade alone.

These circumstances should have suggested caution to say the least, but that was a virtue not known to Milroy. He had four regiments, and sent two of them, he says, to the assistance of General Schurz. The fact is that these two regiments above named moved through the woods straight at the enemy. They were alone- two regiments groping through a coppice in search of Ewell's division. Deep in the woods the unfinished railway embankment already mentioned ran along a flat, marshy piece of ground. Behind this embankment, which was 8 to 10 feet high, the Confederates lay concealed.[61] Stealthily waiting until Cantwell's line had approached within a few paces of them, they sprang up from their ambush and with a wild yell poured a deadly volley full into our faces. In spite of this surprise and shock, the 82nd Ohio charged the embankment and even passed it at one point, when a flanking force showed itself upon our right and obliged us to change front. While directing this movement and gallantly rallying his men, Colonel Cantwell, a most brave and accomplished officer, was struck in the head by a bullet and fell dead from his horse. The 5th West Virginia and 82nd Ohio were driven out of the woods and the 2nd West Virginia, sent forward by Milroy, was pushed back in disorder. Colonel Cantwell's body was left on the field, but was recovered afterward under flag of truce.

This clumsily managed and bloody affair temporarily disorganized Milroy's brigade and weakened the whole line. The enemy at once threw forward masses of infantry to take advantage of Milroy's repulse, and Stahel's brigade had to be brought over from Schenk's division to Milroy's support. Meanwhile the artillery came to our rescue. The battery on Schurz's left was fortunately so placed as to take the advancing Confederates in one flank, while a reserve battery and two of Schirmer's guns struck them upon the other. Milroy, as brave as he was imprudent, rallied his men on his reserve regiment (3rd West Virginia), and held his ground.

During this time, Schurz had been pressing through the woods and had advanced half a mile. The enemy disputed the ground step by step and when Milroy was repulsed, fell heavily upon Schurz's left and center. At the same time heavy columns of Confederate infantry were seen moving upon the right. Schurz's center was broken and thrown out of the woods. Fortunately, Colonel Soest with the 29th New York of Von Steinwehr's brigade (under Colonel Koltes) had come up and

Colonel James Cantwell

"We had just gained the woods when General Milroy rode up and said, 'Go in 82nd and give them hell!' The enemy opened a most terrific fire upon us. Our boys stood bravely for a while, but finally fell back in some disorder. However they were soon rallied by our brave colonel and major and our men were again formed and poured a deadly fire upon the Rebels. It was then that I saw Colonel Cantwell for the last time. He was urging on his men and telling them to stand fast when a rifle ball struck him in the forehead, killing him instantly. He never knew what hurt him. Major Thomson at once took command and brought the men off the field."

~Capt. Solomon L. Hodge, Co. D, 82nd Ohio Infantry

---

[61] The 82nd Ohio struck a 100 yard gap in the unfinished railroad line that became known as "The Dump," named after the piles of stones that workers had placed there preliminary to bringing the section up to grade. "Because it promised to be an unpleasant place for anyone charged with manning it directly, Jackson gathered up his skulkers and stragglers and gave the job of defending the Dump to the army's miscreants." Hennessey, John J. Return to Bull Run: The Campaign and Battle of Second Manassas. New York: Touchstone Books, 1993, pg. 210

deployed behind a fence in the edge of the timber. The fire of this regiment and that of the batteries held the enemy in check and the center soon rallied and recovered its lost ground.

It was not 10 o'clock and the approach of General Kearny's division on Schurz's right was announced. General Reno's troops also came up on the Centreville pike and with Reno's consent three of his regiments and a battery, all under General Stevens, were placed by Sigel on Schenk's right, there relieving Dilger's battery which had held that position all the morning. Two other regiments, with two mounted batteries, were sent to the assistance of Schurz, and slipped in between his brigades. The remainder of Koltes' brigade was also called up. To make room for Kearny, Schurz contracted his right and had no sooner done so than another furious assault was made upon his center and left. The center was driven from the woods in disorder and the enemy advanced to the edge of the timber. The 29th New York, stationed in reserve, was obliged to fall back after delivering several volleys and Krzyzanowski, on the left, had to withdraw, though stubbornly contesting the ground inch by inch.[62] The moment was critical, and again the artillery turned the current of battle. While Schurz was rallying his men, the battery on his left opened fire upon the pursuing Confederates, and at once brought them to a stand. Schimmelfennig had held his ground upon the right, and now the 29th New York and the 54th New York (Lieutenant Colonel Ashby) gallantly advanced in the center and re-entered the woods.

At this moment Schurz was shown a letter which was on its way from Sigel to Kearny, saying that Longstreet was not able to bring his troops in line of battle that day and requesting Kearny to change his front to the left and advance, if possible, against the enemy's left flank. Schurz thereupon ordered a general advance of his whole line, anticipating that Kearny would attack at the same time, as Sigel had requested. It was by this time midday. Schurz's whole division dashed forward and drove the enemy at every point. In this charge the 29th New York distinguished itself for its intrepidity and its brave commander Colonel Soest was severely wounded. The railroad embankment was carried, and on the right General Schimmelfennig's brigade passed beyond it. Krzyzanowski with two mountain howitzers which did effective work from his front line, also carried the embankment. Milroy on the left held his ground. But Kearny did not attack on the right. Had he done so- as he did later in the day- we would, in Schurz's opinion, have crushed the enemy's left wing.

Schurz held the embankment until 2 P.M. His troops and Milroy's had been fighting most of the time since sunrise and were very much exhausted. They had suffered great losses and were nearly out of ammunition. General Hooker's division had come upon the field and at Sigel's request, relieved Schurz's regiments one by one. Milroy kept his place until later. Schurz withdrew his brigades behind the hill on which Krzyzanowski's battery had been posted, and here the men replenished their ammunition and for the first time in the day had something to eat. On the left, Schenk, fighting mainly with his artillery (De Beck's, Buell's and Schirmer's batteries) advanced until he reached the position of Gibbon's brigade on King's battleground of the evening before. Reynolds' division came up on the left of Schenk's, crossed the pike, and established a battery (Cooper's) supported by Meade's brigade on the same ridge on which Jackson's right rested. But the withdrawal of Stahel to support Milroy broke the connection with Schenk and Reynolds, being exposed to a converging fire of the enemy's batteries, deemed it prudent to withdraw from the cleared ground he occupied into the woods. Schenk adjusted his line to Reynolds' new position.

Turning to the extreme right, we find Kearny moving two brigades (Robinson's and Poe's) against Jackson's left. Robinson endeavored to connect with the right of Schimmelfennig's brigade, which had advanced beyond the railroad embankment into a cornfield. But Schimmelfennig was obliged to fall back to the embankment and Robinson, heavily assaulted, was unable to make further progress. Having withdrawn to the road, he was reinforced by four regiments of Birney's brigade and held his ground. Of Hooker's division, Carr's brigade and Taylor's went into the woods to take Schurz's place and this concluded the field movements up to 2 P.M.

General Pope arrived from Centreville about noon. After inspecting the line from right to left, he decided not to push the troops again into action until sufficient time had been given for McDowell and Porter to come in on the left. This, he felt sure, ought to happen very soon. Porter at Bristoe, had received at 5:20 A.M. an order to "move upon Centreville at the first dawn of day." The distance from Bristoe to Manassas Junction is five miles, and from

---

[62] Schurz's report says: "The 74th Pennsylvania, which displayed the greatest firmness and preserved perfect order on that occasion, deploying and firing with the utmost regularity, deserves special praise."

the Junction to the point where Reynolds' left rested, the distance was not over five miles. Moving by way of Manassas, Porter had but ten miles to march in order to come close upon our left, joining Reynolds. Hooker's division had this same day marched that distance before 11 o'clock in the forenoon, and as Porter had been resting 36 hours, he was certainly able to move as rapidly as Hooker.

Near Manassas Junction, Porter was overtaken before 9 o'clock by Pope's order to push expeditiously upon Gainesville. By the joint order issued at 9 A.M., he was additionally instructed to establish communications with the rest of our forces and received the admonition: "It may be necessary to fall back behind Bull Run at Centreville tonight." The Warrenton turnpike, which our lines crossed at Groveton, being the only route by which we could fall back behind Bull Run at Centreville, it was clear that Porter was expected to take a position where he could withdraw by that turnpike if necessary. All this he could do by communicating with the rest of the army as ordered- that is to say, by connecting with Reynolds.

From noonday on, Porter's arrival was momentarily expected and every ear was bent to catch the first sound of his guns. Reynolds' division, after its withdrawal in the morning, was held back and concealed in the woods, awaiting its anticipated support. About 2 o'clock some artillery shots were heard toward Jackson's extreme right, indicating, as was thought, that Porter and McDowell were then approaching the positions assigned them. But the firing in that direction did not continue, and General Pope soon afterward learned that McDowell was coming up the Sudley Springs road and would not arrive until two hours later. Thus the afternoon waned. Meanwhile a heavy cannonade was kept up, some of the Confederate guns throwing spikes, chains, and segments of railroad iron, which as they rushed through the air, produced a horrid medley of unearthly noises.[63]

On all parts of the field, shells were bounding and bursting, and along the skirmish lines there was a loud and continuous rattle of musketry. By 4 o'clock, still no word from Porter. Half an hour later General Pope dispatched a staff officer with the following note addressed to General Porter: "Your line of march brings you in on the enemy's right flank. I desire you to push forward into action at once on the

Confederate View

"I ordered a charge and with a yell the Second Brigade went through them, shattering, breaking and routing them. The struggle was brief, but not a man faltered and with closed ranks their rush was irresistible. They drove the enemy into the railroad cut and out of it."

~Colonel Bradley T. Johnson, commanding Jones' Virginia Brigade

---

[63] The following incidents of the cannonade are mentioned by Colonel Strother: "I remember two of the battery horses on the left performing some singular gymnastics. A shell struck the span and burst between them. They then commenced hopping around and bowing to each other like two over-polite Frenchmen, and having made several circles in this way, they fell plunging and rolling over each other, then rose again to perform this same tour of gymnastics. This continued for ten minutes and I was glad at last to see the poor creatures lying quiet. Going up to them, I found them both stone dead, the shell having carried away the foreleg of one and the hind leg of the other close to the body. Arriving on the ground occupied by a battery of 20-pdr. Parrotts which had been working very industriously and effectively all day, Generals Pope and McDowell (with Sigel and Kearny I believe) with their chief officers, formed a line on the right of the guns and stood for some time reconnoitering the enemy's position. The battery was still working rapidly, and the enemy fighting back with equal spirit, when one of the guns burst, throwing off a heavy fragment of the muzzle, which described an arc immediately over the heads of the lines of officers and fell with a thud, just clearing the last man and horse; two feet lower and it would have swept off the whole party." ~ Lee Note.

enemy's flank and, if possible, on his rear, keeping your right in communication with General Reynolds. The enemy is massed in the woods in front of us, but can be shelled out as soon as you engage their right flank. Keep heavy reserves and use your batteries, keeping well closed up to your right and rear, so as to keep you in close communication with the right wing."

At 5:30 when General Porter should have been coming into action in compliance with this order, General Pope ordered Heintzelman and Reno to attack the enemy. Reno led off in splendid style, accompanied by Taylor's brigade of Hooker's division. Crossing the ridge where our batteries were posted, the blue lines moved with beautiful regularity down the open slope and into the woods where Carr's brigade had relieved Schurz and was now confronted by the enemy in great strength. For half an hour, the roll of musketry along that part of the line was heavy and unceasing. But the attack was repulsed and Carr was obliged to quit the ground over which Schurz had advanced in the morning. Hooker then threw forward General Cuvier Grover's brigade, which on this occasion made a bayonet charge described by General Heintzelman in his official report as "the most gallant and determined of the war." The regiments comprising this brigade were the 1st, 11th, and 16th Massachusetts, 2nd New Hampshire, and the 26th Pennsylvania. Crossing the ridge behind which they had been held in reserve, they descended through open ground, driving before them the enemy's pickets. With fixed bayonets they then rushed upon a heavy line of Confederate infantry, which was driven back over the railroad embankment where it was ten feet high. From behind the embankment another strong line of infantry poured a terrific fire upon Grover's men as they emerged from the woods. Let Colonel William Blaisdell, commanding the 11th Massachusetts, narrate what followed:

> The 11th Massachusetts, being the battalion of direction, was the first to reach the railroad, and of course received the heaviest of the fire. This staggered the men a little, but recovering in an instant, they gave a wild hurrah, and over they went, mounting the embankment, driving everything before them at the point of the bayonet. Here for two or three minutes, the struggle was very severe, the combatants exchanging shots, their muskets almost muzzle to muzzle, and engaging hand to hand in deadly encounter. Private John Lawler of Company D stove in the skull of one Rebel with the butt of his musket, then killed another with his bayonet. The enemy broke in confusion and ran, numbers throwing down their muskets, some fully cocked, and owners too much frightened to fire them. The regiment pursued them some 80 yards into the woods, where it was met by an overwhelming force in front, at the same time receiving an artillery fire which enfiladed our left, and forced it to retire, leaving the dead and many wounded where they fell.

General Kearny's attack was intended to be simultaneous with this, but for some reason was delayed until toward 6 o'clock by which time Grover had been forced back. To prepare the way for Kearny, it was deemed necessary to shell the woods where the enemy was, although many of the wounded of both armies yet lay there. Forty pieces of artillery opened fire and our cannoneers worked with savage energy. Then Kearny, with Poe and Birney holding his front line and Robinson his second, dashed forward, supported on the left by General Stevens. The enemy's infantry was swept up by Kearny's furious onset, causing "the chance of victory," wrote A.P. Hill, "to tremble in the balance." Fortunately for Hill, Lawton's and Early's brigades were nearby and they sprang to the rescue. Kearny and Stevens were both far outnumbered, and were obliged to relinquish the ground they had so bravely won.

It was 5 o'clock or later before General McDowell arrived upon the field. He came by the Sudley Springs road and brought with him King's division, led by General Hatch, General King being sick. While this division was approaching, Kearny made his attack and Pope was seized with the idea that the enemy, worsted on his left, was quitting his positions on that flank, and retreating toward the Gainesville pike. Hatch was therefore pushed rapidly to the front along the pike but instead of finding a retreating column, he encountered Hood's division of Longstreet's corps in line and about to advance. A fierce fight ensued, in which Meade's brigade of Reynolds' division took part on the left. "The struggle was a desperate one," says General Hatch, "being in many instances a hand to hand conflict." General Gordon, in describing it, says "hardly has the Federal line opened fire when Hood's advancing division moved onward, firing as they moved. The storm of Confederate bullets swept through the Federal ranks, and the men bent and swayed beneath its rage, though they breasted it well for a time. The officers urged their men to renewed effort. Field officers and generals set them examples. At one period General Hatch sat complacently on his horse, while every man who approached him pitched and fell headlong before he could deliver his message."

So energetic and aggressive was the resistance of Hatch and Meade that Wilcox's division, which Longstreet had sent over to reinforce Jones' division confronting General Fitz John Porter, was called back to Hood's assistance.[64] Thus reinforced Hood assaulted Hatch with redoubled energy and succeeded in capturing a few prisoners and one piece of artillery. "This gun," says Colonel Law of Hood's division, "continued to fire until my men were so near it as to have their faces burnt by its discharges." Unable to his hold advanced position against such odds, General Hatch withdrew steadily to more favorable ground, and darkness put an end to the fighting.

The battle of the 29th was over. Its conclusion left us in possession of the field and part of the ground which had been wrested from the enemy, but that was all. In the main object, we had failed, and a golden opportunity had been missed. Sigel had seized Jackson's railroad entrenchment, Hooker and Reno had pierced his center, Kearny had rolled up his left, and Hatch and Reynolds had wrestled valiantly with his right wing, but beyond Reynolds, where we expected to hear General Porter's guns thundering upon the enemy's right and rear, there had been dead silence. Porter had not even joined hands with us during the bloody struggles of the day. Let us see where he was and what he was about.

Proceeding from Manassas Junction toward Gainesville, as ordered in the morning, Porter passed Bethlehem Church two miles from the Junction and between 10-11 o'clock arrived at a brook called Dawkins' Branch. Here he halted. In this march (about four miles in two hours) Morell's division led and was followed by Sykes' and then by King's. A short distance beyond the dry bed of the Branch, Rosser's cavalry videttes were perceived. General Butterfield, commanding Porter's leading brigade, passed over the branch with members of his staff to reconnoiter the ground. He directed part of his brigade to follow him, but while engaged in this reconnaissance and when near the enemy's pickets, he saw, to his astonishment, that the regiments which he had ordered forward had disappeared. Riding back, he learned that they had been recalled by General Porter in consequence of something that had occurred between that officer and General McDowell. The latter, in quest of King's division, had just arrived from Manassas Junction and on his way there had received the following note from General Buford of the cavalry: "General Ricketts: 17 regiments, one battery, and 500 cavalry passed through Gainesville three quarters of an hour ago on the Centreville road. (That is they were going toward Groveton, not toward Porter). I think this division should join our forces now engaged at once."

McDowell exhibited this dispatch to Porter. Both officers had by this time received the joint order issued to them by Pope in the morning. Both, from the position where they then were, saw shells bursting in the air and heard the sounds of battle in the direction of Groveton. They discussed together the joint order, and noticed particularly that its instruction that the troops should take a position from which they could reach Bull Run that night or next morning. The signs of battle were spoken of, together with Buford's note, and a column of dust was seen rising above the trees near the pike, indicating that the force which had passed Gainesville was moving, as Buford had reported, toward Groveton, where the battle was. The construction which the two general placed upon the joint order and the action which they took in pursuance of it are thus stated by General McDowell in his statement before the court of inquiry.

> The question with me was, how, soonest within the limit fixed by General Pope, this force of ours could be applied against the enemy. General Porter made a remark[65] to me which showed me he had no question but that the enemy was

---

[64] General Lee so states in his official report: "While the battle was raging on Jackson's left, General Longstreet ordered Hood and Evans to advance, but before the order could be obeyed Hood was himself attacked and his command became at once warmly engaged. General Wilcox was recalled from the right and ordered to advance on Hood's left and one of Kemper's brigades, under Colonel Hunton, moved forward on his left. The battle continued until 9 P.M." ~ Lee Note.

[65] From the court of inquiry testimony of General McDowell. Question- Will you state what that observation was? McD- I do not know that I can repeat it exactly, and I do not know that the accused meant exactly what the remark might seem to imply. The observation was to the effect-putting his hand in the direction of the dust rising above the tops of the trees. 'We cannot go in there without getting into a fight.' Question- What reply did you make to that

in his immediate front. I said to him, "You put your force in here, and I will take mine up the Sudley Springs road on the left of the troops engaged at that point with the enemy," or words to that effect. I left General Porter with the belief and understanding that he would put his force in at that point.

As to the duration of the authority of the chief command bested in him by the joint order, General McDowell testified:

> I decided under the latitude allowed in that order, that General Porter should post his troops in to the right of where the head of his column lay, and that I would take mine away from the road on which out two commands then lay up the Sudley Springs road into the battle, in this way dissolving the joint operations of our two corps and from the moment I left General Porter I considered him no longer under my immediate control or under my immediate command, or my direct orders, but that he came under those of our common commander-in-chief, we not then being on the same immediate ground. The article to which I refer is the 62nd Article of War, which directs that when troops happen to meet, the senior officer commands the whole. I considered that article to apply up until the time that I left General Porter, and broke my command away from his, after which I conceived that his relations were direct to the commander-in-chief.

After the two generals had concluded their conference, McDowell rode back to Bethlehem Church and on the way passed Porter's troops halting in the road. At the church he found and resumed control of King's division, which had been temporarily assigned to Porter, and directed the march of that division up the Sudley Springs road. Arrangements were made for Ricketts' division to follow, as soon as it should arrive, by the same route. On his way from Bethlehem Church to Groveton, McDowell encountered a messenger from Pope bearing a written order to Porter. That was the 4:30 order. Passing on, McDowell reported to Pope, on the field between 5-6 P.M.

The time at which Porter received the 4:30 order has been disputed. Captain Douglas Pope, who was the bearer of it, swears that he delivered it at almost precisely 5 o'clock, and this testimony is strongly corroborated by that of other witnesses. Between 5 and 8 P.M. there were three hours of good fighting time. Within that period Kearny delivered his brilliant assault from the right, Hatch and Meade were engaged until 9 o'clock at night in a desperate struggle with Hood.[66] At 5 o'clock or thereabouts, Grover's brigade crashed through Jackson's center. The mighty clamor of these different conflicts rang out far beyond the position where General Porter's corps lay, summoning every officer and man into line. What did Porter do?

Before him were the enemy's skirmishers, but he did not sweep them away. To the right a column was moving to reinforce Jackson against Hooker, Hatch, and Kearny, but he did not attack it. Morell, at the front, reported that two batteries had come down in the woods on the right and two regiments of infantry in the road, and Porter from Bethlehem Church (two miles back) directed Morell to "move the infantry and everything behind the crest and conceal the guns." Morell replied, "I can move everything out of sight except Hazlitt's battery," and Porter suggested: "I think you can move Hazlitt's or most of it, and post him in the bushes with the others, so as to deceive. I would get everything, if possible, in ambuscade." Assuredly *that* was not the way to engage the attention of Longstreet or to draw him away from Jackson.

Later Morell was directed to "push up two regiments, supported by two others, preceded by skirmishers and attack the section of artillery, giving the enemy a good shelling as the troops advance." Then directly after giving this order, General Porter sent the following to McDowell: "Failed in getting Morell over to you. After wandering about the woods for a time, I withdrew him and while doing so, artillery opened on us. The fire of the

---

remark? McD- I think to this effect. 'That is what we came here for.' Question- Were there any obstacles in the way of the advance of General Porter's command upon the flank of the enemy? McD- That depends upon what you call obstacles. A wood is an obstacle. Question- I mean insuperable obstacles, in a military sense. McD- I do not think we so regarded it at that time. I did not. Question- Was, or not, the battle raging at that time? McD- That battle was raging on our right.

[66] Fifteen months later, Longstreet attacked and was repulsed by Generals Geary and Tyndale in Lookout Valley, Tennessee at midnight. Wellington's last assault at Waterloo was delivered at 9 P.M., and Thursday's fighting at Gettysburg lasted until long after dark. ~ Lee Note.

enemy having advanced, and ours retired, I have determined to withdraw to Manassas. I have attempted to communicate with McDowell and Sigel, but my messengers have run into the enemy. They have gathered artillery, cavalry, and infantry, and the advancing masses of dust show the enemy coming in force. I am now going to the head of the column to see what is passing, and how affairs are going, and I will communicate with you." Later Porter sent another dispatch of substantially the same purport, to Generals McDowell and King, reiterating his determination to "withdraw to Manassas."

It is difficult to comment upon these dispatches with judicial patience. Porter was expected to communicate with McDowell and Sigel, not by messenger only, but with the precipitate momentum of his entire corps. His second dispatch to McDowell begins, "I found it impossible to communicate by crossing the woods to Groveton." If he meant by this that the woods were an obstacle, we may wonder what he would have done had he been required, as, at a later period, other commanders were to communicate in the Virginia wilderness, or amidst the mountain wilds of northern Georgia and the swamps of the Carolinas. Whatever difficulties General Porter may have found, Longstreet it is certain had none (as General Lee's report shows) in "crossing the woods to Groveton." Furthermore, Longstreet was able to cover with two divisions a front not more than half of which Porter was expected to cover with his two.

As to the "advancing masses of dust" referred to by General Porter, we have the following explanation in the official report of General Stuart, commanding Jackson's cavalry.

The next morning (August 29) in pursuance of General Jackson's wishes, I set out again to endeavor to establish communication with Longstreet, from whom we had received a favorable report the night before. I met the head of General Longstreet's column between Haymarket and Gainesville and there communicated to the commanding general Jackson's position and the enemy's. I then passed the cavalry through the column so as to place it on Longstreet's right flank and advanced directly toward Manassas *while the column kept directly down the pike* to join General Jackson's right. I selected a fine position for a battery on the right and one having been sent me, I *fired a few shots* at the enemy's supposed position. General Robertson, who with his command was sent to reconnoiter further down the road *toward Manassas*, reported the enemy in his front. Upon repairing to the front I found that Rosser's regiment was engaged with the enemy to the left of the road and Robertson's videttes had found the enemy *approaching from the direction of Bristoe Station* toward Sudley. The prolongation of his line of march would have passed through my position, which was a very fine one for artillery, as well as observation, and *struck Longstreet in the flank.* I waited for his approach long enough to ascertain that there was at least an army corps (Porter's), at the same time keeping detachments of cavalry *dragging brush down the road from the direction of Gainesville so as to deceive the enemy*, and notified the commanding general, then opposite me on the turnpike, that *Longstreet's flank and rear were seriously threatened*, and of the importance to us of the ridge I then held. Immediately upon receipt of that intelligence, Jenkins', Kemper's, and D.B. Jones' brigade and several pieces of artillery were ordered to me by General Longstreet and being placed in position fronting Bristoe, awaited the enemy's advance. *After exchanging a few shots with rifle pieces, this corps withdrew toward Manassas*, leaving artillery and supports to hold the position until night.

From this it clearly appears that when General Porter reached his most advanced position, there was nothing in front of him but a few brigades of cavalry; that the "advancing masses of dust" from which he assumed the enemy was coming in force were produced by detachments of cavalry dragging brush down the turnpike; and that when notified of Porter's approach, Longstreet could spare and actually sent three brigades of his corps to hold the position which Stuart says was so important. These conclusions are fully corroborated by General Longstreet's report which says:

At a late hour of the day Major General Stuart reported the approach of the enemy in heavy columns against my extreme right. *I withdrew General Wilcox with his three brigades from the left*[67] and placed his command in position to

---

[67] The original disposition of Wilcox's brigades and of the other forces of Longstreet's Corps is thus stated in the official report of General Lee: "Longstreet took position on the right of Jackson, Hood's two brigades supported by Evans being deployed across the turnpike, and at right angles to it. These troops were supported on the left by three brigades under General Wilcox, and by a like force on the right under General Kemper. D.R. Jones' division formed

support Jones in case of an attack against my right. After some few shots the enemy withdrew his forces, moving them around toward his front, and at 4 o'clock in the afternoon began to press forward against General Jackson's position. Wilcox's brigades were moved back to their former position and Hood's two brigades, supported by Evans, were quickly pressed forward to the attack on Hatch. At the same time Wilcox's three brigades made like an advance, as also Hunton's brigade of Kemper's command.[68]

This seems to show conclusively that, as soon as Porter withdrew, or gave signs of withdrawing, Longstreet took away the three brigades which he had detached to resist him and hurled them upon that part of our army as to the defeat of which General Porter had such solemn apprehensions. In a letter published since the war, General Longstreet says, referring to the battle of the 29th: "As we were not engaged, I rode in advance of my line in search of an opportunity to take my share in the battle. Had I thus engaged the day before, it is more than probable that Porter would be *in season to take me on the wing, and in all probability have crushed me*." Porter thought Longstreet was too strong for him, but Longstreet's opinion was different. So was General McDowell was says: "I think and thought that if the corps of General Porter, reputed one of the best if not the best in the service, consisting of between 20-30 regiments and some eight batteries, had been added to the efforts made by the others, the result would have been in our favor, very decidedly."

But without having struck a blow worthy of the name, General Porter decided to "withdraw to Manassas." The joint order had instructed him that the line of retreat, if retreat we must, would be toward Centreville, but he chose a different direction, a direction in which he had already, as we shall now see, taken a preliminary step. About midday, General Sturgis arrived at Dawkins' Branch with Piatt's brigade which had been assigned to Porter's command. At 1 o'clock, Porter sent that brigade back to Manassas Junction, from whence it had just come. Its services would have been of great value anywhere along the front of battle that eventful afternoon, but it was sent to the rear. Piatt continued his march to Centreville, and from thence, of his own accord, he next day moved forward again to the field and took part in the closing scenes of the battle.

After Piatt's brigade had gone, Sykes' division and most of Morell's lay extended to the rear along the Manassas Junction road. Here, countermarching from time to time, these troops remained during most of the afternoon, and some of them were seen as far back as Bethlehem Church by Ricketts' division as it passed by during the evening on its way to the front. But between 5 and 6 o'clock, the intended withdrawal to Manassas was arrested by the 4:30 order. Then Morell, whose pickets were yet at the front, received from Porter a spasmodic verbal order to attack. This was followed by another order in writing, to "put the men in position to remain during the night." Last of all, following the peremptory message to put a final stop to General Porter's movement in retreat, and fitly closed the melancholy history of this day:

Headquarters Army of Virginia, In the field near Bull Run
August 29, 1862- 8:50 P.M.

To Major General Porter:
General:
Immediately upon receipt of this order, the precise hour of receiving you will acknowledge, you will march your command to the field of battle of today and report to me in person for orders. You are to understand that you are

---

the extreme right of the line, resting on the Manassas Gap Railroad. The cavalry guarded our right and left flanks, that on the right being under General Stuart in person. After the arrival of Longstreet, the enemy changed his position, and began to concentrate against Jackson's left." As shown by a previous citation of General Lee's report, as well as by that from Longstreet's report just given, Wilcox's brigades were withdrawn from Longstreet's right in order to support Hood in his attack upon Hatch's division. This left only Jones' division, about 6,000 strong, to confront Porter's corps. Had Porter attacked with half the persistency of Kearny or Hooker, both Wilcox and Kemper would have had altogether too much to do to have been able to lend a helping hand to Hood against Hatch. ~ Lee Note.
[68] With such odds against him, it is no wonder General Hatch had to fall back. ~ Lee Note.

expected to comply strictly with this order and to be present on the field within three hours after its receipt, or after daybreak tomorrow morning.

John Pope, Major General commanding

The forenoon of Saturday August 30 passed quietly. The weather was fair and warm. Our army occupied most of the advanced ground which it had gained the day before, except on the left where Hatch had been driven back. Even there the enemy had retired from our front.

For two days our troops had been almost destitute of food and our cavalry and artillery horses of forage. No reinforcements had come forward. General Fitz John Porter, impelled by the peremptory command of the preceding evening, brought his corps upon the field, but not the whole of it. Griffin's brigade of Morell's division went off to Centreville, and took no part whatever in Saturday's battle. The strong, fresh, and well-equipped corps of Franklin and Sumner came as far as Centreville during the day but approached no nearer. Had the entire Army of the Potomac been brought forward, the Battle of Antietam might have been fought on this day and this ground, as it should have been. General Lee's army had all arrived upon the field, except Anderson's division which was near at hand. Generals Pope, McDowell, and Heintzelman fell into the delusion that the enemy was retreating. Jackson had quit some of his positions on the left, and Hood had disappeared from the front of Hatch's division. Prisoners taken from us on the 29th and afterwards paroled and allowed to return to our lines declared that the enemy was quitting the field. Misled by all this, Pope assigned McDowell "the command of the pursuit." Porter's corps was directed to push forward on the turnpike, followed by the divisions of Hatch and Reynolds. Ricketts was to lead off on the Haymarket road followed by Heintzelman. These orders were issued at noon. Sigel and Reno, not mentioned in the written instructions, were to remain in reserve.

As to whether the enemy was retreating or not, or what his plans were, Sigel was not sure. He therefore, as usual, undertook to investigate the matter for himself and sent out a cavalry reconnaissance to our extreme left with instructions to explore the country in that direction. Lieutenant Colonel Nazer with the 4th New York Cavalry was selected for this purpose and set out about noon. At the same time Sigel sent a regiment of Schenk's division to the left of our position to observe the enemy's movements. In the course of an hour, Nazer reported to Sigel, and also to Buford whom he passed on the extreme left, that the enemy with cavalry, infantry, and artillery, was *advancing against our left*. This information General Sigel communicated immediately to General Pope.[69] Meanwhile, General Ricketts on the right sent word that he had been feeling the enemy's lines and that, so far as from being able to advance, he was by no means sure that he could hold the ground he then occupied. The illusion of Confederate retreat was completely dissipated. Jackson still clung to his railroad embankment, clear down to the turnpike, and on the heights at his right eight Confederate batteries had been posted under Stephen D. Lee. Farther to the right, Longstreet's corps was massed in the woods. While Pope was moving the bulk of his forces north of the pike against Lee's center and left, Lee was preparing a grand assault upon Pope's weakened left flank, south of the pike.

The position of our army, though not especially strong, was a favorable one. With the center advanced and the flanks retired, our formation resembled somewhat that with which the Army of the Potomac afterwards fought at Gettysburg. We held the interior line, which was extremely fortunate as the sequel proved. Our center and most advanced front lay on the turnpike, south of which the ground was high and commanding. Two hills, known as the Henry House Hill and the Chinn House or Bald Hill, were the Round Top and Cemetery Ridge of this battle. North of these hills and close by them the turnpike passed through a deep valley. The Sudley Springs road lay between them. As positions of defense against the assault about to be made on our left, they were invaluable.

---

[69] The correspondent of the *New York Tribune* wrote from Centreville August 31: "I was at General Sigel's headquarters. That general was certain the enemy intended to turn one or the other of our flanks, and said we must ascertain which, or the result was, at best, doubtful, for his scouts had just reported that Lee, with the entire remainder of the Rebel army had come up, and assumed command. The scouts were correct." ~ Lee Note.

Bald Hill

"The 55th Ohio reached the summit of Bald Hill and there formed a line facing north, but perceiving that the attack was coming from the west, it wheeled by regimental front to the left and amid the cheers of the brigade came on the double quick into line. Hood's Texas Brigade, following the turnpike, came forward with tremendous dash and force, but failed to break the stern front of the Buckeye troops and fell back in disorder. General Schenk rode up to the line and cheered on the exultant division (receiving just then a bullet wound in his sword hand which disabled him permanently), but the Confederate line made good their attack on the left, and soon the supporting troops both left and right began to retire from the storms of shot and shell which enfiladed their ranks."

~ Second Lieutenant Hartwell Osborn, Co. I, 55th Ohio Infantry

Up to 4 P.M., the hostilities were limited to skirmishing, maneuvering, and artillery dueling. Heavy blue masses of the National troops moved in fine array into the open ground to the right of the turnpike, and there rested. These were the army corps of Reno and Fitz John Porter, and Hatch's division of McDowell's corps. Reno was in reserve, and Porter and Hatch were waiting the signal to advance. Sigel's corps lay behind Dogan's farm to the right of the turnpike. Banks' corps was yet guarding the trains and stores south of Manassas. Seeing Porter's corps between himself and the enemy, and not comprehending the movement, Sigel sought an explanation. He continued to receive reports from his scouts that the enemy was moving against our left, and it occurred to him that we ought to anticipate and thwart that movement by an attack from our right. He therefore proposed to Porter (who asked him for information on the ground) to shift his (Porter's) corps farther to the right so as to unite with Ricketts and Heintzelman in falling upon the enemy's left flank and rear. This producing no change in Porter's dispositions, Sigel went to Pope with the same suggestions, and urged further that Porter's attack in the center would encounter the enemy in his strongest position, with his artillery massed on commanding ground; and that we ought not to attack from the center, but from the right or left. Pope replied impatiently, "You never understand me; I do not wish to *turn* the enemy's left, I wish to *break* it."

Sigel replied that Porter's attack would not strike the left but the center of the enemy's lines where he was strongest. This remark of Sigel's was based upon his experience of the day before, and upon the facts gathered from his scouts, that Longstreet had crowned the hills in the rear of Jackson's right with batteries. But all this seemed to make no impression upon General Pope. Sigel therefore inquired what he should so with his own corps. "I shall command it myself," replied Pope. "This," says Sigel, "was the last I heard or saw of Pope until the battle of that day was over, except that I received from him an order to send a brigade to the Bald Hill."

Porter's corps rested, at this time, in front of the Dogan house. Morell's division of two brigades held its advance to the left and rear of Morell, and fronting the village of Groveton, Sykes' division was drawn up as a reserve. To his rear, behind the Dogan farm, Sykes stationed as his own reserve his smallest brigade, comprising two regiments and two batteries under General G.K. Warren. Reynolds' division, covering the Bald Hill, held Pope's left and about 4 o'clock took the first step in the general advance. Moving into the thick woods in his front, Reynolds encountered vigorous resistance, and soon discovered that the enemy was massing his forces to turn our left. He reported this back to McDowell, who directed him to retire at once to the Henry House Hill. To connect his line with that of General Reynolds, Sigel had already sent the 55th Ohio and a battery to Bald Hill. He now, by Pope's direction, sent McLean's brigade to occupy and hold that position.

About the same time that Reynolds began his advance above mentioned, Porter and Hatch moved to the attack. Porter attacked only with Morell's division, which was led by General Butterfield, Morell having gone to Centreville with Griffin's brigade. Directly a request came from Porter to McDowell to "push Sigel forward." Thereupon Sigel advanced Schenk's division to the Dogan farm and soon afterwards Schurz took a position behind Schenk with Schimmelfennig's brigade on the right, Koltes' on the left, and

Chinn Ridge

"At 4 o'clock our brigade was ordered forward, we advanced in line of battle and took position in a road that had been dug out, almost as good as a fortification or breastworks for us, and we *paid* them. We took good revenge for the Friday's fight, completely checking their advance in that direction. Major Thomson was in command and no braver man ever met the foe. He was everywhere cheering the men forward, never thinking of his own danger, always in the thickest of the fight. The battle cry the second day was 'Remember Colonel Cantwell!' and the Secesh can vouch that they *did* remember him. "

First Lieutenant Francis S. Jacobs, Co. K, 82nd Ohio Infantry

Krzyzanowski's in reserve. Dilger's battery was posted on the crest of a hill to the right, not far from Dogan's. The enemy's batteries had by this time become very active, and the 1st Corps, though not engaged, suffered severely from their fire. A battery placed upon the high ground quit by Reynolds enfiladed Schurz's brigades, and was particularly annoying, "a most disagreeable fire" as Schurz stated it. Captain Dilger therefore shifted his guns farther to the left, and gave to the obnoxious battery his special attention.

Simultaneously with Butterfield, Hatch pushed forward with his division drawn up in seven lines, and soon Jackson became so hotly engaged as to feel obliged to call for reinforcements, thereby retarding Longstreet's intended movement, already mentioned, against our left. In the face of a heavy fire of musketry and artillery, our assaulting columns dashed forward once more to the railroad embankment, but this time they did not pass that obstacle. Hooker, on the right of Hatch, entered the woods and drove the enemy a short distance, but that seems to have been all that was accomplished by Heintzelman's corps. Along Hatch's front the struggle was obstinate and bloody. General Hatch was severely wounded, the troops on his right made no headway, and those on his left were repulsed. Butterfield's regiments recoiled under the concentrated fire of Stephen D. Lee's batteries, coupled with heavy volleys of musketry. Hatch's division was obliged to withdraw and Butterfield's troops, falling back in disorder passed to the rear through Sigel's lines.

Pursuing Butterfield, the enemy rolled heavily upon Warren's brigade, which had moved up to occupy part of the ground vacated by Reynolds. McLean's brigade and Stahel's also soon became hotly engaged. At this critical moment, Reynolds' division (except one brigade-Anderson's) was ordered to quit the high ground which it occupied and march to the rear of Porter's corps as a support to Butterfield's routed division. This was alike unnecessary and unfortunate. The elevated positions occupied by Reynolds were the key points of the whole field, and they were no sooner quitted than the battle rolled to the left, developing the enemy's real plan of attack. Warren's little brigade was crushed, and a battery of four guns was lost. Anderson's brigade made unavailing resistance and was driven steadily back. Stahel's brigade of Schenk's division was obliged to give ground, and McLean's brigade left by Reynolds' withdrawal without support was assailed in front and flank. Milroy, hurried over by Sigel to McLean's assistance, found a favorable position in the washout of a wagon road and from the shelter of this ditch, his brigade poured volley after volley into the masses of Confederates as they came rushing out of the woods. With fierce energy and splendid effect, Milroy's men reciprocated their bloody repulse of the day before.

But the enemy quickly availed himself of the commanding positions quit by Reynolds, and from thence poured upon us an enfilading fire with his batteries. At the same time, his infantry spread out over the high wooded ground in front of McLean's brigade and on the flank and almost in rear of our center. Forty pieces of cannon ranged upon the Groveton heights united the momentum of their concentrated fire to the sustained rush of Longstreet's corps. "The attack," says Longstreet, "was led by Hood's brigades, closely supported by Evans. These were rapidly reinforced by Anderson's division from the rear, Kemper's three brigades, and D.R. Jones' division from the right, and Wilcox's brigade from the left. The brigades of Featherston and Pryor became detached, and operated with a portion of General Jackson's command."

Such was the assault made upon our unguarded left, and for a time it seemed as if nothing would prevent Longstreet from gaining the turnpike and interposing between our army and Bull Run. At the turnpike itself a most disheartening scene was presented. A mass of stragglers and retreating regiments and batteries filled the roadway, and the fields on either side were clouded with wounded men and fugitives.[70] At the same time, the enemy's cannon shot began to fall among our ammunition and hospital trains, parked along Young's Branch and Bull Run, causing a stampede of camp followers and malingerers, and a rush of wagons for the Stone Bridge.[71]

The moment was critical, and required the most prompt and energetic action. General Pope, says Strother, for the first time in the campaign exhibited strong excitement. His directions, however, were ready and prudent. Reynolds' division was quickly extricated from the wreck of the battle with which it had become entangled and brought back into position to the right of the Henry House. Leaving Reno and Heintzelman to resist Jackson on the right, Pope and McDowell hurried all the troops that could be spared from that quarter over to the strong positions south of the turnpike.

Sigel, left to himself without orders, was prompt in doing his part to meet the crisis. From his position at Dogan's farm he had witnessed Porter's attack and repulse, and then had seen Reynolds' division deliberately withdraw from his left and march over behind his corps. He saw the right wing passive, and had known for hours that the enemy was massing upon our left. He was puzzled and astounded by Reynolds' withdrawal, but he lost no time in doing all he could to retrieve that mistake. On his own responsibility, he sent Milroy to support McLean, but in taking position Milroy left a vacancy of some hundreds of yards between McLean's brigade and his own. Into this vacancy the enemy penetrated, compelling McLean to relinquish, in part, his position on the hill. By Sigel's direction, Schurz sent over Koltes' brigade to help retake the lost ground, and a few minutes later directed Krzyzanowski to move up the wooded slope and support Koltes. In the face of a terrible artillery fire, Koltes and Krzyzanowski moved to their positions where they were at once

---

[70] From the private diary of Captain Fritz Tiedemann of General Schurz's staff, I am permitted to copy the following: "An apparently wounded man of Duryea's Zouaves was being carried to the rear in a blanket by four of his comrades when a shell dropped near the party, and the four men holding the blanket let go of it and fled. Some of us ran to assist the wounded man when, to our astonishment, he jumped off and ran off as fast as his comrades. The 29th New York arrested these worthies and sent them to the front again. ~ Lee Note.
[71] This harmless stampede at the rear gave rise to newspaper reports that a panic, a 'second Bull Run,' had taken place at the front, which was by no means the case. ~ Lee Note.

furiously assailed, both in front and on the left flank. From the edge of the woods, a Confederate battery suddenly opened an enfilading fire upon Koltes' brigade. Colonel Koltes called to his men to "take that battery" and while he was leading the charge, and waving his sword, a shell struck and killed both him and his horse. General Schurz reported that "Krzyzanowski, while showing his men how to face the enemy, had his horse shot under him." The ground was covered with our dead and wounded.

At an opportune moment, General Tower, leading his own and Hartsuff's brigades and Hall's and Leppien's batteries of Ricketts' division, came up by McDowell's orders on the right of McLean. "Tell General Tower to stay right where it is," directed General McDowell in the hearing of the writer, and nobly did Tower endeavor to fulfill the command. The combat on Bald Hill was renewed in the presence of the whole army, and so resolutely was the position held that its defenders were enthusiastically cheered by their comrades on other parts of the field. But our assailants on the hill were reinforced, and their superiority of numbers and weight of metal were overwhelming. Generals Schenk and Tower were wounded, and Colonel Fletcher Webster (son of the Massachusetts statesman) was killed.[72] McLean's brigade was reduced to a shadow, and Koltes' and Krzyzanowski's rapidly melted away. Hood's division, supporting by Evans' brigade and Kemper's division, dashed forward again and again, determined to wrest the ridge away from us, and at last they succeeded. Our forces on Bald Hill were obliged to withdraw.

By Sigel's order, Schurz drew back his brigades under cover of the artillery and formed a new line on the next range of hills to the rear behind the Stone House. "They fell back slowly and in good order. Captain Dilger's battery remained in position to check the pursuit of the enemy, whose infantry rushed upon him with great rapidity. He received them in two different positions, at short range, with a shower of grapeshot, obliged them to twice fall back, and then followed our column unmolested," reported General Schurz. Stahel's brigade and what was left of McLean's followed this movement. Schimmelfennig's brigade was held in reserve on Schurz's right, where it was exposed to an enfilading artillery fire. Under this ordeal, Schimmelfennig's men "stood like trees" says Schurz "until the order to retire reached them." Milroy drew back his regiments without a waver in their ranks, and having replenished his ammunition, took his position on the left of the new line. It is but just to him to say that while he was a nervous and eccentric man, and his excitement in battle sometimes amounted to a frenzy, he was brave even to rashness and at no time during the fighting of this day was his brigade driven from its place; at no time did it retire except in order and by order.

It was 6 o'clock or later when our troops quit Bald Hill. Meanwhile the tide of battle had rolled still farther to the left and the struggle for the turnpike had centered upon the Henry House plateau. Thither Longstreet rapidly pushed his right brigades through the woods and thither Pope hurried every available regiment to meet him. Fortunately, the obstinate struggle that was made by the brigades under Schenk, Schurz, and Tower on the Bald Hill ridge gave time for bringing over our forces on the right and center, and putting them into position on the south side of the pike. Returning from their ill-starred movement to the rear of Sigel, the brigades of Meade and Seymour, and Ransom's battery of Reynolds' division were led into the woods in front of the Henry House and there, with splendid firmness, checked and rolled back the impetuous current of Longstreet's advance. Buchanan's brigade and Chapman's of Sykes' regulars had not been engaged in Porter's attack, and after Butterfield's repulse were called to meet the new emergency on the left. Buchanan's brigade was deployed, with its right resting at the Henry House,

---

[72] "Soldiers of the army still enjoy telling of General Schenk's rage and fearful imprecations at the loss of his sword. It had been in his hand at the moment the ball struck his wrist, and it was thrown some distance from him. The position was very exposed and the staff wanted to carry him instantly off, but he refused to go until his sword should be found. Those about him insisted, but he was peremptory and the missing sword was brought to him before he would suffer himself to be taken to the hospital." General Schenk was wounded in the right wrist so severely that it disabled him from further field service. The Ohioan spent six months recovering from his wound before being assigned to a minor command in Maryland. He resigned his commission in December 1863 to serve in Congress, having defeated the infamous Clement Vallandigham in the fall elections of 1862. Schenk ultimately served another five terms in Congress before losing a reelection bid in 1870, whereupon President Ulysses S. Grant appointed him Minister to England. He died in 1890 at the age of 80 and is buried in Dayton, Ohio. Reid, Whitelaw. Ohio In the War: Her Statesmen, Generals, and Soldiers, Volume I. Cincinnati: Robert Clarke Company, 1895, pgs. 725-738

and Chapman's thrown forward into the woods farther to the left. In these positions, Buchanan and Chapman, two veterans of the Mexican War, fought with lion-like valor, and repelled a series of desperate assaults. After three quarters of an hour Chapman's left flank was turned, and he was obliged to fall back some hundreds of yards.

Then Reno was called. Withdrawn from the center, his division had been massed in squares in support of the left. At the signal to advance, it was deployed in two lines of battle, in which formation, with its leader at its head, it advanced with the evenness of a parade through a hurricane of cannon shot into the woods in front. Immediately a mighty roll of musketry was heard in these woods, and as time passed it resounded with continuous and increasing volume. Four or five furious attempts were made to drive Reno from his ground, but he held it to the last. All efforts to dislodge him failed.

Longstreet's movement was arrested; he had done his worst. The sun went down behind gleaming clouds, and the battle waned and ceased with the light of day. Our army had really begun its retreat with the abandonment of Bald Hill, and General Pope now gave orders to the various corps commanders to withdraw leisurely toward Centreville. When this order reached Sigel, he was discussing with Schurz the meaning of the enemy's quiescence, and the propriety

Major General George B. McClellan and his wife Ellen (Library of Congress)

of assuming the offensive. But Pope's command was peremptory, and Sigel drew back his divisions as instructed "smoothly and with deliberation." His troops, the first to reach the field, were the last to leave it. Schurz, with Schimmelfennig's brigade, and Dilger's battery acting as a rear guard[73] crossed Young's Branch about 9 P.M. The troops moved off in perfect order, turning fiercely upon the enemy whenever he came too near. On the hilly ground between Young's Branch and Bull Run, Sigel drew up his entire corps, and remained in position until all the other troops with their trains had passed over the Stone Bridge, which his rear regiments (Schimmelfennig's) destroyed behind them. Between 1 and 2 o'clock in the morning, he resumed the march toward Centreville.

Thus ended the battle of the 30th of August. The Confederates have called it the Battle of Manassas; we have miscalled it Second Bull Run. In point of fact, it was the continuation of the action of the 29th which has been appropriately named the Battle of Groveton. The fighting of the 30th took place on nearly the same ground as that of the 29th, except on the left flank, where the extension of the enemy's right compelled us to prolong our left. This movement shifted the scene of the conflict eastward to the old Bull Run battlefield. Here our positions were obstinately held until our troops abandoned them of their own accord, and moved off, followed, but not pursued. Longstreet's infantry advanced no farther than Henry House Hill, which we still held for hours after the fighting had

---

[73] "For this office of covering the rear, the 61st Ohio was selected, a regiment which throughout the whole campaign had exhibited the most commendable spirit," reported General Schurz. ~ Lee Note.

ceased. All along the right our lines remained steady to the last. To call the battle Second Bull Run is therefore misleading and unjust. The name "Bull Run" had become synonymous in the popular mind with panic and rout. It implies that Pope's soldiers threw down their arms and ran away, which is the farthest possible from the truth. To the end, they stood bravely to their places repelling the assaults of superior numbers[74] and when they quit the field, they quit it, not to be sure, in the triumph which they had so nobly earned, yet without dishonor. They quit it deserving as much as brave men can the nation's respect and gratitude.

The next morning (Sunday August 31) dawned gloomily enough. The sky was black and mournful, and a chilling rain beat cruelly upon our weary and baffled army. A more dispiriting situation it would be hard to imagine than was presented that morning to those who stood drenched, begrimed, ragged, and hungry in the muddy trenches at Centreville. The army that remained with the colors seemed scarcely so great as the army of sick, wounded, and stragglers, which drifted silently, aimlessly, down the turnpike toward Washington. From General Halleck came the following message to Pope: "My dear General: You have done nobly. Don't yield another inch if you can avoid it. All reserves are being sent forward. Couch's division goes today; part of it went to Sangster's Station last night with Franklin and Sumner who must now be with you. Can't you renew the attack? I don't write more particularly, for fear the dispatch will not reach you. I am doing all in my power for you and your noble army. God bless you and it. Send me news more often, if possible." For ten days we had been hourly looking for these "reserves" promised by General Halleck, and had they come promptly forward and heartily cooperated with us, Lee's army would not have gone into Maryland- at least, not that year.

Before quitting the battlefield, General Pope at 6:30 P.M. on the 30th sent an order to Banks, at Bristoe Station, to destroy all public property there and at Manassas Junction, and withdraw to Centreville. In compliance with this, Banks fired several long railway trains loaded with government stores and moving via Brentsville, reached and crossed Bull Run on the 31st at Blackburn's Ford. Reinforced at Centreville by the two corps of Franklin and Sumner (20,000 men), Pope immediately made dispositions to receive another attack, but none was attempted. The enemy had other plans and early on the morning of September 1st and infantry reconnaissance detected Jackson moving around to our right and rear by way of Sudley Springs and the Little River Turnpike. Jackson was followed, at some distance, by Longstreet. Admonished by the Manassas raid, Pope put his army in motion at once towards Fairfax Courthouse, whither he sent Hooker, instructed to assume command of all forces in that vicinity, and push forward to Germantown. McDowell was directed to move back to Difficult Creek, and connect by his right with Hooker. Franklin was to come in on McDowell's left and rear. Reno was to move north of the Warrenton Turnpike in the direction of Chantilly. Heintzelman's corps was to take post immediately in rear of Reno, Sumner's on Heintzelman's left, and Sigel's and Porter's in conjunction with Sumner's right.

Shortly before 6 P.M., Stuart's cavalry, leading Jackson's march, encountered Reno's skirmishers near Ox Hill, a wooded ridge lying a short distance east of Chantilly. At this time, says Jackson's biographer, "the men of the Stonewall Brigade and their comrades were lying on the side of the road, hungry and exhausted. Jackson, like many of his men, was asleep. Seated at the foot of a tree, which his chin on his breast, as though he had fallen asleep while praying, he slept as peacefully as a child. He was soon aroused; duty called him; and mounting his horse, he took the head of his column, and advanced to deliver battle on another field." Jackson at once deployed his leading column (A.P. Hill's) and moved to the attack. Hill's right rested on the Warrenton Turnpike, and on his left Ewell's division came in, holding the center. On Ewell's left, Jackson's division (under Starke) took its place with its left resting on the Little River Turnpike.

The brigades of Branch and Fields (the latter under Brockenbough) led Hill's attack "and as they advanced into action, a violent storm roared down and lashed the woods with a fury which drowned the noise of the guns. Torrents of rain beat upon the troops, rendering it almost impossible to keep the powder dry; and the forest, now shadowy with the approach of night, was lit up by lightning flashes of dazzling brilliance, succeeded by deafening

---

[74] General Pope estimates his effective force on the field on the morning of the 30th as follows: McDowell's corps, 12,000l Sigel's 7,000; Reno's 7,000; Heintzelman's 7,000; Porter's less the brigades of Griffin and Piatt which ha gone to Centreville, 7,000; total 40,000. ~ Lee Note.

claps of thunder. Amidst this war of the elements," continues Cooke "the two brigades (Branch's and Fields') advanced upon the enemy and engaged him in a close and determined struggle."

But the struggle was quite a determined on our side as on that of the Confederates, and they were staggered and thrown back by the sturdy and aggressive resistance of Reno's line. General Isaac I. Stevens, commanding Reno's left division, ordered his brigades to charge, but while leading them was struck by a bullet and fell dead on the field. His division was heavily assailed in turn, and disconcerted by the loss of its leader, was in the act of falling back in some disorder when Kearny's division came up on its left and the battle was renewed. On the Confederate side, the brigades of Gregg, Pender, Thomas, and Hays were thrown into the fight, and "the conflict raged with great fury," reported General Jackson, the enemy "obstinately and desperately contesting the ground." Of Kearny's division, Birney's brigade came first into action and at once became violently engaged. Seeing a vacancy between Birney's right and Stevens' left and being asked to fill it, General Kearny rode forward to reconnoiter the ground. With his usual disdain of danger, he approached the enemy's lines and in the waning light of that stormy evening, he mistook a Confederate soldier for one of our own. He had no sooner inquired of the man as to the position of one of General Stevens' regiments that he discovered his mistake and turned to gallop away, but too late. The Confederate fired and Kearny dropped dead from his horse. Thus fell the brilliant, ever-faithful, knightly soldier, the most illustrious victim of this ill-starred campaign.[75]

After waiting some time for the missing leader, General Birney assumed command in place of the dead Kearny, and renewed the attack but the storm and gathering darkness soon put an end to the battle. Birney then, unmolested, buried our dead and sent the wounded to the rear. This enemy had been repulsed at every point, and some of his brigades had been badly worsted. In the course of the night, Robinson's brigade and Berry's (under Colonel Poe) came up and relieved Birney. After that, our troops held the battlefield until 3 o'clock in the morning, when they were recalled to rejoin the general movement of the army.

Longstreet came up promptly to Jackson's assistance, but he did not deem it prudent to renew the attack. Next day, by instructions from the War Department, our entire army was withdrawn for rest, re-equipment, and reorganization within the defenses of Washington. The withdrawal was accomplished without interference by the enemy, and thereupon General Pope resigned his command, which was merged at once into that of General McClellan.[76]

Report of Brigadier General Robert H. Milroy

Headquarters, Independent Brigade, Near Fort Ethan Allen, Virginia
September 12, 1862

On the morning of the 29th, at daylight, I was ordered to proceed in search of the Rebels and had not proceeded more than 500 yards when we were greeted by a few straggling shots from the woods in front. We were now at the creek and I had just sent forward my skirmishers when I received orders to halt and let the men have breakfast. While they were cooking, myself, accompanied by General Schenk, rode up to the top of an eminence some 500 yards to the front to reconnoiter. We had no sooner reached the top than we were greeted by a shower of musket balls from the woods on our right. I immediately ordered up my battery and gave the bushwhackers a few

---

[75] General Kearny's dead body, which was carried off by the enemy, was sent over to us next day under a flag of truce. ~ Lee Note.

[76] Pope's exit from the eastern theater was hardly as neat and tidy as offered by Lee. On September 5, the War Department issued Special Order Number 223 which consolidated the Army of the Virginia with the Army of the Potomac and ordered General Pope to appear before a court martial to be convened to try the cases against Generals Franklin, Porter, and Griffin for their poor performances during the campaign. President Lincoln was convinced that McClellan and his subordinates had set Pope up to fail, but he could not afford to relieve McClellan with the Confederate Army nearly at the gates of Washington. An Indian uprising in Minnesota gave Lincoln an out: he relieved Pope and assigned him to the newly formed Department of the Northwest. Pope left the capital embittered, "certain he had been conspired against and his 20 year army career blighted beyond repair." Cozzens, Peter. General John Pope: A Life for the Nation. Urbana: University of Illinois Press, 2000, pgs. 200-201

shot and shell which soon cleared the woods. Soon after I discovered the enemy in great force about three quarters of a mile in front of us, upon our right of the pike leading from Gainesville to Alexandria. I brought up my two batteries and opened upon them, causing them to fall back. I then moved forward my brigade with skirmishers deployed and continued to advance my regiments, the enemy falling back.

General Schenk's division was off to my left and that of General Schurz to my right. After passing a piece of woods I turned to the right, where the Rebels had a battery that gave us a great deal of trouble. I brought forward one of my batteries to reply to it, and soon after heard a tremendous fire of small arms and knew that General Schurz was hotly engaged to my right in an extensive forest. I sent two of my regiments, the 82nd Ohio under Colonel Cantwell, and the 5th West Virginia under Colonel Zeigler, to General Schurz's assistance. They were to attack the enemy's right flank, and I held my other two regiments in reserve for a time. The two regiments sent to Schurz were soon hotly engaged, the enemy being behind a railroad embankment which afforded them an excellent breastwork. The railroad had to be approached from the cleared ground on our side through a strip of thick timber from 100-500 yards in width. I had intended with the two regiments in reserve (2nd and 3rd West Virginia) to charge the Rebel battery which was but a short distance from us over the top of a hill to our left, but while making my arrangements to do this I observed that my two regiments engaged were being driven back out of the woods by the terrible fire of the Rebels.[77]

I then saw the brave Colonels Cantwell and Zeigler struggling to rally their broken regiments on the rear of the forest out of which they had been driven and sent two of my aides to assist them and assure them of immediate support. They soon rallied their men and charged again and again up to the railroad, but were driven back each time with great loss. I then sent the 2nd West Virginia to their support, directing it to approach the railroad at the point on the left of my other regiments, where the woods ended, but they were met by such a destructive fire from a large Rebel force that they were soon thrown into confusion and fell back in disorder. The enemy now came on in overwhelming numbers. General Carl Schurz had been obliged to retire with his two brigades an hour before, and then the whole Rebel force was turned against my brigade and my brave lads dashed back before the storm of bullets like chaff before the tempest. I then ordered my reserve battery into position a short distance to the rear and when five guns had got into position, one of the wheel horses was shot dead, but I ordered it to unlimber where they were and the six guns mowed the Rebels with grape and canister with fine effect. My reserve regiment, the 3rd West Virginia, now opened with telling effect. Colonel Cantwell of the 82nd Ohio was shot through the brain and instantly killed while trying to rallying his regiment during the thickest of the fight.

While the storm was raging the fiercest, General Stahel came to me and reported that he had been sent by General Schenk to support me, and inquired where he should place his brigade. I told him on my left to help support my battery. He then returned to his brigade and soon after being attacked from another quarter I did not see him again during the day. I was then left wholly unsupported, except by a portion of a Pennsylvania regiment, which I found on the field and stood by me bravely during the next hour or two. I then rallied my reserve regiment and broken fragments in the woods near my battery and sent out a strong party of skirmishers to keep the enemy at bay, while another party went forward without arms to get off as many of our dead and wounded as possible. I maintained my ground, skirmishing, and occasionally firing by battalion, during the greater part of the afternoon.

Toward evening, General Grover came up with his New England brigade. I saw him forming a line to attack the Rebel stronghold in the same place I had been all day, and advised him to form his line more to the left and charge bayonets on arriving at the railroad track, which his brigade executed with such telling effect as to drive the Rebels in clouds before the bayonets. Meanwhile I had gathered the remnant of my brigade, ready to take advantage of any opportunity to assist him. I soon discovered a large number of Rebels fleeing before the left flank of Grover's brigade. They passed over an open space some 500 yards in width in front of my reserve regiment, which I ordered to fire on them, which they did, accelerating their speed and discomfiture so much that I ordered a charge. My regiments immediately dashed out of the woods we were in down across the meadows in front of us

---

[77] First Lieutenant Francis S. Jacobs of Company K wrote of this fight that the regiment "had not advanced more than two rods into the woods when a terrible volley was poured in upon us from the front and from behind the railroad embankment on the left, mowing down our men like grass." *Ashland Union,* September 17, 1862, pg. 3

after the retreating foe, but before their arriving at the other side of the meadow, the retreating column received a heavy support from the railroad below them, and soon rallying, came surging back, driving before their immense columns Grover's brigade and my handful of men.

An hour before the charge I had sent one of my aides back after a fresh battery- the ammunition of both my batteries having given out- which arriving as our boys were being driven back I immediately ordered them into position and commenced pouring a steady fire of grape and canister into the advancing columns of the enemy. The first discharge discomposed them a little, but the immense surging mass behind pressed them on us. I held on until they were within 100 yards of us, and having but a handful of men to support the battery, ordered it to retire which was executed with the loss of one gun. I then rallied the shattered remnant of my brigade, which had been rallied by my aides and its officers, and encamped three-quarters of a mile to the rear.

The next morning (August 30th), I brought my brigade into the position assigned them and remained in reserve until about 4 P.M. when I threw it across the road to stop the retreating masses which had been driven back from the front. I soon received an order to move my brigade off to the left on the double quick, the enemy having massed their troops during the day in order to turn our left flank. I formed line of battle along the road, my left resting near the edge of the woods in which the battle was raging. Soon our troops came rushing, panic-stricken, out of the woods, leaving my brigade to face the enemy, who followed the retreating masses to the edge of the woods. The road in which my brigade was formed was worn and washed from three to five feet deep, affording a splendid cover for my men. My boys opened fire on them at short range, driving the Rebels back to a respectful distance. But the enemy, being constantly reinforced from the masses in their rear, came on again and again, pouring in advance a perfect hurricane of balls, which had but little effect on my men who were so well protected in their road entrenchment. But the steady fire of my brigade, together with that of a splendid brass battery on higher ground in my rear, which I ordered to fire rapidly with canister of the heads of my men, had a most withering effect on the Rebels, whose columns melted away and fast recoiled from the repeated efforts to advance upon my road breastwork from the woods. But the fire of the enemy, which had affected my men so little, told with destructive results on the exposed battery in the rear, and it required a watchful effort to hold them to their effective work. My horse was shot in the head by a musket ball while in the midst of the battery cheering on the men. I got another, and soon after observing the troops on my left giving way in confusion before the Rebel fire, I hastened to assist in rallying them, and while engaged in this, the battery took advantage of my absence and withdrew.

I had sent one of my aides shortly before to the rear for fresh troops to support this part of our line, where the persistent efforts of the Rebels showed they had determined to break through. A fine regiment of regulars was sent, which was formed in the rear of my brigade, near the position the battery had occupied. The Rebels came around the forest in columns to our right and front, but the splendid firing of the regulars, with that of my brigade, thinned their ranks so rapidly, that they were thrown back in confusion upon every attempt made. About this time, when the battle raged thickest, Lieutenant Este and Lieutenant Niles of General Schenk's staff reported to me for duty, informing me that General Schenk had been seriously wounded and his command thrown back from the field. Most thankfully was their valuable assistance accepted, and most gallantly and efficiently did they assist me on that most ensanguined field until 8 o'clock at night in bringing up regiments, brigades, and batteries, cheering them on to action, and in rallying them when driven back before the furious fire of the enemy.

Shortly after sunset, my own brigade had entirely exhausted their ammunition and it being considered unsafe to bring forward the ammunition wagons, where the enemy's shells were constantly flying and exploding, and the enemy having entirely ceased their efforts to break through this part of the line and had thrown the weight of their attack still farther to my left, I ordered my brigade back some one-half of a mile to replenish their ammunition boxes and there await further orders. I remained on the field with Lieutenants Este and Niles, my own having been sent to see to my regiments. The enemy continued their attacks upon our left until long after dark, which it required the most determined and energetic efforts to repel.

At one time, not receiving assistance from the rear as I had a right to expect after having sent for it, and our struggling battalions being nearly overcome by the weight and persistence of the enemy's attack, I flew back about one-half mile to where I understood General McDowell was with a large portion of his corps. I found him and appealed to him in the most urgent manner to send a brigade forward at once to save the day, or all would be lost.

He answered coldly, in substance, that it was not his business to help everybody and he was not going to help General Sigel. I told him I was not fighting with General Sigel's corps; that my brigade had got out of ammunition some time before and gone to the rear and that I had been fighting with a half dozen different brigades and that I had not enquired where or to what corps they belonged. He inquired of one of his aides if a certain general was fighting over there on the left; he said he thought he was. McDowell replied that he would send him help for he was a good fellow.[78] He then gave the order for a brigade to start, which was all I desired. I dashed in front of them, waved my sword, and cheered them forward. They raised a cheer and came on the double quick. I soon led them to where they were most needed, and the gallant manner in which they entered the fight and the rapidity of their fire soon turned the tide of battle. But this gallant brigade, like many others which had preceded it, found the enemy too strong as they advanced into the forest and was forced back by the tremendous fire that met them. But one of General Burnside's veteran brigades, coming up soon after dark with a battery, again dashed back the tide of armed treason, and sent such a tempest of shot, shell, and leaden death into the dark forest after the Rebels that they did not again renew the attack.

Perhaps some mighty cheering which I got our boys to send up about that time induced the Rebels to believe that we had received such reinforcements as to make any further meddling with our lines a rather unhealthy business. Feeling certain that the Rebels had been completely checked and defeated in their attempts to flank us and drive us from the field, and that we could now securely hold it until morning, by which time we could rally our scattered forces and bring up sufficient fresh troops to enable us to gain a complete victory on the morrow- I felt certain that the Rebels had put forth their mightiest efforts and were greatly cut up and crippled- I therefore determined to look up my little brigade and bring it forward into position, when we would be ready in the morning to renew the contest and renew the great glorious drama of war. I left the field at 8 P.M. in possession of our gallant boys and with Lieutenants Este and Niles, started back in the darkness and was greatly surprised upon coming to where I expected to find my brigade with thousands of other troops, to find none. I kept on a half mile further in panful, bewildering doubt and uncertainty where I found you, general, and first learned from you with agonizing surprise that our whole army had been ordered to retreat back across Bull Run to Centreville.

Comment is unnecessary. I felt that all the blood, treasure, and labor of our government and people for the last year had been thrown away by that unfortunate order, and that most probably the death knell of our glorious government had been sounded by it. The highest praise I can award to the officers and men of my brigade, in all the hard service and fighting through which we have passed, is that they have bravely, cheerfully, patiently, and nobly performed their duty. Colonel Cantwell of the 82nd Ohio and Colonel Zeigler of the 5th West Virginia deserve particular attention for the coolness and bravery in the long and desperate fight of the 29th with the Rebels at the railroad. In the death of Colonel Cantwell, the country as well as his family have sustained an irreparable loss.[79] No braver man or truer patriot ever lived. He constantly studied the best interests of his soldiers and of the country, and his men loved, obeyed, and respected him as a father. Truly the loss of such an officer in these trying times is a great calamity.

The reported loss for the 82nd Ohio in the Northern Virginia campaign (August 16-September 2, 1862) is given as 24 killed, 99 wounded, and 15 missing, for a total of 138.

---

[78] McDowell remembered this incident somewhat differently, stating that Milroy "came riding up in a state of absolute frenzy with his sword drawn, and gesticulating at some distance off, shouting to send forward reinforcements to save the day, save the country, etc."

[79] Surgeon Jacob Cantwell, under a flag of truce granted Sunday August 31, 1862 recovered the body of his deceased brother from the field. "Everything was stripped off of him, as was the case with all of the balance of our dead who were left on the field. Colonel Cantwell died as he lived: a brave man, knowing no fear, and ready to sacrifice everything in behalf of his country. His health had not been good for two months previous and he was actually not fit or able to be in the saddle that day, but he would never permit or ask his men to go any place that he was afraid to go himself." First Lieutenant Francis S. Jacobs, *Ashland Union*, September 17, 1862, pg. 3

CHAPTER FOUR

All Quiet Along the Rappahannock and Chancellorsville

Following the strenuous efforts and disastrous results of the northern Virginia campaign under Pope, the 82nd Ohio as part of Sigel's corps spent several months recuperating while manning the Washington area defenses. Major General George B. McClellan, now back in the environs of Washington with the entire Army of the Potomac, was tasked with reorganizing and consolidating his army with the tattered remnants of Pope's Army of Virginia, the ultimate mission of this army being the confrontation with General Lee's Army of Northern Virginia. Lee, flushed with success at Second Bull Run, resolved upon an invasion of Maryland and Pennsylvania, crossing the Potomac River in early September. McClellan, demonstrating his notable skill at organization, quickly whipped the army back into shape and pursued Lee for a little more than a week before bringing him to battle along the banks of Antietam Creek near Sharpsburg on September 17, 1862. The battle, the bloodiest single day of the Civil War, halted Lee's invasion and provided the victory that President Lincoln needed to issue the Emancipation Proclamation. But McClellan, displaying the sluggish caution that had landed him in hot water with the administration throughout much of 1862, allowed Lee's battered army to retreat relatively unmolested across the Potomac into Virginia. This was too much for Lincoln, who removed McClellan permanently from command of the Army of the Potomac on November 7, 1862 and promoted Major General Ambrose E. Burnside to lead the army.[80]

Burnside set up about reorganizing the army, and the old 1st Corps of the Army of Virginia (now designated the 11th) was placed in the Reserve Corps under the overall command of Major General Franz Sigel. General Halleck still maintained serious reservations about Sigel's fitness to command a corps, complaining that Sigel was a "damned coward" and suggested that although the 11th Corps "comprised some of the best fighting men we have, it won't do much under Sigel."[81] General Burnside didn't share those reservations, however. The 82nd Ohio was given the honor of being designated the provost guards for the entire corps, and was attached to Sigel's headquarters. Initially pushed out to Gainesville as an "army of observation," the Reserve Corps marched south to join the rest of the Army of the Potomac in their offensive against Lee's army now entrenched at Fredericksburg. The Reserve Corps subsequently did not take part in the Battle of Fredericksburg, observing the battle from the eastern bank of the Rappahannock.

Camp of the 82nd Regt., O.V.I., Gainesville, Virginia
November 17, 1862

Since the memorable campaign on the Rappahannock, terminating with the battles of Groveton and Chantilly, the 11th Army Corps, though seemingly not engaged in active campaigning, has by no means been idle. On the contrary, from the time General McClellan resumed chief command of the Army of the Potomac, General Sigel's command has borne a relation to that army of the utmost importance and performed a most responsible and essential service. First thrown forward from Arlington Heights as far as Fairfax Courthouse with our advance at Centreville, we were charged with the double office of guarding Washington and acting as an army of observation. Our scouts penetrated and scoured a wide range of territory and kept vigilant watch over all Rebel doings east of the Blue Ridge and as far south as Fredericksburg. Now that the grand army has moved southward as far as Warrenton the 11th Corps has been assigned to the duty of closing all avenues of Rebel approach north of that point and thus protecting a large scope of country, including many vital points from any incursion of the enemy.

---

[80] The format for this chapter is to intersperse Captain Lee's letters written to the *Delaware Gazette* with supplementary information drawn from contemporary sources to flesh out the story. Captain Lee's letters will be headed by the date and location where they were written.

[81] Engle, op. cit., pg. 150

Major General Ambrose E. Burnside
(Library of Congress)

The main part of the force is several miles beyond this post; General Sigel, however, still maintains his headquarters here. The gallant 82nd having been detached for the honorable duty of general provost guard has become an accompaniment of General Sigel's domicile. The recent change in the chief command naturally provokes a good deal of comment. But that there is any widespread or substantial dissatisfaction because of it is entirely false. It would be unfair to suppose that the army is more devoted to the interests of any one man than to those of our common country. We soldiers are not yet, I trust, so far the victims of man-worship mania. Besides, even to the most enthusiastic admirers of General McClellan perhaps no one could be more acceptable in lieu of him than the "Hero of Roanoke." In his patriotism, energy and ability there is utmost confidence. "Little Rhody" may well be proud of the noble chieftain she has given us, for indeed there are few of us who do not rejoice at his elevation.[82]

The result of the late elections has caused a good deal of surprise in the army. If there is any unhealthy feeling relevant it is perhaps more on that account than any other. Had not the issue been so clearly taken on sustaining or opposing the policy of the administration, there would be less cause for discouragement. The most energetic measures than can be adopted by the government to subdue the rebellion are certainly the measures and that the policy that will soonest end the war. The more opposition that can be raised to those measures and the more that can be done to embarrass the execution of them, the more will be done to aid the traitors and prolong the war. The army will say today by an immense majority that the emancipation policy is the best. Exposure, fatigue, and all manner of hardships, together with what we have learned by observation, have brought us to our senses in this matter. Let the unpatriotic politicians who have been seeking to ride into power on the hobby of opposition to that policy come and see what we have seen and endure what we have endured in fighting this wicked rebellion and they will soon be converted to a different faith.

---

[82] While Lee may have been pleased at Burnside's elevation, the army high command had serious reservations, starting with Burnside himself. In a meeting with his senior commanders shortly after his promotion, Burnside averred that "he was not fit for so big a command, but since it was imposed on him, he would do his best." Carl Schurz remembered that "there was something very touching in that confession of unfitness. But when a moment later the generals talked among themselves, it was no wonder that several shook their heads and asked how we could have confidence in the fitness of our leader if he had no such confidence himself? This reasoning was rather depressing and destined soon to be justified." Schurz, op. cit.

Slavery is doomed, the edict has gone forth. All the conservatives in Christendom with all their Jesuitical art cannot preserve it. The administration says and the army says that the sooty idol shall fall. Let all Democrats cease their genuflections and stand from under or its fall will grind them to powder. This war is waged for freedom; it is waged to prove that man- not a few men, but all men, mankind- is capable of self-government. It is waged against despotism and tyranny- waged to prove that all men are created free and equal in their rights. It may cost rivers of blood and oceans of treasure, but these facts shall be demonstrated. The creator of man and the God of battles has decreed it. To doubt it is to doubt Him and despair of human nature.

I appeal to every man who has property and life to take them in his hand and stand by the flag. Let every citizen stand ready with his gifts of money and life, fully determined that all shall be laid upon the altar of freedom ere it shall be proven to the world that republicanism is a failure. When the people are ready to do this, no treason nor misfortune, no intervention nor earthly power can prevent our success. As for soldiers their resolution is taken.

P.S. Since writing the above, we have received marching orders. It is supposed we are going to the Shenandoah Valley again.

Camp of the 82nd Regt. O.V.I., Fairfax Court House, Virginia
December 8, 1862

Thousands of times since this war commenced has the questioned been asked, "Will we succeed in subduing this rebellion and restoring the Union?" As often it has been met by the reply "Of course we will." Yet who will not admit that there is a possibility of our failure? This question then arises, where does the responsibility lie? Certainly not in our want of means wherewith to accomplish the end. No loyal man can be found silly enough to broach the opinion that the loyal element of the country has not bone and muscle sufficient to grapple with and overthrow the giant treason of the South. Certainly we have the strength and the power. The danger of failure does not lie in our weakness. That is not the vulnerable point of the great Northern Achilles. Neither is it to be found in foreign intervention. That is only a scarecrow. Our gigantic military power, impaired and crippled as it is, holds Europe in awe. The threats of intermeddling, which came from over the water, are intended to try our pluck and the sincerity and constancy of our determinations. The dynasties of Europe are trying to probe our public sentiment and test its self-devotion and faithfulness to our cause.

Here, then, we have the sure index to the solution of our destiny. These crowned heads desire our overthrow. They know that this cannot be accomplished so long as our people are fixed and unanimous in their determination that it shall not be. But is this the mind of the people? That is just what they want to find out. They are aware that just so much as this is or is not the case, increases or diminishes the probability that we will overcome all opposition and reestablish the Union.

Do the people make anxious inquiries as to the denouement of the war? Their own hearts give them the answer. How do they will it shall be, a success or a failure? There lies the secret. Doubts as to the ability of the administration cannot be entertained. Even if it had not proved itself honest, capable, faithful, and in view of the prodigious difficulties in its way wonderfully successful, it would still be the duty of the people to hold up its arms. To them the administration and the army anxiously turn and make the solemn appeal "will you stand by us?" The answer involves the issue of the war.

True, mistakes may be made. Very few great enterprises were ever undertaken without some errors of judgment. No government can be infallible. Ours is not; yet so long as it exhibits an honest purpose, or even any purpose, to execute the laws and sustain its authority, it is entitled to the full and earnest support of everyone over whom the authority extends. By support I mean property, influence, life, and not a part of these but, if necessary, all. And in case these are withheld, who dare question the right, yea, even much more, of a just and free government to take them?

If this vile rebellion succeeds in fighting itself into respectability, if this wicked treason ever establishes itself as law, if this Union is disrupted, this glorious government destroyed and all the precious blood shed in its behalf made a vain and foolish libation, history will record the fact that it was because the American people lacked courage, faith, patriotism, and determination. We are now establishing our character for all time to come. The future will see us by the light of the events of this struggle. We are necessarily carving out for ourselves an immortality of honor or of shame. God has committed a great cause to our keeping. He has appointed us His chosen instruments to maintain it. Will we be faithful to our trust? Though this war may continue for years, will we stand unswervingly by the right? Let every man honestly propound these questions to himself and mark the echo of his bosom.

After the withdrawal of this corps from Gainesville, General Sigel re-established his headquarters in this ancient and venerable town. The troops are assigned to different positions on the thoroughfares leading from here south. Except a few guerillas, to whom now and then General Stahel pays his respects, the Rebels seem to have mostly retired from our front. Even the ghost of that ubiquitous personage Stonewall Jackson has not lately disturbed our rest. We had our first noticeable fall of snow a few days ago and since then the weather has been very cold. Winter seems to have set in all at once. The cold, biting winds that sweep down upon us from the mountains conclusively demonstrate the insufficiency of our frail shelter, tents, as a protection. In a week's time the men could build log huts that would make them comfortable during the winter. But the time for that seems to have not yet come. Winter quarters is not yet the word. We must still hold ourselves ready for active operations.

One of the most striking features of the landscape about Bull Run and Centreville is the deserted villages that were occupied by the Rebel troops last winter. They consist of log huts covered with clapboards and in fact are more comfortable than tents. It being the fortune of your correspondent to pass a night in one which had been the domain of some Rebel officer, he can verily dispose that it could not have been fitted up more to his liking. There are enough of them to accommodate tens of thousands of troops.

No pen can describe the desolation of this country. After its first settlement the soil was utterly exhausted by the culture of tobacco and then mostly abandoned. Weeds, bushes, and dense pine thickets now mark the place of once flourishing fields. Add to this the blasting and desolating effects of war. Fenceless farms, burned and destroyed houses, long lines of weedy rifle pits, gaping fortifications and here and there a group of neglected graves trace through this land the footsteps of the grim and bloody monster. The village of Fairfax occupies a sight both commanding and beautiful. In times of peace it is, no doubt, a very pleasant country town. The courthouse, an old and antique brick building wherein "Extra Billy" Smith made a speech some years ago in which he predicted a collision between North and South and exhorted his hearers to prepare for it, is now filled with various kinds of warlike stores and equipment.[83] Thus Billy's request has been responded to in the very place where he made it, though he hardly supposed his much abused Uncle Sam would be the respondent. The original courthouse was not located here, but a mile or so distant and was built of logs. This corps is now under marching orders.

Camp of the 82nd Regt., O.V.I., near Stafford Court House, Virginia
December 23, 1862
On Saturday December 13th inst., the 82nd once more bade farewell to Fairfax. The 11th Army Corps had already preceded us several days on the march towards Fredericksburg and General Sigel and staff had followed. The provost guard must bring up the rear in order to arrest lingering depredators and stragglers and protect the trains which were slowly toiling along after the troops over the dreadful roads. The mud defied description. Broken wagons, dead horses and mules, ammunition and equipage strewn by the roadside indicated the enormous difficulty of moving a large force with its necessary appendages over such a route. During our service under the gallant Fremont, we often made 15 miles per day over roads as bad or worse than this. We found we could easily do it now. Not so with a couple of new regiments- the 107th Ohio and 82nd Illinois- which had two days start ahead of us. We overtook them on our first day's march toiling up the banks of the Occoquan River. The heights along this stream have been strongly fortified by the Rebels. These abandoned fortifications are one of the most impressive features of the country. It is an interesting fact, too, that Colonel Frederick Hecker of the 82nd Illinois was general in command of the revolutionary force in Germany wherein General Sigel figured as a colonel.

No pen can describe the utter desolation of this portion of Virginia. The curse of slavery has done for it no less than might have been expected from the whole swarm of plagues that fell upon ancient Egypt. The soil, said to

---

[83] William "Extra Billy" Smith had served several terms as a Congressman from Virginia and was then serving as a colonel in the Army of Northern Virginia.

have been once fertile, is utterly impoverished and one can but wonder how the few wretched inhabitants exist. About two-thirds of the surface is covered with a thick, dense growth of pines, cedars, scrub oaks, etc. Everywhere nothing but pine seems to meet one's gaze until the eye grows weary and heart sick of it. Yet these pine thickets make excellent camping places. Their overhanging branches shield from sun or rain and break off cold winds. The Rebel encampments are almost always in the midst of them.

Thus was the 82nd not many nights ago. The writer hereof had betaken himself to his blankets beneath the overshadowing evergreens and been lulled by the moaning wind to a sleep which proved only too balmy. For, during the wee hours, the rain began to fall in torrents. The first few monitory drops broke the spell of slumber and gave admonition of what was coming. But the warning was unheeded and again I committed all cares to Morpheus. But soon innumerable little streamlets discovered to be slyly creeping under me brought me to my understanding. To find one's self in undress uniform in the midst of a violent rainstorm and compelled to arrange his toilet in pitchy darkness, to say the least, is not an enviable species of fortune.

Stafford Court House hardly deserves the name of a town. A few scattered houses, a gloomy looking prison, and an ancient courthouse are its most noticeable features. The 11th Corps is now encamped here awaiting orders. The 107th Ohio takes the place of the 82nd Ohio in McLean's brigade. The 82nd has been promoted to the honorable duty of General Provost Guard for the grand division of the army under Sigel. The utility of having a general police force of this kind becomes every day more apparent. Straggling, desertion, drunkenness, stealing, etc. are more effectually ferreted out and punished by this means than any other perhaps. Perfect good order in camp and on the march can in no other way be attained.

The late disaster at Fredericksburg has not essentially discouraged the army but the turbulent state of affairs at Washington is somewhat disheartening.[84] The government, the people, and the army must harmoniously work together if this rebellion is to be crushed. Had it been so, the Southern Confederacy would ere this been among the things that were. It is too true that generals and politicians have been too fearful of each other's success to the detriment of their patriotism. Had Fremont captured Jackson, or Pope defeated Lee, it would most likely have elevated either to the head of the army. Hence they were not cooperated with by other aspirants and partisans. And is it not safe to surmise that the pending elections in New York and elsewhere had something to do with the otherwise unaccountable delay of the army on the north bank of the Potomac? At any rate, no one can say there was not a possibility of a design of this kind to disaffect the people toward the administration and its candidates. I know these are startling suggestions, but they are such as occur to our minds, isolated as we are among the pines of Virginia.

With our glorious cause and our immense power, why are there so many different kinds of policy for the prosecution of the war? Is it not because there are so many individuals who want to be king? Oh, for our country's sake, let us have unanimity. Let the people rally around the President and let the two demand and see that the army does its duty. Let every general be held to strict accountability for his conduct. Let common sense displace policy, devotion to our cause supersede devotion to party and individual glory, and love of right dethrone the love of wrong. Then heaven will bless our arms and give us the victory.

Yours for the republic.

Following the battle of Fredericksburg and the Mud March, General Burnside, fed up with being undermined by of some of his generals, resolved to relieve General Joseph Hooker or force Lincoln to accept his resignation from command of the Army of the Potomac. Lincoln chose to accept Burnside's resignation, and

---

[84] Lee's statement that the army was not discouraged ten days after the debacle at Fredericksburg seems to be a deliberate attempt to shield the home front from the unpleasant state of affairs prevailing within the Army of the Potomac. Carl Schurz wrote that "the number of desertions increased alarmingly, and regimental officers in large numbers resigned their commissions." In late January 1863, Burnside attempted another forward movement that bogged down in the infamous "Mud March," where the army found that it simply could not move along the muddy roads in the midst of winter. "It was fortunate that the condition of the roads rendered Lee just as unable to move as Burnside was, for the demoralization of the Army of the Potomac had reached a point almost beyond control." Reminiscences of Carl Schurz, 1907. General Oliver Howard wrote that after he court-martialed two commissioned officers for disloyal language, "mouths were stopped, but discontent had taken deep root."

through General Order No. 20 dated January 25, 1863 he appointed General Hooker as the army's new commander. Hooker's elevation met with general disapproval from many of the general officers of the army, but proved an inspired choice, as least as viewed by the men in the ranks. "To them, he was a soldier's general and they were genuinely fond of him," wrote Hooker's biographer. "They were not concerned about his intemperance nor were they interested in evaluating his moral character."

Hooker soon gave the men of the army abundant reason to have confidence in his leadership. He moved quickly to reorganize his command and correct some major deficiencies that had sapped the strength of what should have been the Union's strongest field army. On February 6th, he abolished Burnside's Grand Divisions, returning to a corps-based organization, but he also consolidated all of the cavalry in the army into one corps. Hooker set the cavalry loose to harass and annoy the Confederates whenever and wherever possible. Army morale was the biggest problem confronting Hooker- at one point, there were 85,000 men absent with or without leave from the ranks of the army. Desertions had sky-rocketed after Fredericksburg, and the lack of pay combined with indifferent rations made the life for the common soldier one of unmitigated drudgery. Hooker tackled both problems with characteristic energy and drive. A system of furloughs was instituted to address the nagging problem of war-weariness amongst the troops. The regular issuance of army rations improved and brigade bakeries made soft bread available to the men. Operating under the premise that a busy army is a happy army, Hooker reinstituted a rigorous regime of drills, reviews, and inspections. Hospital and sanitary conditions received significant attention; the net result of all of these various efforts was that morale recovered and soon surged. A staff officer later wrote, paying tribute to Hooker's efforts, that "the Army of the Potomac never spent three months to better advantage."[85]

Camp of the 82nd Regt., O.V.I., near Stafford Court House, Virginia
February 25, 1863

The weather in this locality alternates strangely between mild and stormy. One morning is clear and beautiful, the birds singing among the pines, the air is pleasant as that of June; the next the earth is enveloped in snow and the elements are so angry as to hardly permit of outdoor movements at all. Then the sun breaks forth again and melts the snow or we have a protracted rain which affects the same result. Thus the light soil of this region, being composed of clay and sand is almost constantly kept in a condition which a little travel will transfer into that of a quagmire. It is easy to see therefore that the present inaction of this great army is not self-imposed. On the contrary everyone is ready to welcome the day when we shall be able to break the spell with which the Mud King has bound us. The lassitude and ennui resulting from our protracted inaction are more oppressive than the hardships of a vigorous campaign. Action is the soldier's element, without it he becomes unhealthy, morose, and miserable.

On Sunday morning last, while a fearful snow storm was raging and when the little huts of the soldiers were many of them almost completely enveloped in the fleecy folds of the soft mantle that had fallen upon the earth, suddenly the deep-voiced artillery began to bellow all along our lines. Surely it must have startled the graybacks who were glowering in their mud forts over the Rappahannock for even many of us did not at first remember that it was the birthday of Washington. How appropriate that we should thus even amid the storm celebrate the memory of the hero who gave us our republic. But how singular the coincidence of our performing this act, at once within hearing of the camps of armed Rebels and of Mount Vernon. Well might the sound of the Union cannon startle the traitors from their dens on such an occasion.

The grand divisions of this army having been dissolved, General Sigel has been re-established in command of the 11th Corps. In General Hooker we all feel that we have emphatically a leader, one who will not send us but lead us against the foe. That is just the kind of a commander we need. In fact, this army needs less commanding than leading. It has long enough been accustomed to obey the behests of those who were themselves unwilling to go to the forefront and show it what to do; fortunately that class is fast being weeded out and shuffled off. The firm course of the government in properly punishing the man who chiefly caused our second defeat at Manassas has slightly

---

[85] Hebert, Walter H. Fighting Joe Hooker. Lincoln: University of Nebraska Press, 1999, pgs. 167-184

wakened up certain partisans, grumblers, and cowards. Let us have more of that kind of policy. If need be, let every general and every subaltern be answerable with his head for misconduct.[86]

The question of arming the Negroes seems to create far less sensation among the soldiers than among certain of their Democratic friends at home who seem particularly jealous of our honor and dignity. A few campaigns have taught us better sense than to claim to ourselves alone the prerogative of being shot and shoveled into trenches by fiendish traitors. Most of us are quite willing to share this privilege even with Negroes. All the twaddle about the impractibility or impropriety of this measure is the most complete humbug. History furnishes us plenty of examples of its successful application. Thiers, in his history of the Consulate and the Empire of Napoleon I, says of the army in Egypt that "the blacks of Darfur, bought and made free, added as many as 500 good soldiers to one of our demi-brigades alone." This complies that many more were employed in other brigades. The valiant French who had won laurels at Lodi, Arcola, and Heliopolis did not feel degradation in fighting even for conquest along with Darfur blacks "bought and made free."

But when our national existence itself is in jeopardy certain nice politicians are offended at such a project. Even in the late war between France and Austria, Louis Napoleon transported from Egypt larger numbers of Turcos, a most savage and bloodthirsty tribe of blacks and sent them along with his splendid Zouaves against the Austrians. And now it is said that he is about to send legions of these despised blacks to assist in the conquest of Mexico. But if even all these examples, and many others might be cited, were wanting, we have that of General Jackson who employed Negroes at New Orleans, and there found reason to compliment them for their bravery and gallantry. But it is not the fear of offending the dignity of the army which disturbs these patriotic politicians. It is their anxiety lest the Negro armed in the cause of freedom may vindicate his manhood, and thus forever disprove their aristocratic notions of caste. They have not forgotten Touissant, who was to St. Domingo what Napoleon I was to France. They are apprehensive that another Touissaint[87] may spring from some obscure Southern plantation and fight his race into respectability. And who denies that such may be the case? God grant that it may.

The health of the army of the Potomac seems remarkably good. There is much less sickness than might have been expected. Snow balling is just now a favorite amusement, two or three companies are often seen engaged in a pitched battle of this kind against many others. Positions are often stormed and carried with as much enthusiasm as a Rebel battery would be. Would that nothing more serious awaited our brave boys than this harmless warfare. God is merciful in not raising the curtain that hides the next campaign.

Long live the Republic!

---

[86] Lee is referencing the court martial of Major General Fitz John Porter, a former commander of the V Corps and an especial favorite of McClellan's, who was accused of insubordination by General John Pope at the Battle of Second Bull Run in August 1862 in that Porter failed to attack when he was directed to do so. He was found guilty of the charge and dismissed from the army on January 21, 1863. Porter spent the balance of his life working to clear his name, was officially exonerated in 1878, and a special act of Congress in 1886 restored Porter's commission.

[87] Lee is referencing Toussaint Louverture, the noted leader of the 18th century Haitian Revolution.

Major General Joseph Hooker (Library of Congress)

CHANCELLORSVILLE

The change in army commanders also produced a change in corps commanders as General Sigel left the Army of the Potomac[88], and was replaced by Major General Oliver Otis Howard, a veteran Army of the Potomac divisional commander who had lost an arm while fighting at Seven Pines in June 1862. "The officers and men of the corps heard of Sigel's departure with keen sorrow," wrote Carl Schurz. "I know, however, that his relations with his superior officers on the eastern field of action had never been congenial. He was always regarded as a foreign intruder who had no proper place in the Army of the Potomac and whose reputation, won in the West, was to be discredited." Schurz was the senior divisional commander in the 11th Corps, and by right of seniority assumed temporary command of the corps, but Hooker installed Howard shortly afterwards. The appointment of Howard, considered an outsider by the men of the corps, was not a popular one. "It soon became apparent that the regimental officers and the rank and file did not take to him. They looked at him with dubious curiosity; not a cheer could be started when he rode along the front. And I do not know whether he liked the men he commanded better than they liked him," commented Schurz.[89] As his men considered him "arrogant, overbearing, and self-righteous," General Howard laconically wrote that "outwardly I met a cordial reception, but I soon found that my past record was not known here. I was not at first getting the earnest and loyal support of the entire command."[90]

For the Chancellorsville campaign which began in late April 1863, the 82nd Ohio served as provost guards for the 3rd Division, 11th Corps, and was attached to the headquarters of General Schurz. Schurz's commentary on the progress of the campaign will suffice to set the scene for the tragedy which unfolded the evening of May 2, 1863. "By the middle of April, Hooker was ready to move. His plan was excellent. Lee occupied the heights on the south side of the Rappahannock skirting the river to the right and left of Fredericksburg in skillfully fortified positions. Hooker set out to turn them by crossing the upper Rappahannock so as to enable him to gain Lee's rear. A cavalry expedition under General Stoneman, intended to turn Lee's left flank and to fall upon his communications with Richmond, miscarried, but this failure, though disagreeable, did not disturb General Hooker's general scheme of campaign. On the morning of the April 27, the 11th, 12th, and 5th Corps started for Kelly's Ford, 27 miles above Fredericksburg which they reached on the afternoon of the 28th. I remember those two days well. The army was in superb condition and animated by the highest spirits. Officers and men seemed to feel instinctively that they were engaged in an offensive movement promising great results. There was no end to the singing and merry laughter relieving the fatigue of the march. A pontoon bridge was thrown across the river and our corps crossed before midnight."

"After our two days' march up stream on the northern bank of the Rappahannock, we now had two days' march down stream on its southern side. We forded the Rapidan, and on the afternoon of April 30th, we reached the region called the Wilderness. We stopped about two miles west of Chancellorsville. The following night, four army corps camped in that vicinity, including the 11th, 12th, and 5th Corps along with the 2nd Corps which had crossed at United States Ford as soon as that ford was uncovered by our advance, a force of 50,000 men. This flanking movement had been masked by an operation conducted by General Sedgwick who crossed the Rappahannock a few miles below Fredericksburg with a force large enough to make apprehend that the main attack would come from that quarter. This crossing accomplished, the 3rd Corps under Sickles joined Hooker at Chancellorsville. Until then, Thursday April 30th, the execution of Hooker's plan had been entirely successful, and with characteristic grandiloquence the commanding general issued on that day the following general order to the Army of the Potomac. 'It is with heartfelt satisfaction that the commanding general announces to the army that the operations of the last

---

[88] Sigel asked to be relieved of command of the 11th Corps in March 1863 due to a combination of poor health, differences with General Hooker, and disgust at the poor treatment of Germans by the War Department. Engle, op. cit., pgs. 156-158
[89] Schurz, Reminiscences, op. cit.
[90] Engle, op. cit., pg. 159, Howard, Oliver Otis. <u>Autobiography of Oliver Otis Howard, Major General United States Army</u>. New York: The Baker & Taylor Company, 1907, pg. 349

three days have determined that the enemy must ingloriously fly, or come out from behind his defenses and give us battle on our own ground, where certain destruction awaits him. The operations of the 5th, 11th, and 12th Corps have been a succession of splendid achievements."

"It sounded somewhat like Pope's bragging order. The impression made upon the officers and men by this proclamation was by no means altogether favorable to its author. Of course, they were pleased to hear themselves praised for their achievements, but they did not forget that these had so far consisted only in marching, not in fighting, and that the true test was still to come. They hoped indeed that the Army of the Potomac, 130,000 strong, would prove able to bear Lee's army, only 60,000 strong. But it jarred upon their feelings as well as their good sense to hear their commanding general gasconade so boastfully of having the enemy in the hollow of his hand, that enemy being Robert E. Lee at the head of the best infantry in the world. Still we all hoped, and we explored the map for the important strategical point we would strike the next day. But the next day brought us fearful disappointment."

"On the morning of Friday May 1st, Hooker ordered a force several divisions strong to advance towards Fredericksburg and the enemy's communications. Our corps, too, received marching orders and started at noon. But the corps was hardly on the road in marching formation when our movement was stopped and we were ordered back to the position we had occupied the preceding night. What did this mean? General Hooker started out to surprise the enemy by a grand flank march taking us into the enemy's rear. We had succeeded. We had surprised the enemy. But the fruits of that successful surprise could be reaped only if we followed it up with quick and vigorous action. We could not expect a general like Lee to stay surprised. He was sure to act quickly and vigorously if we did not. And just this happened. When we stopped at Chancellorsville on the afternoon of April 30th, we might have marched a few miles further and seized some important points, especially Banks' Ford on the Rappahannock and some commanding positions nearer to Fredericksburg. It was then that Lee, having divined Hooker's plan, gathered up his forces to throw them against our advance. And as soon as on Friday May 1st our columns advancing toward Fredericksburg met the opposing enemy. Hooker recoiled and ordered his army back into a defensive position, there to await Lee's attack. Thus the offensive campaign so brilliantly opened was suddenly transformed into a defensive one. Hooker had surrendered the initiative of movement and given to Lee the incalculable advantage of perfect freedom of action. As soon as it became apparent that Hooker had abandoned his plan of vigorous offensive action and had dropped into a merely defensive attitude, the exuberant high spirits which had so far animated the officers and men of the Army of the Potomac turned into head shaking uncertainty. Their confidence in the military sagacity and dashing spirit of their chief 'Fighting Joe' was chilled with doubt."

"Early on Saturday morning May 2nd, General Hooker with some members of his staff rode along his whole line and was received by the troops with enthusiastic acclamations. He inspected the position held by the 11th Corps and found it 'quite strong.' The position might have been tolerably strong if General Lee had done General Hooker the favor of running his head against breastworks by a front attack. But what if he did not? 'Our right wing,' as I said in my official report, 'stood completely in the air, with nothing to lean upon, and that, too, in a forest thick enough to obstruct any free view to the front, flanks, or rear, but not thick enough to prevent the approach of the enemy's troops.[91] Our rear was the mercy of the enemy, who was at perfect liberty to walk right around us through the large gap between Colonel von Gilsa's right and the cavalry force stationed at Ely's Ford.

---

[91] General Howard described his location thus: "Here were stunted trees, such as scraggy oaks, bushy firs, cedars, and junipers, all entangled with a thick, almost impenetrable, undergrowth, and criss-crossed with an abundance of wild vines. In places all along the southwest and west front the forest appeared impassable, and the skirmishers could only work their way through with extreme difficulty. The position was never a desirable one." Major General Oliver Otis Howard, "The Eleventh Corps at Chancellorsville," Battles and Leaders of the Civil War, Vol. 3. New York: The Century Co., 1888, pgs. 189-202

Major General Carl Schurz
(Library of Congress)

"As we were situated, an attack from the west or northwest could not be resisted without a complete change of front on our part. To such a change, especially if it was to be made in haste, the formation of our forces was exceedingly unfavorable. It was almost impossible to maneuver some of our regiments, hemmed in as they were on the old turnpike by embankments and rifle pits in front and thick woods in the rear, drawn out in long deployed lines, giving just room enough for the stacks of arms and a narrow passage; this turnpike road being at the same time our only line of communication we had between the different parts of our front. Now, the thing most to be dreaded, an attack from the west, was just the thing coming."

"Not long after General Hooker had examined our position, I was informed that large columns of the enemy could be seen from General Devens' headquarters moving from east to west on a road running nearly parallel with the plank road on a low ridge at a distance of a mile or more. I hurried to Talley's where I could plainly observe them as they moved on, passing gaps in the woods, infantry, artillery, and wagons. Instantly it flashed on my mind that it was Stonewall Jackson, the "great flanker," marching towards our right to envelop it and attack us in flank and rear. I galloped back to corps headquarters at Dowdall's Tavern and on the way ordered Captain Hubert Dilger (Battery I, 1st Ohio Light Artillery) to look for good artillery positions fronting west as the corps would, in all probability, have to execute a change of front. I reported promptly to General Howard what I had seen and my impression, which amounted almost to a conviction, that Jackson was going to attack us from the west. I urged this view as earnestly as my respect for my commanding officer would permit, but General Howard would not accept it. He clung to the belief which, he said was also entertained by General Hooker, that Lee was not going to attack our right but actually in full retreat to Gordonsville."

Schurz, appalled at Howard's failure to recognize the perils of the situation, galloped back to his division headquarters at Hawkins' Farm and dispatched two regiments (the 58th New York and 26th Wisconsin) to face west, and a little southeast of those two regiments placed the 82nd Ohio in line. A shallow rifle pit was dug just east of corps headquarters at Dowdall's Tavern, but "this was all, literally all, that was done to meet an attack from the west," commented Schurz. "As for the rest, the absurdly indefensible positions of the corps remained unchanged. There we were then. That the enemy was on our flank in very great strength had become more certain every moment."

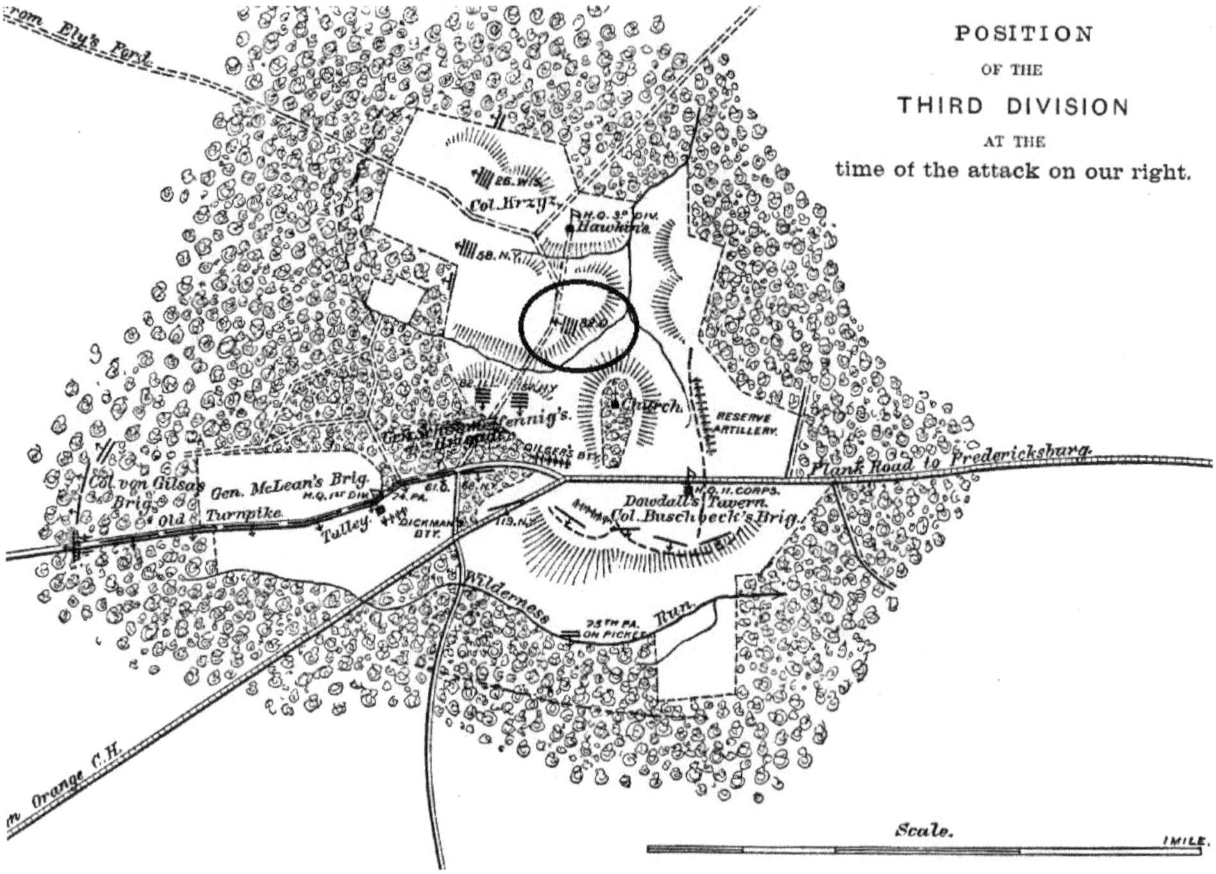

This map of the encampment of the 11th Corps on the right flank of the Army of the Potomac at Chancellorsville on May 2, 1863 was included in General Schurz's official report. General Howard described the position thus: "The old plank road and the old turnpike coming from the east are one and the same from Chancellorsville to and across Dowdall's opening; there the road forked, the plank continuing west, making an angle of some 20 degrees with the pike. North of the plank, in the Dowdall's opening, is the Wilderness Church; Hawkins' house is in the small glade-like space about a quarter mile north of the church and Dowdall's Tavern, was southeast of the church and also south of the main road. The next opening to Dowdall's westward was called Talley Farm. The highest ground was at Talley's near the pike and at Hawkins house, there was only a small rise at Dowdall's. Except the small openings, the forest was continuous and nearly enveloping. Generally the trees were near together with abundant entanglements of undergrowth." In the map above, the initial location of the 82nd Ohio is circled; the regiment retreated southeast and made its stand in the rifle pits dug near the reserve artillery just east of Dowdall's Tavern.

"Schimmelfennig had sent out several scouting parties beyond our regular pickets. They all came back with the same tale, that they had seen great masses of Rebel troops wheeling into line. The pickets and scouts of McLean and von Gilsa reported the same. In fact, almost every officer and private seemed to see the black thundercloud that was hanging over us and feel in his bones that a great disaster was coming. It may be fairly said that, if there had been a deliberate design or a conspiracy to sacrifice the 11th Corps (of course there was not), it could not have been more ingeniously planned. This was the situation at 5 o'clock in the afternoon."[92]

[92] Schurz, Reminiscences, op. cit.

Captain Alfred Lee's letter to the *Delaware Gazette*:
Camp of the 82nd Regt. O.V.I., Six miles north of Falmouth, Virginia
May 11, 1863

We broke camp at Stafford on Monday morning April 27th. The men were heavily loaded, having eight days' rations, 60 rounds of cartridges, and a change of clothing to carry, in addition to their guns and equipment. Yet full of confidence and good spirits, they traveled well and on Tuesday evening reached the Rappahannock at Bremen's Ford. The most powerful glasses could discover but few traces of the enemy on the other side and preparations were at once made to cross. About 12 o'clock at night the 82nd steadily tramped over the pontoons and found itself on the right bank of the Rappahannock. We continued marching until about 3 o'clock in the morning. On Wednesday our corps continued its advance, and evening found us on the bank of the Rapidan. The Rebels were building a bridge here and were captured, bridge and all. They only had a few timbers raised and our pontoons had to be laid, which was accomplished with trifling opposition. About midnight the 82nd crossed the roaring torrent, moved upon the heights of the right bank and waited for the day. On Thursday the army commenced its advance down the plank road towards Fredericksburg. On Friday there was considerable skirmishing with the enemy, but no general engagement on our flank (the right) of the grand army, though I believe there was very severe fighting on the left. We were under arms most of the day Friday and Friday night.

On Saturday morning, the sun dawned clear and beautiful and though we all looked for a general engagement, everything was comparatively quiet. There were a good many random volleys of musketry and some cannonading, but with that exception the day wore away quietly. About 3 P.M. it was announced to us that the enemy were retreating; that one of our brigades was following them, capturing their train and securing many prisoners. Our men were jubilant over the good news, talked of marching to Gordonsville on the morrow, cheerfully ate their frugal supper, and began to think of preparing for one quiet night's rest after so many of sleepless watchfulness. While seated on the ground with my two lieutenants (1st Lieutenant John H. Ballard and 2nd Lieutenant Thomas J. Abrell) eating our evening meal, Captain George H. Purdy (Co. I) came to us and jovially remarked about our good living, smiled, and walked away. Alas, it was the last smile, the last word from him to me on this earth.

About half an hour afterwards we were startled by some random musket shots on our right. Almost immediately there followed the most terrific, the most tremendous, the most deadly volley of musketry that in all of my war experience I ever heard. The Rebels instead of retreating had turned our right flank and in heavy force had stolen up within a few paces of our unsuspecting lines. It was a complete surprise. Our men flew to arms and stood waiting for orders and watching the result of the dreadful conflict on our right. Soon troops of stragglers swarming from the woods indicated but too plainly that our lines were broken. The Rebels followed them closely into the open field. All was now hurry and confusion. We were ordered this way and that, changing position every minute, yet doing nothing decisively. Oh, for a Napoleon at that critical juncture! He would have had but five minutes, but even in that time he might have made dispositions that would at least have covered our retreat if not checked the enemy. The German regiments, of which of corps is unfortunately chiefly made up, acted any way but bravely. Many of them threw away their arms and ran without scarcely firing a shot.[93]

Our own regiment, although comparatively cool and determined, narrowly escaped disorganization in the hurry and confusion. It was decided at length to move our regiment to the rear and post it behind a slight earthwork that had been thrown up during the day. I rallied my company while moving up toward the entrenchment, got every man in his place and filed my men into the ditch in good order.[94] The air was now darkened with the smoke of battle, bullets, shells, and canister shot sung, whistled, and howled about our heads and the enemy were coming on

---

[93] The Confederate flank attack was spearheaded by General Alfred Iverson's brigade (5th, 12th, 20th, and 23rd North Carolina), and General George P. Doles' brigade (4th, 12th, 21st, and 44th Georgia).

[94] First Lieutenant Stowel L. Burnham of Co. G recalled that the 82nd Ohio executed this movement "as calmly as if on battalion drill. I have been with the regiment since its organization and in every battle and I must say in justice to the men that they never exhibited any more of the qualities of tried and veteran soldiers." *Hardin County Republican*, May 22, 1863, pg. 3

pell-mell, driving before them a herd of cowardly Germans, some of whom every moment were paying a dreadful penalty for their want of pluck. I got my company into the ditch without a man being hurt except one sprightly little German whom I had sent to Captain Purdy's company to equalize it. He, poor boy, was killed before reaching the embankment. Captain Purdy was also struck down dead at about the same moment and was left where he fell. We had no sooner got our position in the breastwork than hundreds of our stragglers came swarming over us in their efforts to escape. Of course we had to withhold our fire until they had passed.

They had no sooner done so than I gave the word to my men to commence firing and they went at it not only with a will but with coolness and deliberation. Hardly a man but seemed perfectly resolved to stay there and die rather than run. The breastwork was very frail, being only about two and a half feet high and so thin that the bullets went through it. Yet there we intended to stay. But alas, though the enemy was checked in front of us, our flanks were left entirely exposed and the enemy came right down on our right and left. Three minutes more and would have to die in our places or be captured. Colonel James S. Robinson saw the danger and ordered a retreat. It was an awful moment. Between the breastwork and the woods in our rear, a distance of about 150 yards, we were entirely exposed to the fire of the enemy. Yet there was no alternative- we had to run for life or be taken. Previous to the order to retreat, I had but two men hurt- the little German above referred to and one sergeant- but ere we passed that 150 yards, 2nd Lieutenant Thomas J. Abrell and one man was killed and ten were wounded. The carnage was sickening. I saw men dropping all around me- saw faces streaming with blood-but let me not rehearse the sad details.

The Dutch had all run, and though we had checked the enemy sufficiently to give them ample time to form a new line of battle for us to rally behind, yet none was formed and there was no alternative but to continue our retreat until we had fallen behind the lines of the 2nd and 3rd Corps. Thus the 82nd was the last regiment to leave that bloody field. We left it not because we were demoralized, not because we were cowardly (for there is no better fighting material in the Army of the Potomac), but simply because we had three things to choose: death, a Richmond dungeon, or a retreat. Perhaps we ought to have taken one of the first two rather than the last, and I have since heard many regrets that we did not, but would it not only have aggravated the disaster? Had the German regiments fought at all, had they stood firmly upon our flanks as we expected they would, in short had they rendered us any assistance worth naming, I have no doubt at all but the enemy would have found himself unable to pass the breastwork and would have been driven back in confusion. [95]

But the men who have always made themselves notorious in the army by their thieving and straggling were not the men to depend on in the

Confederate View

"About 4 P.M. we reached Hooker's right flank. We were in a thick woods and the enemy was 200 yards in front in an open field. They were making coffee and evidently unconscious of so formidable a foe. It was very hot. Everything was about ready for the attack. Stonewall Jackson was sitting on a log by our company when a member of our company, seeing the attack was imminent, suggested we all kneel while he prayed. Jackson dropped his head and the others likewise. Immediately after the short prayer, the attack was ordered."

"We were right among them before they could turn their cannon on us. They broke, and the rout was complete. We pursued them, killing and capturing them for two miles. Many who were not killed or captured 'did not stop south of Baltimore.' All that I saw were foreigners, mostly Germans."

~ Private John H. Traylor, Co. B, 4th Georgia Infantry

---

[95] Lee's disgust with the conduct of the German troops of the 11th Corps was commonly held by many of the Ohio soldiers within the 11th Corps. One soldier of the 82nd Ohio acidly remarked that "most of them were Blenkers, better at killing hogs or stealing and plundering than at fighting the Rebels" and "if our regiment has been with some regiments from our own state instead of the Blenkers from New York, we would have whipped the Rebels." *Harding County Republican*, June 5, 1863, pg. 1

hour of danger as we found out to our sorrow. About 8 P.M. our regiment was rallied in an open field by the clear moonlight. But alas, how many vacant places there were in our ranks. My own company, I can say with sorrow and pride, suffered more than any other in the regiment and I have good reason to believe hurt the enemy some. The Rebels, not satisfied with the defeat of the 11th Corps, came pouring down in heavy masses upon the lines of the 2nd and 3rd Corps. Crazed with whiskey and intoxicated with success, they seemed determined to break our lines regardless of the cost. But as well might they have dashed against the rock of Gibraltar. This night battle was indescribably, grandly, and awfully terrible. No language of mine can give you any adequate idea of it. The bellowing of scores of cannon vomiting fire and smoke against the moonlit sky, the shrieking shells, the howling of canister, the constant and tremendous roaring and rattling of musketry and intermingled in an awful discord that seemed supernatural and made one think himself suddenly sunk to the lowest depths of pandemonium. Three of four times the Rebel tide came surging down upon our lines and as often it was rolled back by our brave hearts with awful slaughter. After a while, the storm of battle lulled and ceased for the night.

Early next morning (Sunday), the 11th Corps was moved to the extreme left and posted behind entrenchments. We had hardly got our positions when the battle commenced again in front and on the right. The 11th Corps was not engaged. The fighting was mostly done in the midst of a thick forest which was soon fired by the artillery. The wounded not carried off must have either suffocated or burned. For hours the bellowing of artillery and the roaring of musketry was deafening. General Hooker, placing himself at the head of the Gibraltar Brigade of the 2nd Corps (it includes the 4th Ohio Infantry) went in and drove the enemy, captured colors, and made himself a beau ideal hero.[96] The Army of the Potomac loves Hooker as it never loved McClellan. He is our man and must lead us. About noon the battle lulled again and there was no more fighting save picket skirmishing.

The Rebels meant to drive us into the river and failed. We had held our position and beaten them back. For three days and nights our regiment was kept under arms, and often was summoned to arms expecting to go out and meet the enemy. Rebel bullets would sometimes come rattling about our ears in our bivouac. On Tuesday evening a cold, chilling rain set in. Our clothes were saturated with water, yet we could have no fire. I sank upon the ground and slept but soon awoke shaking as though I had an ague. When the morning dawned cold, damp, and cheerless, we were tramping through the mud on our way back to the left bank of the Rappahannock. On Wednesday evening we reached one of the old cantonments of our army near where I am now writing. How it rained! There was no room to lie down, so I sat by the fire and nodded the night away. Next day we went into camp where I now write and that night I had the first good night's sleep I had had for 11 days.

Our troops never fought better than they did in the battles I have been describing. I speak of the army generally. To any who inquire after Captain Purdy, please give the circumstances of his death as I have detailed them. He was a brave man, a true patriot, and a fast friend. If at any future time it can be done, I will endeavor to secure his body and have it sent to his friends if they desire it. The citizens of Delaware ought to give him a monument.

Years later, General Howard wrote that when the attack came, "I heard the first murmuring of a coming storm- a little quick firing on the picket line, the wild rushing of frightened game into our very camps and almost sooner than it can be told, the bursting of thousands of Confederates through the almost impenetrable thickets of the wilderness, and then the wilder, noisier conflict which ensued. It was a terrible gale! I could see numbers of our men, not the few stragglers that always fly like chaff at the first breeze, but scores of them rushing into the opening, some with arms, some without, running or falling before they got behind the cover of Devens' reserves and before

---

[96] This story appears to be a mix of camp rumor and fact; General Joseph Hooker had been knocked senseless early in the battle on May 3, 1863, but the men of Hooker's old division under the command of General William French, including the Gibraltar Brigade led by Colonel Samuel S. Carroll, succeeded in driving off a Confederate attack and freeing portions of two Zouave regiments that had been captured on May 2. Moreover, Private Thomas McLaren of Co. E, 4th Ohio Volunteer Infantry captured a set of colors with "Williamsburg" and "Seven Pines" inscribed upon them during this engagement. "The 4th Ohio in the Battle of Chancellorsville," *Harding County Republican,* May 15, 1863, pg.2 The key point of Lee's comment remains consistent for the remainder of his correspondence- he continued to hold General Hooker in high regard throughout the war.

General Schurz's waiting masses could deploy or charge. The noise and smoke filled the air with excitement, and to add to it, Dieckmann's guns and caissons, with battery men scattered, rolled and tumbled like runaway wagons and carts in a thronged city." Howard's horse became uncontrollable, and the general was unceremoniously thrown to the ground.[97] Reserve batteries, most notably Hubert Dilger's Battery I, 1st Ohio Light Artillery, deployed and were soon shelling the Plank Road and the woods, right over the heads of the retreating troops from the First Division. Corporal Sidney S. Allen of the battery recalled that "our battery took position and did nobly- not a man left his post. We stayed until our infantry were all gone and the Rebels were within ten rods of us. We sweetened them nicely with canister. Captain Dilger took my gun out into the road and I kept it clear, for as often as they would fill it up, it was cleared with a few rounds of canister. General Schurz came up and inquired what gun came down the road. The captain told him, and he came and shook hands with all of the men. He said he never saw such determined bravery in his life."[98]

The 82nd Ohio, upon orders from General Schurz, fell back into the rifle pits near Dowdall's Tavern and opened fire on the approaching Rebels. "Our officers obeyed every command, and gave the commands without the least excitement, appearing as cool when the destructive missiles of the enemy thinned our ranks as though they were miles away from danger," wrote one veteran. "We took position on the extreme right of the regiment, fully determined to hold any position assigned to us, and the whole regiment felt fully as determined as we did. We held our position in the rifle pits until the Rebels had us hemmed in on both of our flanks and if we remained two minutes longer, we would all have been taken prisoners."[99] Yet, it was not the isolated determined stands of units like the 82nd Ohio or Battery I that would be reported in the press- it was the panic.

Before the Army of the Potomac had even settled back into its camps near Falmouth, news of the disgrace of the 11th Corps on May 2nd was front page news. The *New York Daily Tribune* led the charge with an account from their special correspondent "J.R. Sypher." The relevant portion of this article, presented below, set the stage for a page four editorial that lambasted the "dishonored" 11th Corps:

> It was now about 5 o'clock in the afternoon and thus far all the movements undertaken had been successfully executed. Suddenly, a most firm and heavy charge was made on the right flank and rear of Howard's corps. Regiments, brigades, and divisions broke and fled in the most terrible confusion. One brigade alone fought bravely until to attempt longer to hold a position would have been madness, then it stubbornly withdrew. The casualties among the men were slight. Thirteen pieces of artillery were left to the enemy; most of them by some unaccountable accident were spiked. The retreating train, the withdrawal of the artillery, and the jumbled and confused mass of stragglers and frightened soldiery that blocked the roads and occupied the fields and woods produced a degree of confusion that was truly alarming. The enemy,

Chancellorsville

"When the firing began, we were eating our supper but we soon stopped that and took place in line of battle. The Rebels were so much stronger than we that they drove our pickets at once, and Schimmelfennig's brigade retreated in great disorder. These men rushed through our brigade, which was then exposed to a most galling fire. The 119th stood well against great odds, until they saw old regiments break and run right through them, when it was impossible to keep them in line. They broke and retreated by companies, slowly though not in good order. Rally them we could not. I got a little group around the colors, but when the boys who had never been under fire before saw the others running, they could not be kept together."

~ Adjutant Theodore A. Dodge, 119th New York Infantry

---

[97] Howard, Battles and Leaders, op. cit., and Howard, op. cit., pg. 370

[98] "From Battery I, 1st O.V.A.," *Portage County Democrat (Ohio),* May 20, 1863, pg. 3

[99] "Army Correspondence- From the 82nd Ohio Regiment," *Hardin County Republican,* June 5, 1863, pg. 1

flushed with a most brilliant success, came rushing forward toward the rear of the right and center with yells and cheers that made the air hideous with ill-omened sounds.[100]

Horace Greeley, editor of the *Tribune*, laid the blame for the failed campaign squarely at the feet of the men of the 11th Corps, stating that if "the 11th Corps had held its ground, the defeat and destruction of Jackson would have been inevitable, but when they fled, it became necessary to recall Sickles and the whole maneuver was foiled. Gen. Howard who commanded it is a brave and skillful general, but neither his efforts nor those of Gen. Devens and Gen. Schurz could arrest the panic. We trust that swift justice will overtake the regiments that broke; that if it be deemed too rigid to shoot them all, they may at least be decimated and then dissolved."[101]

The competing *New York Herald* was equally denunciatory if more colorful in its description of the disaster. Correspondent T.M. Cook wrote that "when an overwhelming body of the enemy fell upon our right flank with a violence that we were unable to withstand, the 11th Corps broke in confusion under this attack and fled from the field in a panic, nearly effecting the total demoralization of the entire army." Cook's confused account of the battle drew a vivid picture of the panicked stampede of the "flying Germans" and bears inclusion here as these stories helped to stoke the fire of controversy which followed:

> Headed by their commander, the gallant Howard, the German corps charged boldly up to the Rebel lines. Here they were met as the Rebels always meet their foe with shouts of defiance and derision, a determined front, and a heavy fire of musketry. The German regiments returned the fire for a short time with spirit, but at a time when all encouragement to the men was needed that could be given, some officer of the division fell back to the rear leaving his men to fight alone. At the same time, General Devens was unhorsed and badly wounded in his foot by a musket ball. Thus losing at a critical moment the inspiring influence of the immediate presence of their commanders, the men began to falter, then to fall back, and finally broke in complete rout. The men were panic stricken and no power on earth could rally them in the face of the enemy.

> I must confess that I have no ability to do justice to the scene that followed. It was my lot to be in the center of the field when the panic burst upon us. May I never be a witness to another such scene. On the one hand was a solid column of infantry retreating at the double quick in the face of the enemy who was already crowding their rear; on the other hand was a dense mass of beings who had lost their reasoning faculties and were flying from a thousand fancied dangers as well as from the real danger that crowded so close upon them, aggravating the fearfulness of their situation by the very precipitancy with which they were seeking to escape from it. On the hill were 10,000 of the enemy, pouring their murderous volleys upon us, yelling and hooting to increase the alarm and confusion; hundreds of cavalry horses, left riderless at the first discharge of the Rebels, were dashing frantically in all directions. A score of batteries of artillery were thrown into disorder, some properly manned and seeking to gain position for effective duty, and others flying from the field; battery wagons, ambulances, horses, men, cannon, caissons, all jumbled and tumbled together in an apparently inextricable mass, and that murderous fire still pouring in upon them.

> To add to the terror of the occasion there was but one means of escape from the field, and that through a little narrow neck or ravine washed out by Scott's Creek. Towards this the confused mass plunged headlong. For a moment it seemed as if no power could avert the frightful calamity that threatened the entire army. On came the panic stricken crowd, terrified artillery riders spurring and lashing their horses to their utmost, riderless horses dashing along regardless of obstacles; ambulances upsetting and being dashed to pieces against trees and stumps; men flying and crying with alarm, a perfect torrent of passion. But by the blockade of the main passage, the stampede of the artillery and the cavalry had principally been checked. Once halted, reason began to return to those who had previously lost it, and much of the artillery, properly manned, was quickly brought back upon the field.[102]

General Schurz noted that the period after Chancellorsville was one of the most trying periods of his service. "Every newspaper that fell into our hands told the world the frightful story of the unexampled misconduct of

---

[100] "From Hooker's Army," J.R. Sypher, *New York Daily Tribune*, May 6, 1863, pg. 1
[101] "Chancellorsville," *New York Daily Tribune*, May 6, 1863, pg. 4
[102] "Operations on Saturday," *New York Herald*, May 7, 1863, pgs. 3-4

the 11th Corps, how the 'cowardly Dutchmen' of that corps had thrown down their arms and fled at the first fire of the enemy, how my division led in the disgraceful flight without firing a shot, how these cowardly Dutch like a herd of frightened sheep had overrun the whole battlefield and come near stampeding other brigades or divisions, in short, the whole failure of the Army of the Potomac was owing to the scandalous poltroonery of the 11th Corps. We procured whatever newspapers we could obtain- newspapers from New York, Washington, Philadelphia, Boston, Pittsburgh, Cincinnati, Chicago, Milwaukee- the same story everywhere. I was thunderstruck."[103] General Schimmelfennig was the first to file an official protest, writing a caustic letter on May 10th to General Schurz demanding succor from the vicious criticisms of the press. "The officers and men of this brigade of your division, filled with indignation, come to me with newspapers in their hands, and ask if such be the rewards they may expect for the sufferings they have endured and the bravery they have displayed," he wrote. "The most infamous falsehoods have been circulated through the press…it would seem as if a nest of vipers had but waited for an auspicious moment to spit their poisonous slander upon this heretofore honored corps. I am an old soldier. To this hour, I have been proud to command the brave men of this brigade, but I am sure that unless these infamous falsehoods be retracted and reparations made, their good will and soldierly spirit will be broken. I demand that the miserable penny-a-liners who have slandered the division be excluded, by public order, from our lines and that the names of the originators of these slanders be made known to me and my brigade, that they may be held responsible for their acts."[104]

The newspaper criticism stung because there was a kernel of truth to the charge. The first units struck by Jackson's flank attack were of Brigadier General Charles Devens' First Division, consisting of Von Gilsa's brigade of the 41st New York (German), 45th New York (German), 54th New York (German), and 153rd Pennsylvania (German), while the five regiments of Brigadier General Nathaniel C. McLean's included the relatively new 17th Connecticut, three veteran Ohio regiments (25th, 55th, and 75th) that had distinguished themselves at Bald Hill and Chinn Ridge on August 30, 1862 at Second Bull Run, and the new 107th Ohio (German). Once they were struck in the flank, the entire Federal line in this sector collapsed as a result, but it was the flight of these predominately German units that became the commonly accepted narrative that was applied to the entire corps. Numerous letters were written to clarify that it was Devens' division that broke first; Schurz tried to persuade Howard then Secretary of War Edwin M. Stanton to publish his after action report to clear the names of his men, but to no avail. He even tried to appeal for a hearing before the Congressional Committee on the Conduct of the War, but received no response. "I found myself driven to the conclusion that there was in official circles a powerful influence seeking to prevent the disclosure of the truth; that a scapegoat was wanted and that the 11th Corps could plausibly be used as such a scapegoat."[105]

Major General Oliver O. Howard, soon after his return to camp, couldn't help but notice the damaging news coverage and the pronounced effect it had on the men of his command. He issued the following general order touching upon the recent disaster at Chancellorsville and expressing his confidence in the men:

Headquarters, Eleventh Army Corps, May 10, 1863
General Orders No. 9

As your commanding general, I cannot fail to notice a feeling of depression on the part of a portion of this corps. Some obloquy has been cast upon us on account of the affair of Saturday May 2. I believe that such a disaster might have happened to any other corps of this army and I do no mistrust my command. Every officer who failed to do his duty by not keeping his men together and not rallying them when broken is conscious of it and must profit by the past.

I confidently believe that every honorable officer and every brave man earnestly desires and opportunity to advance against the enemy and to demonstrate to the army and to the country that we are not wanting in principle or

---

[103] Schurz, Reminiscences, op. cit.
[104] Alexander Schimmelfennig, *Sandusky Commercial Register (Ohio)*, June 8, 1863, pgs. 1
[105] Schurz, Reminiscences, op. cit.

patriotism. Your energy, sustained and directed under the Divine blessing, shall yet place the Eleventh Corps ahead of them all.

O.O. Howard, Major General, commanding

But General Howard, outside of issuing this general order, took little action to clarify what happened at Chancellorsville or to accept his portion of the blame for the disaster- as a result of this silence, his soldiers laid the blame at his feet. It was clear what had happened, from the lowest private in the ranks to generals commanding divisions. Private Henry C. Hennery of the 55th Ohio refrained from naming the guilty party, but stated that "a decent respect for the truth would compel me to say that the impression was notoriously current all day Saturday that the enemy were trying to flank us, and that this impression was not founded on mere conjecture, but was the natural inference from the report of our pickets."[106] Corporal George W. Iden of the 25th Ohio complained that "General Howard made a poor display of generalship in my estimation, and in the estimation of all who had an opportunity of knowing. It is reported that General Sigel takes command of our corps again. It would afford universal satisfaction throughout the entire corps for all think well of Sigel as a general."[107] First Lieutenant Oscar D. Ladley of the 75th Ohio wrote that "we have, through the ignorance of our generals, suffered a complete surprise. I don't know who to blame, whether Hooker, Howard, Devens or who, but whosoever the fault it was they have brought disgrace to our troops."[108] Captain Barnet T. Steiner of the predominantly German 107th Ohio stated that "a great blunder was committed in leaving the right in such a weak condition, but it is not our province to attach the responsibility on any particular person."[109] One of his fellow officers in the 107th Ohio, writing under the pen name "Tuscarawas," wasn't shy about assigning blame to Howard. "General Howard must share its disgrace for to him belongs the generalship. He was warned by Colonel Lee and others that the Rebels were massing on his right. But like many others whose great military knowledge was gained at West Point, he would take no advice. A disgraced corps, a defeat, and the dishonor should be borne by him."[110]

Colonel John C. Lee of the 55th Ohio[111], who resigned his commission in the wake of Chancellorsville, declared that "there was no corps within the armies of Hooker's or Rosecrans that could withstand that attack, disposed as we were. Much has been said of the running of the 11th Corps. I am sorry to admit that there is some truth in it, but I am very sorry to know that there has been a great deal said in reference to it that is not true."[112] Lee claimed in 1885 that he and his men had witnessed Confederate troops moving west on multiple occasions during the day on May 2nd, and had tried to convince his brigade commander General McLean and his division commander Devens of the grave import of those sightings. Lee reported three times that he sent messages to both McLean and Devens indicating that infantry and artillery were moving toward their right flank, but the messages were ignored. On the third try, Lee insisted that action be taken. General Devens refused, stating that "it was not worthwhile to be scared before we are hurt." Lee soon was caught up in the attack that he had been warning all day was going to occur, and laid the blame for the rout on his superiors. "If the corps and army headquarters had the facts showing the impending attack that brigade and division headquarters had, then the responsibility rests there (Howard and Hooker). If not, then they ought to have been furnished these facts by the division commander (Devens). The rank

---

[106] "From the 55th Ohio," *Wooster Republican (Ohio)*, May 21, 1863, pg. 3
[107] "Twenty-Fifth Ohio Regiment," *St. Clairsville Gazette (Ohio)*, May 21, 1863, pg. 2
[108] Becker, Carl M. and Ritchie Thomas, editors. Hearth and Knapsack: The Ladley Letters, 1857-1880. Athens: Ohio University Press, 1988, pgs. 120-131
[109] "From the 107th Regiment," *Stark County Republican (Ohio)*, May 21, 1863, pg. 1
[110] "From the 107th Ohio Regiment," *Tuscarawas Advocate (Ohio)*, May 22, 1863, pg. 2
[111] Colonel Lee had temporarily led the First Brigade, First Division, 11th Corps during the battle when General McLean assumed divisional command in the wake of General Devens being wounded.
[112] "Speech of Col. Lee," *Tiffin Tribune (Ohio)*, June 5, 1863, pg. 4

and file of the 11th Corps are no more to be blamed for the rout than the pins in a bowling alley for falling when struck by the ball." [113]

Members of the non-German units quickly took to the papers to separate themselves from their German brigade mates, but the broad brush that painted the entire 11th Corps as a pack of cowards led to widespread grumbling throughout the army about the corps and its woebegone troops. One soldier of the 82nd Ohio wrote that "we have served under General Rosecrans in western Virginia, General Schenk, General Milroy, and General Sigel, and always had a good reputation, unsullied or unstained with any mean or cowardly acts, and now the 11th Corps is marked as cowards by Mr. Greeley. If Mr. Greeley and his reporter had been a little nearer to our regiment or the scene of action, they could then have perhaps noticed the conduct of our regiment, and not condemned the innocent with the guilty. Mr. Greeley is not gaining much good will by his remarks. It makes our boys feel bad after doing their very best and doing all that men could do to be pronounced fugitives." [114] Surgeon Gibboney Hoop of the 84th Pennsylvania spoke the common opinion of many soldiers of the Army of the Potomac when he wrote "our men behaved splendidly, except the 11th Corps. They broke on the right wing and disgraced themselves forever. May the devil pound them for their cowardly conduct." [115]

Interestingly, the defeat at Chancellorsville did not appear to impact overall troop morale as negatively as the debacle at Fredericksburg. Journalist William Swinton observed that at Chancellorsville General Hooker had been beaten, but not his army. "The rank and file were puzzled at the result of a battle in which they had been foiled without being fought, and caused to retreat without the consciousness of being beaten." [116] Historian Bruce Catton wrote that "actually the army was not in a bad way at all. It was not in the least demoralized, and if it was downhearted, the mood did not persist for long. Indeed in a remarkably short time the army settled back into its old routine." [117] A regular series of inspections and drills took place and soldiers resumed their illicit commerce with their erstwhile enemies across the Rappahannock, trading Yankee coffee for Confederate tobacco.

For the 11th Corps in the aftermath of Chancellorsville, however, the entire command structure was shuffled. As General Devens had been seriously wounded at the battle, command of the First Division was given to hard fighting 28 year old General Francis C. Barlow, while the First Brigade would continue to be led by Colonel Leopold von Gilsa (who Barlow had arrested shortly after taking command of the division) and the Second Brigade gained the competent General Adelbert Ames. General Nathaniel C. McLean who had led the Ohio brigade so well at Second Bull Run was shelved after Chancellorsville and given a desk assignment in Ohio under General Burnside. Hooker had found a want of fighting qualities in the division and the promotions of Barlow and Ames were an attempt to restore the fighting spirit found missing at Chancellorsville. The second division retained General von Steinwehr, but he gained two new brigade commanders. Colonel Charles R. Coster took over the First Brigade as Colonel Buschbeck went on leave; Colonel Orland Smith took command of the Second Brigade, formerly led by General Barlow. In Schurz's Third Division, the First Brigade would continue to be led by General Schimmelfennig. The 82nd Ohio was relieved from provost marshal duties and assigned to Colonel Wladimir Kryzyanowski's Second Brigade, serving alongside the 58th and 119th New York regiments, the 75th Pennsylvania, and the 26th Wisconsin. In the course of the reorganization, a few regiments were shuffled from brigade to brigade. To help better direct the field artillery, all of the batteries of the corps were removed from brigade control and placed into a separate artillery brigade, led by Major Thomas Osborn.

[113] Colonel John C. Lee, "Criminal Blundering at Chancellorsville," originally published March 19, 1885 in *National Tribune*; Cozzens, Peter, editor. Battle and Leaders of the Civil War, Vol. 6. Urbana: University of Illinois Press, 2004, pgs. 230-236

[114] "Army Correspondence-From the 82nd Ohio Regiment," *Hardin County Republican (Ohio)*, June 5, 1863, pg. 1

[115] "Army Correspondence," *Clearfield Republican (Pennsylvania)*, May 20, 1863, pg. 1

[116] Swinton, William. Campaigns of the Army of the Potomac. Secaucus: Blue & Grey Press, 1988, pg. 307

[117] Catton, Bruce. Glory Road: The Army of the Potomac. Garden City: Doubleday & Co., 1952, pgs. 214-215

General Howard's headquarters up to the early evening of May 2, 1863 at Chancellorsville was located at Dowdall's Tavern located near the center of this drawing by Alfred Waud. The troops of Colonel Adolphus Buschbeck's Brigade are depicted at rest along the Plank Road while the hint of smoke in the dim distance indicates that Jackson's flank attack had just begun. The 82nd Ohio fell back from their position at Hawkins' Farm to a line of slight breastworks near Dowdall's Tavern before being driven from the field. The 82nd Ohio's losses in this battle were not included in the official reports, but totaled roughly 81 men: 9 killed, 3 died of wounds, 48 wounded (6 of these were captured), and 21 captured or missing. (Library of Congress)

A war-weary Captain Alfred E. Lee in 1864; note the combined 11th and 12th Corps badge. (Larry M. Strayer Collection)

CHAPTER FIVE

Reminiscences of Gettysburg

"Now for the fight! Now for the cannon peal!
Forward through blood, and toil, and cloud, and fire,
Glorious the shout, the shock, the slash of steel,
The volley's roll, the rocket's blasting spire,
There was a lack of woman's nursing, there was a dearth of woman's tears"[118]

The Battle of Gettysburg was the supreme crisis of the war. All the circumstances under which it took place conspired at the time and will ever conspire to draw upon it the world's attention as the culminating point in the struggle. Everything was staked upon its issue. Had it resulted in a decisive defeat to the federal army, the National cause would, in all probability, have been lost. There was practically but one obstacle to prevent the Confederate army from going where and doing what it pleased, and that obstacle was the Army of the Potomac. Had that army been overwhelmed, New York, Philadelphia, Baltimore, and Harrisburg would have been in peril of seizure by the enemy, the national capital would have been isolated, and the national government captured or put to flight. All the great trunk line railways between east and west would have been broken up, and the fierce mobs already in preparation to resist the draft would have welcomed the triumphant Confederate host to all the principal seaboard cities.[119]

What would have saved the Union? Raw, undisciplined militia would have been of but little avail to resist the march of such an army as that of General Lee. That army had reached the summit of its power and prestige. It believed itself to be invincible. It was skillfully led, well equipped, and composed of such fighting material as only Americans seasoned and trained in war can make. Excepting the forts around Washington, there were no formidable artificial obstructions in its path. It was in a productive country, where it could subsist indefinitely. The armies of the West, even after the surrender of Vicksburg, could not have spared adequate help to resist it. Those armies, as was soon demonstrated at Chickamauga, had quite sufficient use for all their strength in their own field of operations. The success of Lee at Gettysburg would have freshly imparted a tremendous impetus to the secession movement.

On the other hand, the permanent ebb of that cause began with the repulse of Longstreet on Cemetery Ridge. The little coppice which Pickett aimed for, and beside which Armistead fell, was indeed "the high water mark of the Rebellion." From the moment the supreme effort failed on the afternoon of July 3, 1863 until the final collapse at Appomattox, the Confederacy steadily lost ground and, what was worse, lost heart, hope, and prestige. Its mightiest army, under its greatest leader, had done its utmost and failed; the entire North was fired anew with patriotic resolve and there was no reasonable hope left for the independence of the South. Had reason prevailed rather than pride and passion, the bloody logic of Gettysburg would have been accepted, and the war would have ended then and there.

---

[118] Lee is quoting from the Napoleonic-era poem "The Battle Hymn of the Berlin Landstrum" by the youthful German poet and soldier Karl Theodor Koerner. Koerner died of battle wounds at age 21 in 1813.

[119] The text of this chapter is a combination of Captain Lee's introduction to his book The Battle of Gettysburg written in 1888 while he was secretary of the Gettysburg Memorial Commission of Ohio, along with an article he wrote entitled "Reminiscences of Gettysburg" that was published on page 1 of the February 26, 1864 issue of the *Delaware Gazette*.

Viewed in its physical aspects, we are amazed at the magnitude and fierceness of the battle. Never was there a more tremendous shock of arms. Greater armies have fought each other, but the concentrated rush and grapple of force at Gettysburg were perhaps unequaled. The fight continued three days and nights; its theater covered a space of 25 square miles and when it ended nearly 50,000 men lay dead or wounded on the field. Nearly 5,000 horses were slaughtered in the conflict.

Forests through which the rage of battle blazed were struck dead as by fire, and fields and hilltops were plowed by hurricanes of shot and shell such as the eye of man had never before witnessed. Fighting as desperate took place afterwards in Grant's Wilderness campaigns, where the contending armies were for the most part hidden from each other by dense forests, but never was there such a prodigious duel as here between two armies in full sight of each other.

Gettysburg had been called the most dramatic battle of the war, and the arena in which it was fought was one well adapted to lend it scenic grandeur. The ancient Greeks, in constructing their open air theaters, were accustomed to place the

Major General Oliver O. Howard
(Library of Congress)

stage so as to bring some striking object into view as a suitable setting to the play. The chances of war contrived a like appropriate setting for the mighty tragedy, the issue of which was to be the life or death of this republic. The country around about Gettysburg has many striking and attractive features well worthy to be associated with some great historic event. Its wide reaches of luxuriant and variegated landscape, bounded by blue lines of distant mountains, are well adapted to kindle an artist's inspiration, or a soldier's heroism. The plains of Marathon or of Waterloo afforded no fitter theater than this upon which to arbitrate the world's destiny.

The topography of the battlefield is too familiar to the public to need any extended description. The town, or borough rather, from which it takes its name, itself lay within the whirlpool of the conflict. At first the National troops held it, then the Confederates having gained possession of it, stretched their lines of battle through its streets and General Lee (at one time) established his headquarters in its public square. Many of its buildings still bear traces of the battle. Westward from the town, the South Mountain Range, ten miles distant from its nearest point, comes up from the southwest and trends away to the northeast. Two outlying ridges extend in the same general direction, one of them less than a mile west of the town, and the other just east and south of it. Upon the western ridge stands the Lutheran Theological Seminary, and upon the eastern lies the village cemetery. The one height is therefore known as Seminary Ridge, and the other as Cemetery Ridge. The highest point on the first named is known as Oak Hill, and the highest on the other is a bold promontory, directly overlooking the town, known as Cemetery Hill. These two eminences stand about one mile asunder. Half a mile west of Seminary Ridge, Willoughby Run courses between the two other ridges less commanding.

Following Cemetery Ridge south of the town, we soon reach a small oak forest- much larger at the time of the battle than it is now- known as Ziegler's grove. Beyond the grove for the distance of a mile the ridge is quite commanding, and affords very fine views over the country to the westward, bounded in the distance by the South Mountain Range. Further on the ridge descends to the marshy basin of Plum Run, beyond which it reappears, and terminates in two steep granite peaks, separated from each other by a narrow ravine, and known as Round Top and Little Round Top. The loftiest and most distant of these peaks is Round Top, which rises to a height of 400 feet above the waters of Plum Run. East of Gettysburg and of Cemetery Hill, the ridge terminates in a precipitous, forest-covered height known as Culp's Hill, which is separated by the ravine of Rock Creek from another eminence known as Wolf's Hill.

The collision of the two armies on this field was an accident. Neither commander had planned to meet the other here. Each one hoped to fight in a defensive position, and each expected to choose his own ground for so doing, but neither of them seems to have thought of Gettysburg in this connection, or to have been at all acquainted with the country thereabouts. The advance columns of the Confederate army had approached the Susquehanna and were about to move on Harrisburg when they were given pause by General Hooker's menaces upon their line of communications in the Cumberland Valley. To checkmate any movement of Hooker's in that direction, General Lee determined to cross over the mountains to the east, and throw himself upon the broad open highways to Philadelphia and Baltimore. In this way he hoped to compel the National army to defend its own line of communications, or to uncover Washington and fight, perhaps, at the gates of Baltimore or Philadelphia. Accordingly on the 29th of June, he gave orders which, if carried out, would have concentrated the whole Confederate army at Cashtown, on the eastern slope of South Mountain, ten miles from Gettysburg.

The itinerary of the campaign prior to this time may be briefly stated: on the 1st of June the armies of General Hooker and General Lee confronted each other along the Rappahannock, in the vicinity of Falmouth and Fredericksburg. Their positions were those assumed directly after the Battle of Chancellorsville. On the 3rd, Lee, leaving A.P. Hill's corps to watch and detain Hooker, started the corps of Ewell and Longstreet on their northward march via Culpeper. Longstreet reached Culpeper on the 7th and Ewell arrived there also on the 9th. Stuart's cavalry (9,500 strong with 30 guns) was at Fleetwood Hill near Brandy Station. On the 5th, Hooker directed a reconnaissance by the 6th Corps of which Howe's division crossed below Fredericksburg and encountered Hill's corps in position. On the 7th Hooker ordered a reconnaissance towards Culpeper by the cavalry, now under General Alfred Pleasanton. On the 9th, Pleasanton supported by two brigades of infantry (Ames' and Russell's) encountered Stuart at Fleetwood and, after a severe action, had to withdraw but not without unmasking Lee's movement. General Hooker now proposed to cross the Rappahannock and move on Richmond, but President Lincoln demurred, telling him that Lee's army and not Richmond was his "true objective point." Hooker therefore began shifting his army to the right and rear, corresponding to the movements of his adversary. Placing General John Reynolds in command of his right wing (comprising the 1st, 3rd, and 11th Corps and the cavalry), he directed him to proceed with it along the line of the Orange & Alexandria Railroad towards Manassas. This movement began on the 12th, on which date the 11th Corps, marching from Brook's Station on the Aquia Creek Railroad arrived at Catlett's Station. The 3rd Corps at the same time took position at Rappahannock Station, and the 1st Corps at Bealton.

Meanwhile Ewell's corps, comprising three divisions and 20 batteries and preceded by two brigades of cavalry under Jenkins and Imboden, having quit Culpeper on the 10th, pushed rapidly northward via Sperryville and Flint Hill, crossed the Blue Ridge at Chester Gap, and on the 12th penetrated the Shenandoah Valley at Front Royal. With two divisions, Early's and Johnson's, Ewell moved from Front Royal directly to Winchester while Rodes' division pushed ahead via Berryville towards Martinsburg. At this time General Robert H. Milroy was in command in the valley under General Robert C. Schenk as department commander at Baltimore. Milroy's force comprised 7,000 effectives of which one brigade, under Colonel McReynolds, was at Berryville.

Unadvised of and not suspecting Lee's movement, Milroy withdrew McReynolds from the path of Rodes but remained at Winchester, where he was surprised and virtually surrounded by Ewell on the 14th, and lost most of his command in killed, wounded, and captives. On the evening of the same day Rodes attacked the small garrison under Colonel Tyler at Martinsburg, and obliged it to fall back to Harper's Ferry. Pursuing Milroy's fugitives, Jenkins crossed the Potomac at Williamsport on the 14th and on the 16th entered Chambersburg. At the same time

Imboden, advancing from Romney, seized and broke up the Baltimore & Ohio Railroad and on the 17th occupied Cumberland. Awaiting the arrival of Longstreet and Hill, Ewell's three divisions remained at Williamsport and south to Winchester until the 19th, Rodes' division being at Williamsport.

Quitting Culpeper on the 15th, Longstreet moved along the eastern base of the Blue Ridge, crossing it at Snicker's Gap, he neared Winchester on the 19th. This movement was covered by Stuart's cavalry, keeping to the right and falling into frequent combats with Pleasonton's troopers while endeavoring, though not successfully, to dispute with them the passes of the Bull Run Mountains. Most notable among these combats were those at Aldie on the 17th, at Middleburg on the 19th, and at Upperville on the 21st, in all of which the Confederates were worsted. Forcing back Stuart, Pleasonton's squadrons gained the summit of the Blue Ridge and from thence observed the movements of Lee's whole army down the valley.

Admonished by Ewell's advance on Winchester, Hooker, on the 13th, put the 2nd, 5th, and 12th Corps in motion northward, and A.P. Hill, being thus relieved from further necessity of watching the Rappahannock, immediately set out upon the track of Ewell to rejoin Lee. General Hooker now kept his army well in hand, covering Washington and Baltimore. On the 22nd, the 11th and 12th Corps, supported by the 1st at Guilford, were on the line of Goose Creek near Leesburg, the 5th Corps was at Aldie, and the 2nd Corps was at Hopewell and Thoroughfare Gaps, supported by the 3rd Corps at Gum Springs. Pleasonton's cavalry, having withdrawn to Aldie, covered the approaches to Leesburg.

Having concentrated his army on the banks of the Potomac, Lee now gave it the signal to advance into Maryland and Pennsylvania. Ewell's corps, of which Johnson's division had already been posted at Sharpsburg, led off with instructions to move on Harrisburg. On the 24th and 25th, A.P. Hill's corps crossed the Potomac at Shepherdstown and Longstreet's at Williamsport, and on the 27th united their columns at Chambersburg. Taking with him the divisions of Johnson and Rodes, Ewell pushed rapidly up the Cumberland Valley and reached Carlisle on the 27th, while Early, to cover the flank in the absence of Stuart's cavalry, kept further to the right with instructions to move on York, break up the Central Railroad, burn the Susquehanna bridge at Wrightsville, and rejoin Ewell at Carlisle. Early reached Greenwood and Gettysburg on the 26th, Berlin on the 27th and York and Wrightsville on the 28th. On the 27th, Jenkins, preceding Ewell's column, arrived at Kingston, from whence he advanced, skirmishing, within three and four miles of Harrisburg. Gordon's brigade, which advanced to Wrightsville, intended to cross the Susquehanna at that point, and move by the left bank on Harrisburg, but was thwarted by the Pennsylvania militia which fired the bridge and destroyed it. On the 29th, Hill was at Fayetteville with two divisions of his corps, the remaining division (Heth's) being thrown forward from Cashtown. On the same day Longstreet moved from Chambersburg to Greenwood, leaving behind him Pickett's

Second Winchester

"The Rebels were posted in the woods and in a railroad cut while we were in the open field in the road. Our regiment was in the advance and charged on their batteries three different times and drove them from their guns twice, but had to fall back. It was one continual war of musketry for nearly two hours as grape shot flew as thick as hail. It seemed to me that every man in our regiment would fall, but Colonel William T. Wilson sat on his horse as coolly as if it was nothing but rain or hail."

"After fighting this way for an hour or more, Col. Ely hoisted the white flag and surrendered. It was grinding for Colonel Wilson and the rest of us to surrender to the ragged Rebels, but there was no help as we were by this time surrounded by some 30,000 Rebels."

~ *Private Robert N. McConnell, Co. F, 123rd Ohio Volunteer Infantry* division to guard the trains. Early's division had meanwhile been recalled from Carlisle to join in the intended advance, in force, on Harrisburg, and on the 30th encamped near Heidlersburg.

Adjusting himself to Lee's movement, General Hooker led his entire army across the Potomac at Edward's Ferry and grouped it around Middletown and Frederick. The 1st, 3rd, and 11th Corps comprising the left wing, crossed on the 25th, the remaining corps with the cavalry on the 26th and 27th. The 12th Corps, under General Slocum, proceeded to Knoxville within three miles of Harper's Ferry, with instructions to unite with the garrison there in following closely upon Lee's rear, and severing his communications with Virginia. With his army thus concentrated and the South Mountain defiles in his possession, General Hooker was prepared to precipitate his entire force into the Cumberland Valley, in support of Slocum, or to continue his movement northward along the eastern base of the mountain as circumstances might require. Upon learning that the enemy was at York and Carlisle he determined, says Doubleday, "to throw out his different corps in a fan shape toward the Susquehanna, and advance in that direction with three corps on the left to defend that flank, in case Longstreet and Hill should turn east, instead of keeping on toward the north. At the same time it was his intention to have Slocum follow up Lee's advance by keeping in his rear, to capture his trains and couriers, and to cut off his retreat should he be defeated."

In the meantime, the governor of Pennsylvania had issued a proclamation calling out 60,000 militia to assist in defending the state. To organize and command this force, and the new Department of the Susquehanna, General Darius Couch was taken from the command of the 2nd Army Corps, which thereupon devolved upon General Winfield Scott Hancock. Hooker requested that Couch should be subordinated to his own direction, and that the garrison at Harper's Ferry should be withdrawn from that post- which it was no longer important to defend- and added to the active forces in the field. Both these requests being denied by General Halleck, General Hooker, deeming his plans thwarted, asked to be relieved of his command which, by direction, he transferred on June 28th to General George G. Meade, then commanding the 5th Corps.[120] Couch's department was at once subordinated to Meade, who was also permitted (although Hooker had been forbidden) to withdraw the Harper's Ferry garrison to Frederick.

General Meade affirmed that he was not aware of Hooker's plans. However that may be, he decided to move forward at once on the main line from Frederick to Harrisburg, extending the wings of his army on both sides as far as consistent with rapid concentration, and intending to continue this movement until the enemy should be obliged to turn from the Susquehanna and give battle. Accordingly on the 29th of June, the Army of the Potomac, directed by its new commander, resumed its march and spread its moving columns out like a fan with Buford's cavalry on the left, Gregg's on the right, and Kilpatrick's in advance.

The 1st and 11th Corps, being the vanguard of the army, reached Emmitsburg on the evening of June 29th. Previous to that date the movements and whereabouts of the enemy were to us a profound secret. There were faint rumors that Stuart's cavalry was ravaging the Cumberland Valley, but beyond this we knew little.[121] At midnight of the 30th, a mounted orderly galloped to Colonel James S. Robinson's quarters and delivered a message. It was manifest from his hurried manner that he brought marching orders. Accordingly, Sergeant Major Jasper S. Snow soon came around warning us to be up betimes and be ready for an early movement. It was not, however, until 8 A.M. that the regiments had filed out of their camps into the road and were well on the march. It was understood that we were going to Gettysburg 11 miles distant. Many of the men were nearly barefoot, but all were cheerful and each one ready and anxious to perform his part in driving the invading traitors from loyal soil. At 10 A.M. we crossed the

---

[120] Hooker's disappointment is evident in the farewell address he issued to the army on June 28, 1863. "Impressed with the belief that my usefulness as the commander of the Army of the Potomac is impaired, yet I part from it with the deepest emotion. Sorrow of parting with comrades of so many battles is relieved by the conviction that the courage and devotion of this army will never cease nor fail."

[121] General Schurz remembered that the men of his division camped around St. Joseph's College, a young ladies' school carried on by a religious order. Schurz requested permission to use one of the buildings for divisional headquarters, and one of his officers began to play the organ in the chapel "which he did to the edification of all who heard him. The conduct of my troops camped around the institution was exemplary," Schurz proudly remembered. "We enjoyed there as still and restful a night as if the outside of the nunnery had been as peaceful as daily life was ordinarily within it." Schurz, Reminiscences, Vol. 3, op. cit., pg. 3

Brigadier General Wladimir Krzyzanowski
(Library of Congress)

line separating Maryland from Pennsylvania. The regiments from the latter state greeted the "Old Keystone" with enthusiastic cheers, their drums and colors saluting and bands playing.

At 11 A.M. the distant and ominous booming of artillery gave us our first intimation that we were in the vicinity of the enemy. The dull and occasional thunder sounded directly in advance and told us plainer than words of what we were approaching. But its influence upon the soldiers was far from depressing. On the contrary, I never knew them to be so confident and cheerful on the eve of battle. Those inclined to straggle were shamed out of it, and the provost guard was commended for driving forward the cowardly at the point of the bayonet. The column pressed forward with alacrity and without halting. The cannonading grew louder and more frequent. Pale and anxious looking women, whose solemn countenances plainly indicated what their hearts were too full to express, stood by the roadside giving drink and food to the hurrying soldiers who could snatch them and go on.[122]

At length reaching the crest of a plateau, a wide undulating plain unfolded itself to our view. It was the amphitheater in which was about to be enacted the greatest tragedy since Wagram and Austerlitz. About one mile in front at the foot of the plateau, the town of Gettysburg loomed up in the dull, vapory atmosphere. Just beyond it, dense puffs of white smoke indicated where the Cerberean mastiffs whose baying we had heard, were executing the prologue to great drama. At this moment a heavy shower of rain began to fall which dangerously dampened our muskets and cartridges. By the time we had entered the village, however, the rain had entirely ceased and the air had become pleasantly cool. The town was in a tumult of excitement. The heavy trains of the infantry, the rumbling and rushing of the artillery carriages hurrying to the front, the clanging of sabers, the clatter of horses' hooves, the gleaming of arms, the sweaty, excited countenances of the troops, the shouts of command, and the booming of the deep-throated guns made up a scene whose vivid picture will burn upon thousands of memories to the end of life.

The column was not allowed a moment's rest, but hurried through the town as fast as it could walk. Groups of men and women, stood showering upon us their benedictions. The prattling child joined the young maiden and the trembling matron in waving "God bless you" to the troops. On the far side of the village we met the cavalry just returned from the front. They brought news that the gallant General Reynolds had baptized the soil of his native

---

[122] General Schurz had ordered the division forward on the double quick upon receiving a dispatch from General Howard reporting that the 1st Corps was engaged at Gettysburg. Along the road, the troops met fugitives from the town. "I remember especially a middle-aged woman who tugged a small child by the hand and carried a large bundle on her back," remembered Schurz. "She tried to stop me, crying out at the top of her voice: 'Hard times at Gettysburg! They are shooting and killing! What will become of us?" Schurz, op. cit., pg. 5

state with his blood, and had perished almost within the atmosphere of his home. Yet they gave encouraging accounts of skirmishing and were enthusiastic over a wild rumor that a whole brigade of Rebels had been captured.

Filing from the road into the open fields beyond the town, the brigade immediately took its position. The regiments being hastily formed into double columns, ours was put in the rear in support of one of the batteries that was now vigorously playing upon the enemy. The Rebels replied no less vigorously, and the shot and shell plunged wildly over the fields. Just as we halted in our position a poor fellow was knocked flat upon the earth by a cannon shot, which nearly severed his leg from his body. Soon another was struck and the regiment shifted slightly its position. An order was then given to call the rolls, and amid the roar of artillery, each man gave his unfaltering answer "here." And there many a one who so answered, now lies where he fell, with his face to the foe.

The enemy could be plainly perceived forming his evolutions along the slope of a series of elevations that skirted the western border of the landscape. The columns of the 1st Corps appeared on our left front, moving gradually to the attack. Soon the random shots cracked spitefully; then came the crashing volleys, and in a few minutes the Rebels were seen running like frightened sheep. A loud cheer followed this success and officers who watched the maneuver through their glasses declared that we were getting along swimmingly. But the enemy had strong reserves and soon rallied. In fact, it began to be suspected that we were being dallied with by a greater superior force with the design of decoying the left wing of the army beyond supporting distance that the right might be circumvented and overwhelmed. The suspicion soon grew into a positive belief: for the captain of the skirmishers on our right front, hastened back with the news that the enemy in heavy masses was endeavoring to turn our right flank. The ground was admirably adapted for this, a ravine circling in that direction masked the movement.[123]

This piece of news was at once communicated to the general (Krzyzanowski). It made his face grow pale and distressed. It was apparent to his mind that a great crisis had come- that the enemy must be met at once and that he must be met halfway and in the open plain. Accordingly the brigade was ordered to change front, which was done in splendid style, the regiments moving in double columns. A general advance of the line through the open fields now began. The fences obstructing the way, the soldiers were ordered to "take hold of them" and in a twinkling of an eye, they were levelled with the ground. The enemy's batteries completely swept the plain from two or three different directions. The shells and shot howled, shrieked, and plunged through the air like infuriate demons. There was no shelter, not even a stump or tree. Grandly the line swept on in almost perfect order. Now a huge iron nugget plowed its way through the living mass, leaving in its track eight poor fellows torn and bleeding. The deadly thug and a submissive groan or two is all that is heard- the gaps are closed and the heroes of the Peninsula and the Rappahannock move on with a steadiness worthy of Napoleon's Old Guard.

Confederate View

"After advancing to within a half mile of the town, we discovered the enemy on our right flank and within a short distance of the right of this regiment, the right having just reached the road. The enemy came up within 30 to 40 yards of us. As soon as it was discovered that we were flanked, we made a wheel to the right , faced the new foe, and began to fire on him. Thus checked in his movement, he faced us and opened a severe fire upon is. We soon charged over two fences, across the turnpike, under a raking fire from some batteries near the edge of the town, firing grape at us as we crossed the road. But nothing seemed able to stand the impetuosity of our men. Immediately after crossing the road, we put to rout the party that flanked us. In this engagement, we lost 10 killed, 48 wounded, and 9 missing."

~ *Major William H. Peebles, 44th Georgia Infantry*

---

[123] The 82nd Ohio was arrayed opposite the 44th Georgia Infantry of General Doles' brigade, the same brigade that had spearheaded the Confederate flank attack at Chancellorsville roughly two months before and the same that had battled the 82nd Ohio in the rifle pit near Dowdall's Tavern. The results of this fight at Gettysburg proved remarkably similar to that of Chancellorsville.

Again and again the jagged fragments of iron sweep destructively through the ranks, but there is no wavering- no backs turned to the advancing foe.

The gray lines of the Rebels now began to be unmasked from the ravine and to push steadily up to the level surface of the plain. Their crimson banners surmounted by the blue cross containing the cabalistic stars of treason floated saucily in the air and seemed to challenge combat. On they came, one line after another, in confident array. Our troops now steadily deployed and the firing, hitherto reserved, began. Quick as thought the bullets swept by, and one after another, strong men toppled over and stretched upon the green turf. Each instant someone fell or went to the rear wounded. The combatants approached each other until they were hardly 75 yards apart. No obstacle intervening to shelter or hinder either party.

The firing grew terrific. Both parties fought with the obstinacy of desperation. The ground became strewn with the helpless wounded and the dead. It seemed that not a man could survive the withering leaden storm except by a miracle. The line became dreadfully thinned, yet there were no reserves at hand. Many of the dampened muskets could not be discharged, and the excited soldier rammed in load upon load. Fiercer and faster came the pitiless volleys, gathering momentum from the closing masses of the enemy. It was impossible to maintain the ground against such odds. The thinned and broken line was ordered to fall back towards the town. The enemy was too much crippled to charge, but maintained a sweeping fire under which the troops made the best of their way back to the heights east of Gettysburg. Here they rallied under the protection under the reserves and held the Rebels at bay until the arrival of the main body of the army. But such a retreat could not be executed except at a fearful loss. For a distance of half a mile, the plain was strewn with mangled victims of the fray. Scores of men in an agony of pain cried for water and for help. It was enough to make the pitying heavens weep.

The enemy did not venture to charge, but maintained a severe fire, to which our response in the act of falling back was necessarily feeble. Forgetful that I had in my belt a good revolver, with five good loads in it, I picked up a musket and asked a soldier for a cartridge. He gave me one, remarking as he did so that he did not think it would 'go,' as his ammunition had been dampened by the morning rain. My next impulse was to load the musket and get at least one parting shot at the enemy. While I was thus engaged, a poor fellow dropped at my side. "Oh, help me," he cried. Giving him my hand, he struggled to rise, but could not. He sank back again and with a look of utter despair, he exclaimed "Oh, I'm gone, leave me." The bullets came fiercer and faster reaping a rich harvest of death, and drenching the green sward with crimson. Success seemed to intoxicate the merciless foe, and he followed with infuriate yells. It was not long until I, too, felt the sting of a bullet and felt numb with pain. It was a sudden singular metamorphosis from strength and vigor to utter helplessness. Calling to the nearest man for assistance, he answered by a convulsive grasp at the spot where a bullet at that moment struck him. He passed on, limping as he went, and in a moment more the last blue blouse had disappeared and the field was alive with hooting Rebels. The cannonading was yet active and the unexploded shells ricocheted in dances across the plain. The influence of pain was not sufficient to entirely dispel a wounded man's anxiety in regard to their unwholesome pranks. But there was no alternative but to lie still and take the chances.

The musketry firing having slackened, the enemy's line of battle advanced in fine style preceded at a few paces by skirmishers. The crimson flags floated in the air more saucily than ever and the entire Rebel personnel breathed the language of impertinence. One of our wounded soldiers, rising upon his elbow to ease his aching pain, a curly monster dressed in gray hurled at him the most bitter curses. With his musket at a ready the brute ordered him at once to lie down or he would shoot him dead, accompanying the threat with the vilest epithets. The helpless soldier obeyed the inhuman mandate and sank back upon the turf where, in a few hours afterward, his brave and noble spirit left its mangled clay. The line of Rebel skirmishers now passed me and I was within the hated dominion of the traitors. One of them, a young fellow whose countenance betokened mildness, approached. He had picked up the sword of one of our disabled officers and carried it swinging from the belt which was thrown over his neck. To the inquiry, whether the wounded would be molested by his companions in arms, he replied, "No, you need not be afraid. Ten minutes ago, I myself would have shot you in a minute, but now a prisoner, you will not be disturbed." Taking my revolver, he passed on.

The Rebel infantry now faced by their right flank and moved off in a direction perpendicular to that by which they had been approaching. Looking about, I discovered my friend Lieutenant Stowel L. Burnham lying a few

Gettysburg

"While in this position one of my sergeants rode up to me and stated that a wounded Federal officer was lying near the battery, and had expressed a wish to see me. General Early heard this, and in a kind manner said to me; "Go back and see what he wants." I did so, found lying between one of my caissons and a gun, a Federal officer (Captain Alfred E. Lee). I got off my horse, told him I was captain of the battery, and wished to know what he wanted. He stated to me in a manly way that he was helpless from the effect of his wound, and asked me to remove him to a place of safety. I immediately said to him "Certainly, that shall be done." Four of my men took him up and laid him in the corner of the fence nearby. I rode over to where he was, and had some conversation with him. I raised his head and placed his overcoat under it to make him more comfortable. At this he expressed much surprise, and intimated that he did not expect such kindness from a Confederate soldier. I remonstrated with him for such a sentiment. He had on a handsome pair of field glasses, which he offered to me. At first I declined them, reminding him of General Lee's strict orders in regard to such things. He insisted, however, that I should take them, saying that they would be a temptation on account of their value for some Federal or Confederate who might pass by, to knock him in the head. I at last accepted the glasses as a present."
~ *Captain James McDowell Carrington, Charlottesville Artillery Battery*

yards beyond. "Is that indeed you, lieutenant?" But he hardly gave me the look of recognition when a Rebel battery came up at a brisk canter and unlimbered its guns upon the ground where we lay.[124] They seemed about to commence firing upon the town through which our troops were now retreating. Fearing the shots that would be fired by our batteries in return as well as the trampling of the horses attached to the caissons, I requested the cannoneers to remove me. Two of them kindly complied, and very gently placed me under the shade of a shrub, in the corner of a fence. They then brought poor Lieutenant Burnham who had received two or three frightful wounds and laid him close by me. His sufferings were indescribable. "Oh this is terrible, terrible," he groaned. The Rebel artillerymen spoke with sympathy to him and their browned faces evinced sincere compassion. They endeavored to arrange for him an easy posture, but in vain; all were painful. They gave him water to quench his feverish thirst, but it only served as an emetic. Singularly thoughtful, they brought a testament which a soldier had dropped upon the field. He opened it and tried to read, but the distracted torment of his wounds would not permit it. "Oh, I cannot," said he despondingly, and the book fell at his side.

It was now 5 P.M. The artillerymen were summoned away and the columns of Rebel infantry quietly filed off to their different stations in front of Gettysburg. Our troops having taking position on Cemetery Hill, the enemy chose to postpone his assault. A comparative calm settled over the field, where the whirlwind of battle had so lately arisen and spent itself. Save the ceaseless moaning of the wounded, mingled with their frantic cries for water and assistance, there was little to disturb the stillness of the evening air. Here and there a Rebel soldier sauntered around, either from curiosity or in quest of plunder, or perhaps, occasionally one more humane, cooling feverish lips with water from his canteen and saying with looks of pity how sorry he was that "you'uns were all out here against us this way."

Lieutenant Burnham seemed to have not a moment's rest from his excruciating agony. I asked him where he was wounded, and he said in the bowels. This was his mortal wound. He also had a severe wound in the thick part of one of his thumbs. I think he also had a wound in his legs. The Rebels were very kind to us. They gave us water and whiskey from their canteens, but the adjutant could not get anything to stay in his stomach. As often as he drank anything he vomited. He begged piteously that some surgeon would come and do something, anything that might ease him or his dreadful pain. The clammy dews were upon him and he was now plainly sinking. "I shall die," he said "and oh that I might escape this

---

[124] This battery was the Charlottesville (Virginia) Artillery led by Captain James McDowell Carrington.

Gravestone for Adjutant Stowel L. Burnham in North Windham, Connecticut.
"How sleep the brave who sink to rest, with all their country's wishes blest."
December 13, 1837-July 1, 1863

misery." A Rebel, in whose heart remained a dint of pity, stooped over him and expressed sorrow that by giving himself to a bad cause he had brought upon himself so great a misfortune. But in words mildly reproachful and with a heroism stronger than death, he spurned such sympathy. The setting sun neared the verge of the horizon. The clouds that hung around its disc were magnificently tinged with golden light. Up through their brilliant volumes seemed to reach a gorgeous vista, to whose end the human eye could not pierce, but which seemed to die away in serene splendor. It was not hard to fancy that it was the shining road along which the souls of heroes were ascending from the bitter cross of the battlefield to the crown of glory and infinite peace.

The soft light fell upon the feverish brow of Lieutenant Burnham. It was as if the pitying angel's hand was supplying the gentle baptism of an absent mother's. "Oh, that I could look upon that once more," he said, and the Rebel bolstered him with a knapsack, so that he might gaze upon the sweet pageant of nature, whose beauty too truly symbolized his sweetly ebbing life. He caught one glimpse and only a glimpse, for the posture was too painful and he sank back again upon the ground. Bending over him, the pitying Rebel asked, "Is there anything I can do for you? I will do anything in my power." He helped me conceal my field glass so that it might not be stolen. He offered to get us a surgeon or an ambulance if he could. The dying man sighed a negative, he pressed the farther inquiry. "Is there any message or any article that you wish me to deliver to your friends. If there is, I will cheerfully attend to it at my first opportunity." "Yes," said he. "Here is my watch; send it to my uncle Lester Hunt." The Rebel took the name, address, and repeated his promise to faithfully perform this dying injunction. The sun dropped behind the western hills and Lieutenant Burnham departed with the day. He lay beside me calm and still. He was dead.[125]

---

[125] The compassionate Confederate was a cavalryman named James O. Marks of Lynchburg, Virginia, who was then serving as a courier on General Jubal A. Early's staff. Adjutant Stowel Lincoln Burnham, a native of North Windham, Connecticut, was visiting his sister in Kenton, Ohio in the fall of 1861 when he chose to enlist in Co. A of the 82nd Ohio Volunteer Infantry. "Soon after the battle of Chancellorsville, he was appointed adjutant of the

Night drew like a pall over the dreadful scene; her curtain through which the stars looked down like eyes of angels, full of tears. Quiet pervaded the sanguinary field disturbed only by the beaming supplications of unattended and friendless sufferers. The shadowy form of the plunderers glided like phantoms among the wrecks of battle. A sepulchral gloom curtained the damp, uneasy couches of the wounded and shrouded the ghastly upturned faces of the dead. But the pulseless form at my side recalled my mind to other features of the impressive scene. I thought of the far off New England home of which I had heard those mute lips speak so tenderly. I thought of the hearts there who would look and sigh in vain for the return of that pallid face with its wonted beaming at the home threshold. My fancy portrayed their grief at his loss, and heard them envy me my poor privilege. I grieved to think how inadequately I had supplied their places in his dying moments. Yet his fate needed not to be mourned by them or me. Rather might we envy it. He was "freedom's now and fame's," not needed he aught of earth's stupid pageantry to make him glorious as he lay silent and painless, upon his soldier's bier with the night dews and I for his only weepers.

The 82nd Ohio Volunteer Infantry went into action on July 1, 1863 at Gettysburg with 22 commissioned officers and 236 men; and of these 20 officers and 161 men were killed, wounded, or captured, leaving only two officers and 75 men, a casualty rate of 70%.

82nd Ohio Volunteer Infantry Monument at Gettysburg National Battlefield

regiment. He was ever found willing, prompt, and capable, and enjoyed in a high degree the confidence and esteem of all with whom his duties and relations brought him in contact. Youthful, brave, and promising, he was ever a shining mark for the swift messengers of death but until the battle of Gettysburg had never sustained serious injury. Receiving a severe and painful wound in the hand, he was ordered by his commanding officer to the rear, but insisted upon remaining at his post and did remain until his horse had been shot under him and was again severely wounded by a ball passing through his thigh. He then attempted to leave the field and in doing so was wounded a third time- this time mortally." *Hardin County Republican,* July 31, 1863, pg. 3 Adjutant Burnham was buried with impressive military ceremony in his hometown on July 22, 1863. "Funeral of Adjutant Stowel L. Burnham," *Hardin County Republican,* August 7, 1863, pg. 2

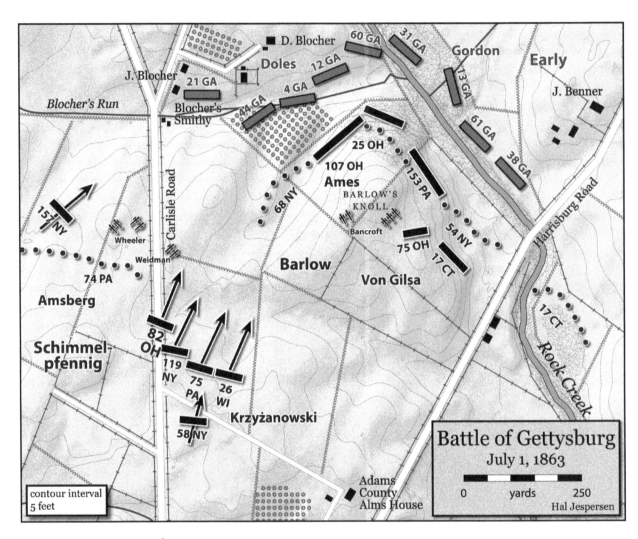

The desperate fight of the 11th Corps north of Gettysburg on the first day of the battle ended nearly as disastrously for the corps as the debacle at Chancellorsville. Captain Lee was severely wounded when his regiment started to retreat from the field and remained in Confederate hands for the remainder of the battle. The 82nd Ohio suffered a 70% casualty rate at Gettysburg.
(Hal Jespersen, www.cwmaps.com)

CHAPTER SIX

To the West

Now a prisoner of war, Captain Lee was moved by carriage to the John S. Crawford House, which was the headquarters of General Richard Ewell, and received care from Mrs. William Smith who was a member of the Crawford household. "Among his fellow captives there was General Francis C. Barlow of New York. From the Crawford House he was conveyed after the battle to the 11th Corps field hospital at the George Spangler barn, in and about which were lying at the time, about 1,500 Union and Confederate wounded. Among the Confederates was the famous General Lewis Armistead, who fell in Pickett's Charge, and died in a shed a few yards from the haymow in which Captain Lee, with the other wounded, were placed." General Schurz walked the field of battle and visited his wounded men in the hospitals scattered around town. "The houses, the barns, the sheds, and the open barnyards were crowded with moaning and wailing human beings and still an unceasing procession of stretchers and ambulances was coming in from all sides to augment the number of sufferers. Many of the wounded men suffered with silent fortitude, fierce determination in the knitting of their brows and the steady gaze of their bloodshot eyes. Some would even force themselves to a grim jest about their situation or about the 'skedaddling of the Rebels.'" [126]

Back in Delaware, Ohio, the initial report from the battlefield was that Captain Lee was dead. "We regret to notice among the deaths in the late battle at Gettysburg our young friend and correspondent Capt. A.E. Lee," noted the July 10th issue of the *Delaware Gazette*. "He was a young man of decided ability, a good soldier, and his whole heart was enlisted in the cause for which he gave up his life."[127] Imagine the surprise when Captain Lee arrived the following day in Delaware and took up quarters in the American Hotel. "We were not a little surprised as well as gratified to hear, Saturday morning (July 11th) that he had arrived at the American the previous evening and though seriously was not mortally wounded and was doing very well. He is shot through the upper part of the left thigh and as the bone is supposed not to be touched, the injury will not be likely to prove a permanent one," the *Gazette* reported. "We congratulate the gallant captain upon his escape from death and safe arrival among his friends."[128]

Within a few days of being recaptured by Union forces, Captain Lee was sent to a hospital in Baltimore where he procured a leave of absence from Middle Department commander General Robert Schenk, his former brigade commander from the McDowell campaign. Local physician Dr. M. Gerhard described Lee's wound as entering the "middle of the dorsum of the ilium, and emerging in front a little below the anterior superior spinous process, passing in close proximity to the hip joint." The doctor thought Lee would need at least three months to recover, but by the end of August, Lee was making rapid improvement and was getting about town on crutches. Lee remained at Delaware recuperating until late September when, hearing of the probable advance of the Army of the Potomac, he set out for Washington "though not entirely recovered." Captain Lee, hobbling on crutches, reported to the Board of Officers in Annapolis for examination on September 25th, and was sent to the general hospital at Annapolis, Maryland "for admission and treatment." Lee was discharged from the hospital on October 12, 1863. In the meantime, he had missed the movement of the 11th Corps when it went west, and rejoined his regiment at Bridgeport, Alabama on October 21, 1863.[129]

---

[126] General Armistead died on July 5, 1863. Schurz, op. cit., pgs. 39-40

[127] "We regret to notice…," *Delaware Gazette*, July 10, 1863, pg. 3

[128] "Still worth a dozen dead men," *Delaware Gazette*, July 17, 1863, pg. 3

[129] Lee, Alfred E. The History of the City of Columbus. New York: Munsell & Company, 1892, pgs. 900-901, and *Delaware Gazette*, September 25, 1863, pg. 3; also see Military Service Record of Captain Alfred E. Lee, Form 86, National Archives and Records Administration

Brigadier General G. Hector Tyndale. Captain Lee remembered Tyndale as a "brave man of rare intellectual ability and accomplishments."
(Memoir of Hector Tyndale)

In the wake of the disastrous losses sustained by the 11th Corps at Gettysburg, the command was again reorganized and the 82nd Ohio was placed in the First Brigade of the Third Division under Brigadier General G. Hector Tyndale of Pennsylvania. Tyndale, returning to service after spending nearly nine months recovering from a head wound sustained at the Battle of Antietam, took command of the brigade on July 13, 1863. His new command consisted of the veteran 82nd Illinois, 45th New York, 61st Ohio, and 82nd Ohio regiments, all of which had seen hard service with the 11th Corps. The 143rd New York, pulled from the defenses of Washington, was added to the brigade in early July. The composition of the brigade changed again once the troops arrived in Alabama, as the 82nd Illinois was transferred to another brigade and the 101st Illinois substituted in its place. Captain Lee and the 82nd Ohio would serve in this brigade for the remainder of the war.[130]

Ulysses S. Grant's victory at Vicksburg in July 1863 dovetailed with the Union victory at Gettysburg and turned the tide of the war decisively against the Confederacy, but the Rebels soon demonstrated that they had plenty of fight left. With the war in Virginia appearing to enter a period of relative quiet, reinforcements were dispatched from the Army of Northern Virginia to Braxton Bragg's Army of Tennessee and this enlarged force struck William S. Rosecrans' Army of the Cumberland in the two day battle of Chickamauga on September 19-20, 1863. In this bloodiest battle of the western theater, Rosecrans' army suffered defeat and was driven back to Chattanooga where the army soon found itself besieged. The War Department had already dispatched troops from Grant's Army of the Tennessee to reinforce Rosecrans prior to Chickamauga (they were in route), but news of the defeat prompted Secretary Stanton to revisit the issue of sending Rosecrans additional reinforcements. It was determined to send two corps from the Army of the Potomac (the 11th and 12th) under the command of Major General Joseph Hooker to Tennessee to help Rosecrans break the siege at Chattanooga.

The decision to send the 11th and 12th Corps away from the Army of the Potomac was made easier due to the fact that neither corps had won a particularly warm place in the affections of the eastern army. The 11th Corps had received the bulk of the blame for the defeat and Chancellorsville and their performance on the first day of the Battle of Gettysburg had not removed the stain of that defeat. The 12th Corps, while free of any stain, had been cobbled together just before Antietam and hosted a large proportion of the army's western regiments. But neither General Howard, commanding the 11th Corps, nor General Slocum, commanding the 12th Corps, had a good

---

[130] The format for this chapter is to intersperse Captain Lee's letters written to the *Delaware Gazette* with supplementary information drawn from contemporary sources to flesh out the story. Captain Lee's letters will be headed by the date and location where they were written.

relationship with General Hooker, Slocum going so far as to tender his resignation rather than serve under Hooker again. Lincoln managed to pacify Slocum's concern by promising him a command away from Hooker in the future, and in late September, the two corps started to leave their camps in Virginia for the nearly 1,200 mile journey to southern Tennessee.

News of the corps' impending departure from Virginia hit the men like a bolt from the blue. General Howard recalled that he was enjoying the relative monotony of peaceful camp life when he received General Meade's order directing him to have his corps in readiness to move the following morning, September 25th. "The two corps quickly started up from their scattered camps in regiments, loaded up their tents and luggage, and marched to the nearest railway station. We were to leave our army wagons behind. Our artillery and horses went with us. Instead of having a single long train, we were furnished with several short ones; as soon as the first one was loaded to its full with our material, animals, and men, it moved off, to be followed by the second, filled in like manner. As several stations were used at the same time, it did not take long to embark everything which was allowed. At first, our destination was a secret to everybody."

Howard disembarked at Washington and reported to General Hooker for orders, finding him at Willard's Hotel. "He at once informed me that my corps and Slocum's were to move by rail to the west and join Rosecrans as soon as it could be done." As the series of trains barreled west, the troops took the opportunity to ride atop the freight cars and bask in the enthusiastic welcome provided by the populations of Ohio and Indiana. General Howard wrote that "multitudes filled the streets of the towns we passed and gave us refreshments and hearty words and other demonstrations of their appreciation. At Xenia, Ohio, little girls came in flocks and handed up bouquets of flowers to the soldiers; children and ladies were the bearers of little housekeeper bags, needle books, and bright flags, each bringing some small thing for use. Nothing ever inspired our men more. The loyal feeling, sympathy, and kind words prevailed."[131]

In one of the most impressive achievements of the wartime railway system, this large force, totaling more than 15,000 men, 5,000 horses, and 700 wagons, arrived in theater within two weeks of leaving Virginia. By early October, the two corps had settled into camps across southern Tennessee and northern Alabama, tasked with guarding the railroad line that led into Chattanooga, repairing roads, and rebuilding bridges that had been destroyed during the summer campaigns.[132] "The next morning, October 4th, we passed on to Bridgeport, Alabama where the greater portion of the 11th Corps had already arrived and bivouacked as well as it could without wagons and with its mixed up baggage," wrote General Howard. "The artillery was there, but the horses had not yet arrived. It was singularly rough country- nothing but abrupt hills and mountains, nothing except the broad river and the crooked railway. Though early in October, the air was very chilly; and the old camps left by the Confederates as they withdrew to the south shore were, as old camps mostly are, very uninviting. At first everybody was homesick."[133]

It didn't take long for the soldiers to acclimate themselves to rear area duty in quiet northern Alabama. Major Lewis D. Warner of the 154th New York wrote gleefully from Bridgeport in late October that "the corps which could steal mit Blenker, fight mit Sigel, and run mit Howard, can dig like 'ter tyvel' as the Dutchmen say."[134] The nattily dressed Easterners proved quite the novelty to the Army of the Cumberland veterans, but they soon learned that the Potomac veterans were more than just fancy dressers. Private Charles Le Isle of the 9th Ohio Battery stationed at Tullahoma, Tennessee marveled at the Easterners' propensity to rob the citizenry. "The continual passing of Eastern troops has subsided and I presume the citizens ain't sorry for it," he averred in a letter home. "I imagine they can beat us Western fellows all hollow for the quantity of tar that's on their fingers, as everything they touch seems to stick to them. They've shocked my ideas of propriety amazingly by their strategic movements upon storekeepers. When the trains have stopped 'half an hour for dinner,' parties of them, model soldiers to we Westerns, assailed the stores, completely gutting them, not confining themselves to edibles, but watches, boxes of

---

[131] Howard, op. cit., pgs. 449-456
[132] Hebert, op. cit., pgs. 251-254
[133] Howard, op. cit., pg. 457
[134] Newspaper articles of the 154th New York Volunteer Infantry, New York State Military Museum and Veterans' Center

cigars, brass jewelry, tin ware, or anything they placed their paws on had to come- excepting bibles, prayer books, and such like reading." The woebegone 11th Corps and the hard hand of war learned in Virginia had arrived in the West. In the forthcoming operations that raised the siege of Chattanooga, the 11th Corps would successfully work to remove the stains of Chancellorsville and Gettysburg, proving their worth as veteran soldiers, but the habit of foraging and depredations against the civil population proved hard to break.[135]

Headquarters, 82nd Ohio Vols., Lookout Valley, Tennessee
November 12, 1863

On the morning of the 27th of October, the 11th Corps followed by Geary's division of the 12th Corps, commenced its march up the left bank of the Tennessee towards Chattanooga. Thus was inaugurated as the sequel has proved one of the boldest, most successful and important movements of the war. The brave Army of the Cumberland was starving. New communications must be opened for it, or within five days' time it must be brought to the painful necessity of a disastrous retreat. Upon the veterans of the Potomac devolved the vast responsibility of seizing by one bold sudden stroke the mountain bulwarks that range along the south bank of the Tennessee River, of making that beautiful stream a highway for Union navigation and or rendering Chattanooga the eagle's nest- the impregnable stronghold of freedom.

The first day's march was accomplished without special incident and we encamped at night among the mountain defiles, resting our weary limbs beside a swift little stream denominated Running Water. Next morning we had slung knapsacks and were again pursuing our march before old Sol had bestowed his morning kiss upon the gray, angry brow of Lookout Mountain. Signs of the desolation of war began to present themselves in deserted homes, burned railroad bridges and weedy untilled fields. From straggling citizens we learned that a small Rebel force had picketed the road the night before and had leisurely retired before the advance guard, yet there were no emphatic signs of resistance until 10 A.M. when we began to hear the ominous thunder of artillery far in the advance. Some incredulous ones said it was accidental thumping on a drum but more practiced and veteran ears detected its real meaning as easily as the schooled hunter interprets the distant rumbling made by a galloping herd of bison.

The Rebels were shelling our passing columns from Point Lookout. This towering mountain spur is the abrupt termination of the Lookout range, and it lifts its rocky crest 2,400 feet above sea level, directly in front of Chattanooga. Near the top it is permeated by a large stratum of rock 50 feet in thickness, the faces of which are perpendicular thus rendering a direct assault next to impossible. Upon the very pinnacle of this crag the Rebels have managed to plant a battery of light guns. The road along which we were compelled to pass led us under the fire of this battery for about one mile. There was no chance of replying and our nerve and grit was fairly tested by the merciless nuggets of iron that came shrieking down upon us like howling demons.

Confederate View

"Soon after the fighting on the left began I was notified that a column of troops was moving from the camp on my right along the road in front. I directed my skirmishers to retire to the line of battle, and allowed the head of the column to get opposite my left before firing. One volley scattered it in the fields beyond the road, where it attempted to reform and move on but a second fire again dispersed it. While this was taking place, other troops were coming up from the right and, our position having now been disclosed, they turned to attack it. Their line of attack was formed obliquely to our own, their left coming in contact with our line first and striking it near the right. The first attack was easily repulsed. The second was made in heavier force with a like result at all points of the line except one, at the junction of the 44th and 15th Alabama regiments. Here the enemy, forced in by the right of the line upon a vacant space in our own, broke through the line. Parts of both regiments gave way. When the firing had almost ceased I gave orders, for the whole line to retire to the hill on which it had first formed, thence into the hollow behind it."

~ Brigadier General Evander McIver Law , C.S.A.

---

[135] "Our Military Correspondence: From the 9th Battery," *Jeffersonian Democrat (Chardon, Ohio),* November 20, 1863, pg. 1

This photograph of Whiteside Valley in 1864 by noted photographer George N. Barnard shows the rough-hewn if bucolic aspect of the countryside through which the 11th Corps passed during their march to Chattanooga.
(Library of Congress)

We marched at quick time and most of the men kept their places well though the jagged pieces of exploded shells tore up the ground and rattled among trees, houses, and fences like iron hail. But why should the heroes of Gettysburg and Chancellorsville shrink at this? Had they not faced a hundred times worse on dozens of immortal fields? Rapidly but firmly moved the column almost entirely unshaken, though now and then a blood-bespattered artillery horse or a ragged indentation in the soil pointed out the danger they were passing.

Very few casualties occurred in passing this Rebel blockade. Emerging from the thick woods that skirted the road into the open fields we saw standing upon the summits of a series of heights on our right, groups of darkly clad men whom we knew to be soldiers but were they Rebels? No, for there in the clear air of the evening was the glorious old flag of the Union waving us welcome. Then came such volleys of shouts as made the welkin ring and the mountains echo. Shouts such as we heard come only from the throats of freemen. Then the bands struck up "Hail Columbia" and other airs that must have brought sad reminiscences to many a Rebel heart. The Army of the Potomac had greeted the Army of the Cumberland. There are episodes in the life of a soldier which are worth a century's enjoyment of luxurious pleasure. Such was the one I have just described.

We now encamped for the night but just as our minds were beginning to soothe tired nature with fancy pictures of home and dreamland, we were aroused by heavy and continuous volleys of musketry in the direction from which we had come. Longstreet's Rebels were trying to pounce upon our trains and intercept Geary. Our men fell shivering into line for the night was bitter cold and the moon shone too brightly and the stars twinkled too merrily for such a scene. Tyndale's brigade of the Third Division, 11th Corps was ordered to the front on the double quick. The enemy had occupied a series of precipitous wooden heights on our left and we were completely ambushed by the dark shadows of the timber. They saw our columns passing in the moonlight and fired on us. The bullets rattled, whizzed, and spattered in their old familiar way, some going too high, some too low, and others here and there striking a soldier.

Arriving at the base of the wooded heights, two companies of the 82nd, by the personal direction of General Hooker, were ordered to reconnoiter them. Deploying as skirmishers, we began to advance cautiously. We could hear the rebels far above us and expected warm work. But they fled hastily before us, not even firing until at a safe distance. Our skirmishers advanced to the crest of the mountain, the Rebels giving way before us, scampering through the bushes like frightened rabbits.[136] We remained in our position until daybreak, looking down on rebel camps and listening to Rebel conversations and commands. While these things were going on in Schurz's division, Von Steinwehr's men had made several successive assaults upon another height on our left and after repeated and most brilliant charges had carried it. In this gallant affair I regret to say that Captain Buchwalter, one of the most brave and patriotic hearts that beat, ceased to beat upon the field of the Wauhatchie; he was mortally wounded but his life's sun has set in the immortal glory which will forever crown the death of those who in this war have given up their lives to sustain the cause of justice and republican freedom.[137]

Von Steinwehr had no sooner won these fresh laurels for his brave division when General Geary's men put to rout greatly superior numbers and established his communication with us. Our victory was thus complete, the communication opened, Chattanooga saved, and the battle scarred and much-abused soldiers of the Peninsula, of Chancellorsville, of Cross Keys, and Fredericksburg were vindicated upon a western field. Such was the Battle of the Wauhatchie, and while I do not desire to indulge in self-praise or make individual distinction, let me say that the scandalous and foolish tongues of those who sit by their firesides, planning campaigns and criticizing generals and who have no more idea of the real vastness of this war or the proper method of conducting a campaign than an insect has of the motions of the spheres; these twaddlers I say cannot so falsify history as to cheat the brave men of the 11th and 12th Corps, particularly in the former, of the laurels they have gained in redeeming Chattanooga, any more than they can deprive them of those more hardly won on the bloody fields of the Old Dominion.

We are now strongly entrenched and have no doubt as to our ability to maintain our position. Our picket lines are in close proximity to those of the Rebels and conversation passes freely between the insurgents and our soldiers. Deserters come in by scores. Mutual agreements are made with our pickets by which they can enter our lines. A few nights since, over 30 came inside the 11th and 12th Corps lines with seven of whom I conversed immediately afterward. They were intelligent and freely gave all the information they could. They belonged to the 46th Alabama, almost all of whom they represented as ready to desert. They had even gone so far as to construct a raft to ferry themselves over Lookout Creek but were deprived of an opportunity to escape. They said Bragg's men are living on one-fourth rations of corn bread and are greatly disaffected. This morning one waded across Lookout Creek in broad daylight and in full view of the Rebel pickets. While his pantaloons were still wet, he told me his comrades did not fire on him because they wanted to follow him. He said that many of the commissioned officers were actively engaged in trying to persuade their companies and regiments to disband and go home. Such is a deserter's story and I give it for what it is worth.

Let every patriot hope that the beginning of the end has come. And may the all-wise God who is able to control the hearts and minds of men as well as their destinies, hasten a returning sense of reason to these deluded victims of ambition and prejudice, and bring to a speedy close this cruel war.

The *Delaware Gazette* was delighted to resume its correspondence with Captain Lee, pointing out to its readers that "the gallantry and courage of our correspondent needs not to be vouched for. He has been in some of the

---

[136] In this assault on what became known as Tyndale's Hill, the 82nd Ohio faced the veterans of Henry L. Benning's Georgia brigade, consisting of the 2nd, 15th, 17th, and 20th Georgia Infantry regiments.
[137] Captain Luther M. Buchwalter of Company A, 73rd Ohio Volunteer Infantry was killed in action October 29, 1863.

hardest fought battles of the war and the severe wound he received in the thickest of the fight, and in the front ranks, speaks louder than words of his noble bearing."[138]

General Tyndale wrote the following regarding his brigade's actions at Wauhatchie and the fortification of what became known as Smith's and Tyndale's hills. "The force led by Hooker up Lookout Valley was composed of the 11th Corps of about 6,000 men, one brigade of the 12th Corps of about 2,000 men, some batteries of artillery, and a few cavalry, making in all about 8,500 men. My own brigade, the largest in the 11th Corps, had about 1,500 muskets. On the afternoon of October 28, 1863, this command arrived and bivouacked near to closely pressed Chattanooga, in and about which were great expressions of joy upon our coming, and of gratitude for the relief we brought to its brave and much enduring army under General Thomas."

"On our march upward from Bridgeport, Alabama through Lookout Valley, a part (about 2,300 men of Geary's division of the 12th Corps) had been left behind between the railroad station of Wauhatchie and Kelly's Ferry- a very important point on the Tennessee River and one necessary for holding that river open for supplies. Geary's position was about two and half miles from the bivouac of the 11th Corps. In this upward movement, we cut the enemy's lines and drove them from the valley back upon Lookout Mountain. Observing the situation, I thought the proper thing for the enemy to do was to make a heavy attack upon us that night, before we had organized and entrenched our positions. I, therefore, ordered the men of my brigade to sleep in regular regimental formation, behind their stacked arms, and that the commanders of regiments and their staffs, as well as my own, should be ready for instant motion. I issued other brigade orders, as to the disposition of regiments in case of a movement."

"There had been a continuous angry picket firing since sundown, which gradually swelled in volume, until about 11 o'clock when it became a pretty heavy and long outpost chain of fire. Lying with my staff not far from Hooker's quarters, just before midnight I heard him give orders to an aide for General Howard of the 11th Corps 'to move at once with his whole corps to the relief of Geary who is sorely pressed.' Within four minutes from that time, my five regiments (the 45th and 143rd New York, 61st and 82nd Ohio, and 101st Illinois) were in rapid march towards the heaviest firing, which very soon burst into the roar of battle. This very rapid movement, followed soon, upon my left and rear, by Colonel Orland Smith's brigade, saved Geary's command from destruction, as the enemy's attacking force greatly outnumbered his, for my brigade cut off their line of battle and supports from their reserves, the latter of which my brigade and that of Colonel Smith attacked, driving them, and causing the instant withdrawal of their attacking line, which was pounding Geary terribly, and his fate hung upon minutes of time."

---

[138] "Army Correspondence," *Delaware Gazette*, November 27, 1863, pg. 3

General Hector Tyndale

Brigadier General G. Hector Tyndale of Philadelphia was described as "eminent for his heroism and love of truth. Firmness and loyalty to his convictions were his chief characteristics and he was naturally earnest and sincere in language and action. He was gentle and affectionate to his friends, attentive and helpful to the brave men under his command, and just and considerate to all who approached him. Great integrity, a strong and masculine intellect, and a feminine tenderness of heart were so happily blended in him that they produced the harmonious effect of an admirable and exalted character."

Tyndale's services in the war, starting with the 28th Pennsylvania Infantry and leading a hard hitting brigade at Antietam where he received a severe head wound, were of such a distinguished character that he was awarded a brevet promotion to major general of volunteers in 1865.

"The instantaneous spring of my brigade had sent it a pretty long way to the front, where a very fortunate deflection from my line of march upon the regular road, through or into a large open space, made by me in order to move more directly upon the firing, saved my own, it if did not our other brigades, from great peril, perhaps from destruction. The enemy's reserves, as it subsequently appeared, lay on hills covered by dark woods, through which our roadway ran, and were placed there, doubtless, to intercept our relief and to conceal their movements. Now, had my brigade entered those woods in following the road, we should have been at a great disadvantage to say the least, and had the head of our column been destroyed or even checked, it would have been most disastrous. The country was entirely unknown to us, and as it afterwards proved, the roadway was the proper approach to Wauhatchie because of deep muddy grounds in the fields."

"It was a bright moonlit night, and our movements in the open field were plainly visible to the enemy, while his positions and forces were hidden from and unknown to us. The battle, raging in our front, was also entirely invisible to us, being in dense forests, from which came only the increasing crash of musketry and the roar of artillery. Geary's command was, evidently, in sore straits and we pushed on quickly and steadily past the enemy's, then unknown, positions of reserve. After moving about a mile in the open field and being about the same distance from Geary, my skirmish line was suddenly stopped by a muddy branch, the position of which was reported to me by the officer in command of the 45th New York, who was acting as skirmishers. The enemy seeing the halt, and not knowing the cause and believing, I doubt not, that (because we had left the road and now seemed to be making dispositions for attack) we knew of his positions for interception, and further, in order to check my movement, which would have soon thrown my command upon the rear of his line of battle, opened fire on us at long range from what was afterwards known as Tyndale Hill No. 1"

"This was the first intimation I received of the enemy being on my left, as well as in my front. I at once changed front and forming line with supporting columns, attacked the hill and with persistent and vigorous efforts, carried it at the point of the bayonet. After clearing away the base of the hill, the 61st Ohio (Colonel McGroarty) and the 82nd Ohio (Lieutenant Colonel Thomson), formed and swept up the steep and rugged hillside to the very top, driving the enemy at every toilsome step. Captain William McGroarty[139], brother of the colonel, and others of both regiments were killed on the very crest- the enemy's line making a last stand there before it was pushed down the opposite slope. With the first opening of the fire upon my brigade and our attack on the hill, firing against Geary suddenly ceased and the enemy fell back through the dark woods, as their line of retreat was imperiled, and had we known the country and our position, it was possible that it would have been lost to them. From the gaps at both ends of the hills and from my right, there was now lively skirmishing, both parties feeling in the dark. The 45th New York was thrown back upon my right, which was threatened by the enemy then withdrawing from Geary's front, which we knew, as all sounds of battle from his position, had so suddenly died away. After this, the 143rd New York (Colonel Boughton) and the 101st Illinois (Colonel Fox) drove the enemy's covering force from a hastily formed breastwork in the gap between the Tyndale hills and carried the latter hill about daybreak."

---

[139] Captain William H. McGroarty died of wounds November 17, 1863.

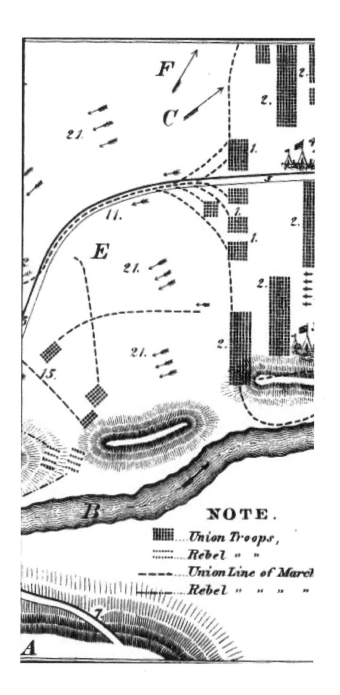

Wauhatchie Encampment

October 28, 1863

At left is General Tyndale's map of the 11th Corps encampment near Wauhatchie on the night of the battle. Note how he depicts the regiments as camping in regular regimental order to facilitate a rapid deployment in the event of a night attack.

Index to the Map:
B: Lookout Creek
C: Direction of Chattanooga, distance about three miles from that point
E: Open fields and country, through which the supporting columns of the 11th Corps moved to the front
F: To Brown's Ferry, distance about two miles
1. Position of bivouac of Tyndale's Brigade
2. Position of bivouac of other troops of 11th Corps
3. General Hooker's Headquarters
4. General Howard's Headquarters- nearby was General Schurz's headquarters
5. Common road from Bridgeport to Chattanooga
15. Colonel Orland Smith's advance on Smith's Hill
21. Supporting columns of 11th Corps

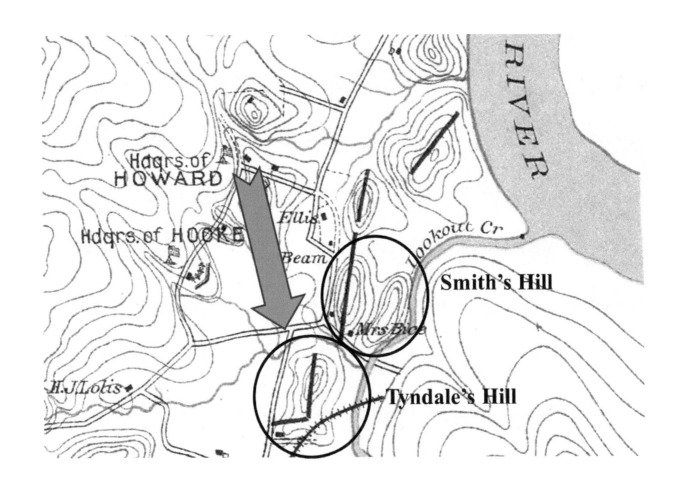

Battle of Wauhatchie, Tennessee, October 28-29, 1863 (Author's rendition)

"Skirmishing all along the line, entrenching our positions and throwing up long and strong works, connecting with other commands upon the right and left, occupied us all the following day and for many weeks thereafter. Lasting all the succeeding night was one of the coldest and heaviest of storms. We had no food, no shelter tents, and the men and officers alike were in light fighting trim and all suffered greatly. Added to this, we were under a constant and annoying fire of shell from Lookout Mountain. The Battle of Wauhatchie afforded a good test of the courage of our soldiers. Awakened about midnight and hastened into unexpected action, they behaved in the handsomest manner and with the coolest discipline, showing what Napoleon desired in his troops- 'two o'clock in the morning courage.' Wauhatchie was one of the most important minor battles of the war in its results."

"As Lookout Creek was, for several weeks afterwards, the only line between our pickets and the enemy's, we were very hard at work every day and often at night, making rifle pits, breastworks, and battery works. During this time, the enemy's fire from Lookout Mountain was incessant, though not rapid, and some few men and animals were lost by their shells. The works were made pretty strong, abatis put up and large spaces of timber slashed, notwithstanding the fire so that Smith's and Tyndale's two hills- the two or three taken in the night attack- became strong points, defensive or offensive. During this time the desertions from the enemy became so frequent that their commissioned officers stood along the posts to guard the sentinels."[140]

---

[140] McLaughlin, John. <u>A Memoir of Hector Tyndale</u>. Philadelphia: Collins Printer, 1882, pgs. 60-61, 74-80

Battle of Wauhatchie

"Our skirmishers ascended the dark woods silently. There was a moment of remarkable stillness. Then, we heard about half way up a ringing voice calling out: 'What regiment do you belong to?' Another voice, a little farther away, responded, naming a Georgia regiment. Thereupon promptly followed a shot and then a rattle of musketry. Then three of our regiments rushed up after our skirmishers, the firing became more lively, and soon our men were on the crest and descended the opposite slope, the enemy yielding as our men advanced. The affair occupied not much more than a quarter of an hour, but it cost of two killed and ten wounded."

~ *Major General Carl Schurz*

On the night following the Battle of Wauhatchie, while his company was engaged with fortifying Tyndale's hill, Captain Lee was visited by General Tyndale on a round of inspection. The two men, both cultured gentlemen of letters who had been wounded on the field of battle, struck up a quick friendship. Tyndale likely noted that Lee's hip wound would make duty as a line captain exceedingly difficult, a fact the Tyndale no doubt appreciated given his own struggles in battling the effects of his own wound. Despite their pain, both men were in the field and performing duty. Tyndale needed good staff officers and being suitably impressed with the Ohioan, he appointed Captain Lee as acting assistant adjutant general for the First Brigade, Third Division, 11th Corps on November 13, 1863. Lee appreciated this kindness and enjoyed a warm relationship with Tyndale, later writing that the general "was one of those rare men whom, once intimately and thoroughly known, one never could be able to and never would forget. The period of my acquaintance with him was one of the most eventful in my life. It was a period, for him especially, of great trials and responsibilities; a period that would thoroughly test any man and show what materials he was made. I found him, under these trials, one of the manliest and bravest of men. He was the soul of true chivalry and his sense of honor was of that knightly quality which would feel a stain like a wound." Captain Lee would spend the rest of the war on the brigade staff; being on staff duty would allow him to ride a horse much of the time, sparing him much pain from his hip wound.[141]

Lookout Valley, Tennessee
December 20, 1863

Not often in the annals of war have been recorded greater achievements with an equal loss than those accomplished within the four weeks just passed by the combined armies commanded by General Grant. Within a brief and comparatively bloodless campaign of 25 days, some of the most formidable strongholds on the continent have been wrested from the Rebels. East Tennessee has been permanently redeemed to the Union and the insolent army of Bragg has been discomfited and compelled to seek safety in disgraceful flight. And yet the inherent grandeur of these results can scarcely challenge more of our admiration than the skill, vigor, intrepidity, and harmony of movements by which they were achieved.

On the calm and beautiful morning of Sunday November 22, the Third Division of the 11th Army Corps received the stirring order to march to Chattanooga at 1:30 P.M. At the time stated our long blue lines of infantry began filing out of their camps and winding up through this valley. The Rebels from the eyrie on Point Lookout watched our movements and at each opportunity sent a hurtling shell to execute some puerile vengeance upon some detachment or train that ventured within range. But we had listened too long to the shrieking of those savage but generally harmless messengers from our

---

[141] Tyndale's divisional commander Carl Schurz maintained a warm regard for his Pennsylvania brigadier. "His was the natural refinement of a mind animated with high ideals, pure principles, perfect honesty of intelligence, a chivalrous sense of honor, and added to all this, artistic instinct. A strict disciplinarian, he was at first not popular with his soldiers, but they gradually perceived that his apparent sternness sprang from an overruling sense of duty and conscientious care for their welfare, and then their respect turned into affection." Schurz, op. cit., pgs. 53-54

erring brethren to care much for this parting testimony of ill will. Encamped for weeks under the very muzzles of those guns without suffering but a few casualties, we had learned to despise those frantic efforts at our destruction.

Night had fallen and the moon gleamed on the water and illuminated the gorgeous landscape as we tramped over the long pontoon bridge across the Tennessee. Passing under the dark shadows of the cliffs, we ascended to the plateau upon which Chattanooga is built and bivouacked under the guns of Fort Wood. It began to be whispered about that the result of our movements would be an attack upon the enemy's position next morning. An early reveille aroused us before the stars had been dimmed by dawn, yet not until 10 A.M. did we receive the suggestive order to march at a moment's notice. What that meant with the enemy's pickets within a few hundred yards of us and his camps plainly visible on the slope of Mission Ridge in front we well understood.

At 10 A.M. the troops of the 14th Corps began to move to the front. The two divisions of the 11th Corps were formed in columns in reserve. It was a magnificent sight, seeming too much like a grand review or parade to be meant for a real demonstration against an enemy. The Rebels who observed our slightest movements from Mission Ridge and Lookout I have no doubt really thought our movements only ceremonial or at most a mere sham demonstration or reconnaissance. With perfect regularity and order, the 14th Corps advanced as far as the outposts and entered the neutral ground that had lately separated the two armies. In breathless suspense we watched their movements until suddenly white puffs of smoke are seen and the cracking of rifles breaks the silence. Our skirmishers and Rebel pickets had simultaneously fired and the first blow of this great campaign was struck. The Rebels bounded back into their rifle pits, rapidly pursued by our glorious fellows. Without scarcely a check, forward goes the blue line until it reached the base of a small elevation between the plateau of Chattanooga and Mission Ridge. The cracking of rifles had grown almost to the magnitude of volleys and we now anxiously feared a defeat. But no, the living moving wall of blue sweeps right up the slope, reaches the crest and disappears into the Rebel entrenchments and a ringing cheer announces that the heights are ours.

Missionary Ridge at Chattanooga, Tennessee (Library of Congress)

It is now our time to move. Schurz's division goes immediately to the front and takes its position under a heavy fire from the Rebel batteries and begins skirmishing with the enemy. The 42-pounders of Fort Wood fired directly over our heads, answering savagely to the lighter caliber of our foes on Mission Ridge. Thus the contest continues until night closes upon the scene and all is still save the rattling of axes and the clicking of spades. Day dawns and finds us immovably fixed in our position with rifle pits and abatis covering the weaker points. The enemy, nevertheless, grows more restive and skirmishes with us briskly for a few hours but at length finding we cannot be dislodged ceases to annoy us.

In the afternoon a terrific battle breaks out upon our right. It is Hooker storming Lookout. A dense fog has settled around the mountain concealing his movements from our view. In the absence of correct information to go on, for an instant we supposed that the fancied Gibraltar of the rebellion was being attacked. By common consent it had been agreed upon as one of the things our army would never attempt to do. But the daring hero of Williamsburg and his compeers of the Potomac are underestimated. That huge, precipitous, towering pile of rock, though strengthened if strengthened if it could be, by rifle pits and batteries was actually being assaulted by Hooker and his dauntless braves. The terrific contest ended not with the day. Long after night had fallen and the stars had come forth in the clear blue sky, the quick fierce twinkling of rifles could be seen far up the dark, craggy side of Lookout. In the face of a sweeping fire of artillery and musketry our soldiers had gained a foothold among those rocks, from which they could not be driven. They held their position firmly during the night and when the day dawned, in triumph unfurled from the summit their shot-torn colors to a new baptism of glory. Such was the storming of Lookout, a theme for the painter, poet, and historian for all coming time.

While these operations were going on, Sherman was not idle. With admirable celerity and skill he had thrown a sufficient force across the river above Chattanooga to gain a footing upon the northern extremity of Mission Ridge, this completely turning the enemy's right flank. The 11th Corps was now ordered to affect a junction with Sherman and did so on the 25th, marching to him directly up the left bank of the river. But the enemy defeated on every hand was now thinking only of flight. His retreat commenced with the darkness of night and by dawn on the 26th he was well on his way southward. He was at once followed by our army and compelled to leave immense stores, and larger numbers of guns and prisoners in our hands. Deserters came into our lines by scores and hundreds, glad to escape from the army of treason.

At Ringgold, the enemy attempted to rally in the gorges of the mountains and by a desperate resistance redeemed something of his discomfiture. But again he was met by the heroes of Lookout and ingloriously driven from his chosen position. Thus ended the operations in the immediate vicinity of Chattanooga. Though glorious and successful, almost beyond hope or expectation, they did not complete our task. Ominous rumors were daily coming in from the vicinity of Knoxville that Burnside was in great danger- we must hasten to his relief. On the 29th of November, the 11th Corps forming temporarily a part of General Sherman's command, began a march of 150 miles. The troops were supplied with three days' rations which they were ordered to make last six.[142] Their shoes and their food gave out at the same time. They were enjoined to live cheerfully on meal until their comrades at Knoxville should be relieved. This was hardly needed. With the fortitude of the noblest true soldiers, they marched over the frozen ground from day to day with nearly bare feet and at night ate cheerfully their scanty fare. The Hiawassee was crossed and the Tennessee reached at Loudon. The enemy had destroyed the bridge at this point and the river was not fordable. Diverging from a direct course our columns sought the Little Tennessee, a less formidable stream. Bridges of wagons were thrown across it by which the infantry passed over, the artillery fording.

The evening of December 5th found us at Louisville, one day's march from Knoxville. Here we learned with regret that Longstreet had raised the siege of Knoxville and made good his escape and that it was unnecessary for us to advance farther. Resting one day, we began our retrograde march on the 7th. We were 80 miles from Chattanooga- that is, 80 miles from supplies of any kind, yet very many of the troops were barefoot, many sick, and all compelled to subsist entirely upon the country. The continual labor, watchfulness, and exposure to which they

---

[142] "We marched in the lightest kind of order- no tents, no wagon trains, the men carrying only their blankets and knapsacks, if they had any, with something to eat in their haversacks and plenty of ammunition in their cartridge boxes," remembered General Schurz. "But they were in fine spirits after the great victory and bore the fatigue of the forced march with excellent cheer. We usually started at daybreak and went into camp about dark, having in the meantime crossed rivers and creeks with or without bridges, mountain passes, sometimes over roads hardly worthy of the name. We saw no enemy in our front except some cavalry detachments." Schurz, op. cit., pg. 78

had been subjected with scarcely an intermission seven weeks began to tell upon the men. I have seen their stalwart forms shoeless and in rags, prostrate and trembling with feverish exhaustion. Yet few would complain. The American soldier scarcely knows the word complain. If God has given to any man above another a noble nature it is to him. I have heard his agonizing groans upon the bloody field, in the hospital, on the march, but very rarely have I heard him complain of any hardship or suffering that came upon him in the line of duty. Forgetting myself, I cannot but say God bless the men who thus dare, do, and suffer for the welfare of mankind.

The night of the 16th will be ever memorable to the Third Division. Halting at nightfall, a drenching rain set in and a settled gloom which our hundreds of glaring camp fires could scarce annihilate. The shelter tents had been erected and the men were preparing for rest when an imperative order came to march six miles further at once. At the same time the rain came faster and the night grew more dismal. Six miles further on such a night! Yet it must be done, even though we had already marched 20 miles before nightfall. Leaving their fires, their only comfort, our soldiers plunged into the darkness and pressed forward. The lightning occasionally revealed to us each other's presence and gleaming along our watery path. These glimpses of the column reminded me of the solemn train of lost beings treading the gloomy regions of Dante's Inferno. God pity the sick and shoeless on such a march.

At 1 A.M., the division halted. Pitilessly fell the rain, making fires next to impossible. The sun's eye opened at length, but saw few sleepers. Yet our soldiers complained not, but seemed rather to cheerfully congratulate themselves that they were men able to cope with and overcome such painful trials of their fortitude. That evening saw them again in their old camps or at home as some called it. They had reached them by traversing Mission Ridge and Lookout, where three weeks before they had seen the enemy lodged as it seemed impregnably. Proud of their conquests and forgetting their privations, their thoughts travelled homeward in many an affectionate line- a weakness by the way even of your A.T. Sechand.

The night march of December 16th alluded to by Captain Lee proved especially memorable as a night of misery by General Schurz. After a long day's march through the mountains, Schurz came across a perfect meadow to camp the fatigued men of his division. A clear stream ran through the meadow, which offered abundant wood, water, and space for the entire division. Schurz resolved to camp there for the night and sent a staff officer to so notify General Howard. "After the lapse of about an hour, when a large part of my command had come in and were beginning to build fires and to prepare such food as they had, an officer returned from corps headquarters with the positive order that I must, without loss of time, continue my march and proceed about three miles further, where a camping place would be assigned to me. I thought there was some mistake and I dispatched a second staff officer to represent to corps headquarters that to start my men again would be downright cruelty to them, and I begged that they be allowed to stay for the night where they were, unless there was real necessity for their marching on. In due time, the answer came that there was such necessity. Now nothing was to be done but to obey instantly."

"My division bugler sounded the signal. There arose something like a sullen groan from the bivouac, but the men emptied the water, which was just beginning to boil in the kettles, upon the ground and promptly fell into line. We had hardly been on the way half an hour when a fearful thunderstorm broke upon us. The rain came down in sheets like a cloudburst, driving right into our faces. In a few minutes we were all drenched to the skin. I wore a stout cavalry overcoat with a cape, well lined with flannel over my uniform. In an incredibly short time I felt the cold water trickle down my body. My riding boots were soon full to overflowing. One may imagine the sorry plight of the poor fellows in rags. They had to suffer, too, not only from the water coming down from above but also from the water coming from below. We were again passing through a hilly district. The road ran along the bottom of a deep valley with high ridges on both sides. From these the rain water rushed down in streams, transforming the road into a swelling torrent, the water reaching up to the knees of the men and higher. Meanwhile the thunder was rolling, the lightning flashing, and the poor sufferers stumbling over unseen boulders under the water, and venting their choler in wild imprecations. At last, having struggled on in this way for about two hours, we emerged from the wooded hills into a more open country, at least I judged so as the darkness seemed to be a little relieved. The storm had ceased."

An officer from corps headquarters met Schurz in the middle of the road, and gave the order that Schurz was to encamp his men on both sides of the road. "It was so dark that I could not distinguish anything beyond a half dozen feet. I did discover, however, that on both sides of the road were plowed fields. There was water from the rain standing in the furrows and the ridges were softened into a thick mire. And there my men were to camp. Nothing remained but to stay where we were. The regiments were distributed as well as possible in the darkness. The men could not stretch themselves on the ground because the ground was covered or soaked with water. They had to sit down on their knapsacks, if they had any, or on their heels and try and catch some sleep in that position. About midnight, the wind shifted suddenly and blew bitterly cold from the north, so bitterly indeed that after a while our outer garments began to freeze stiff on our bodies. I thought I could hear the men's teeth chatter. I am sure mine did. There we sat, now and then dropping into a troubled doze, waiting for the day to dawn. As soon as the first gray of morning streaked the horizon, there was a general stir. The men rose and tossed and swung their limbs to get their blood into circulation. The feet of not a few were frozen fast in the soil, and when they pulled them up, they left the soles of such shoes as they had sticking in the hardened mud. The pools of water left by the rain were covered with solid crusts of ice, and the cold north wind was still blowing. I started my command as soon as possible in order to get the men in motion, intending to have them prepare their breakfast further on in some more congenial spot. The ranks were considerably thinned, a large number of men having strayed away from the column and trudged on in the darkness of the night. As we proceeded we saw them crawl out from houses or barns or sheds or heaps of straw or whatever protection from the weather they had been able to find. The hard, frozen, and stony road was marked with streaks of blood from the feet of the poor fellows who limped painfully along."

"And finally it turned out that all this had been for nothing. Headquarters had been disturbed by a rumor that the enemy was attempting a cavalry raid in our direction, which might have made a drawing together of our forces necessary. But the rumor proved quite unfounded. I have told the story of that dismal night so elaborately to show that even in an ordinary campaign, soldiers are sometimes exposed to hardships not always necessary, which their effect are now and then no less destructive than powder and lead."[143]

---

[143] Schurz, op. cit., pgs. 81-84

Typical army encampment outside of Chattanooga, Tennessee in early 1864. The Third Brigade returned to spend the winter near Bridgeport, Alabama in log huts similar to those shown above. (Library of Congress)

CHAPTER SEVEN

Bridgeport to Kolb's Farm

"The 82nd Ohio had scarcely recovered from the effects of the Knoxville campaign when it declared anew its devotion to the country by veteranizing. Out of 349 enlisted men present, 321 were mustered into the service as veteran volunteers on January 1, 1864," reported Whitelaw Reid. Within days, the regiment started home for Ohio on veterans' furlough. The regiment arrived in Columbus, Ohio on the evening of January 21st and the men were dismissed to their homes for 30 days from January 24th. The members of the regiment reconvened at Camp Chase on February 23, 1864 with 200 new recruits added to the ranks. The 82nd Ohio retrieved their muskets and in conjunction with the 21st Ohio Infantry, started south on February 26th. The 82nd Ohio rejoined its brigade at Bridgeport, Alabama on March 3, 1864.

Notes in Dixie Vol. I

Bridgeport, Alabama

March 1864

One of the most remarkable features of the war for the Union is the wonderful application which has been made of the principles and discoveries of science in the use of our military resources. Civilization has been proven to be self-defensive. As it advances our military power is not diminished but increased in a ten-fold ratio. The more we know, the more we gain not only in moral but physical strength. The discoveries in chemistry, pharmacy, mechanics, and the mechanical arts have been found no less available in crushing the rebellion and fighting barbarism than gunpowder and projectiles. Steam and electricity are as essential to the successful carrying on of this war as saltpeter and the weapons adopted for its use. The physical supremacy of civilization over barbarism, of human liberty over oppression, and of republicanism over despotism in America is no longer secure without these new and powerful agents. Our armies advance with the locomotives. The railroads and rivers are their strategic lines and they are the vital arteries through which their lifeblood circulates. The electric wires are the nerves which join them to the nation's loyal head and heart and to its central executive power. Over them its thoughts, feelings, and volitions reach the camps and bivouacs on lightning wings. Our hundreds of thousands of soldiers and our vast armaments are obedient to the clicking of the magnet. Steam brings the soldier his food, supplies him with raiment, and carries his messages of affection to and from his friends and loved ones. A million soldier tongues have learned to utter daily blessings on steam. The sick and wounded bless it, as it swiftly bears them from the hospital and battlefield to the quiet comfort of their homes. The scarred and sun-burned veteran blesses it as it gently sets him down at his own loved fireside, and she blesses it who with anxious eyes has long watched for his coming.[144]

To justly estimate the achievements of the Army of the Cumberland it must be remembered that it has steadily and persistently beaten the enemy back into the interior of his own territory a distance of over 300 miles. Three hundred miles of railroad now joins that army to its proper base of supplies. Much of that immense line passes through a country infested with guerillas who, if they could sever one foot of it, would place the army at their mercy, and though the road is well guarded, yet at many points the enemy daily and nightly listens to the whistling of our

---

[144] The format for this chapter and all succeeding chapters is to allow Captain Lee's "Notes in Dixie" letters series carry the story of the war to its conclusion with less of the supplementary information seen in some of the previous chapters. "Notes in Dixie" totaled 33 letters, all of which were published in the *Delaware Gazette* between 1864 and 1865. The reader will immediately note that the style of these letters differs significantly from the postwar articles and early war letters that comprise the first six chapters of the book; "Notes in Dixie" is more literary in character as opposed to strict military history.

passing engines and vigilantly awaits his opportunity to obstruct or destroy the track and thus sever the thread upon which hangs a nation's hope and destiny.

At Bridgeport, Alabama, the point at which the railroad crosses the Tennessee, the river is divided into two branches by an island. The bridges spanning these two arms of the river were destroyed by Bragg when he retreated before Rosecrans. They have since been beautifully and substantially rebuilt by the government. Another very large bridge was also destroyed and has been rebuilt at Whiteside. To destroy these bridges is, no doubt, a pet project of the enemy and one to accomplish which he would be willing to sacrifice a great deal. Fortunately, however, they are greatly protected by the adjacent mountains through the passes of which the enemy can alone approach them. A part of the 11th Corps is now guarding these important points, and it may be relied upon that they will not be yielded to any attack the enemy can make. The command on the south side of the river has been entrusted to Colonel James S. Robinson of the 82nd Ohio. He has force enough at his disposal to make the enemy rue the day that he attempts the capture of this post. On the north side of the river General Geary commands a force adequate to all possible emergencies.

There is a touch of beauty in the scenery along the Tennessee which is just now made doubly charming by most delightful weather. The climate of this region has been not inaptly compared to that of Italy. But it is now unusually fine for the season. True, there are occasional gusts of rain but they are like the fretful showers of an Ohio April. The sun smiles forth from the clouds ere the raindrops have ceased falling, just as a child sometimes breaks into laughter in the midst of its tears. Morning leaps from her rosy couch behind the gray crest of Raccoon Mountain as joyously and complacently as though the dreadful sounds of war had never broken the quietude of these valleys. And the nights, how surprisingly lovely! How stilly and grandly the dark shadows of the mountains loom up against the gemmed dome of the "celestial sphere, so rich with jewels hung that night, doth like and Ethiop bride appear."[145]

How finely their inverted images are mirrored in the star-spangled surface of the river! How musical the bugle's clarion call rings out upon the bracing air of incense-breathing morn, how gently at dewy eve the dying echoes of the cadenced tattoo melt away in the distant valleys! Such a climate and such a country, one would imagine to produce a superior race, an exalted type of manhood, "a combination and a form, indeed, Where every God seemed to set his seal, to live the world assurance of a man."[146] But alas for earth's loveliness and man's goodness, if the one were to be always judged by the other. The noblest minds are not rocked into existence by summer zephyrs. The purest hearts are not matured beneath unclouded skies. The men who stand foremost in the advance of time and who think and act for the rest of mankind are not the pampered pets of luxury and ease. They have rarely come from the perennial bloom of the equator. They are children of harsher climes. The Northern nations have always held the balance of intellectual and physical power. They will always hold it.

These things are truer than they ought to be of the people who dwell in the delightful valley of the Tennessee. Their lamentable condition is not the result of the climate alone. In spite of that they might have been free, opulent, and happy. But they are oppressed, poor, and miserable. They might have been refined, educated, and intelligent. They are coarse, ignorant, and stupid. And why are they so? It is all summed up in one word: slavery. They have been victimized by a monstrous crime, that of human oppression. By it they have been brought to a state of absolute barbarism, aye more; they have been led into a wicked war for barbarism. That war has brought them to poverty, shame, and starvation. But even this is not all. It is one of the rarest things to find a man, woman, or child among them who can read or write. The dynasty of Austria and the autocracy of Russia opens the door of education to the humblest, but the oligarchy of Southern slavery closes the door of knowledge against freemen in God's own free land. The Negroes were bondsmen born, but the white people of the South are verily slaves by consent.

There are scores of destitute families in this neighborhood who are now being supported almost entirely by the government. Every ten days rations are issued to them by the brigade commissary. Troops of hard-featured haggard-looking women come from far and near begging bread of that government which their natural protectors have vainly endeavored to destroy. One poor creature trembling with the weight of 60 years told me she had come

---

[145] A quotation from "Nox Nocti Indicat Scientiam" by English poet William Habington (1605-1646)
[146] Lee is quoting from the third act of "Hamlet" by William Shakespeare.

12 miles on foot! Widows come whose husbands have fallen with the dagger of treason in their hands. Wives and children come who have been left to starve by those who should feed them, in order that human rights might be overthrown. Maidens come at whose instigation brothers and lovers have given their lives to the vilest of despotisms. And the human and generous government dispenses its bounty to them all and asks in return only a renunciation of past misdeeds and future loyalty.

Looking at these poor creatures in their faded and homespun rags, it is difficult to withhold from them the feeling of pity. All of them are not the self-made victims of want and suffering. Some who have been steadfastly opposed to the rebellion have lost their friends by the sweeping and merciless conscriptions. Others, too weak to think for themselves, have been induced by designing knaves to give their votes and influence to the rebellion, and now suffer the consequences of stupidity rather than crime. But the social condition of these people is not less lamentable than their physical one. Slavery has in a great measure destroyed their instincts, and annulled the restraints of civilized society. The marriage rite and its sacred obligations are scarcely more observed among them that it was in France at the period of the revolution. Mixture with the blacks is by no means uncommon. Yet here are the chivalry who have so sneeringly decried the Northern people for their "free love" doctrines and amalgamatory inclinations! What more than Egyptian darkness has beshrouded the Southern mind? Thank God, the dawn is breaking for them. Heaven hasten the coming of the noonday sun.

The influence of association is strikingly illustrated in the dialect almost universal in the South. It is clearly and emphatically the Negro brogue. It is by no means eschewed in the highest circles through somewhat modified. But among the lower classes it is almost precisely the phraseology of the African. But the adoption of this language is doubtless one of the means used by Southern philanthropists for the elevation of the Negro. The wickedest and vilest of mankind has an inalienable interest in the cause of truth and human progress. The soldiers of the Union are fighting, not for themselves alone, but for their very enemies. They are fighting civilization into the Southern heart and mind. They are fighting barbarism out of them. They are stripping from these manacles more oppressive and inhuman than the chains of the slave. They are enfranchising the Negro not more than they are the white man. It is the Anglo-Saxon of America whom they are giving their lives and comfort to save. They are rescuing him from his own insane efforts at self-destruction. History will rapturously record how the patriots of 1863 offered themselves up by hecatombs for the salvation of their very foes. The glowing muse will never weary of recounting:

How they went forth to die,
Counting themselves as the unvalued dust,
Trod by a nation; bearing on its trust,
Content if but their sunken graves should be,
The footprints of the progress of the free."[147]

---

[147] Lee is quoting from a poem entitled "To the Sanitary Commission" published in the March 12, 1864 issue of *Harper's Weekly*.

Lieutenant General William Tecumseh Sherman (Library of Congress)

Bridgeport, Alabama
April 5, 1864

That the war being waged by the Southern states is wholly unjustifiable cannot be doubted by any enlightened and impartial mind, and that it is base, cruel, and barbarous, that it had its origin in ambition and avarice, that it is prosecuted for the overthrow of free institutions, that it has not the palliation of a single humane principle or feeling, that it is a conspiracy against the best interests, the noblest impulses, and the highest destinies of mankind which are propositions that will meet no dispute when time and civilization shall have dissipated the baleful influences of prejudice and barbarism.

But much as we may denounce the crime of the South, the criminals are not wholly underserving of our charity. Our humane and free government has all along been administered in view of this generous supposition. It is even now worried to know how it shall sustain the destitute families of thousands of men who today stand in Rebel ranks. It extends a hand of kindest forgiveness to all who, willing to renounce the madness and treason of the past, accept for the future the immunities of loyalty and good citizenship.

The rebellion of the South is the rebellion of an oligarchy. It is the adventure of a few rash and desperate capitalists who manage and own the whole concern. Its success is designed not to promote the interest of the many but of a few; not to elevate the masses but to trample them down. The despotism of Jefferson Davis is one of the most arbitrary, cruel, and unrelenting that ever existed. It drags the youth of 17 summers and the trembling dotard of 60 from the purity and comfort of home to the corruption and suffering of the camp. With troops of bloodhounds, it hunts the lover of liberty like a wild beast from hospitable caves and forests. It holds the knife at the throats of helpless women and children and counts the hours during which a loved father, husband, or son shall be betrayed to a merciless conscription, or they, as hostages, pay the penalty of their lives. It hangs, shoots, burns, devours men for no other crime than that of loyalty to truth, to country, and to God. It courts the alliance of the savage and appeals to all the basest instincts of human nature.

But the tyranny of the Davis government is after all mildness compared to the tyranny of that public opinion which it molds, owns, and controls. The bitter sneer, the taunting jest, the scornful innuendo have driven more young men from their homes to the Rebel camps than the conscription agents ever dragged. And in this, women have been the chief workers. The insinuations of cowardice have fallen upon them from lips too fair to be questioned, too winning to be resisted. The female garb has tendered to men whose love of country was only surpassed by their pride and whole physical courage but too far outdid their moral. Those whose loyalty and good sense attempted to withstand the tide of popular hate and passion were, by these female harpies, hooted from society and made targets for all the tea-table venom of the neighborhood. What wonder the thoughtless youths and even those of mature years should under such influences give themselves up to the deceitful and attractive delusion of a Southern Confederacy? What wonder that with the prejudices of locality, the bias of education, the fever of political excitement, a prurient love of adventure, a mistaken patriotism, an arraigned manhood, together with the tender influences of the social relation to warp and blind the judgment, that thousands, both learned and unlearned, ignorant and intelligent, should flay to the embrace of treason, arrayed in the stolen garb of freedom? At any rate, let us not judge them too harshly, nor forget the sentiment warbled by Ohio's sweet poet:

> "Among the pitfalls in our way,
> The best of us walk blindly;
> So man be wary, watch and pray,
> And judge your brother kindly."[148]

---

[148] Lee is quoting from the poem "The Heaven That's Here" by Ohioan Alice Cary. Alice was only 17 when she and her sister Phoebe had a volume of verse published in 1849; their work gained popularity and the sisters moved to New York City in 1850 where they continued to write. Alice Cary died in 1871.

It was, not long since, the fortune of the writer to have an interview with a lady of Rebel proclivities just after she had heard of the death of her son. Induced by a wily traitor of the neighborhood, the lad at the age of 17 had, as thousands of others have done, left his home in violation of parental injunctions, and joined the Rebel army. He was captured by the Union forces and paroled, afterward retaken under suspicious circumstances and sent to Camp Chase, Ohio. Thence he was sent to Rock Island, Illinois and there he was taken sick with small pox and died. The unutterable agony of that mother when the news of her son's calamity reached her! Sinking to the ground, her heart seemed to melt in tears. "Poor little fellow, said she, "I begged him, pleaded with him not to go, but that wicked Glover coaxed him away and now he has died in a strange land. Oh how can I endure it?" The poignancy of her grief seemed too intense for comfort, yet in the midst of it she frankly avowed that the wicked leaders of the rebellion were responsible for all her sorrow. Would that the voice of her piteous wailing, joined by that of every bereaved Southern mother might unceasingly resound in the ears of those who have misled, hoodwinked, and abused the Southern people for their selfish purposes.

The extensive railroad bridges spanning the Tennessee at this point have a history which is somewhat interesting. They have been twice destroyed and as often rebuilt. General Mitchel[149] soon after the capture of Huntsville by his forces, led a small detachment in the direction of Stevenson, Alabama. Without serious resistance he reached a small stream called Battle Creek, six miles below Stevenson. Here he encountered one General Leadbetter[150] with a brigade of Rebels. Mitchel made a bold and sudden attack and drove Leadbetter hastily back toward Bridgeport. Following close upon the heels of the flying Rebels he soon appeared upon the banks of the Tennessee and opened a brisk cannonading upon Leadbetter's forces. Leadbetter, thinking only of flight, pushed his column over the railroad bridge connecting the right bank of the river with the island. So rapidly did the frightened Rebels crowd upon this narrow passage that numbers were crowded off and falling into the river were drowned. Leadbetter had no time to fire the first bridge and after the passage of his troops so hotly was he pressed by the energetic Mitchel. But the second bridge, joining the island with the left bank of the river, being a covered one, and a large quantity of flammable material having been previously collected in it, was quickly fired by the enemy and so rapidly consumed that it could not be saved. Thus General Mitchel's pursuit was suddenly checked.

But not so the redoubtable Leadbetter. So completely disgusted had he become with Yankees and Yankee tricks that he embarked his command upon a railroad train and, abandoning his camp equipage and supplies, then set out at once for Chattanooga. In a day or two General Mitchel sent a small detachment over in canoes and made a bonfire of Ledbetter's stores and equipage. Pursuing the skedaddling chivalry to Shellmound, a railway station seven miles further up the Tennessee, Mitchel's brave fellows discovered a large quantity of bacon bearing C.S. brands. Piling it upon some abandoned cars, the soldiers started the vehicles towards Bridgeport. The grade being quite steep the cars needed only the impulse of gravitation to make them go and the merry captors jumping aboard had a free ride at Confederate expense. Nearing the river the boys, unmindful of the destruction of the bridge and forgetting in their sport to put on the brakes, found themselves driven to the paradoxical alternative of losing their bacon in order to save bacon of a more precious quality. So leaping from the cars they committed their swinish trophies to the engulfing waters of the Tennessee. General Mitchel not designing to hold the place, now destroyed the remaining bridge and thus completely severed Rebel connections by rail between Chattanooga and Nashville.

After the retreat of Buell and the advance of the Rebel army into Kentucky, great efforts were made by Bragg for the reconstruction of the bridges. But in all rebeldom (as Union citizens aver) engineers could not be found who were capable of accomplishing the work. The same authorities positively assent that Bragg sent emissaries to the North who by the influence of Confederate gold and the pledge of protection secured the services of a Northern firm by whom the bridges were rebuilt. This is no idle story but comes well authenticated and bears

---

[149] Major General Ormsby MacKnight Mitchel (1810-1862) was known by his troops as "Old Stars" for his pre-war work as an astronomer. Mitchel was noted for his role in seizing important points along the Memphis & Charleston Railroad in the spring of 1862 which led to his promotion to major general. He was transferred to the Department of the South along the South Carolina coast where he soon contracted yellow fever and died.
[150] Brigadier General Danville Leadbetter (1811-1866) led a brigade in the District of East Tennessee into the summer of 1862, then served in a series of engineering assignments.

upon its face the marks of plausibility. It is also affirmed that the persons who undertook this perfidious enterprise were from Ohio, even from Cincinnati. Can it be possible that while the squirrel hunters of the Buckeye State were rushing by the thousands to the defense of the Queen City, infamous scoundrels were accepting the bribes of traitors to facilitate its destruction? For humanity's sake, for Ohio's sake, let us hope not.

After the discomfiture of Bragg and at the time of his retreat before the victorious Rosecrans, the Rebel general marched his columns and drove his artillery and trains across these same bridges and destroyed them. They were at once reconstructed by the government and on the 1st of January last were ready for the passage of trains. What vicissitudes they have yet to pass time along can determine.

Notes in Dixie Vol. III

Bridgeport, Alabama
April 26, 1864

There is an inexhaustible charm for the true lover of nature in the valley of the Tennessee. The scenery possesses a rare and enduring loveliness which, though it may be modified, is never lost by any changes of the seasons. There is a stately grandeur in the mountains, a touch of Arcadian voluptuousness in the vine-hung forests, a romantic dreaminess in the cliff-girt river, which retains perennial freshness and fascination. To the beauty of the scenery is added a climate almost devoid of extremes, and delightfully tempered both as to heat and cold. There is a genial and softly bracing atmosphere which diffuses the gentle flow of health and animates and restores the dropping invalid.

Nor are there less attractions for the utilitarian than for the health seeker and the admirer of nature. The soil of the lowlands and plains is rich and fertile, producing nearly all the staples common to both north and south. The mountains are stored with vast treasures of mineral wealth which lie waiting for the hand of enterprise and industry to reach forth and take them. Great facilities are afforded for the profitable investment of manufacturing capital and for the home production of an endless variety of comforts and luxuries of civilized life. In short, all that is needed is an enterprising, cultured, and intelligent population to render this one of the most desirable abodes of man. When it shall have been decided that free government is to be maintained in America, when the barbarism of slavery shall have ceased to oppose the progress of a free civilization, when the hand of free labor shall till these fertile valleys, when the genius of enlightened republicanism shall have gained a permanent lodgment among these mountain fastnesses- when all these things shall be added as they will be- to the amenities nature has bestowed upon the Tennessee Valley, it will not only be one of the most inviting sections of this continent, but will proudly rival the most famous land of the Orient. It will then be indeed worthy of the proud title of American Italy.

No one who climbs the rocky steeps of Lookout or of Raccoon Mountain and surveys from the summit of either the glorious exhibition of nature's beauty and grandeur spread before him can fail to appreciate the truth of these observations. Nor will he fail to be inspired by new and lofty conceptions of the present and future glory of that vast confederacy of states joined in one free republic which Southern madmen are trying to destroy. He will thank God for a country so great, so free, so sublimely beautiful. The very breath of freedom will seem to inspire him in the cheerful breeze which animates his frame, and the music it makes among the solemn pines will sound like the chant of her holy and unceasing anthem. His heart will, silently perchance, but none the less truly, join the sublime paean with its weak, human utterances such as these:

"My native country thee, Land of the noble free,
Thy name I love.
I love thy rocks and rills, Thy woods and templed hills,
My soul with rapture thrills,
Like that above."[151]

---

[151] Lee is quoting from the second verse of "My Country 'Tis of Thee" written by Samuel Francis Smith in 1831. The song gained much popularity by the outbreak of the Civil War.

The view from the summit of that portion of Raccoon Mountain which lies opposite Bridgeport, Alabama and which has received the local sobriquet of Sand Mountain, though it cannot be compared to the incomparable one from Point Lookout, is nevertheless extremely fine. Far to the westward and northward the Cumberland Mountains heave against the horizon their massive billowy shapes ever and anon overtopped by some "beetling crag" or aspiring peak and tinted by God's own hand with a shade of blue as deeply pure and ethereal as mortal eye ever dwelt upon. For 50 miles away off to the southeastward the eye follows the meandering Tennessee wandering hither and thither among its mountain suitors until like a coquettish maiden weary of her dallying, it loses itself in their softly dim embrace. At one's feet the deep valley expands itself, threaded by gleaming rills and rivulets, swept by the stately river which clasps a romantic little island set like a jewel in its bosom, animated by the steaming locomotive hastening to and fro on its swift errands, and by the dark moving forms and the evenly ranged camps of thousands of soldiers. Dumb must be the soul that would not be intoxicated by such a sight, dead the heart that it would not inspire with an almost unearthly fervor. Of such and one it may well be said, as it has been so aptly of him that "hath no music in himself" that he "is fit for treasons, stratagems, and spoils, the motions of his spirit are dull as night, and his affections dark as Erebus."[152]

To these scenes each day's progress of this war attaches an additional and historical interest. Upon mountain stream and valley the boys in blue are fastening associations which will challenge the reverence and wonder of all coming generations. Thither through all the years to be the lovers of human liberty will repair to bless the soil baptized by the blood of so many patriot martyrs for the cause of free government. The plains of Waterloo and of Austerlitz will be tame in glory beside Chickamauga and Mission Ridge. While the former names can but forever stain the page of time, the latter ones will illuminate it with an imperishable and soul-inspiring beauty.

The crescent and the star have been merged- the 11th and 12th Corps are blended into one. Singular vicissitudes in campaigning have kept these two organizations in close connection since the autumn of 1862. During the winter of that year they formed the fourth Grand Reserve Division of the Army of the Potomac under Major General Franz Sigel. They were closely allied in the battles of Chancellorsville and Gettysburg. In September last they were sent to the Army of the Cumberland under Major General Hooker and shortly afterward joined in the important work of opening the river and railroad communication between Bridgeport and Chattanooga. During the battles of Lookout Mountain and Mission Ridge, though still nominally belonging to the same command, the two corps by a series of singular chances became separated and participated in entirely different operations. They joined company again however at the termination of the campaign. By an edict from the War Department the two veteran organizations are now made to fuse themselves into a new creation, the 20th Corps. The composition of the divisions and brigades has been announced and the soldiers who carried the star to the summit of Lookout and those who unfurled the crescent from Mission Ridge are learning to fraternize under the new regime.[153]

Yet the breaking up of these old organizations of the army is no trivial matter, and should not be done except for the gravest reasons. Their names, numbers, and symbols became entwined with the powerful associations of the camp and campaign, and accumulate a charm and prestige no less dear to, than they are potent in their influence upon every soldier. They are the nucleus of that esprit du corps which is the slow growth of time, and which, though far from being least of the moral forces of the army, lives and dies with the organization that nurtures and sustains it. The torn and weather-stained colors that have been borne through the flame and storm of a dozen campaigns, the old regiments, brigades, and divisions which have together withstood the shock of many a battle,

---

[152] Lee is quoting the fifth act of "The Merchant of Venice" by William Shakespeare.

[153] This consolidation of the 11th and 12th Corps allowed General Hooker the opportunity to get rid of both General Carl Schurz and General Adolph von Steinwehr, both divisional commanders of the 11th Corps with mixed combat records. Tyndale's brigade was designated the Third Brigade, First Division of the 20th Corps and consisted of the 82nd Illinois, 101st Illinois, 45th New York, 143rd New York, 61st Ohio, and 82nd Ohio regiments. Brigadier General Alpheus S. Williams led the First Division and General Hooker led the 20th Corps. It was at this same time that General Tyndale was granted medical leave which eventually ended his military service; Colonel James S. Robinson of the 82nd Ohio assumed brigade command in late April 1864 and would lead the brigade for the rest of the war with Captain Lee serving as his assistant adjutant general.

attain a sort of sacredness in the estimation of the soldiers which it is next to sacrilege to violate by innovations and substitutions not absolutely necessary.[154]

It is not strange therefore that the demise of these two old organizations, venerable for their years and hallowed by so many memories should be generally lamented. The men who have followed the star and the crescent for so long and so faithfully who have been guided by them through the smoke and flame of so many contests, who have borne them through so many weary marches and fixed them upon so many strongholds of the enemy, cannot give up these old emblems without sadness. Yet all are willing to hope that the new luminary which appears in the military horizon, blending the brilliancy of the star with the soft and constant gleam of the crescent, may ever shine with a steady, increasing, and enduring glory. May it meet with no inglorious eclipse, nor its splendor cease to burn until it shows the flag of the Union floating above the last dark lurking place of treason and rebellion.

Notes in Dixie Vol. IV

Cassville, Georgia
May 20, 1864

A lull in the hitherto incessant marching and fighting of the 20th Corps enables me, my dear *Gazette*, to give you a summary account of the late glorious operations of the armies commanded by Major General Sherman. Screened from the broiling Georgia sun by the shade of a tent fly, your correspondent writes from a point near Cassville, Georgia. Over the ground the brave men of the First Division swept before them the Rebels of Hood's corps only two hours since. Just beyond, the enemy made a determined stand and seemed resolved to resist our farther advance. Skirmishing continued until a late hour last night but at daybreak not a Rebel was to be seen. They have resumed their southward flight from the "Yankee vandals." General Schofield's corps[155] has just gone forward in pursuit, but Hooker's ironclads are lying to for a few hours rest.

The various divisions and brigades of the newly organized 20th Corps had not been assembled until the order came to move to the front. They were scattered from Chattanooga to Nashville, engaged in guarding railroads, posts, etc. They made their first acquaintance as members of the same organization within sight and sound of the enemy's guns. The First Division under General Williams marched from Bridgeport on the 2nd of May. On the evening of the 3rd it reached the front of Point Lookout and encamped in Chattanooga Valley. On the 4th, the division marched on, passing through Rossville and near the battlefield of Chickamauga. On the other hand, as the column passed, could be seen the horrible evidences of intensity and violence of the storm of battle that had here arisen and spent itself. The scarred, broken, splintered trees, the debris of battle strewn about the forests and fields, the sadly frequent groups of clay mounds from which now and then a protruding bony limb pleaded with rightful eloquence for a few shovelfuls of kindred dust- all these things spoke with fearful impressiveness of the horrid work war had made among these now silent and dismal forests.

On the 6th Williams' division joined Butterfield's near Taylor's Ridge and in front of Buzzard Roost. Palmer's 14th Corps had already taken its position on the left and made threatening demonstrations upon the enemy's stronghold. McPherson's command consisted of three corps was rapidly coming up from Chattanooga. The 4th and 23rd Corps were hastening down from London. Altogether an immense army was being hastily but quietly gathered in front of the Rebel army of Johnston, and the latter was being rapidly brought to the alternative of a fight or retreat.

---

[154] General Tyndale's medical certificate signed May 21, 1864 stated that Tyndale was suffering from "great nervous excitability, fits of despondency and aggression of spirits supposed to be connected with a wound of the head received at Antietam." A subsequent certificate also cited partial paralysis of the extremities in connection with head trauma. Tyndale wrote, in a letter to General Hooker in 1870, that "the mere physical act of writing and the fixed attention it required caused me acute suffering, so much so that the mere signing of my name to official papers became a torture." Tyndale resigned his commission August 24, 1864, writing that "my physician declares that I require many months of rest before I can regain strength for duty of any kind." Tyndale resumed peaceful pursuits in Philadelphia and received a brevet promotion to major general to date March 13, 1865. He died from the effects of several heart attacks March 19, 1880, five days shy of his 59th birthday. Tyndale Memoir, op. cit.

[155] Major General John M. Schofield led the Army of the Ohio which included the 23rd Corps.

Major General Alpheus S. 'Ol' Pap' Williams of Michigan proudly displays the red star badge on his hat denoting the First Division, 20th Corps. (Library of Congress)

On the 7th the column crossed Taylor's Ridge at Nickajack Gap and reached Trickum Post Office. McPherson was by this time pushing his command down the Snake Creek Gap thus threatening the enemy's rear at Resaca. On the 10th the 20th Corps followed in the same direction and on the 13th arrived in position in front of the enemy's works around Resaca. By this time the enemy had been driven from his positions at Dalton and Buzzard Roost and was being pushed down the railroad toward Resaca by the 4th and 23rd Corps. On the 14th the connection was formed by these corps and the remainder of the army which had debouched from Snake Creek Gap. Thus the enemy's position at Resaca became completely invested by the vast army of General Sherman on at least two sides. General Logan's corps (15th) kept his attention occupied in front while the 20th Corps was quickly shifted to his right, the weakest portion of his line. In the meantime a portion of McPherson's commanded succeeded in crossing the Oostenaula and again threatened the enemy's rear. Hooker, Howard, and Schofield now vigorously pressed the enemy's right. At 5 P.M. on the 14th, Hood's Rebel corps succeeded in forcing back Stanley's division of the 4th Corps. General Williams' division of the 20th had just arrived and was in the act of taking position in the woods when the Rebel columns swarmed down after Stanley's discomfited regiments. The enemy at once made for the 5th Indiana Battery which was posted in an open field and the infantry support of which immediately gave way. On came the confident foe intoxicated by success. The battery men stood manfully by their guns and kept their deep throats gleaming with rapid and incessant volumes of flame. The enemy was permitted to approach within 100 yards of the battery when General Williams ordered the Third Brigade of his division to unmask itself from the timber and display itself in the rear of the battery and take the heights beyond. This gallant brigade, led by Colonel James S. Robinson of the 82nd Ohio, sprang forward with cheers and within the time it takes to tell it opened a tremendous fire upon the unsuspecting foe. It was a sublime movement. In a moment not only was the battery saved but Hood's Rebels were turned back in complete rout. It was by this time quite dark and the pursuit could not be continued.[156]

---

[156] Robinson's attack was delivered in "Army of the Potomac style," the regiments of the brigade formed in ranks, each regiment behind the other. The first regiment delivered its fire, then went to ground; the second regiment fired, then went to ground, etc. "Shocked, staggered, and shredded, the Confederates turn and flee," wrote historian Albert Castel. "Robinson's troops follow, still blasting away with their devastating volleys until the bugles call a halt."

On the 15th it was resolved that the strong points of the enemy's line upon his right must be assaulted and if possible captured. The 20th, 23rd, and 4th corps were to act in concert in this undertaking. At noon, Butterfield's division moved out to the attack supported by Williams' division, all of Hooker's Corps. The enemy's entrenchments were formed along the crest of a difficult ridge, the slope of which was covered by a dense forest so thick and tangled that the troops made their way through it with great difficulty. But they pushed bravely forward and soon a tremendous musketry fire opened along the entire line. The Rebels were driven from their first line and forced back to the second. This line was very strong and the enemy held it with great obstinacy. Butterfield maintained his position but could not succeed in advancing further. His losses were very severe but there was no flinching on the part of the veteran soldiers who had learned their first lessons of war in Virginia. They maintained their ground firmly in spite of a terrible storm of bullets, shells, canister, and every sort of missile the enemy could hurl at them. General Williams' division was now ordered to move forward and take position on the left of Butterfield's. This was done in handsome style and without serious resistance. Williams' brigades formed their line along the crest of the ridge. Thus the last series of hills covering Resaca on our left came into possession of our troops.

The Rebels, exasperated by our success and reduced to a desperate extremity, resolved to drive Williams from his position and turn our left flank. Stewart's division of Hood's Corps was formed four lines deep and led the onslaught. The Rebel troops quickly emerged from the dense woods and moved rapidly across the open field intervening between the railroad and General Williams' line. Our troops at once poured in on them a terrific fire. But their masses were too strong to be suddenly checked. They replied vigorously to our fire and steadily advanced. Colonel Robinson's brigade being on the extreme left of the line was now in imminent danger of being turned. The brave men of this brigade stood firmly in their places and with faces blackened with powder and streaming with sweat and blood they poured upon the Rebel lines one of the most terrific musketry fires ever heard. The enemy checked his advance, staggered, and fell back. Then ran along the Union line one of the wildest and most inspiring cheers that could be imagined. But the enemy, though whipped, was not discomfited. He rallied and again came forward to the assault. He met with the same reception as before but showed great persistency. He pushed his column until they arrived within a few yards of General Williams' line of battle. But the fierce storm of bullets was too much for him and again our brave fellows had the satisfaction of seeing the enemy withdraw not only whipped but routed. He left his dead and wounded, one battle flag, and hundreds of small arms lying upon the field.[157] It now became quite dark and the fighting along Williams' line entirely ceased. The quiet of evening was disturbed only by the

Robinson's counterattack halted the Confederate flanking effort. Castel, Albert. <u>Decision in the West: The Atlanta Campaign of 1864</u>. Lawrence: University of Kansas Press, 1992, pgs. 165-166

[157] The 3rd Wisconsin of General Thomas H. Ruger's Brigade, Williams' Division captured the colors of the 18th Alabama General Henry D. Clayton's during the battle of May 15, 1864. The colors of the 38th Alabama Infantry, also of Clayton's brigade, were captured by Captain Thomas J. Box of Co. D, 27th Indiana Infantry of Ruger's brigade the same day. Captain Box would be awarded the Medal of Honor in 1865 for capturing this flag. Sherman praised the action at Resaca, stating that "all our men showed the finest fighting qualities."

weird notes of the whippoorwill and the heart-rending cries of the Rebel wounded who were left uncared for between the hostile lines. The brave men of the Third Brigade were too humane to listen indifferently to these moanings of distress. Parties sallied out into the woods even beyond the picket lines and brought in poor helpless victims of a fiendish rebellion.

To cover his retreat the enemy made a night assault upon Butterfield's lines. He was gallantly repulsed and immediately began to retreat across the Oostenaula. By daybreak his columns had entirely disappeared and were in full retreat southward. The army immediately began the pursuit. Hooker's Corps being upon the left flank, crossed the Coosawatee on the 16th. The column passed in its march over that portion of the battleground occupied by the Rebel army. The entire country in the vicinity of Resaca is densely wooded, the forests being so thick as to be almost impenetrable. Where the surface has been cultivated the timber has been cut and the trunks left standing, giving a sort of somber aspect to the scenery. The natural features of the battlefield of Resaca are therefore very inviting. Besides, there were strewn about the dense jungles the most horrid evidences of the carnage that had been made in the Rebel ranks. Mangled and blackened corpses were left lying among heaps of rubbish and debris no more cared for than if they had been the carcasses of beasts. In one desolate place where General Hindman's division hospital had been located was found the living form of wounded man stretched upon the operating table for the amputation of a limb and abandoned by the rebel surgeons before the operation had been completed. Though still breathing his face had become black and mottled with the lines of death. Thus the rebel Confederacy cares for its soldiers.

But let me not dwell upon these sad and dreadful scenes. Hooker's Corps moved rapidly in pursuit of the enemy's right wing. The country traversed by his columns, never very fertile, presented a singularly abandoned appearance. The dwellings were mostly desolate, the doors swinging idly at the mandate of the wind. Now and then a family of women and children were found but never an able-bodied man. Inquiry developed the fact that all such were in Rebel service. The third and fourth days' march brought us into a better country though similarly depopulated. There were very few Negroes to be seen, those who have not escaped to our lines having mostly been transported to central Georgia. The inhabitants displayed much less bitterness than might have been anticipated. They all express themselves heartily tired of the war and anxious for peace upon any terms.

On the 19th General Hooker's columns came up with the Rebels under Hood, Polk, and Hardee as described in the beginning of this article. Our forces now possess Kingston to which trains of cars from Chattanooga have already followed us. We are also in possession of Rome. The citizens hereabouts seems greatly chagrined at the presence of our troops, they having been assured that if they would but feed the Rebel army it would maintain its position at Dalton. They are now opening their eyes to the scandalous deceptions that have been practiced upon them by the Rebel leaders.

Johnston's army is now falling back to another mountain stronghold at Etowah, where it is reported that the enemy is about to make another stand. How much of this is true remains to be seen and will soon be tested. In such places as Lookout Mountain, Missionary Ridge, and Buzzard Roost were not impregnable to the boys in blue; it is doubtful whether there is any other place in the Confederacy that will be. If the enemy is driven from Etowah he must inevitably fall back to Atlanta. There he will be driven to the alternative of fighting a fair pitched battle or of seeking his last ditch still farther toward the Gulf of Mexico.

This George N. Barnard view of the Resaca battlefield shows the tumbled and tangled nature of the heavily wooded ground over which Robinson's Brigade fought on both days of the battle. The brigade's counterattack against A.P. Stewart's division which helped save the 5th Indiana Battery may have been the unit's finest moment in the Atlanta Campaign; it was certainly the most noted. General Alpheus S. Williams wrote "on the 14th we moved through thickets and underbrush to the rear and in support of Butterfield's Division, and in the afternoon received a hurried order to move rapidly farther to the left to support Stanley's division of the 4th Corps. I reached the ground just in time to deploy one brigade and to repulse the Rebels handsomely. They had broken one brigade of Stanley's division and were pressing it with yells and were already near one battery (5th Indiana) when I astonished the exultant rascals by pushing the brigade from the woods directly across the battery, which was in a small open in a small valley. They skedaddled as fast as they had advanced, hardly exchanging a half dozen volleys. They were so surprised that they fired wildly and didn't wound a dozen men. I was much complimented for the affair and General Howard, commander of the 4th Corps, came and thanked me." The following day, the men of Williams' division captured the battle flag of the 38th Alabama Infantry including the colonel and several hundred prisoners. A lack of support from the raw recruits in General Alvin P. Hovey's division drew Williams' and Lee's ire; the erroneous newspaper reports in the Cincinnati press that gave credit to Hovey's troops embittered both men. Captain Lee wrote that the newspaper accounts were totally false, and reported that Hovey's men refused to advance while under shellfire despite repeated requests delivered by him personally on behalf of Colonel Robinson and General Williams. "But those men, so valiant on paper, could not be induced to budge an inch toward the desired point. Yet for the injustice done to the brave men who actually did the work, of which the whole credit was given to others, while they whose blood bought the victory were not even mentioned, no attention would have been paid to this scandalous misrepresentation." (Library of Congress)

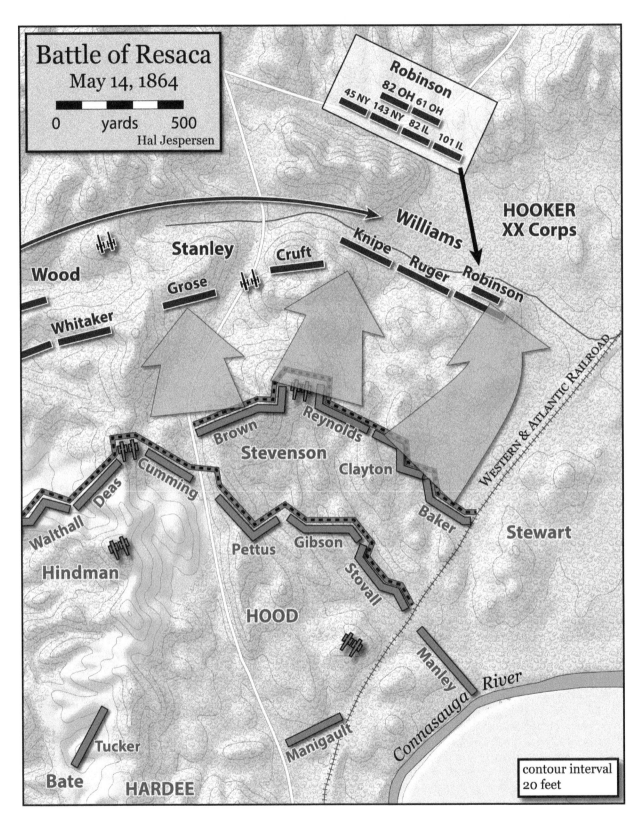

Battle of Resaca
May 14, 1864

0 yards 500
Hal Jespersen

Robinson
45 NY 82 OH 61 OH
143 NY 82 IL 101 IL

Williams

HOOKER
XX Corps

Wood

Stanley

Cruft

Knipe Ruger Robinson

Grose

Whitaker

Brown Reynolds

Stevenson

Clayton

Cumming Deas

Walthall

Hindman

Pettus Gibson

Baker

Stewart

WESTERN & ATLANTIC RAILROAD

Stovall

HOOD

Manley

Connasauga River

Tucker

Manigault

Bate HARDEE

contour interval
20 feet

Battle of Resaca, Georgia, May 14, 1864
(Hal Jespersen, www.cwmaps.com)

Near Acworth, Georgia

June 17, 1864

       From the outbreak of this war the political element has been the bane of our army. It is a lamentable fact that among the thousands of unselfish patriots who, taking their lives in their hands, sprang at the call of their imperiled country, very many of that worthless class of men known as politicians attached themselves to the army for mere ad captandum purposes. The exigencies of the country opened a new road to place and power, of which the political tricksters were neither the last nor the least zealous in availing themselves. However unfitted by nature or experience for the vast and sacred responsibility of commanding men, there was no military office or appointment too high for the scope of their ambition or the reach of their intrigues. Bringing with them a very small proportion of brains, but a very large propensity for wire pulling, many of them quickly wormed themselves up to the positions for which they had neither ability or adaptation. Such men were no sooner in power than they began to use their patronage and influence in such a way as best served their party purposes and secured the greatest amount of newspaper glorification and lying praise of everything they did. Thus many a military quack has been carried up and kept up by mere political inflation. The severe ordeal of actual service has shown up the true caliber of large numbers of these scheming pretenders and they have been accordingly weeded out or sloughed off. Abandoning the army they again betook themselves to political gambling, and almost invariably became the antagonists of the war policy of the government. To cover their own incapacity they turn and rend the country they have cheated.

       Though our armies have been well rid of large numbers of this class, there are still many who cling to them for the emoluments and political eclat of the service. Where they control, disaster invariably attends our arms. It is to such true soldiers and mere soldiers as Grant, Sherman, Thomas, and others of their class that we must look for the proper management of our vast military operations. If they cannot succeed it is idle, it is foolish to attempt to supply their places by pretentious demagogues and politicians.[158]

       During the brief repose allowed by General Sherman to his army after the battle of Resaca and the occupation of Kingston, a circular was issued by the general commanding, in which, after stating that the impression had become prevalent that the mails to and from the army had been prohibited, which impression he declared to be wholly unfounded in fact, and declaring that he desired that the soldiers should have the best possible opportunities for full and free communication with their friends. He concluded as follows: "What the commanding general does discourage is the maintenance of that class of men who will not take a musket and fight, but follow an army to pick up news for sale, speculating upon a species of information that is dangerous to the army and our cause, and who are more used to bolster up worthless and idle officers than to notice the hard working and meritorious, whose modesty is generally equal to their courage and who scorn to seek the cheap flattery of the press."[159]

       In this language the miserable perversion of the press which has been made by a set of sycophants and party tools for the support of demagogues in shoulder straps receives a merited denunciation. In late issues of the Cincinnati papers occur certain statements in regard to the performances of Hovey's division of the 23rd Corps during the assault of the army on Resaca on the 15th of May. The statements referred to are utterly false, and must have been made by someone who was either ignorant of the facts or else designed a misrepresentation of them. It is asserted that Hovey's men repulsed the attacks of the enemy and the most extravagant praises are bestowed upon Hovey's "recruits" for the brilliant feat. Now for the facts.

---

[158] One is left to wonder which specific general officers Captain Lee is referring to in this scathing commentary on the undue influence of the political generals, but the balance of the letter may imply that his target was General Alvin Peterson Hovey of Indiana.

[159] General Sherman issued this circular on May 20, 1864 at Kingston, Georgia.

The enemy was not repulsed by Hovey's men, and they fired scarcely a shot during the whole fight. He was repulsed by Brigadier General Williams' veterans of the 20th Corps. General Williams' division was in position a full hour before any portion of the 23rd Corps arrived. When it did arrive, Hovey's division was formed in the rear and in support of Williams, and, so far as the writer could see, lay perfectly flat upon the ground to avoid the bevies of bullets that constantly filled the air during the battle. The left of General Williams' line was held by Colonel Robinson's Third Brigade, which on the previous evening had so gallantly turned the rout of Stanley's division into a victory. Upon this brigade the enemy made two assaults with forces massed four lines deep, and in each instance was repulsed with terrible loss. During the fight Colonel Robinson fearing that his left, which was exposed, might be turned by the enemy, made repeated efforts to get only a regiment or two of Hovey's "recruits" to support the exposed flank. But those men, so valiant on paper, could not be induced to budge an inch toward the desired point. Of all these facts the writer is personally cognizant, he having himself delivered the earnest requests of Colonel Robinson to the officer commanding the "recruits" of General Hovey. Yet for the injustice done to the brave men who actually did the work, of which the whole credit was given to others, while they whose blood bought the victory were not even mentioned, no attention would have been paid to this scandalous misrepresentation.[160]

After three days of rest in the vicinity of Cassville and Kingston the vast army of General Sherman resumed its advance against the enemy. The troops, provided with 20 days' rations and stripped for battle, were cautioned that they were about to launch into the interior with little regard for communications or bases of supply. It was understood that Johnston's army was lodged in the fastnesses of the Allatoona Mountains in the vicinity of Etowah, on the line of the railroad. This position, like that at Resaca, was capable of being turned by means of a practicable road leading over the mountains and debouching into the open country at Burnt Hickory opposite Dallas. Once at Dallas General Sherman would be in the rear of Johnston at Allatoona and have an open road to the Chattahoochee.

On the 23rd General Hooker's corps led the advance from Cassville and on the same day crossed the Etowah at Enharlee Mills. On the 24th the corps without serious opposition arrived at Burnt Hickory. On the 25th the march was resumed toward Dallas. The three divisions moved abreast on nearly parallel roads. General Williams was upon the right on the main road to Dallas. All went smoothly on

Resaca

"A very rapid fire of canister was opened on the advancing foe, which quickly cleared the field, the greater portion of the enemy's troops going into the woods toward our left. The pieces were immediately turned by hand to the left, and spherical case and shell were used, canister being held in readiness in case they gained the hill on our immediate left. Some few of the rebels reached the road at the foot of the hill, within fifty yards of the battery, but the main body appeared to be greatly disconcerted by the firing. They made one more endeavor to get over the hill more to our left, but were met in this attack at first by the fire of the battery with canister, and as they turned, by a volley from Robinson's brigade, of Williams' division, of General Hooker's corps, and who immediately charged and drove them clear over the hill out of sight in great confusion."

~ *Captain Peter Simonson, 5th Indiana Battery*

---

[160] Lee is referring to the second day at Resaca when General Williams' division was attacked by A.P. Stewart's division. The two brigades of General Alvin P. Hovey's division, the 1st Brigade under Colonel Richard F. Barter (120th, 124th, and 128th Indiana) and the 2nd Brigade under Colonel John McQuiston (123rd, 129th, and 130th Indiana), took position on Williams' left but "came under shellfire and promptly went to ground" where they would remain "in spite of all orders and pleas to get up." The inaction of the Hoosiers infuriated General Williams, who referred to one of the Indiana colonels as a "damned cowardly son of a bitch." Castel, op. cit., pgs. 176-178

until 3 o'clock P.M. when General Williams received an order to face his division about and move at once to the support of Geary who had encountered the enemy and became dangerously engaged. The head of the column was by this time within five miles of Dallas. The command promptly turned about and taking a by-path reached Geary's line at 4:30 P.M. General Hooker ordered General Williams to immediately prepare to attack the enemy, directing that the division push the Rebels back about two miles and take and hold a point which it was important should be at once brought into our possession. General Williams formed his division into three lines, a brigade in each, with the Third Brigade leading. The 61st Ohio was deployed as skirmishers and at once relieved the skirmishers of Geary. The troops being formed stood waiting the signal to advance. It was a thrilling moment. These brave men were about to open the tragedy of battle. Upon them were the eyes of their beloved commanders, the calm intrepid Hooker, the sober earnest gaze of Thomas, the steady and determined glance of Williams. Freemen, patriots, standing quietly at their muskets waiting for the call to go forward and do or die in defense of the holiest trust ever committed to patriot keeping; holding in their hands the rights and destinies of man, bearing in their beating hearts the hopes and purposes of a nation. There was something sublime in their firm quiet bearing betokening a manhood adequate to the emergency, a solemn and fixed determination that duty must at all hazards be done.

The final orders and instructions having been hurriedly given, the bugle sounded the advance, the line moved forward through the thick forest and the roar of battle at once began. The enemy fell back stubbornly, leaving some prisoners in our hands. But there was no hesitation, not the slightest wavering on the part of Williams' veterans. On went the steady line until about three-quarters of a mile had been gained, when the ammunition running low, General Ruger's brigade was ordered to relieve Robinson's which now retired to the rear with the calmness and order of drill. General Hooker, who was present from the beginning of the fight, complimented them upon the ground, declaring that its conduct was "splendid." General Ruger's troops now pressed the enemy one half mile farther when the Rebel artillery opened upon the line with shells and canister, and the battle became bloody and obstinate. The fight continued without intermission until 6:30 P.M. when Colonel Robinson's brigade was ordered to go again to the front. The order was obeyed with alacrity and the men who had opened the battle had the satisfaction of closing it. Arriving upon the line they immediately reopened their fire. The enemy's artillery made fearful havoc among them but not one inch would those devoted men yield. They remained firmly in their position until all their ammunition was gone. They then searched the cartridge boxes of the wounded and dead and thus managed to keep up the fire until the battles was ended by the darkness of night which slowly settled upon that mountain forest.

Thus closed the first day's fighting south of the Etowah. It was a sanguinary contest as the losses attest. The Third Brigade lost 35 killed and 200 wounded. The entire division behaved with great credit and seems to have convinced our western fellow-soldiers that men from the Potomac Army *will* fight.[161]

Notes in Dixie Vol. VI

Near Kennesaw Mountain, Georgia
June 23, 1864

War has its seasons of storm and calm very much as the weather has. Even in the midst of active operations the destructive elements that compose armies have their fits of quietude as well as of turbulence. Were it not so, my dear *Gazette*, the name of A.T. Sechand would be one of the rarest of your collection and would (what a blessing to your readers) very seldom make its appearance in your columns. But fortunately, or unfortunately, a brief period of calm in the murky atmosphere of war enables me to submit to the charitable consideration of yourself and readers a few more crude pencilings from my notebook.

Permit me, dear *Gazette*, to felicitate myself upon being farther into Dixie than when I last wrote you. My progress since then has been slow but sure, and has been (it is needless to say) considerably regulated by the movements of General Sherman's vast army. I now write from about the most southward point in the "land of cotton" attained by us Northern vandals on this route since the outbreak of the rebellion. To be more exact, it is southwest of Kennesaw Mountain and five miles from Marietta. To describe to you by what route I have reached

---

[161] Lee is referring to what became known as the Battle of New Hope Church fought May 25, 1864.

this point would be like defining the meanderings of a bird of passage. Perhaps I may give you a general idea of it. Fixing our starting point at position of the 20th Corps in front of the enemy's works at Dallas, let me conduct you (in imagination) by bridle path and plantation roads through a wild, densely wooded mountainous country in a northeasterly direction to Lost Mountain. Such was the route traveled by Hooker's Corps from the 2nd to the 6th inst. At Lost Mountain (which is nothing more than the lofty and abrupt termination on the right of a series of hills which end in the peaks of Kennesaw on the left) we find the enemy in strong force and presenting a bold front. Accordingly our line of battle is formed and we display a threatening aspect in order to cover the movement of the remainder of the Army of the Cumberland and also of the armies of the Tennessee and Ohio, all of which are, in like manner, shifting to the left. It is a sort of hand over hand movement in the direction of the railroad.

By the march across the Etowah and to Burnt Hickory, we compelled Johnston to abandon his strong mountain lodgment at Allatoona and obtained possession of the railroad from Kingston to that point. It was evidently Sherman's intention to march directly to Atlanta had not Johnston determined to risk a battle rather than permit him to do so. Johnston quickly seeing his danger precipitated his entire army directly across Sherman's path at Dallas, and taking advantage of the mountainous character of the country, constructed field works which rendered his position very strong before our army could concentrate. Sherman therefore now moves his army to the left, towards the railroad, and Johnston is again compelled to abandon his works and make corresponding movements. Thus the two armies came to confront each other along the series of heights extending from Lost Mountain to Kennesaw. Sherman's left extended across the railroad south of Acworth by the 8th inst. Hooker remained in front of Lost Mountain until the 15th inst. At that date, the movements along our immense line had been such as to compel Johnston to refuse his left. He evacuated his position at Lost Mountain and Hooker plunged forward and pushed him back to a new and more formidable line of entrenchments.

Geary's division, supported by Williams', established our line within 100 yards of the enemy's rifle pits. Here our forces entrenched amid the incessant fire of musketry on the night of the 15th. On the morning of the 16th the hostile parties found themselves so close to each other that they bandied epithets and exchanged verbal as well as leaden compliments. Neither party could show himself without attracting a salute of a larger number of guns than are allowed to persons of the same rank by the army regulations. Day and night the bullets whizzed incessantly like fiendish sprites among the trees. Your A.T. Sechand lay himself down by a tree and endeavored by all the subtle arts he knows of to compose himself to sleep. But in vain. The wicked leaden-winged elves kept up a horrible midnight carnival above and all around him. Each little Rebel fiend seemed to come nearer and to make a more unseemly noise than any that preceded it. Thus wore the night away-a night that will never be forgotten.

On the night of the 16th, the Rebels abandoned their works and withdrew. On the morning of the 17th we had the satisfaction to enter one of the finest lines of field fortifications I have ever seen. Advancing about two miles we found the enemy posted behind another series of works equally strong. We entrenched again within about 1,000 yards of the Rebel line. Active skirmishing and desultory cannonading immediately began, and continued until the night of the 18th, when the enemy again abandoned his works and fell back. We pursued him on the morning of the 19th and again had the satisfaction to take possession of one of the finest lines of field works that could be imagined. The question naturally arose as to how the enemy could afford to spend so much pain and labor upon these works of temporary defense. There is a report that Johnston has an immense corps of Negro laborers which he keeps constantly at work upon the fortifications of this kind as the prospective movements of his army will probably develop the necessity for.

Hooker's Corps now advanced to find the enemy in a new position near Kennesaw Mountain. General Howard's Corps joined us on the left and General Schofield's on the right. The skirmishing and artillery dueling immediately began again and continued incessantly. Though there was no general engagement yet hostilities were never for a moment suspended. Indeed such has been the state of affairs almost constantly since the commencement of the campaign. Without any very general engagement the troops are kept constantly under fire and their nerves always in a state of anxious tension. Sometimes the battle storm breaks out at some point of the line with immense fury and a general engagement seems imminent. But it finally proves to be a merely local matter and though a battle in itself yet does not bring the two armies into an unreserved grappling with each other. They are generally caused by an advance of some portion or other of our line with a view to wrenching from the enemy some position of

Major General John Geary
(Library of Congress)

importance to him. Thus the fighting continues day after day and week after week. Now it will break out upon the right, now upon the left, and again in the center. All the time our line keeps steadily advancing and the enemy is crowded back mile after mile and from position to position.

On the 20th General Hooker moved Williams' division to the right and put it in position on the plantation of a rebellion Negro trader named Atkinson. The lord of the manor had migrated southward some weeks before, taking with him his most "likely" human chattels. His infirm and decrepit Negroes were left to the tender mercies of the vandal Yanks, whose advent his flight had anticipated. The poor creatures spoke very naively of their master's defection, but seemed to be not very seriously affected by the bereavement. Perhaps this is not much to be wondered at in view of the fact reported of him that his chief occupation was that of raising (let me not say breeding) Negroes for the market. O humanity, for shame!

On the morning of the 22nd General Hooker notified his division commanders to keep their commands in readiness for an advance. At 10:30 A.M. General Williams moved his division forward one mile. The position now taken, and in which the division still remains, was most important. Being southwest of the Rebel position at Kennesaw Mountain and overlooking and threatening their left flank, it became a matter of great importance to dislodge us from it. The enemy attempted this during the afternoon of the 22nd but signally failed.

The Rebel General Hood plunged his entire corps against our line, but it was beaten back with terrible slaughter. Once more the enemy was taught that to trifle with Williams' veterans was dangerous work. Twice at Resaca, once at Dallas, and once here this splendid division under its brave and popular commander has fairly measured swords with the enemy and always with the same result. I believe a more valorous and noble body of soldiers does not exist than Williams' division of the 20th Army Corps. I must defer a full description of the battle of the 22nd for the present. Perhaps at another time I may give you some account of it.

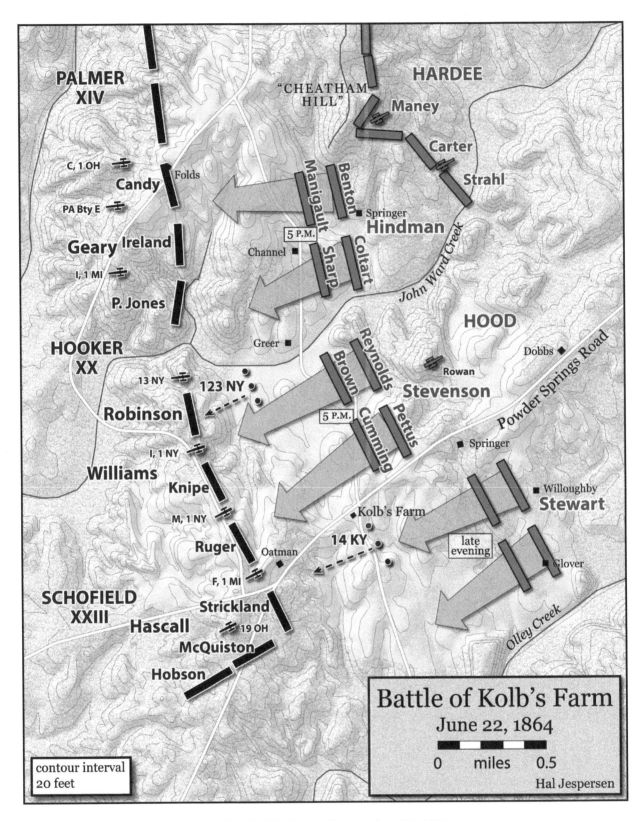

PALMER
XIV

HARDEE

"CHEATHAM
HILL"

Maney

Carter

Strahl

C, 1 OH

Candy

Folds

PA Bty E

Geary   Ireland

I, 1 MI

P. Jones

Manigault
Benton
Springer
5 P.M.
Hindman

Channel
Sharp
Coltart

John Ward Creek

HOOKER
XX

Greer

HOOD

Dobbs

13 NY

123 NY

Robinson

I, 1 NY

Williams

Knipe

M, 1 NY

Ruger   Oatman

F, 1 MI

SCHOFIELD
XXIII

Hascall

Strickland

19 OH

McQuiston

Hobson

Reynolds
Brown
Cumming
Pettus

5 P.M.

Rowan

Stevenson

Springer

Powder Springs Road

Willoughby
Stewart

Kolb's Farm

14 KY

late
evening

Glover

Olley Creek

Battle of Kolb's Farm
June 22, 1864

0   miles   0.5

Hal Jespersen

contour interval
20 feet

Battle of Kolb's Farm, Georgia, June 22, 1864
(Hal Jespersen, www.cwmaps.com)

Near Kennesaw Mountain, Georgia
June 25, 1864

     The month of June has been, in a double sense, a month of storms in Georgia. While vast armies have been struggling for the mastery and destruction of each other, nature has seemed to catch the contagion of man's ill humor and doffing her smiles has put on the most ungenial looks. Rain, rain, incessant rain has fallen day after day and night after night, drenching our soldiers, saturating their clothing and blankets, and making the trenches where they have to constantly confront the enemy beds of watery mire. On the 22nd however there were indications of better weather, the day dawning bright and clear and a light breeze sweeping the last shreds of humid vapor swiftly from before the smiling sun. Yet another storm was brewing- the dreadful and destructive storm of battle. At 9 A.M. General Hooker ordered his division commanders to hold their commands in readiness to advance. A reconnaissance had developed the presence of the enemy in our front and the reconnoitering detachment had taken possession of and fortified a very important position overlooking almost his entire line. There had been the usual amount of skirmishing on the picket lines during the previous 36 hours, showing that the enemy was still looking out for us and as yet had no intention to retreat.

Lieutenant Colonel David Thomson, 82nd Ohio
(Richard Fink Collection)

     At 10:30 A.M., General Williams' division was in motion. The respective positions of the brigades having been previously designated, they moved successively, each to a particular point to occupy in the line. Along the crest of a high wooded hill was placed Robinson's Third Brigade, the left of which connected with the division of General Geary. Robinson's position overlooked an open space 1,200 yards in width and skirted on the farther side by a thick forest along the edge of which the Rebel skirmishers were arrayed, covered by well-built rail barricades. This point also commanded a fine view of the peaks of Kennesaw, three miles distant to the left and rear, and overlooked the country in the direction of Marietta a distance of five miles. It was in short a most excellent position for defense and within easy artillery range of the wooded plateau occupied by the enemy.

     On the right of the Third Brigade General Knipe's brigade extended the line along the crest of a more unpretending hill considerably in advance of the one occupied by Robinson's command. This disposition was rendered necessary by the conformation of the ground. It had its advantages also in giving it a converging fire upon the enemy's position. On the right of General Knipe was formed Ruger's brigade (the Second), thus completing an immense concave line half a mile in extent. Along this concave were ranged three batteries, one being in the center or most retired point of the line supported by the Third Brigade and the other two upon the wings. The extreme right covered the main road to Marietta and was entirely unsupported. Schofield's Corps was hastening to join us on that flank but had not yet arrived. The vast importance of its coming quickly will appear in the sequel.

The division being in position the skirmishers were pushed forward and established their line 200 yards from that of the enemy. The artillery raked the Rebel line from one end to the other, some of the shots being really splendid. But each Rebel skirmisher had a little fortification of his own, and by keeping well down in his pit could in most instances avoid the flying missiles. Soon however the enemy attempted to relieve his line and boldly marched out a detachment for that purpose. The Johnnies are quickly descried by the artillery men and in a moment a half dozen shells are hustling through the air bearing with lightning speed General Williams' (or 'Old Pap' Williams as he is more familiarly called) compliments to the traitors. White puffs of smoke instantly show where the shells have exploded close to the Rebel detachment. The enemy immediately scatters and breaks for the woods, and the Rebel picket is 'relieved' in double quick time.

Thus the day wore away. During the afternoon several assaults were made on Knipe's skirmishers, the enemy thus incontinently intimating his hostile intentions toward our right flank. Will Schofield come in time, thoughtfully meditated everyone. The enemy under cover of the woods was evidently massing his forces for some purpose. Could it be a defensive or offensive one? And if the latter, what if he should plunge into our thin unsupported line before Schofield would arrive? Such was the question for which we were anxiously seeking a satisfactory answer when the welcome news came that Schofield was in position and that the danger that our flank would be turned was past. But then our line was still very much extended, and being devoid of support, might not the enemy by a desperate dash break through it? Let us see.

Of all the words in the English language, the term butternut best describes the color of the dress worn by Johnston's soldiers. Back in the distant recesses of the woods we could discover a butternut-colored column moving to our right. It is partially concealed by the foliage but enough is seen to show our artillerymen where to direct their aim. Again General Williams sends his compliments to the butternuts and the Rodmans of Winegar's Battery[162] speak more loudly and effectively for the Union than ever did windy politicians in the halls of Congress. The column disappears in the deep foliage and once more there is tolerable quiet along the line.

The evening comes on apace but in that there is no assurance that a battle will not occur. On the contrary it is proverbial that from 3-8 P.M. is the fighting portion of the day. The heaviest work of battle is almost invariably done during that period. Accordingly at about 6 P.M. the firing on Knipe's line suddenly began to grow more fierce and rapid. The enemy was advancing. He quickly drove the skirmishers back upon the main line and debouched from the timber in heavy and well sustained masses. Now the deep volleys begin to roll and Knipe's men are enveloped in the battle smoke. The quick flashes leap from the deep-throated cannon and their bellowing thunder mingles savagely with the sharp cracking of musketry.

Confederate View

"We advanced and soon struck the enemy, driving him quickly before us from his advanced works which consisted of one line of logs and rail works complete, and one partially constructed. The fire under which this was done was exceedingly heavy and the artillery of the enemy, which was massed in large force and admirably posted was served with a rapidity and fatal precision which could not be surpassed. The nature of the ground over which we passed was most unfavorable to such a movement- the two right brigades moved for much of the way over open fields, the two left through dense undergrowth. The line thus became more irregular and broken every moment, and when the two right brigades had driven the enemy into their main works the line was so much broken and mixed up that it was not deemed practicable to carry the works by assault. The commands were halted and the best possible line under the circumstances was formed. My loss was heavy- 807 killed and wounded."

~Major General Carter L. Stevenson, commanding division

---

[162] Battery I, 1st New York Light Artillery under Captain Charles E. Winegar was formerly known as Wiedrich's Battery, and had been re-equipped with 3-inch Rodman rifled guns in September 1862 after the five of the battery's six guns were disabled during the Battle of Second Bull Run in August 1862.

Kolb's Farm

"Our skirmishers now came swarming out of the woods at thrice quick time, not even looking back. They had no occasion to for not more than 15 rods behind them came a long line of battle, four ranks deep, at double quick. For 30 minutes the scrap was animated and everybody kept busy. Their whole force then moved forward under cover of the hill and firing slackened. We distinctly heard the order "Fix bayonets," and we were expecting them to try a rush upon us. From the beginning of our service we had never been budged from any place we tried to hold, and we had no thoughts of being driven then."

"I was at the right of my gun when a ball crashed through the top of the head of a man standing at arm's length from me. He was a young fellow, about 17. He fell on his back and every muscle seemed strained to its utmost tension. His captain, standing near, raised him to his feet; the man opened his eyes and exclaimed 'Captain, am I killed?' But he was dead, and did not hear the captain's reply."

~ Sergeant Frank Elliott, Battery M, 1st New York Light Artillery

But our attention is suddenly called away from Knipe's line of brave unyielding hearts by the developments in our own front. Quick as thought the Rebel skirmishers have leaped from their lurking places and are coming right down upon those of the Third Brigade. Winegar sees them and again his Rodmans speak with tongues of flame their words of iron. The missiles went hustling through the air nipping the huge branches from the trees like merest twigs, and bursting about the field or heaving up huge volumes of earth as they bound away over the yielding surface. But the enemy is deployed and has too many chances against them. Right on he comes and our skirmish line is compelled to withdraw. The Rebels pursue and soon their heavy columns debouch from the woods into the open field. General Williams, who has been puffing away at his pipe with as much complacency as an old salt would while giving orders in a moderate gale, now exclaiming, "There, Winegar, there, see them, see them, let them have it!" And Winegar did let them have it with a good will, making some magnificent shots. The shells exploded in the midst of the Rebel columns scattering them as a hurricane whirls in air freshly-built ricks of straw. The rebels broke and fled in utter confusion and soon disappeared behind bushes, fences, everything that could afford shelter or concealment. Nor did they venture to display their columns again before Winegar's terrible Rodmans.

The firing on General Knipe's line now slackened and the enemy withdrew completely repulsed at all points. Their skirmishers hastily sought their barricades again, bearing with them their wounded. At length the sputtering fire of the pickets and the heavy overhanging cloud of powder smoke remains the only tokens of the battle storm that encroach upon the quiet air of the evening. Thus ended the affair of the 22nd, one of the most brilliant of this campaign. Allow me to clear, dear *Gazette*, by proposing three cheers for "Pap" Williams old Red Star Division.

Map of the Atlanta defenses in July 1864 with the location of the 20th Corps circled. Directionally, north is on the left of this map. (Library of Congress)

CHAPTER EIGHT

At the Gates of Atlanta

Notes in Dixie Vol. VIII

Near Kennesaw Mountain, Georgia
July 3, 1864

You are aware, dear *Gazette*, that this is the anniversary of the glorious Battle of Gettysburg. One year ago today the Rebel army now fighting at the gates of Richmond fiercely plunged itself against the Army of the Potomac on Pennsylvania soil. One year ago today that proud Rebel host spent its fury and its strength in one last desperate effort to sweep over the serried barrier of Union bayonets which alone prevented its unfurling of the emblems of treason over Faneuil Hall and the pinnacles of the Monumental City. One year ago tonight that army began to march southward and has not since reversed its direction. Tomorrow, the nation's birthday, also brings the first anniversary of that glorious day when Grant's victorious army unfurled the standard of the Union from the frowning battlements of Vicksburg. Verily this should be out national thanksgiving time- the holy week of the Republic.

True our cause is not yet wholly triumphant and the rebellion is not only not crushed but presents a strong and dangerous front. The past year has been marked by reverses as well as crowned with victories, and there yet remains much to fear as well as hope for. But it is nonetheless true that the clock of the world has moved forward since July 4, 1863 and the shadow of the dial plate of civilization has since advanced many degrees. Were there no other object in this war than merely the overcoming of resistance to law and the restoration of the supremacy of the central government, we might have reason to be discouraged. But it is not so much to save our government that we fight as to establish the principle that underlies it. We fight to demonstrate the great truth that men have the right and the ability to frame and administer their own government and are not borne to be creatures of an arbitrary will. We fight to prove that the principles of justice, humanity, and patriotism are stronger in the hearts of men than injustice, inhumanity, and treason. We fight, in short, to prove that the form of government which conceded that man is free, that government is made for him and not he for the government, and that his own mind and heart are the safest repositories of justice and law and liberty, is the correct form. It is for this that we expend our blood and treasure; for this our great nation groans and travails in bloody sweat.

The progress of truth has always been slow and tedious. We should never be so over-sanguine of speedy triumph when right is arrayed against wrong. But this should be no cause for discouragement. We should exhibit it a patient firmness and an inflexible determination worthy of the great and glorious cause committed to our keeping. Even if it takes a score of years to re-establish this nation free and undivided, let us sternly resolve to fight on until we achieve that consummation.

Such, Mr. *Gazette*, is my 4th of July oration. And now the last sentence is hardly penned until here comes the stirring order to march. Again the enemy has abandoned his formidable line of entrenchments and we are to pursue him. I therefore respectfully beg pardon for this abrupt leave-taking, promising, however, to renew our interview at the first opportunity which the exigencies of the campaign will afford me.

Chattahoochee Heights, Georgia
July 7, 1864

Since the 2nd of May when we marched from our trim winter camps beside the majestic Tennessee, the soldiers of this division have lived a decidedly sylvan and nomadic sort of life. It would puzzle any one of them to make his way back over precisely the same route traveled by the division during the present campaign. It must not be supposed that this vast army in sweeping down through the wild mountainous country of northern Georgia has moved in a single column or marched only along the main roads and highways. On the contrary the army has moved in almost as many columns as there are divisions composing it. The divisions move as nearly as possible in parallel lines, carefully keeping up their connections with each other, in order than when the enemy is encountered there may be no vacancies in the line. Thus this immense army, stretched out in one continuous line from seven to twelve miles in length sweeps along over creeks, rivers, mountains, forests, and fields in pursuit of Johnston's rebellious legions. Only a portion of the troops move on the beaten roads and highways. Usually most of the columns march by the most unfrequented paths and byways, pursuing the pine-clad crests of mountain ridges, threading the dense and tangled forests, and bivouacking and fighting amidst their wild copses and jungles. Thus our soldiers for more than two months past have been marching, fighting, and entrenching in the midst of these Georgian wildernesses, seeing and enjoying little more of civilized life than did the legions of Darius when they plunged into the uninhabited wilds of ancient Scythia.

On the crest of one of the forest-clad heights overlooking the Chattahoochee River and beneath a dark umbrageous canopy of southern foliage, I am tonight penning these lines. Among the silent trees gleam the myriad of lights of the encampment, while far above in the soft azure of a Southern sky, the pure lights of heaven shower down their gentle benisons of peace on earth and good will to men. The quiet of the evening air is comparatively unbroken save by the bands that here and there discourse inspiring strains of martial music, and by the unmelodious notes of musketry which at regular intervals resound discordantly along the picket lines. Unmindful of war's alarms the soldiers one by one sink to rest upon their earthly couches and dream of their peaceful homes in the far off Northern land not cursed by the devastating tread of armies.

By a series of strategic movements, which it would be difficult to describe minutely, this army has at length succeeded in forcing the enemy to abandon all his formidable works and next to impregnable positions and has compelled him to fall back to the line of the Chattahoochee. Since the army crossed the Etowah its progress has been slow, but suffering no serious reverse, it has steadily pressed the enemy back from one stronghold to another, and with comparatively small losses, has achieved results truly marvelous. Twice the army has entirely abandoned its communications to the mercy of the enemy and relying entirely upon its own strength and the genius of its leader, has swung off into a wild and destitute country and moving right across the enemy's flank, has compelled him to evacuate positions which it would have been next to impossible to take by direct assault. It was by a bold, daring movement of this kind that the Rebel leader was forced to yield the line of the Etowah and his boasted citadel of Allatoona Pass. By a similar movement the formidable line of the Kennesaw Mountain became an easy prey to the Union army.

On July 2nd, the Army of the Tennessee, marching behind the Army of the Cumberland as a curtain, moved rapidly to the right and directly down on the Rebel left flank towards the Chattahoochee. The Army of the Ohio, already upon the extreme right, joined in the movement and extended its line as far as Oily Creek. The enemy, from his watchtower on Kennesaw, observed our slightest movement and quickly intercepted General Sherman's designs. Under the cover of night, he evacuated his works and withdrew. On the following morning the flag of the Union gloriously greeted the first gray streaks of dawn from the peaks of Kennesaw. The army was in motion by 6 A.M. and shortly afterwards marched into the enemy's breastworks. No more formidable lines of field works were probably ever constructed. The main breastwork was riveted with heavy timbers and covered by an embankment of earth from four to sixteen feet in thickness. Loopholes for musketry were constructed by placing a heavy timber called a head log on top of the embankment and elevated a few inches from its surface. Thus the enemy completely sheltered himself from both bullets and shells. But the Rebels were not satisfied with this. Our brave boys might easily leap their ditches, dash over breastworks, and bayonet them in their trenches.

To guard against a contingency of this kind the less brave than cautious enemy constructed a continuous line of chevaux-de-frise a few yards in advance of this breastwork. This obstacle consisted of sharp stakes closely set in the ground and protruding from it at an angle of about 45 degrees. Again a few yards in front of this there was usually a line of abatis constructed with the tops of trees so trimmed as to leave the branches protruding from the stem like a many pronged fork. Beyond the abatis the timber was felled with the tops outward so as to make a tangled and almost impassable surface over which no line of battle could advance in any sort of order. Add to all this the natural strength of the positions invariably chosen by the enemy and something like an adequate conception can be formed of the kinds of works from which this brave army has time and again compelled the enemy to withdraw. Such were his works at Kennesaw, and such have been his works in every position from which he has been driven.

He who examines them and at the same time carefully studies the geographical and topographical features of this country cannot but be amazed at the achievements of this army.

Between Kennesaw Mountain and the Chattahoochee the Rebel general had another line of entrenchments behind which he posted his army. Our forces presented themselves before this new obstacle on the evening of the 3rd. General McPherson now pushed his column forward and reached the Chattahoochee near the mouth of Nickajack Creek. Thus the Rebel left flank was completely turned and the enemy was again forced to leave his works and retreat. He withdrew during the night of July 4th, this time not to stop until he had gained the heights that form the right bank of the Chattahoochee. Our army closely followed him, the line stretching from right to left like an immense seine. The 4th Corps on the extreme left reached the river on the 5th and the corps forming the center of the army on the same day pressed the enemy back into his entrenchments on the heights already named. Thus the army forms an immense crescent, both ends or flanks of which rest upon the river and which completely envelops the smaller crescent formed by the Rebel army in its new defensive position. Such is the present position of the main portion of the army. Our cavalry has already crossed the river and a certain portion of the infantry is already on its way to follow it. It is rumored that only Hardee' Corps remains in front of us, the rest of the Rebel army having crossed the river in order to checkmate certain movements of ours.

Chattahoochee Heights, Georgia
July 8, 1864

It is now understood that General Sherman has established a sufficiently strong tete-du-pont on the left bank of the river to ensure the crossing of the entire army if necessary. The grand movement which will probably result in the capture of Atlanta or a great battle at its gates is not likely to take place until the troops have had a few days rest from their arduous toils. General Thomas has promised his command that it shall now have a brief opportunity to refit and recuperate before the active operations of the campaign shall be resumed. The Army of the Cumberland therefore now quietly regales itself under the shadows of these Georgia forests and keeps itself as cool as possible with the enemy in front and the thermometer at 97 in the shade. The hot weather of the season has now fairly set in and from 9 A.M. to 4 P.M. the heat knows no mitigation and the sun's eye "scorcheth all it glares upon."

Desertions from the enemy's ranks are becoming more and more frequent as the tide of the rebellion ebbs southward. The northern Georgians and Tennesseans come in by companies and almost by regiments at each retrograde movement. They invariably express themselves ready for any measure that will stop the war and restore them to their homes. Now and then a rabid Rebel is taken who still holds to his "Southern principles." None of them, however, can give any intelligible account of what they are fighting for. "Pat Cleburne," said one of them the other day, "tells us we are fighting for vengeance." Cleburne commands a division in Hood's Rebel corps.

From many points of our present line the city of Atlanta can be distinctly seen, on an eminence eleven miles distant. Here and there over the wide landscape the smoke of the busy mills and factories rises into the dull heated atmosphere, showing that the threatening proximity of the vast Yankee army has not yet suspended the everyday employments of the people of the doomed city. The curiosity of our soldiers to see Atlanta when it first came into view was amusing. The trees all along the line immediately became peopled with blue blouses, each eager watcher trying to obtain the highest point and the best view of the Gate City of the South. Atlanta is also plainly visible from the peaks of Kennesaw near Marietta, which illustrates to how wide an extent the enemy could carry his observations while he yet held that stronghold.

It is rumored that the enemy is already preparing to fall back upon Macon. Whether this be true or not it may be depended upon that this army will go forward and by the help of God will unfurl the starry banner of liberty over many another stronghold of the rebellion ere the leaves of autumn gild the ground. Under the leadership of our brave old Tecumseh and with the favor of Divine Providence, we ardently hope to scent the fragrance of this summer's magnolias beside the Ocmulgee and Altamaha. Brethren in Virginia, all hail!

Notes in Dixie Vol. IX

Chattahoochee Heights, Georgia
July 16, 1864

The aristocrats of the South have boldly set their claims to superiority of race. They affect to despise the free laborers of the northern states and to spurn all political and social union with them. They regard toil as a menial office of mankind. In such base estimation do they hold it that they deem it not even worthy of reward, but regard it as a sort of price by which a wretched class of human beings is destined to purchase a miserable subsistence. They hold further that it is inflexibly decreed in the law of nature that the superior or non-laboring class shall have the right to buy, sell, own, and enslave the inferior or laboring class. They claim also that this is rendered necessary inasmuch as the inferior class is created weak, abject, and totally dependent on the superior one.

Such is the philosophy of Southern aristocracy- the aristocracy which Southern slaveholders are today fighting to establish. Upon these theories rests the peculiar social system which the Southerner claims has made him superior to the Northerner. He insists that the latter in removing from his social system the barrier separating the laborer from the capitalist, and thus destroying the only solid foundation for an aristocracy under a free government has degraded himself in the scale of moral and manly existence. Instead of being the aristocrat he might have been, he has made himself a mudsill; instead of owning labor he has honored it; instead of degrading the laborer to a serf he has elevated him to the proud position of a freeman. Here lies the whole fault of the North and the whole secret of Southern hate. Because of the reputed encroachments of the free labor system, the Southern people have attempted to destroy this Union and to establish a government which shall recognize and sustain an aristocracy founded on the enslavement of labor. This object of the rebellion is therefore to degrade labor. This, indeed, is the chief cornerstone of the Confederacy.

To overthrow these vain and wicked theories the Northern people are contending. To establish the nobility of labor, to destroy a false, artificial, and selfish aristocracy, and to refute the assumption, as wicked as it is false, that the man who lives upon the unrequited toil of others is superior, superior forsooth, to the man who withholds not from the laborer his hire, our vast armies are grappling with this giant rebellion. I know this is not the whole object of the war, but it is an important part of it. It is a part of which fossilized conservatives and Copperheads doughfaces at the North have vainly tried to ignore. But the soldiers recognize it, all true patriots recognize it, and he who does not recognize it is fearfully ignorant or desperately wicked.

This war goes on. In the meantime, the cotton presses stand idle, the tobacco and rice fields are bare, and a strange and solemn silence broods over the half-tilled plantations where so lately the groans and prayers of gangs of enslaved men went up daily to the ear of an avenging God. The mansion of the proud master is tenantless and its unlatched doors sway to and from at the idle mandate of the wind. No cringing human chattels do the servile bidding of capricious insolence through its richly-adorned and lofty-sounding halls. With its broken gateway and weedy untrodden avenue, it exhibits enough of dingy stateliness to tell impressively of something which was but is not, and stands a gloomy spectral watcher for that which is to be. It is the relic of an old era. The dawn of a new one begins to illuminate the land. True it as yet but glimmers through the battle smoke and mingles in the lurid lightning of war. Yet it gives promise of the coming day and reveals to us the flag of our country still floating in tranquil glory far above the clouds and baptized by heaven's own blessed light.

The war goes on. Daily some patriot falls and daily the letters of oppressed bondsmen are broken. And let this be our consolation while the best blood of the land is being shed, that our just and equitable government each day makes some new recognition of the rights and nobility of man. We are not approaching an aristocracy, an oligarchy, or a monarchy, but we are constantly receding further from it. We are daily growing in our appreciation of the immutable principles of justice that underlie the government of our fathers.

The climate of the South, it has been claimed, develops a superior race of men. Nothing could be more absurd. All history and analogy proves the contrary. Yet if genial climate, beautiful scenery, and a soil rich in every resource could develop a lofty type of manhood, those of the South should certainly do it. These gorgeous summer skies where voluptuous clouds softly float in slivery volumes and amorously roll themselves into ten thousand bewitching shapes are enough to swell an angel's soul with rapture. These sublime mountains, romantic rivers, and Arcadian groves are worthy of a race of heroes possessed of Godlike minds and man's noblest impulses. Alas, that such a country should be the asylum for the worst of tyrannies and the basest of barbarisms. The Southron superior! He, the model of virtue, the paragon of patriots, the quintessence of chivalry! He the oppressor of a weaker race simply because it is weaker, the self-styled aristocrat, the despiser of honest toil! Hard-headed freemen of the North, it is a false and baseless assumption and every day your good right arms are proving it so. The appreciation and respect so ungenerously withheld from the plough and the loom you are rapidly conquering upon many a bloody field. The lily-handed lords who sneered at you are learning to do you reverence.

A remarkable illustration of the principles and tendencies of this war is found in the nomination of two such men as Abraham Lincoln and Andrew Johnson for the next presidency and vice presidency of the United States. They are both sons of toil. They were both nurtured in the rough cradle of self-dependence and have alike risen to their present lofty standing from the humble walks of labor. Under the benign influence of republican liberty a friendless backwoodsman and an untutored tailor have by their own persevering efforts attained the proud position of being the almost spontaneous nominees of a great people for the highest places known among men. And such is the true manhood, such is the genuine nobility, the stamp of which bears nature's own signet. And who will not say with Bishop Thompson that it is grand to see a man thus "rising as a granite mountain by volcanic fires, piercing the super incumbent strata, and looking down beneath its crown of snow upon a continent at its base while the aristocratic fossils of successive epochs repose upon its flanks."

The boundary of freedom has been advanced from the Tennessee to the Chattahoochee. The banner of the Union floats at the very gates of the metropolis of northern Georgia. The 20th Corps still reposes in the shade of Chattahoochee Heights. From many points of the line the distant roofs and spires of Atlanta can be distinctly seen. The entire rebel army has crossed the river, abandoning a line of field works of amazing strength. Block houses with bomb proof coverings crown every hilltop. These are joined by substantial breastworks with loopholes for musketry and awnings of brush. The usual lines of sharpened stakes, abatis, and slashed timber cover the earthworks. But there is a new feature in these fortifications which adds enormously to their strength. This consists of heavy slabs of wood set perpendicularly in the ground and forming an almost impassable wooden wall about eight feet in height. These lines are usually built a few yards in rear of the trenches and have narrow openings through which the enemy might retire if driven out of his rifle pits. These lines are arranged with recreant angles so as to give the advantage of a converging fire against an assaulting party. To capture such works by a direct assault when defended by a determined foe would be next to an impossibility. Nothing but the danger of losing his communication with which Johnston is almost constantly threatened could have induced him to evacuate a position of such strength.

A portion of our forces have now crossed the Chattahoochee and the cavalry under Stoneman is reported to have severed the railroads leading southward from Atlanta. The time for the army to set forward again on its march toward the Gulf seems to have not yet fully come. But when Tecumseh shall give the word and this mighty host shall gather itself up again and resume its southward journey, the pillars of the rebellion will tremble and Atlanta will surely fall. The army needs rest and refitting, hence the present inactivity. In the meantime let all its friends be patient. The work before it is enormous but it will be performed in due time.

Notes in Dixie Vol. X

Near Buckhead, Georgia
July 19, 1864

The army has crossed the Chattahoochee. Early on the morning of the 17th, a lively cannonade began to violate the Sabbath quiet of our sylvan encampment. It was a lovely morning. A copious rain had fallen the previous night, dampening the ground, reviving vegetation, and diffusing coolness and fragrance through the atmosphere. A light breeze whispered in the foliage and convolved the soft summer clouds that floated athwart the pure azure sky. The hoarse bellowing of artillery could not but break unpleasantly upon the quiet of such a morning and foreboded something very different from that calm rest which God designed men should enjoy one day in seven.

By 10 A.M. it was apparent that a movement was afoot and that the 20th Corps was expected to participate in it sometime during the day. Early in the afternoon the final order to march came and in a very few minutes the 1st Division was in motion. Very few positively knew our destination but it was the general impression that the grand final movement against Atlanta had begun. At 5 P.M. the column reached Pace's Ferry on the Chattahoochee. Here two pontoon bridges had been laid in spite of considerable opposition from the enemy. The troops filed rapidly over them causing the light canvas boats to oscillate considerably. The Chattahoochee at this point is narrow and shallow and can hardly be called a beautiful stream. It compares quite favorably with the stately Tennessee and the swift-flowing romantic Etowah. Its banks are high, abrupt, and wooded and devoid of those exquisite touches which adorn the scenery along our northern rivers.

After reaching the south bank of the Chattahoochee the 20th Corps immediately advanced into the interior in a direction parallel to the line of works covering the Rebel position on the river; the 14th Corps had already crossed and now extended its line from Pace's Ferry toward Buckhead. The 20th Corps at once formed a continuation of this line along the north bank of Peach Tree Creek and thus occupied the center of the Army of the Cumberland. On the left of the 20th, the 4th Corps prolonged the line in a southwesterly direction towards the Georgia Railroad. Such is the disposition of General Thomas' command at the present writing. It will be seen that the enemy's position on the Chattahoochee is completely turned and that Atlanta is being attacked from the northward and eastward. But this is not all. It is understood that McPherson's and Schofield's commands which crossed the river at a point much higher up are already well on the way to Stone Mountain. The design of this movement can be easily seen. It is to sever railroad communication between Atlanta and Augusta and threaten the other railroads leading from Atlanta southward. The Rebel metropolis will thus soon be threatened from at least three different directions. General Thomas is now within seven miles of the city and General McPherson is expected to be much nearer within a few hours. This vast army is now executing one of the grandest movements of the war and that it is terribly in earnest and means to accomplish a great purpose will be soon seen.[163]

Four and a quarter miles north of Atlanta, Georgia
July 21, 1864

The great struggle for Atlanta has now fairly begun and its first sanguinary scenes have already transpired; on yesterday occurred the most bloody and obstinate battle which this army has yet fought during the campaign. Almost the entire Army of the Cumberland was engaged, but perhaps on no portion of the line was the battle so fierce and so hot as along that part occupied by General Hooker's Corps.

Early on the morning of the 20th, Hooker's three divisions crossed Peachtree Creek and took their respective positions on the chain of hills extending along the south bank. The enemy was discovered in strong force in front but it was determined to press him vigorously in order to create a diversion in favor of McPherson who had reached the Georgia Railroad, destroyed the track, and was now advancing upon Atlanta from the direction of Stone Mountain. Nothing being thought of but an advance against the enemy the usual precautions against attack were thought unnecessary. The troops were allowed the rest quietly in the shade after building temporary rail barricades and were not troubled with constructing heavy lines of breastworks which almost invariably cover the line of battle. Williams' Division held the right of the line, Geary's the center, and Ward's the left. Between Geary and Williams lay a deep, woody hollow which occasioned a vacancy in the line and was covered only by the pickets.

Thus matters continued until noon. There was comparatively little firing in front and so far as human sagacity could determine everything seemed to be going on well. Thomas' usually serious countenance wore the light of a smile and Hooker's fine features indicated nothing within to vex their wonted imperturbability. Williams chatted and laughed with as much unconcern as if the cares of war were not worth minding, while Geary, so ordinarily restless and active, seemed for once to have but little to disturb him. But this was not to last. Early in the

---

[163] John Bell Hood's elevation to army command marked a shift towards an offensive-minded Confederate strategy to defend Atlanta; Hood launched three successive attacks on Sherman's army in the 10 days following his appointment, Peach Tree Creek on July 20th being the first, followed by the Battle of Atlanta on July 22nd and finally Ezra Church on July 28th. All three battles ended badly for the Confederates with high casualties that did little to break Sherman's grip on the city. General Jacob D. Cox wrote that most Union officers were relieved to learn that Hood now led the Army of Tennessee. "The patient skill and watchful intelligence and courage with which Johnston had always confronted them with impregnable fortification had been exasperating," he wrote. "They had found no weak joints in the harness and no wish was so common or so often expressed that he would only try our works as we were trying his." Cox, Jacob D. Sherman's Battle for Atlanta. New York: Da Capo Press, 1994, pg. 148

afternoon the enemy began to grow restive suddenly and about 2 P.M. a heavy discharge of musketry was heard on the left of Williams. In a moment more of the storm began to burst along Williams' front and everyone sprang instinctively to his feet. The portend of the firing was unmistakable: the enemy was advancing. Whiz, whiz came the bullets directly over the ridge where the 1st Division lay grouped in the woods. General Williams immediately ordered his brigades into position. Robinson's started on the double quick along the crest of the ridge and had hardly formed its line of battle until the enemy in heavy masses came sweeping down upon it, having taken advantage of the hollow previously named to mask his movement. The First Brigade quickly formed on the right of Robinson's and also became immediately engaged. The battle now raged with indescribable fury. Robinson's men became mingled with the enemy in an almost hand to hand conflict and captured several prisoners. The Rebels seemed determined to break the line and at all hazards capture the hill. If they could accomplish this, they possess themselves of the key to the whole position and probably inflict upon us an irretrievable disaster.

But in vain did the Rebel masses surge against General Williams' lines. Though the carnage was awful and the ground became strewn with the bleeding forms of scores of brave men, yet not one inch was yielded to the enemy. Perhaps not in the annals of this war has been seen a more terribly sublime spectacle than that presented by Williams' brave division in the height of this conflict. It is impossible to describe it. No pen, no tongue is adequate to the task. He alone who has felt the terror, the grandeur, and the awful solemnity of such an occasion can properly appreciate it. There is much, alas too much about it that the heart sickens to think or tell of. To see the forms and faces you love streaming with blood or staggering in the dizzy reel of death; to see the motionless limbs and glassy eyes of those whom you so lately met in lusty life; to hear the heart-rending call for help from those whom it is beyond your power to assist; to feel amid all this that the next moment you too may be alike slain or helpless. Oh, it is a terrible ordeal. The stoutest heart need not be ashamed to acknowledge this, and he who has grown so unfeeling as not to appreciate it needs to be pitied.

The enemy was finally compelled to withdraw a short distance into the timber, which movement abated but did not end the battle. It continued to rage until the slanting beams of the setting sun shot redly through the battle smoke and finally withdrawing from a scene so dreadful, disappeared behind the western horizon. Then it ceased, for the enemy was repulsed at all points and withdrew to his entrenchments. Our troops at once threw up a short line of defensive works and then slept upon their arms. The enemy still remains in front of us in large force though he has not ventured to precipitate himself against the veterans of Pap Williams' Division and it is not likely that he will. His loss in the attack of yesterday was very great and the woods were strewn with his dead and wounded. Polk's and Hardee's Corps seem to have been chiefly engaged in the attack on Hooker. There seems to be little doubt that Johnston has been relieved from the chief command and that the Rebel army is now commanded by Hood. [164]

Confederate View

"We moved out of our works on the left and nearly parallel with the Pace's Ferry and Atlanta road at 2:30 P.M., moving by right of companies to the front. I soon became engaged with the enemy's pickets and drove them in and pressed on, my left capturing a portion of the enemy's works and a few prisoners. My right did not get into the works, being directed to keep dressed with the brigade on its right. Shortly after entering their works the enemy poured an enfilading fire down my left flank and compelled the brigade to fall back some 75 to 100 yards. I ordered Major Preston to move a battery to a position on the left of the road and drive the enemy from my left flank. The battery did noble service and kept in position until it had fired its last round of ammunition. Now having no protection on my left, and the troops on my immediate right having fallen back, the brigade fell back 100 yards further."

"My whole brigade did not exceed 540 effectives, including the 9th Arkansas; my loss was 6 killed, 52 wounded, and 9 missing."

~ *Brigadier General Daniel H. Reynolds, commanding brigade*

---

[164] Robinson's brigade clashed with General Daniel H. Reynolds' brigade at Peachtree Creek; the brigade consisted of the 1st and 2nd Arkansas Mounted Rifles (dismounted), and the 4th, 9th, and 25th Arkansas Infantry regiments.

Peach Tree Creek

"There was a ravine to the right of the 13th New York Battery on our right where the lines did not meet. Seeing this, the Rebs came pouring through the gap. But Major John A. Reynolds, our chief of artillery, detected it just in the nick of time. He sprang to the front saying 'Men, are you going to see them take those guns?' All who were within hearing of his voice rallied about him, charged the now confident Rebs, and drove them out of the gap."

"The guns were manned and double shotted with Minie balls taken from the infantry ammunition boxes that were thrown down near the guns. They were hastily broken open, and the men would tear off a leg of their drawers and others a leg of their pants and after tearing the cartridge from the ball, would fill these up with balls, load them in the guns and hurl them at the advancing foe."

~Private Daniel Simms, Battery E, Pennsylvania Light Artillery

Three miles from Atlanta, Georgia
July 23, 1864.

The enemy abandoned his works in our immediate front on the evening of the 21st. He withdrew to a new line 2 ½ miles from Atlanta and seems bent on making an obstinate defense of his new position. Having failed in his attempt to crush the right wing of the army he massed his force and plunged them against McPherson on the left yesterday. An obstinate and bloody battle has been fought, concerning which we have as yet received few particulars. If movements contemplated and which by this time ought to be nearly executed are successful, there can be little doubt that the flag of the Union will float over Atlanta ere many days. The city is now plainly in sight from many points of the line and almost within range of the artillery. There are said to be many Union citizens in the place who refuse to go South and are anxiously awaiting the entrance of our army. May God speed that event and hasten the downfall of treason and rebellion.

A lively artillery duel is going on this morning and perhaps I ought to say (by way of apology at least) that the concluding portions of this paper have been written under fire of Rebel batteries. The iron missiles actually make dismal noises overhead and convey to one's sensibilities hints which are not hard to appreciate. Excuse, therefore, an abrupt close.

Report of Colonel James S. Robinson, 82nd Ohio Infantry, commanding Third Brigade, of operations May 1-July 24.

HDQRS. THIRD BRIGADE, FIRST DIVISION, 20TH CORPS,
Near Atlanta, Ga., July 24, 1864

CAPTAIN: I have the honor to submit the following report of the field movements and operations of my command since the 1st of May, 1864:

On the 2d day of the month just named the command of this brigade devolved upon me from the hands of Brigadier-General Tyndale, who had received a leave of absence on account of illness. On the same date the brigade marched from Bridgeport, Ala., where it was then stationed, to join the remainder of the division at Whiteside's, Tenn. The latter point was reached during the ensuing evening, and the brigade for the first time met its associate brigades of the new organization, known as the First Division, Twentieth Army Corps. The brigade, as at that time organized, consisted of the following regiments: 61st Ohio Veteran Volunteers, commanded by Col. Stephen J. McGroarty; 82nd Ohio Veteran Volunteers, Lieut. Col. David Thomson; 143rd New York Volunteers, Col. Horace Boughton; 45th New York Veteran Volunteers, Col. Adolphus Dobke; 101st Illinois Volunteers, Lieut. Col. John B. Le Sage; 82nd Illinois Volunteers, Lieut. Col. Edward S. Salomon. The march

---

Interestingly, the Ohio-born General Reynolds also attended Ohio Wesleyan a few years prior to Captain Lee. He later moved to Arkansas to practice law.

Brigadier General James Sidney Robinson, whom Captain Lee wrote was "a true patriot, a brave soldier, and a noble-hearted man."
(Library of Congress)

was continued from Whiteside's on the 3d, and was pursued without being marked by any event especially important until the arrival of my command with the remainder of the division at Trickum Post-Office, on the East Chickamauga, May 7. Here the brigade was rejoined by the 61st Ohio Veteran Volunteers, which regiment had been absent on veteran furlough since the 13th of March, 1864.

The command marched again from the Trickum Post-Office at midnight of the 10th, and arrived at Sugar Valley, at the mouth of Snake Creek Gap, on the 12th. On the 13th the command was pushed forward toward Resaca, and during the afternoon formed line of battle and assisted in building a line of entrenchments near Camp Creek. On the 14th the position was shifted one mile farther to the left, where the entire division was held in reserve of the division of General Butterfield until 4:30 p.m. At that hour I was directed by the brigadier-general commanding division to move my brigade by the left flank and lead the division in marching toward the Dalton road, near which at that time the Fourth Corps was engaging the enemy. By 6.30 p.m. the head of my column reached a high wooded ridge, overlooking a narrow open valley, along which extended the main road leading to Dalton. On the farther side of the valley was another thickly wooded hill, and upon a slight knoll in the open field at our feet stood the 5th Indiana Battery, supported by a portion of Stanley's division, of the Fourth Corps. The division itself was at that time engaging the enemy some distance beyond the farther end of the valley, and from the character of the firing it was evident that General Stanley's lines were falling back; in fact that they were giving way in some disorder.

By direction of General Williams I immediately formed my brigade in line of battle along the crest of the ridge parallel to and overlooking the valley. I had four regiments in front and two in rear, thus forming two lines, one in support of the other. In my first line were the 101st Illinois, 82nd Illinois, and the 143rd and 45th New York Volunteers, and in the second the 61st and 82nd Ohio Volunteers. I had hardly gotten my command into position until the enemy swarmed out of the woods in pursuit of Stanley's men, and with defiant yells made for the battery, the infantry support of which immediately fled.

The enemy came confidently on, apparently unaware of our presence. He was rapidly nearing the battery, when I was directed by the brigadier-general commanding division to precipitate my entire command into the valley, and, wheeling it upon the right flank, bring it up to the support of the battery. This order was at once communicated to the regiments of my brigade, and in a moment the whole was in motion. The evolution was executed with enthusiasm and with no less precision and regularity of movement than might have been expected upon drill. Arriving at the front of the battery the 82nd Illinois, 61st Ohio, and 143rd New York Volunteers poured a tremendous fire upon the overconfident foe. The 101st Illinois was directed to move at once upon the hill on the left, now in possession of the enemy. That gallant regiment at once advanced in perfect order to the crest and drove from it the enemy's skirmishers. Meeting with such severe and unexpected resistance, the enemy at once gave way and confusedly sought his entrenchments back in the woods.

The troops now bivouacked in line of battle, and remained in the position thus taken up until 12 m. of the following day. At that time I was directed by General Williams to march my brigade, following that of Brigadier General Ruger, down the Dalton road. After proceeding about half a mile, and having entered the dense forest covering the enemy's position, I was ordered by the brigadier general commanding division to form my brigade on the left of the road in line of battle, the regiments being in column. Butterfield's and Geary's divisions had already actively engaged the enemy, and the firing upon my right had grown severe. Upon further consultation with General Williams, I moved my brigade to the crest of the hill in front of the line then occupied, and directly afterward moved my command forward half a mile and placed it in position on the left of General Ruger's brigade, and upon the left flank of the division, and in fact the left flank of the army. My brigade was formed in two lines, the 101st Illinois and the 143rd New York Volunteers, deployed, composing the first, and the 61st Ohio, 82nd Ohio, 45th New York, and 82nd Illinois the second line, supporting the two regiments of General Ruger's brigade, and the two regiments of my own brigade deployed in the front line. My first line rested along the base of a slight declivity. Shortly after my brigade was thus formed, I was directed by General Williams to send a regiment to support the battery of Captain Woodbury, which had been placed in position upon a wooded hill some distance to the rear.

I immediately dispatched the 45th New York Veteran Volunteers, which regiment remained with the battery until the morning of the 16th. At about 5 p.m. the enemy was discovered to be massing his troops in the forest that skirted the farther side of the open field in my front. I immediately moved the 82nd Ohio to the crest of the slope, and stationed it behind the breast-works immediately in rear and support of the 150th New York Volunteers, of Ruger's brigade. The 101st Illinois Volunteers was then deployed and formed in continuation of the line on the left of the 150th New York Volunteers. The 143rd New York Volunteers was next deployed and formed on the left of the 101st Illinois. The two latter regiments were unsheltered by any species of breastworks or other obstacle to the fire of the enemy. The dispositions just described had been hardly made until the enemy boldly emerged from the woods and began the attack. He at once opened a heavy fire of musketry, which was repaid with interest. He had not advanced far into the open field until his progress was checked by the sweeping fire which was poured upon him. In about twenty minutes his lines, broken and confused, withdrew to the woods, and the firing ceased.

The 82nd Illinois Volunteers was now deployed and placed in the position previously occupied by the 150th New York Volunteers, which regiment was relieved. The 61st Ohio Veteran Volunteers was also deployed and kept in hand ready to strengthen whatever might prove to be the weakest point. These dispositions were no sooner made than the enemy again advanced to the attack. He came forward with a reckless desperation, which indicated a determination to break our line at every hazard. But his rash purposes were doomed to the same signal failure as before. He approached in heavy and well sustained force within seventy-five yards of my line, when the fire of musketry became so destructive that he again hastily withdrew, leaving dead and wounded, hundreds of small-arms, and about 20 prisoners in our hands. It was now 6:30 p.m. No further attack was made upon my lines during the evening or night. On the ensuing morning, it being discovered that the enemy had withdrawn, I sent out my pioneer corps to bury the dead of the enemy in front of my line. The officer in charge of the corps afterward reported that he buried 85 dead rebels, including 5 commissioned officers, in front of the brigade.

The march in pursuit of the retreating enemy was begun at 9 a.m. on the morning of the 16th. My command crossed the Connesauga River above Resaca at 1 p.m., and encamped on the right bank of the Coosawattee at 6 p.m. The march was pursued on the 17th as far as to a point four miles east of Calhoun. On the 18th the brigade resumed its march, and arrived at 9:30 p.m. at a point near Spring Mills, and six miles east of Adairsville. At 1 p.m. on the 19th the march was continued as far as Two-Run Creek. Here the enemy's cavalry and flankers were encountered at 4 p.m., and the brigade was immediately formed in battle order. By direction of General Williams, and under the

Union entrenchments near Kennesaw Mountain, Georgia, 1864. (Library of Congress)

personal superintendence of Lieutenant-Colonel Asmussen, of General Hooker's staff, I advanced my brigade in two lines, one in support of the other, at 5 p.m. The troops moved steadily forward over steep hills and through tangled forests and marshes, compelling the enemy to remove his light artillery and cavalry and fall back upon his infantry supports. The latter were encountered in strong force near the village of Cassville just at dusk. My command closed up well upon the enemy and threw up a breastwork under cover of the darkness. The rebel forces withdrew during the night, and on the following day I encamped my brigade in the suburbs of Cassville.

On the 23d of May active operations were resumed, the brief repose permitted to the army having expired. My command marched from Cassville at 5 a.m., and at 2 p.m. crossed the Etowah River near Euharlee Mills. On the 24th the brigade marched by mountain paths and by-ways to Burnt Hickory, where it encamped at 4 p.m. On the morning of the 25th the 45th New York Volunteers, was, by order of General Williams, detached from the brigade to guard the division ammunition train. (This regiment remained thus detached until June 28, and, therefore, participated in none of the subsequent operations and engagements of the brigade up to the latter date.) At 6 a.m. my command marched from Burnt Hickory and crossed the Pumpkin Vine Creek about noon. Shortly after passing this stream, and while the column was marching on the main road to Dallas, and was about three miles distant from that place, I was suddenly ordered by General Williams to face my command about and march it to the relief of General Geary's division, which, I was informed, had encountered the enemy. I quickly reversed the direction of the march, and my brigade, having been the rear of the division, now led the advance. Recrossing Pumpkin Vine Creek, the column moved up that stream about two miles, then crossing it ascended a high wooded ridge, and continued the march along its crest.

At 5 p.m. my brigade came up with Geary's division, and immediately formed in line of battle preparatory to an advance against the enemy. The 61st Ohio Veteran Volunteers was deployed as skirmishers, covering the brigade front. The other four regiments, viz, the 143rd New York Volunteers, 82nd Ohio Veteran Volunteers, 101st Illinois Volunteers, and 82nd Illinois Volunteers, formed the main line from right to left, in the order named. My brigade was supported by Brigadier General Ruger's command. Everything being ready the signal to advance was given, the troops moved forward, and the action opened immediately. My troops, I am happy to say, moved with great steadiness, and there was not the least sign of hesitation or wavering. The enemy's skirmishers were compelled to withdraw precipitately, and some of them were taken prisoners. The brigade moved steadily forward for a distance of about one mile, when it was, by order of General Williams, relieved by the brigade of General Ruger. My regiments retired by the left of companies, permitting General Ruger's to pass through, then reformed in line of battle. The fight continued about one-half hour longer, when General Ruger's ammunition getting low, the general commanding the division directed that my brigade go again to the front. The troops of my command instantly advanced to the front line and reopened their fire. The enemy swept the line with shell and canister in addition to the musketry, thus occasioning many fearful gaps in the ranks, but not the loss to us of one inch of ground. The already depleted cartridge-boxes of my men were soon emptied of their remaining contents, and the boxes of the wounded and dead were resorted to. The ammunition thus obtained enabled the troops to maintain their fire until, under cover of the darkness, they were relieved. Some of my regiments went to the rear with scarcely a single cartridge remaining.

During the night the troops rested upon their arms a few hundred yards in rear of the front line. They remained in this position during the 26th and 27th. On the 28th, having been directed by General Williams to report with my command to the officer having charge of the ordnance train of the army headquarters, to escort the same to Kingston and return, my brigade marched at daylight and reached Pumpkin Vine Creek, where the train was to be collected at 6 a.m. Much time was consumed in unloading and preparing the wagons, and the march could not be resumed until about 1 p.m. Stilesborough was reached on the 28th and Kingston at 3:30 p.m. of the 29th. The train was immediately loaded with ordnance, subsistence, and sanitary stores, and at 7 a.m. of the 30th was on its march back to the front. The entire command reached Burnt Hickory early on the morning of the 31st. Here the ammunition was shifted to another train and my brigade, having completed its duty as escort, rejoined the division at the point where it had left it, at 6:30 p.m.

On the 1st of June, the army having commenced its movements to the left, my brigade marched four miles in that direction. On the 2d the movement was continued one mile farther, and my command formed a line of battle on the left of Carlin's brigade, Fourteenth Army Corps, and threw up a line of breast-works. The brigade remained in this position on the 3d and 4th, keeping a strong line of skirmishers in front, which engaged the enemy both day and night. On the 5th, being relieved by Mitchell's brigade, of Davis' division, Fourteenth Army Corps, the movement to the left was resumed.

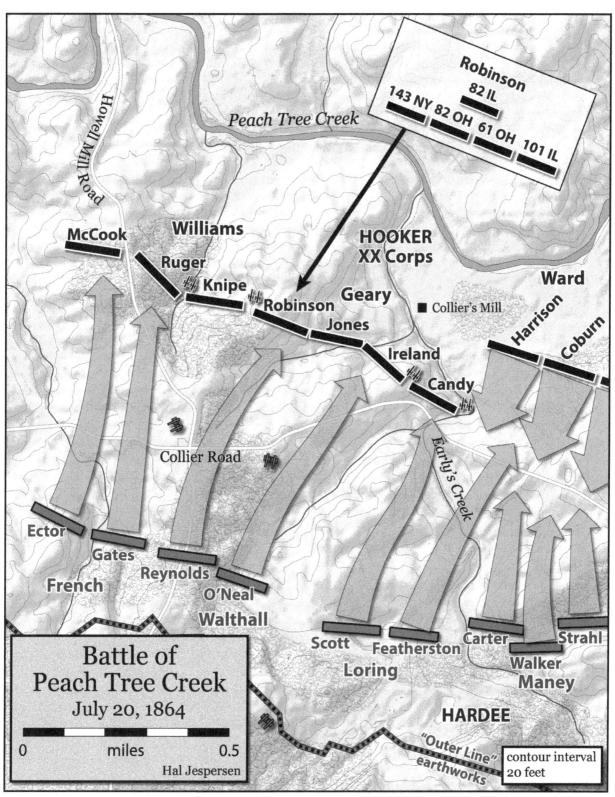

Battle of Peach Tree Creek, Georgia, July 20, 1864
(Hal Jespersen, www.cwmaps.com)

At 3 p.m. my command encamped near the junction of the Acworth and Marietta roads five miles from Acworth. On the 6th the brigade marched again, and after proceeding about three miles, formed in line of battle, and threw up a line of breast-works. This position was changed during the afternoon, and a new line of breast-works built at a point on the Sandtown road two and a half miles north of Lost Mountain. The position of the brigade remained substantially the same until the 15th. On that date, a general advance being made, the line was thrown forward two miles on the Sandtown road. General Geary's division, having encountered the enemy, and become engaged with him in his trenches, General Williams directed me to support him with my brigade. I moved my command in line of battle up to within a few yards of Geary's line, and, as ordered by General Williams, constructed a breastwork under cover of the darkness of the evening. On the 16th, being relieved by Geary s troops, I was ordered to withdraw my command a few hundred yards, which was accordingly done.

Early on the morning of the 17th my brigade joined in the pursuit of the enemy, who had abandoned his works during the previous night. The advance continued about one and a half miles, when the enemy was again discovered in a strongly fortified position. The picket became immediately engaged with him, and the brigade formed a new line of battle, which was at once strengthened by breastworks. The position thus taken remained unchanged during the 18th. During the night, however, the enemy abandoned works of immense strength, and which, if not impregnable, seemed to have at least exhausted the last resources of military science and human ingenuity to make them so. My brigade marched in the pursuit on the morning of the 19th and went into position in front of the enemy near Kennesaw Mountain at 1 p.m. Active skirmishing immediately began, which resulted in the killing and wounding of several men of my command. At 7 a.m. on the 20th the brigade marched to the right, and at 7 p.m. encamped in line of battle on Atkinson's plantation. On the 21st my line was strengthened by breastworks, the position remaining otherwise unchanged.

At 10:30 a.m. on the 22d my brigade advanced about one mile directly to the front and went into position on the left of General Knipe's brigade on the crest of a high wooded hill. The troops were concealed by the timber. My line overlooked an open field and hollow about 1,000 yards in width, on the farther side of which the Rebel skirmish line was plainly visible. There was no serious demonstration in my immediate front, and no movement of my command until 5:30 p.m. About that time the enemy, having massed his forces under the concealment of the woods, suddenly debouched from the timber and advanced to assault the hill occupied by my brigade. General Knipe, on my right, had already become heavily engaged, and the enemy's masses, preceded by a strong skirmish line, came boldly forward, apparently bent upon carrying my position at every hazard. As directed by General Williams, I marched my brigade out of the woods, formed it in line of battle along the brow of the hill, and made all possible preparations to receive the enemy's expected onslaught. Lieutenant Winegar's battery (I), of the 1st New York Artillery, which was supported by my line, opened a vigorous fire as soon as the enemy began to advance and plunged so well directed and rapid a fire of shell against his masses that they soon became checked and confused, and were finally compelled to withdraw.

In the meantime, General Knipe's line being dangerously pressed, I was directed by General Williams to send one of my regiments to form on the left flank of that brigade, to prevent the enemy from turning it. I immediately dispatched the 61st Ohio Veteran Volunteers with directions to report to General Knipe and remain with his command subject to his orders. During the battle this regiment suffered considerably. Excepting this, my brigade, not being much engaged, suffered but little, and that chiefly from the enemy's shells. The fight substantially ceased at sundown, and as soon as safe to do so, I strengthened my line with breastworks. The enemy, repulsed at all points, retired, and the battle subsided into the irregular firing of the pickets. The position of my brigade remained unchanged until the 3d of July.

On the 27th of June it was held in readiness to participate in the assault then made upon the enemy's works, but was not moved from its entrenchments. During the night of July 2d the enemy again retreated, leaving his fortifications in our front vacant; at 7 a.m. on the ensuing morning my command marched inside of them. The pursuit was continued about five miles, when the brigade was put in position in front of the enemy, who was again discovered strongly entrenched. On the 4th the position was slightly changed, preparatory to an anticipated advance, which, however, was not made. At 5 p.m. the command moved one and a half miles to the right and encamped. On the morning of the 5th it was discovered that the enemy had again retreated, and the troops at once began the pursuing march. Passing through a broken and wooded country by unfrequented roads and by-ways, the column came up with the enemy in his fortifications on the right bank of the Chattahoochee River at 6 p.m. The brigade was put in position along the summit of one of the series of heights skirting the river and overlooking the city of Atlanta.

On the 6th of July I received an order of Major-General Thomas transferring the 45th New York Veteran Volunteers from the Third Brigade, First Division, to the Fourth Division, Twentieth Corps, and directing that the 31st Wisconsin Volunteers, then at Nashville, Tenn., immediately report for duty with my brigade. At noon of the same day my command marched from its position on the height crowning the right bank of Nickajack Creek, and crossing that stream, went into position again on the right of the Fourteenth Corps. Here the troops threw up breastworks and otherwise strengthened their line. No further event occurred to mark the history of the brigade, until the night of the 9th, when the enemy disappeared from its front, having retreated over the river. The position of my command remained the same up to the 17th of July. On that day it marched in conjunction with the other brigades of the division to Pace's Ferry and crossed the Chattahoochee River at that point. On the 18th, in obedience to an order from General Williams, I detailed the 82nd Ohio Veteran Volunteers to accompany a reconnaissance, under Colonel Carman, of the 13th New Jersey Volunteers, to Island Creek. The reconnoitering party encountered and engaged the enemy's cavalry early in the forenoon, but no serious loss occurred to the regiment from my command. The brigade marched at 2:30 p.m., and crossing Nancy's Creek, encamped near Buck Head. Here it remained until the evening of the 19th, when it marched on the road leading to Atlanta, and encamped at 8:30 p.m. on the north bank of Peach Tree Creek.

Early on the morning of the 20th my command crossed Peach Tree Creek, and ascended the chain of hills skirting the left bank. It being understood that the line was to be pushed forward and the enemy pressed during the day, care was not taken to put the troops regularly into position or to entrench the line. The picket was pushed forward far enough to feel the enemy and discover his whereabouts. No special precaution was taken against an attack, for none was anticipated. At 2 p.m., however, a heavy discharge of musketry was heard in the direction of General Geary's division. The storm quickly rolled along toward the right, and it became suddenly apparent that the enemy was advancing in heavy force. Preparation was immediately made to meet him. At the instance of General Williams, I marched my brigade by the right flank at double-quick time along the crest of the hill, then formed in line of battle and moved a short distance down the eastern face of the hill into the timber. This movement was not fully executed when the enemy opened a heavy fire of musketry upon my line, and received a similar compliment in return. The battle at once grew fierce and bloody, a portion of my troops becoming mingled with those of the enemy in an almost hand-to-hand conflict. The 143rd New York, 82nd Ohio, 61st Ohio, and 101st Illinois Volunteers, being in my front line, bore the brunt of the attack. The 82nd Illinois Volunteers was formed a short distance in rear, and in support of the other regiments. The first onslaught of the enemy was finally repulsed, and he sullenly withdrew a short distance, still, however, maintaining a considerable fire.

In the meantime the battle grew very warm along General Knipe's line on my right. I was directed by General Williams to send two regiments to reinforce General Knipe's brigade, and in compliance with the order at once dispatched the 101st and 82nd Illinois Volunteers. These two regiments reported to General Knipe, and remained with his command during the remainder of the battle. The fight continued to rage with irregular fury until sundown, when the enemy, being repulsed at all points, withdrew his forces. I regret to say that this sanguinary engagement cost my brigade many valuable officers and men. It would be invidious to mention names where all alike performed their part so nobly. Never was the hardihood and temper of my entire command more completely and thoroughly tested. The battle was sprung upon it at an unexpected moment, and with a fury not hitherto exceeded in the annals of the campaign. Yet officers and men sprang with alacrity to the post of duty and danger, and met the shock of battle with a courage, promptitude, and determination that ought to command the most lasting and exalted admiration.

On the 21st my brigade was joined by the 31st Wisconsin Volunteers, over 700 strong, from Nashville. The position of the troops remained the same as on the evening of the previous day, except that it was covered by a line of defensive works. On the 22d, the enemy having fallen back during the night previous, my command advanced one and a quarter miles directly toward Atlanta and formed a new line, the right of which rested upon the road by which the advance was made. A strong breastwork, covering the line, was immediately constructed under fire of the enemy's artillery and sharpshooters. The position thus assumed remained unchanged until the 24th instant, at which date, owing to severe illness, I was compelled to request the brigadier general commanding division to relieve me temporarily from command. The request was promptly granted, and Col. Horace Boughton, of the 143rd New York Volunteers, assumed command of the brigade.

I cannot close this report without expressing my high appreciation of and sincere thanks for the gallantry, ability, and hearty spirit of co-operation displayed by the commanders of the regiments of my brigade throughout the period of my command. Their names and regiments, to mention which affords me mingled pride and pleasure, are as follows: Col. Stephen J. McGroarty, 61st Ohio Veteran Volunteers; Col. Horace Boughton, 143rd New York Volunteers; Col. Francis H. West, 31st Wisconsin Volunteers; Lieut. Col. David Thomson, 82nd Ohio Veteran Volunteers; Lieut. Col. Edward S. Salomon, 82nd Illinois Volunteers; Lieut. Col. John B. Le Sage, 101st Illinois Volunteers, and Lieut. Col. Adolphus Dobke, 45th New York Veteran Volunteers. To the different members of my staff my hearty thanks are also due for their willing and able performance of their arduous duties. To them all I am deeply indebted, and shall hold in lasting remembrance their names, which are as follows: Capt. F. S. Wallace, topographical engineer: Capt. B. Reynolds, inspector-general; Capt. Cyrus Hearrick, acting aide-de-camp; Capt. R. Lender, aide-de-camp; Capt. Alfred E. Lee, acting assistant adjutant-general; Capt. Charles Saalmann, acting commissary of Subsistence; Lieut. H. Rocke, acting assistant quartermaster, and Lieut. George Young, provost-marshal.

Notes in Dixie Vol. XI

Three Miles from Atlanta, Georgia
July 27, 1864

The Gate City is not yet ours, the newspapers to the contrary notwithstanding. For three weeks its roofs and steeples have been in sight and General Sherman's iron lines have been daily closing nearer and nearer upon the devoted metropolis. It is now within range of the artillery and shells have been thrown into the suburbs if not into the city itself. The huge forts that cover its approaches loom up, frowning around its finely shaded avenues, and above them the flag of rebellion gleams insolently in the bright Southern sun. The three corps of the Army of the Cumberland confront the northern, northeastern, and northwestern faces of the city, like the three sides of a polygon; the 20th Corps occupying the center, the 14th Corps the right, and the 4th Corps the left of the line. The hostile forces are almost within a stone's throw of each other; the sly Yanks having built their breastworks under the very noses of the incautious Rebs. Through the long summer days the two parties lie in entrenchments, screened from the sun by awnings of brush and amusing themselves by passing leaden compliments at each other. To raise one's head above the friendly embankment is due to draw upon it a Rebel bullet. Consequently it is not considered safe to make one's appearance visible above the plane of the parapet, and few have the temerity or rather indiscretion to do so. But by keeping yourself well down you may pretty confidently defy the sharp-shooting foe and laugh at the furiously musical hum of the minnies.

A young man of delicate sensibilities would find here an excellent schooling for his nervous system. At night he would be composed to slumber by the mild fusillade of the pickets, the soporific effects of which would be highly increased by the soft and very peculiar whiz of rebellious bullets at a moderate proximity to his ear in the clear night air. At the first gray streak of dawn the lassitude of sleep would be gently dispelled by the breezy call of a few shells which at that time of day the chivalry usually amuse themselves by pitching at our works. This delightful pastime is indulged in by both armies at irregular intervals, both day and night, and has had a wonderful influence in cultivating the grace of humility. I have seen dashing lieutenants, gay captains, handsome colonels, and even august brigadiers hugging rocks and trees as though they were the dearest friends they had on earth. If any sensitive young man was therefore given to haughtiness of spirit, it would be amusing to see how soon in a certain contingency he would find himself wilted.

Along the line of our breastworks each regiment displays its colors in full view of the Union-hating Johnnies. They no doubt consider this an unchivalrous provocation, for the brave old stars and stripes are often made a special target by both their artillery and sharpshooters. Sometimes they succeed in cutting away the staff and bringing the flag to the ground, which no doubt affords great gratification to the traitors as is evinced by their yells of exultation. But our gallant boys soon replace the colors and usually higher than ever. There is no traitorous Rebel who can dare so much to tear down that flag but that there will be some brave loyal heart ready to leap into the breach and sacrifice more to replace it. They who think otherwise forget that it is the 'flag of the free hearts, hope, and home, by angel hands to valor given.'

Major General Thomas has just made known to his command the aggregate results of the battles of the 20th and 22nd in the following order:

(Circular)
Headquarters, Department of the Cumberland
Near Atlanta, Georgia, July 25, 1864

The Major General Commanding congratulates the troops upon the brilliant success which has attended the Union arms in the late battles, and which have been officially reported as follows:

In the battle of the 20th inst., in which the 20th Corps, one Division of the 4th Corps, and part of the 14th Corps were engaged. Total Union loss in killed, wounded, and missing, 1,733. In front of the 20th Corps there were put out of the fight 6,000 Rebels, 563 of them were buried by our troops and the Rebels were permitted to bury 250 additional themselves. The Second Division of the 4th Corps repulsed seven assaults of the enemy (which must swell the Rebel loss much beyond 6,000), captured 200 prisoners, and seven stands of colors.

In the battle of the 22nd, the total Union loss in killed, wounded, and missing is 3,500 and 10 pieces of artillery. Rebel loss: prisoners captured 3,200; known dead in front of the 15th, 16th, and one Division of the 17th Corps; 2,142. The other Division of the 17th Corps repulsed six assaults of the enemy before it fell back, which will swell the Rebel loss in killed to at least 3,000. There were captured from the enemy in this battle 15 stands of colors and 5,000 small arms.

Brigadier General Garrard, commanding the Second Division of Cavalry, has just returned from a raid upon the Georgia Railroad, having lost two men and brought in 200 prisoners and a fair lot of fresh horses and Negroes. He destroyed the railroad bridge across the branch of the Ocmulgee and the depots at Conyers, Covington, and Social Circle.

By order of Major General Thomas
W.D. Whipple, A.A.G.

It will be seen that in both engagements great damage was inflicted upon the enemy at comparatively small expense to the Union army. The new Rebel commander Hood has undertaken to inaugurate his peculiar style of tactics, which is that of massing his forces and suddenly precipitating them against his antagonist. In no less than four instances during this campaign has the Red Star Division of the 20th Corps met these reckless dashes of Hood, and in each instance the enemy was not only repulsed by terribly punished. Johnston was too cautious and too economical of his strength to thus idly waste it. Instead of attacking us, he rather chose to wait behind his formidable entrenchments for us to attack him. Not so Hood. He is too impatient to endure the cool calculating work of strategy, and therefore, dashes himself to pieces against our serried lines, and we all say, let him dash. This kind management of the armies of the Rebellion is just what we want. Let it be continued until, like the fabulous ram, the spiteful thing has butted itself all away except that portion which is said to have remained to tell the sad tale of the Kilkenny Cats.

I believe that it is consistent with the character of these notes to make mention of anything noteworthy that I hear or see, without much regard to connection in the subject. I will therefore tell what I heard a soldier say the other day while he was shoveling earth in the trenches. "Some officers," said he "are very brave when they get a canteen of whiskey slung on their neck. We privates, though, have to go into the fight without it." Ah, what irony! I wish that every officer of this army and every other army to whom it applies might have it ringing, ringing in his ears until it would make him ashamed of himself. Much is often said about the gallantry in battle of General A. or Colonel B. when the doughty knight had borrowed from John Barleycorn all the courage and obliviousness of danger for which credit is thus given him. Surely in such a case as this at least, the devil ought to have his due, and it is unfair in newspaper correspondents to bestow upon others the credit properly belonging to him. Besides it is absurd to call him brave who cannot, or does not, depend upon his own inherent strength of will to face danger. True courage does not consist in ability to disparage peril, or in using artificial means to destroy the sense of it. The real hero is the man who, while he clearly discerns and fully appreciates the danger to which he is exposed, has yet within himself that powerful self-control and strength of purpose which enables him to go forward and do his duty at every hazard.

Again, if it is right for an officer to go besotted into battle, it is right for the private soldier, and if it is proper in one instance, it is proper in all. To carry out the idea, whenever our army is about to have an engagement it ought to convert itself into a drunken crazy rabble in order that the moral weakness resulting from the natural sense of danger may be neutralized. The propriety of a thing so absurd needs not to be discussed. In my humble opinion (and it is one founded upon long and careful observation), the efficiency of the army would vastly improve by the total abolition of the whiskey ration and by the rigid enforcement of the article of war against intoxication on the part of the officers. Careful research will develop the startling fact that at least half of all the disasters of this war, and consequently the loss of half of the lives which it has cost us, is directly traceable to the intemperate habits of those who have been charged with our military operations. There are those who will scoff at this statement, but it is terribly true. Let the temperance men investigate this matter and they will soon be convinced of what I have said is a very moderate representation of the facts. They will perceive, too, what great necessity there is for a speedy correction of the evil. The great heart of our country has not poured out its patriot sons to be immolated upon the shrine of Bacchus. Yet I have heard men high in military authority talk slightly in their cups of matters involving the lives of thousands of soldiers, and the happiness and hope of many a home and hearthstone. Oh God, how great is the folly of men!

Exactly how much longer the great struggle for Atlanta will last is difficult to tell. Many confidently anticipated that our army would be in possession of the city within a few hours several days ago. But they were disappointed. The importance of the place to the enemy as a railroad center and strategic point is immense, and it is not hard to see why he should make the most desperate efforts to hold it as long as possible. Once in our possession, it forms a substantial base from which we may operate against Augusta, Milledgeville, Macon, Montgomery, and even Mobile, Savannah, and Charleston, hardly excepting Richmond. There is no place in the Confederacy in the fate of which there is more of the destiny of the rebellion involved.

South of Atlanta, the mountain ranges of the Cotton States substantially cease and the rivers flow directly southward into the Gulf and southeastward into the Atlantic. There is therefore in the natural features of the country no longer any material obstacle to military operations. There is no longer a mountain barrier or a deep river to obstruct the invasion of almost any portion of the territory. We are inside of the last circle of national defenses which guards the life of the slaveholding Confederacy. And what wonder if yet devolves upon this army the real work of destroying the rebellion. And if this be the vital point, for surely Richmond is not, why keep an immense army in Virginia struggling against almost insurmountable obstacles for the accomplishment of a secondary end? Would it not be better to leave a sufficient force to guard the line of the Potomac and defend Washington, and send the remainder of the vast Army of the Potomac to cooperate with General Sherman? What are Richmond and Virginia worth to the enemy if he loses the Carolinas and Georgia? Let us occupy the Cotton States, let us get possession of their cities, mountains, and mines, and the rebellion will be a nullity. Here it was cradled and nurtured up to gigantic proportions, and here it must be destroyed.

Respectfully submitting these reflections for the consideration of yourself and the Secretary of War, I remain very truly yours…

Notes in Dixie Vol. XII

Three miles north of Atlanta, Georgia
July 30, 1864

Major General Joseph Hooker, has, at his own request, been relieved from the command of the 20th Army Corps. Being entitled through the death of General McPherson and by virtue of his rank to the command of the Army of the Tennessee which was denied him, he felt that his self-respect required that his connection with this army cease.[165] Whether the course pursued was or was not justifiable for the reason named- the officers and men of the 20th Corps cannot but sincerely regret the contingency that has deprived them of their gallant and beloved commander. In their memory and affections the name of General Hooker occupies an exalted place and can never perish. Their beau ideal of courage, gallantry, and soldierly grace and bearing, he was doubly endeared to them by reason of long association reaching back through many a campaign and hard-fought battle. Always present with his men in the thickest of the fight, sharing their toils and exposures, and exhibiting the most sublime contempt for danger, he quickly won by a sort of majestic influence their most unreserved admiration and esteem. From Williamsburg to Wauhatchie, and from Lookout Mountain to Kennesaw and Peach Tree Creek, the name of Hooker has been to the veterans of this corps a synonym for all that is brave, gallant, and heroic in an officer and soldier.

The removal of General Hooker places Brigadier General Alpheus S. Williams of the Red Star Division temporarily in command of the corps. Brigadier General Knipe succeeds General Williams in the command of the division. Major General Oliver O. Howard, who formerly commanded the 11th Corps but more recently the 4th Corps, has been assigned to the command of the Army of the Tennessee. Major General David Stanley succeeds General Howard as commander of the 4th Corps. Such are the changes which have followed the death of the lamented McPherson and the removal of our gallant Hooker.

The enemy still clings to Atlanta with desperate tenacity. The batteries of the 20th and other corps fire regularly upon the city and, as prisoners say, are causing considerable destruction of property. This morning at daybreak the pickets of the 1st Division dashed suddenly forward upon those of the enemy and captured almost the entire line. The men of the Third Brigade captured a company of the 46th Alabama regiment almost en masse, including the lieutenant commanding the company. But one man out of a party of 22 seemed to regret his capture. All the rest, including the officer, seemed as cheerful and contented as if they considered falling into the hands of the Yankee vandals a great piece of good fortune. [166]

Since the battles of the 20th and 22nd, Tecumseh has made a new disposition of a portion of his host. The Army of the Tennessee has been moved from the extreme left to the extreme right and now forms the right wing. It is now in such a position as to seriously threaten the Macon Railroad, the only communication of the enemy which remains open. Atlanta has thus become invested on three sides, north, east, and west. General Sherman's army stretches around it in the form of a huge semicircle and slowly but surely closes in upon the devoted city. Occasionally a terrific artillery duel breaks out and varies the monotony of what may, without much impossibility, be termed the siege. At such times one would think the very demons of war were let loose. The explosions of the guns and the bursting shells, the howling of the iron missiles as they dart through the air, and the frightful noises made by the jagged fragments as they fly in all directions make up a discordant concert indescribably terrible. Yet the execution done usually compares but insignificantly with the amount of noise made. Though the shells burst above and all around the trenches filled with troops, yet it is but seldom that any one gets seriously hurt by them. It is the insidious and lightning-winged bullet and not the shrieking shell that does the real work of death.

The Northern people are doubtless impatient for the capture of Atlanta. I fear they do not fully appreciate either the difficulties already overcome or those which still interpose themselves to the occupation of the place. It is true that General Sherman has a magnificent army and that his troops are greatly superior to the enemy in point of numbers, discipline, and morale. But it must be remembered that this army is now operating at a vast distance from its base and with a line of communication which in point of length and exposure to hostile raids is paralleled only by that of Napoleon during some his most daring campaigns. One misstep, one disaster might work the ruin of the whole army. An enemy is before it savage and Argus-eyed. Eagerly does he watch for an opportunity to take advantage of his antagonist. Thus far during the campaign the wary yet daring Sherman has given him no opportunity. On the other hand he has steadily forced him back from position to position, capturing works of enormous strength and wrenching from him an immense tract of territory inherently of great value to the enemy and

---

[165] Hooker's resignation from the Army of the Cumberland had long been sought by General Sherman who nursed a animus against the easterner, regarding him as "envious, imperious, and a braggart." Hebert, op. cit., pg. 286
[166] The 46th Alabama Infantry was part of Brigadier General Edmund W. Pettus' brigade, Stevenson's Division, Cheatham's Corps.

including many of the strongest natural positions in the South. Not until this campaign comes to be fully investigated and better understood than it is at present will the splendid achievements of this army be properly appreciated.

Three miles north of Atlanta, Georgia
August 3, 1864

Since the above was written another movement has transpired which bids fair to either bring an engagement or compel the evacuation of Atlanta. The Armies of the Tennessee and the Ohio have now both been transferred from the left to the right wing. Tecumseh evidently has some scheme in view not designed for the best interests of the Rebel commissariat. He doubtless intends to teach the enemy some practical lessons in the great truism that "armies like serpents go upon their bellies" and that huge forts, bristling abatis, and all that are but cold comfort to a starving soldiery. But the Rebel leader already understands this too well to remain in his works until our extended flank shall be thrown across his railroad communication. Hence it is fair to conclude that he will soon either venture another desperate onslaught upon our lines our evacuate Atlanta.

The weather is delightful; copious rains have cooled and freshened the air which is continually stirred by a delicious breeze that carries off the miasma of the camps and leaves the atmosphere pure and as clear as crystal. The thermometer usually averages about 85 in the shade. The country being broken there are plenty of springs affording the troops an abundance of good water. Could they have a proper supply of vegetables there would be but little disease among them. As it is, there is much scurvy and there will be vastly more unless the men are provided with a larger proportion of anti-scorbatic diet. Let the Onion Society folks not forget the army before Atlanta.

The army has watched with deep interest the course of affairs in Virginia. There is no particular surprise at the attempt of the enemy to make a diversion by invading Maryland, neither has it created any serious alarm. The raising of the siege of Petersburg or a defeat of the Army of the Potomac would be tenfold more disastrous to the army here than Rebel raids in Maryland and Pennsylvania can be to the country at large. Such an event would enable the enemy to send a portion of his Virginia army to threaten General Sherman's communications and then perhaps compel him to fall back upon Chattanooga and lose the valuable results of this long and difficult campaign. It is therefore of the utmost importance that the Rebel army at Richmond be kept so occupied that no portion of it may be detached and sent in this direction.

Of late there seems to be a good deal of talk outside the army about peace and even the semblance of a peace negotiation seems to have been recently enacted over the dark vortex of Niagara. It is proper to say that in the army there is but one sentiment on this subject, and that sentiment is expressed by the President in his "short, sharp, and decisive" letter to the nondescript Rebel emissaries. Peace without Union? How absurd! If such a thing ever were reasonable or even possible, it was before the loyal people of the nation became involved in this gigantic war to maintain its integrity. If we were to give up the government of our fathers we should have done so before scores of thousands of lives and untold millions of treasure were expended in its defense. That government, so precious by reason of the great principles it involves, is now rendered doubly so by the vast sacrifice of our best blood which it has cost us. To yield it now would be a base betrayal of the patriots who have given their lives to maintain it. It would be a humiliating concession to the enemies of the constitutional liberty and a cowardly recreancy from the greatest holiest trust ever committed to the keeping of a loyal people. Besides, the obstacles to a peaceful division of the country into two independent governments are just as great now as they ever were. It would be just as difficult to mark the boundary between freedom and slavery now as it would have been at the outbreak of the rebellion. The same perplexing questions that would have arisen then would arise now and would be found quite as remote from amicable and honorable adjustment.

Had the war been a total or even partial failure upon our party, there might be some excuse for seeking the best terms of reconciliation with our enemies. But such has not been the case. Considering the immense disadvantages under which the war has been waged, it has been a marvelous success. Anyone who takes a map of the country and fairly and intelligently compares the present limits of the rebellion with its boundaries as they existed three years ago must be filled with wonder and admiration at the vast achievements of our armies. The enemy is now driven to the wall. His armies have reached those points from which it is impossible for him to retreat without bringing sure and swift ruin upon his cause. The evacuation of Atlanta would be a virtual confession of the utter futility and hopelessness of any further effort to maintain the rebellion.

Let the war therefore continue, not only so, but let the war be waged with redoubled energy and with that irresistible determination which never admits the thought of failure. Let the people unite to sustain the army with all possible moral and physical support, and resolve that nothing shall be left undone that can strengthen the arms and encourage the hearts of those who fight the battles of the Union. Then shall we soon see the beginning of the end and the dawn of that lasting and substantial peace which is founded upon the immutable principles of justice and truth. The monstrous rebellion will disappear as a morning cloud and be chronicled among the things that were, its authors covered with the scorn of the civilized world, will sink to deserved oblivion and that blessed time so long hoped and prayed for will come. Yours for the war.

> "When bloody Mars is known only among the stars,
> And his armor with its thousand scars,
> In a niche as a curious thing is bound,
> And peered into and nothing found,
> When some sweet bird of the South,
> May build in every cannon's mouth,
> Till the only sound from its rusty throat,
> Shall be the wren's or the bluebird's note,
> When doves may find a safe resort,
> In the embrasures of every fort." [167]

Notes in Dixie Vol. XIII

Near Atlanta, Georgia
August 13, 1864

As the triumphant march of our armies more and more contracts the limits of the rebellion and accordingly hastens its downfall, the enemies of the government both North and South seem to increase in bitterness and fury. Upon the part of the armed Rebels, who not only disown all allegiance to the government but avowedly seek its overthrow, this course is not at all surprising. Being enlisted heart and soul in the work of establishing an independent Confederacy, it might be expected that they would grow more exasperated and uncompromising as they begin to realize that the daring schemes for which they have made such immense sacrifices are being thwarted and annulled. It conforms well, too, with their absurd notion of chivalry for the Southern leaders (not people, for they have no voice in the matter) even after events have forced them to a conviction of utter hopelessness of their cause, to wage rebellious war with more fierceness and desperation than ever. This false guide teaches them that to tamely succumb under any circumstances would be a shameful humiliation. They are therefore determined to die with arms in their hands, and to glorify their expiring hour by the very highest reach of sublimized hate and mistaken patriotism.

All this is natural enough and finds an easy solution in impulses which, however base and wicked, are nevertheless native to the human heart. But how strange, how passing strange, that men professing loyalty to the government should be guilty of an analogous course of conduct, and yet such men seem to be by no means uncommon in the loyal states. As the war for the Union approaches a triumphant consummation, they exhibit a more bitter hostility to every measure damaging to the Rebel cause. The more hopeless that cause becomes, the more sympathy do they manifest in its favor. The more nearly the administration attains the overthrow of the rebellion, the less they have to say in its praise. The Rebels themselves are surpassed by them in their denunciation of acts and policy. They would have us believe that it is the most corrupt and untrustworthy government that ever presided over

---

[167] Quotation from "The Wagoner of the Alleghenies: A Poem of the Days of Seventy-Six" by American poet and painter Thomas Buchanan Read published in 1863. Read later painted the famous picture depicting Sheridan's Ride at the Battle of Cedar Creek.

the destinies of any nation. They charge it with having wrested from the people the right of speech and of the press and every other right guaranteed by the constitution. In reviling it, they exhaust the language of invective, being careful, however, to very rarely say a hard word against the rebellion or its instigators. They present every argument that could possibly be adduced for the enemy to tax every resource and strain every nerve to keep up the war to the bitter end. These arguments are repeated in Rebel newspapers and bandied through Rebel camps. At every opportunity the enemy flings them at our soldiers with the taunting insinuation that "your own papers are authority for it." The writer himself has been met by quotations from the *New York World* and the *Cincinnati Enquirer* when discussing with violent Rebels the merits of their cause.

It is easy to see, therefore, upon which side of this great contest the class of men just described properly belong. In fact it is impossible to play the political hypocrite at such a time as this. The events of this war are as strongly and irresistibly developing the innermost characters of men as the poet conceived in his vision:

"I dreamed of a marvelous harvest,
I dreamed of a threshing floor,
Where men like grain, by angels twain,
Were garnered in measureless store,
All bound in sheaves, like corn in the leaves,
And flailed from husk to core." [168]

There is no difficulty in determining who are the friends and enemies of the country now. While the true patriot stands forth in more bold relief than ever, the traitor, stripped of his disguises, stands unmasked before the world. He who loves liberty and Union is just as distinct from him who hates them as day is from night. Nor is there any medium class. In the very nature of the case such a thing is impossible. The only distinguishing marks among the friends or enemies of the Union are their different methods of maintaining it or opposing it. There can be no other. Every sane man must range himself upon one side or the other of the great question. Merely criticizing or opposing the administration as such is not culpable. It is the insane and reckless abuse of it as the government of the country, and when charged with the immense responsibilities of war like this, with which I have to find fault. Common sense ought to teach us to be thankful that amid the fearful political perils through which we have passed during the past three years, we have had an administration that has committed so few mistakes. It ought to teach us also that at such a time as this it is the duty of every true patriot to rather ignore the faults of the governing power than to be constantly endeavoring to expose and magnify them. We ought to realize, too, that it is a time when the people should bring all possible moral and physical support to the executive arm of the government and should by no means either in word or deed give any countenance or encouragement to the traitors in arms.

Such as my conclusions upon these matters dear *Gazette*, as I have thought them over behind the rifle pits in front of Atlanta. I venture them as a soldier's opinion, believing, however, that they are the sentiments entertained almost universally throughout this army. Just beyond the picket line I regret to say there is a very different state of feeling, as I am painfully informed there is also in certain benighted districts of Ohio. This latter is to a large extent no doubt the result of the impending draft, and probably finds its proper origin in that disgust for villainous saltpeter which among persons of that class is believed to be surpassed only by their hatred of the African.

We soldiers, it is true, are inclined to be somewhat 'radical' in our Union sentiments. Bayonets and bullets are radical; Rodmans and Parrotts are radical; and war itself is the very perfection of radicalism; and we who have grown accustomed to the daily use of these kind of arguments with Southern Disunionists, are radical by virtue of necessity as well as inclination. Whatever utopian peace or compromise fantasies enter the minds of Northern conservatives, it is perfectly certain that the soldiers of this army demand and expect nothing less than the unconditional submission of every armed rebel to the Union, the whole Union, and nothing less than the Union.

---

[168] Lee is quoting "Harvest and Vintage" by Augustine Joseph Hickey Duganne; Massachusetts-born Duganne served as lieutenant colonel of the 176th New York Infantry before being captured June 23, 1863 at the Battle of Brashear City in Louisiana. He wrote a book entitled <u>Camps and Prisons, Twenty Months in the Department of the Gulf</u> describing his Civil War experiences in 1865.

Union graves at Peachtree Creek battlefield in 1864.
(Library of Congress)

They expect also that the government will exercise sufficient license of power to suppress every treasonable element throughout the land, whether North or South. They desire nothing more than to see the government arise fearlessly in its might and lay its hand of iron upon the throat of resistance to its authority wherever and in whatever form is may be manifested. They feel that the Union of these states must, at every cost, be restored and maintained. To this end, they expect the loyal people to make all necessary sacrifices, not only of money and men, but even of their personal liberties. No government can be perfectly free when assailed by open and armed rebellion upon the one hand and domestic treason upon the other. The power necessary to overcome such elements of opposition must to a certain extent be arbitrary and untrammeled. And what true patriot is not ready to consent that it should be so rather than to have his country divided? That people only is worthy of free institutions which has the intelligence to appreciate the necessities of a great crisis, and is willing to submit to whatever temporary suspension of natural rights may be necessary for their preservation and perpetuity.

The siege of Atlanta still continues. The position of the 20th Corps, except a slight advancement of a portion of the line, remains substantially the same as it was 15 days ago. The troops, being constantly confined to their entrenchments and not allowed their usual freedom of motion, grow weary of the changeless tedium of rifle pit life. The time often hangs heavily upon their heads and is mainly beguiled by discussing the thousand rumors that are wafted to them from no one knows whither. Dispatches from the "grapevine telegraph" and "canteen rumors" continually agitate the camps from one end of the line to the other. The variety of these reports and the rapidity with which they circulate are wonderful. They embrace all sorts of news, both good and bad, and receive the usual amount of enlargement as they pass from lip to lip. Each officer and soldier seems to be always provided with his own particular budget of "latest information" which is almost invariably "official" or traced to some official source. The mutual exchange of these treasures affords a sort of amusement which, after all, is worth something. Meanwhile the pickets keep up a lively fusillade along the lines and the batteries ever and anon belch their thunder in discordant interludes. We have many quite heavy pieces in position which daily and nightly shower upon the rebellious city of Atlanta a worthy baptism of flame and iron. Even while I write, their deep bellowing breaks wildly forth upon the calm air of night and is followed by the far distant explosion of the shells in the direction of the devoted city.

The enemy scarcely perched behind his fortifications ventures no attack upon our lines, but quietly awaits our assault or the expected flanking movement which is to deprive him of his communications. He seems bent upon holding Atlanta to the very last moment, and is determined not to yield the vast advantages of his present position except when compelled by the most desperate extremities. That those extremities are near at hand there is but little doubt, and we live in almost daily anticipation of occupying the Rebel metropolis. May it soon be realized.

Notes in Dixie Vol. XIV

Near Atlanta, Georgia
August 24, 1864

The temperature at the moderate altitude of 78 in the shade, a delicious breeze softly whispering among the dark branches of the overshadowing pines and dallying with the pliant canvass of my tent, the emerald earth breathing aroma from its lately moistened bosom now covered with a dappled carpeting of light and shade, blue patches of Southern summer sky interspersed by snowy clouds whose radiant whiteness seems almost too pure and stainless for earth, the golden tongue of music vexing the lazy air with amorous echoes through the hills and valleys- such, my dear *Gazette,* are some of the circumstances and surroundings amid which I propose once more to continue these notes. Nature retains something of her loveliness even while great armies confront each other and reserves a voice of harmony and a touch of beauty even for the war-worn soldiers, provided he will turn aside to listen and observe. And so powerful is the charm during these rich and glorious summer days that it subdues all the distractions of the camp and silently steals upon the mind despite the unnatural influences and associations occasioned every day and every hour by the angry strife between man and his fellow. The sun smiles, the dew glitters upon the grass, the songsters twitter in the groves, day declines in serene glory, night dons her jeweled mantle of gemmed ebony, and nature day by day calmly and serenely pursues her course, diffusing peace and beauty everywhere as if to shame guilty men who devote night and day to the destruction of their lives and happiness.

A strange medley life is this of mingled pleasure and pain. Sublimity and horror, calm and unrest. Thrilling in its episodes, almost unbearable in its monotony, severe in its privations, terrible in its trials, noble in its aims, demoralizing in its tendencies, grand in its events, fearful in its perils, mysterious in its uncertainties, it develops some of the best, worst, and most singular traits of human character. Among the latter may be ranked the utter abandon which army life cultivates. Having surrendered the control of himself and his destinies to others, the soldier learns to be forgetful of the past, unmindful of the future, and almost regardless of the present. The extreme test of continual exposure to danger breeds in him a sort of careless unconcern about matters less important than life and death, and cultivates a power of will and strength of manhood which death itself can scarcely daunt or subdue. It is emphatically true that the experience of war makes men strong, and it is probably fortunate that this severe schooling has befallen this great people, inasmuch as it will bring them up to a lofty standard of manly strength and heroism which otherwise would probably have never attained. Let those be commiserated who are too ignorant to appreciate, or too weak to avail themselves of the glorious opportunities of this great crisis. Without the manhood and courage to stand by the truth, they fain would stoop in humble submission to traitors and surrender the dearest holiest trust ever committed to the keeping of a free people. Unworthy inheritors of freedom! Unworthy of the sublime history of the past and the sublime one of the present, unworthy of their day and generation, unworthy of the land of their birth!

Next to the engagement itself, there is perhaps nothing about a battle which attracts more interest than the place where it occurred. It was my sad pleasure to revisit recently the scene of the fight near Peachtree Creek on the 20th of July. It was a calm quiet evening and the mellowed light of the declining sun fell softly upon the freshly made graves of our fallen heroes. Southern songsters whistled their vesper melodies undisturbed among the trees, newly scarred and splintered by shells and bullets and the cricket chirped his evening ditty along the lonely sward so lately crimsoned by the blood of patriot and Rebel. Winding along the crests of the hill and through the thick, somber forests the hastily built breastwork pursued its zig-zag course and marked the position of our line as it was formed and held during the sanguinary conflict. All the ground was strewn with the rubbish and debris of battle and told all too plainly of its hurry, its terror, and its destruction. The dead had been gathered and carefully buried in groups, their names and regiment spelled by the unlettered muse being plainly carved on boards which were fastened to the graves. And there in that lonely Georgian forest those patriot martyrs for our country's cause "each in his narrow cell forever laid" peacefully sleeps their long last sleep disturbed no more by the angry thunders that still echo about their quiet resting place than by 'summer evening's latest sigh, that shuts the rose.' And their sepulchers though obscure and unfrequented are not unhonored. Around them in perennial freshness are entwined the memories and affections of all who admire valor and love liberty and law. Nor is there any wreathed monument needed to perpetuate the fame or enhance the glory of their occupants. It is as imperishable as the rights of man, immutable as truth when their open enemies and doubtful friends shall have perished and have been forgotten, their names will be spoken as household words and will live and burn immortal.

> "They do not die, they do not die,
> Souls of the brave and just.
> It's not a cowards thought to say,
> Ye pass again to dust!
> Ye live through every age- ye are given,
> To breathe in hearts of slaves,
> The patriot flame ye drew from heaven,
> That sleeps not in your graves." [169]

I had hoped to be able by this time to record the triumphant entry of our army into the Gate City of the South. But such is not yet my good fortune. Our immense line, about 14 miles in length, encircles the city upon three sides lying across the Georgia Railroad on the extreme left and almost reaching the Macon & Western Railroad on the extreme right. The Army of the Tennessee now holds the center, the Army of the Ohio and the 14th Corps of the Army of the Cumberland the right, and the 4th and 20th Corps still in their old positions on the left. The entire line is now so strongly entrenched as to be impregnable against any force liable to be brought against it. The troops idly lie in camp behind their breastworks and wile away the long summer days as best they may. All sorts of devices are resorted to to vary the monotony and give buoyancy to the dragging hours. One of these is the manufacture of trinkets of every shape and species which soldiers ingenuity can suggest. The copper fuses from the enemy's shells are manufactured into rings, the elaborate finish of which would do credit to a finer material than copper, and a more complete toolkit than a pen-knife.

The regular bombardment of Atlanta is kept up day and night, the guns firing at stated intervals and dropping the shells directly upon the city. Great destruction of property has been effected in this way and there is little doubt that very many of her sons have been killed and wounded by both our artillery and musketry in the very streets of the devoted city. During the quiet evenings the shells can be distinctly heard whizzing away on their destructive mission, furiously crashing among roofs, walls, or whatever obstacles they may meet, and finally bursting in the very heart of the war-scourged metropolis.

The musketry firing has very much abated along the line during the last few days, the hostile pickets having a sort of mutual understanding that they will not shoot at each other without having first given due notice. "Take care Yank" or "Look out Reb" is usually the preliminary warning given when either party deems it necessary to reopen the fire. At this injunction all spring to their rifle pits and commence the usual fusillade upon each other. This being ended the combatants again venture slowly out of their pits and a "peace negotiation" is set on foot which usually results in the exchange of a quantity of Yankee coffee for a certain amount of rebellious tobacco, and quite often on the bringing in by the "boys in blue" of a Rebel soldier or two who have made up their minds to abandon the waning Confederacy.

The cavalry under dashing Kilpatrick had just returned from a raid around the rear of Atlanta. They report having destroyed two depots and an important bridge on the Macon Railroad, and having torn up several miles of track. Just how long the enemy will be able to endure so many successive interruptions of his communications it is

---

[169] Lee is quoting from "Napoleon at Austerlitz" by Irish/English poet George Croly.

difficult to tell, but it is fair to presume that he already finds the question of supplies a very troublesome one to solve. Events are probably not far distant which will render it still more so. [170]

A few days since preparations were made for a grand movement of the entire army which it was intended should cut short the siege of Atlanta by its complete investment or by compelling the enemy to leave it. Whether General Sherman intended the whole arrangement as a feint or whether some unforeseen event spoiled his plan seems to be not yet fully understood; but at all events, the whole movement was suspended just in its incipiency. The enemy, suspecting that something was going on, furiously shelled our lines early on the morning of the 18th, upon which day the great movement was to culminate. Doubtless to his great dismay and chagrin he found the Yanks still in their works and apparently without any intention of leaving them. On the following morning, the anxiety of the Rebs to know our whereabouts was anticipated by our batteries, which opened about an hour before daybreak one of the most tremendous cannonades that ever "woke snakes" in Georgia. Peal on peal the thunder rose all along the line in one uninterrupted deafening explosion. The gleaming of the guns, the streaming through the air of the lighted shells and the quick lightning-like flash of their explosions illuminated the shades of early morning with a pyrotechnic display which it would be idle for me to attempt to describe. The batteries fired in volleys or else in that quick succession which resembles file firing in musketry. The enemy scarcely replied a single shot, but seemed to be thinking only how to preserve himself amid the terrific storm of iron being poured upon him. The firing finally subsided to its ordinary proportions and the Rebels crawling from the dens and caves in which they had sought refuge were doubtless convinced that the Yanks had not gone yet. And they were right.

Notes in Dixie Vol. XV

Montgomery Ferry, Georgia
September 1, 1864

The compensating advantages of fortifications for inferiority of numbers have been demonstrated in no portion of this war more fully than in General Sherman's operations around Atlanta. For months previous to the approach of our army to the city the enemy, understanding that it would be the objective and key point to the coming campaign, had industriously and with perseverance employed every available means in encircling the place with a cordon of forts, breastworks, redoubts, abatis, and every conceivable obstacle known to the science of fortification. Besides this, knowing the flanking proclivities of his daring antagonist, he carefully covered his railroad communication with a line of defensive works extending far south of Atlanta and so constructed as to be almost next to impregnable against anything less than a regular siege. The commanding site of Atlanta and the rolling character of the country in its vicinity added much to the strength of these various works. They also possessed the vast advantage of forming an interior defensive line built at leisure and without any hindrance as to a choice of ground. The attacking party must of necessity assume an exterior line which, in order to protect the flanks, must be drawn out to a much greater extent. Such were some of the inherent and artificial advantages of position possessed by the enemy.

To these must be added still others found in the peculiar arrangement of his railroad communications. Since the enemy's position was so effectually guarded against assault, there remained for our armies but two alternatives: either to lay siege to his works, or to cut his communications. General Sherman chose the latter. In doing so he undoubtedly selected the one least difficult, but nevertheless full of obstacles and embarrassments. Two railroads lead out of Atlanta southward and one northward. The direction of these three roads as they proceed from their common junction near the center of the city is such that lines drawn from one to the other, at points equidistant from

---

[170] However "dashing" Kilpatrick may have seemed to Lee, his reputation amongst his fellow general officers was that of a reckless ne'er do well, or in General Sherman's colorful words, "a damned fool." Kilpatrick's troopers nicknamed him "Kill-Cavalry" for his propensity for ordering bold, bloody charges; his raid around Atlanta nearly ended in disaster for his command and this failure finally convinced Sherman that the only way to break the stalemate at Atlanta was to swing around a large portion of his army to Hood's remaining railroad line and force a battle. The subsequent Battle of Jonesboro fought August 31-September 1, 1864 finally broke Hood's hold on Atlanta.

that junction, are equal to each other and form an isosceles triangle. By this arrangement, the longest possible line is required to hold all three of the railroads at the same time. Our own communication of course must be covered. To abandon it entirely, as was done at Kingston and Kennesaw, would not do now with the Chattahoochee River in our rear and the enemy lodged in fortifications which he could hold with half of his force. But to lay hold of the two lines of Rebel communication (with Augusta and Macon) and at the same time sever its own communication with Chattanooga was too much even for the vast army of General Sherman. The Augusta road was seized and held by our forces on the left, but after extending the line nearly 14 miles, it was found impossible for those and the right to envelop the enemy's fortifications and reach the road leading to Macon.

It became apparent that to accomplish this object, the same bold flanking policy which gave us Allatoona Pass and the lines of Kennesaw must be resorted to again. Nothing but starvation would loosen the enemy's desperate grasp upon Atlanta. But to starve him we must obtain possession of the Macon road. That involved not only the abandonment of our lines in front of Atlanta but, by the greater part of the army at least, of its line of communication. It was resolved therefore to detach one corps, the 20th, to hold the Chattanooga railroad while the main body of the army would move boldly upon the enemy's rear. Such was the daring plan conceived and now partly executed by General Sherman. During the night of August 25th, the great movement began. For some days previous to that date it had been understood that some great adventure for the entire army was impending. The picket firing had gradually dwindled along the entire line until almost the only hostile demonstration remaining was the incessant bombardment of the city by our batteries.

The sun of the 25th went down in serene glory. A Roman would have said the omen was auspicious for the great undertaking, involving the interests and destinies of a nation about to be inaugurated amid the gathering gloom. To withdraw a great army from the immediate presence of another great and hostile force is always a delicate matter, but particularly so when that withdrawal initiates a grand offensive strategic movement. As the evening shades began to gather a sort of anxious feeling pervaded the mind of everyone from the major general down to the humblest private. A random musket shot, the jolt of an artillery carriage, the too bright gleam of a camp fire, the strange glimmer of a distant light, any unusual or seemingly unusual sight or sound excited the nerves and quickened pulsations that seemed to feel and beat in common throughout the army. Shortly after nightfall the artillery began to withdraw. The carriages were hauled out slowly and cautiously one at a time. What if their irrepressible rattling should waken up the iron fiends which had so often swept that ground with a tempest of shell? Would they continue to repose thus harmlessly behind their gaping embrasures until our now helpless guns were out of range, or would they at the first intimation of our movement with vengeful gleam belch upon us their vomit of shrieking shell? Though each moment their booming thunder would scarce have startled anyone, they kept strangely quiet. While everything was astir in our camps, hardly a sound emanated from those of the enemy. Either he was not apprised of our leaving, or being anxious to be well rid of troublesome neighbors, did not desire to hinder us.

It was arranged that the troops should leave their trenches at precisely 8 o'clock P.M. At 7:30 the artillery had been all gotten out of the way without accident. As the time for the movement of the infantry drew nigh, the men silently gathered in their places in line. It was wonderful how soft footed they were-they moved like shadows. All being ready, at exactly eight o'clock the buglers stepped up to the breastworks and a blew a long soothing tattoo (for the Rebels) and while its last echoes were reverberating away over the hills and hallows toward Atlanta, the dark silent column displayed itself moving out in the pale moonlight. In ten minutes the chain of hills in the rear of and commanding those just abandoned was reached and the troops were placed in position, concealed by the dark shadows of the timber and prepared to receive the enemy should he dare to come out of his works and follow us. But he manifested no disposition to dispute us in the least. The solemn silence of night remained unbroken by a single shot and scarce a sound disturbed the quiet save the cricket's chirp and the answer shrill of the gauze-winged katydid.

While the 20th Corps was thus engaged in withdrawing from its entrenchments, the 4th Corps had also quietly abandoned its position on the left and was now rapidly moving to join the main body of the army which had at the same time begun its movement to the right and toward the rear of Atlanta. The 20th Corps was retained in position until after midnight in order to cover this movement of the 4th. This task being accomplished, the different divisions moved quickly off toward their assigned stations, covering the bridges and fords of the Chattahoochee.

Gen. Alpheus Williams' Red Star Division was appointed to guard the approaches to the railroad bridge near Montgomery Ferry. The troops arrived safely in position shortly before daybreak, and in a few hours strengthened their line by strong breastworks and abatis.

Almost seven days have elapsed since these movements occurred. Yet scarcely a word of intelligence has been received from the army. "Where is it?' everyone asks. Echo answers "where." It is remarkably quiet all along the Chattahoochee. Only the occasional booming of a very distant gun can be heard in the direction of Atlanta. Brave old Tecumseh with his magnificent legions has disappeared far down in the enemy's country. Where he has gone or what he is doing no one seems to know. He and his host seemed swallowed up in the flood of the rebellion. But we all feel that it is only the settling of the leviathan who will shortly appear again at the surface bringing with him the trophies of the deep. The army is safe not merely because Sherman leads it, but because it is strong in its reliance upon its ability to take care of itself, and because God himself befriends it. Never was any army blessed with more uniform and unadulterated success that this one has been during this 120 days' campaign. And the tide of fortune is not going to change now. It is still at the flood and will bear onward, still onward, the standard of victorious freedom. Tremble traitors, for your doom is nigh! The thunders of the North are at your castle gates, and the Union tocsin swells in high and pealing notes over Southern hills and valleys.

Montgomery Ferry, Georgia
September 3, 1864
Hurrah! The flag of the Union floats over Atlanta! The great citadel of the rebellion in the cotton states has at length fallen, and the boys in blue, led by the victorious Sherman, have hoisted over it the starry emblem of liberty and union. All its gaping forts and bristling abatis are harmless now, except to traitors. Defended by loyal hearts and true, they must ever remain the impregnable stronghold of freedom in Georgia.

The enemy began his retreat during the night of August 31st. The last of his forces did not abandon the city until the night ensuing. At midnight of the 1st, a multitude of loud thunderous explosions, like the rapid firing of artillery, began to be heard in the direction of Atlanta. They grew more and more frequent until a deep monotonous road like that of a heavy battle filled the midnight air. Almost everyone took it for granted that a severe engagement had suddenly sprung up in the darkness. A great light loomed up against the atmosphere which was construed to be caused by burning houses which had been fired by shells. But all these suppositions and theories have been proved to be incorrect. It was the explosion of vast quantities of Rebel ammunition. The enemy was retreating, and a blazing ruin lit up his track.

On the following day (September 2), reconnoitering parties were sent out by General Slocum, commanding the 20th Corps, and the evacuated city was occupied by our troops at 5 P.M. General Williams with two of his brigades left his position at Montgomery Ferry en route for Atlanta. The gallant old Third Brigade now commanded by Colonel Horace Boughton of the 143rd New York Volunteers was left to guard the railroad bridge. Thus our noble fellows who have braved so many dangers and expended so much toil and blood to capture the Gate City have not yet been blessed with a sight of it. But they doubtless will be soon. For the present, it suffices them that it is ours. That it is, let God be thanked.

Notes in Dixie Vol. XVI

Atlanta, Georgia
September 5, 1864
"Move your brigade forward to this place starting tomorrow morning at an early hour." Such was the order sent from Atlanta by General Williams to Colonel Boughton, commanding the Third Brigade on the evening of September 3, 1864. Two regiments from the brigade (the 101st Illinois and 82nd Ohio) had already gone forward from Montgomery Ferry and were among the first to carry the stars over the Rebel battlements and hoist them on the pinnacles of the Gate City. And now we were to follow. The thought caused a joyous thrill which none could know but those who for 120 days had been toiling and marching through sun and rain and had during that time fought through five bloody battles, to reach the end now about to be so easily attained.

It needed no reveille to remind the men of the Third Brigade of the approach of day on the morning of the 4th inst. Its stirring notes, as they echoed up and down the war-scathed banks of the Chattahoochee, fell upon ears from which the film of sleep had already been brushed away. The proud thought "I have helped to take Atlanta and now I'm going into it" was more animating than early bugle and drum calls, and forestalled any complaining. The troops were not only up before time, but quickly on the march, each man pressing forward with eager step and joyous heart, as if some festive or holiday occasion awaited his anxious feet.

By 11 A.M., the column filed through an opening in the breastworks which our troops, a few weeks before, had thrown up in the face of the enemy and under the very muzzles of his guns. It was all abandoned now and the debris of the deserted camps and trenches loomed gloomily in the bright light of the Southern sun. A hundred paces or so beyond the Union works brought us to those of the enemy. And such works! Let me, if I can, convey some idea of the barriers which these mistrustful Confederates raised up against an assault by their daring antagonists. First was a line of rile pits from 50 to 100 yards in front of the main line. These were occupied by pickets. Next came lines, usually three in number, of bristling abatis. These were partly formed by sharp stakes firmly set in the ground and protruding outwardly, and partly by heavy rollers constructed of timbers through which two rows of long wooden pins was passed by means of holes bored at right angles with each other. Next to these abatis was a line of timber ten feet high, set perpendicularly to the ground with narrow crevices or loopholes between for the musketry. Close behind this formidable obstacle was the main breastworks from four to six feet in thickness. Add to all this the strong redoubts built on prominent points of the line, manned with artillery which swept with a crossfire all the approaches from the outside, and some idea can be formed of the kind of fortifications with which the Rebels have completely encircled the city of Atlanta.

The column halted for a breathing spell in the shade of the pine trees that grow in comfortable profusion all about the suburbs of Atlanta. This gave us an opportunity to observe something of the execution done by our artillery. Along this portion of the line were many handsome suburban residences, once models of comfort and the abodes of wealth and fashion. Those that had stood between the hostile entrenchments were completely demolished. Others that stood behind the enemy's line were ruined monuments of the waste and devastation of war. Near one of the Rebel forts, on a commanding site just opposite the position occupied during the siege by the Third brigade, was the wreck of what had been a beautiful edifice. Around the hand of industry and taste had strewn more of the comforts, conveniences, and charms of a civilized home than I had seen almost anywhere in the South. But owing to its prominent position, it be had been fearfully riddled by our artillery. Its fine balconies were a pendulous wreck, its painted walls full of gaping holes, it stucco ceiling mutilated and stained, its marble mantle pieces displaced and broken, its broad polished stairways strewn with rubbish, its piazza hedged up with bricks and broken timbers. The yard where rich palms, ferns, flowers, and a great variety of other rare and beautiful plants had bloomed in delicately cultured beauty was now a trampled, tangled jungle. Such is the fate which befalls the homes of traitors; such is the retribution which sooner or later must overtake their crimes.

After a few minutes the bugle rang out its shrill summons, the soldiers sprang to their places, and keeping step to the inspiring cadence of martial music, the column, with colors flying and arms at right shoulder shift, began its entrée into the city. Marching down Marietta Street until near the railroad depot, it filed up Peachtree Street. We did not expect of course that the rebellious citizens of Atlanta would prepare an ovation for us or receive us enthusiastically. Nor did they. But in silent groups and with sullen or expressionless countenances they watched us pass. The bands entertained them with the thrilling strains of "Hail Columbia" and "Rally Round the Flag," which, if they had not forgotten the meaning of those inspiring airs, must have either awakened some regrets or else smothered them with aggravated hatred. But to the noble men who "carried the flag and kept step to the music of the Union," there was something particularly gratifying in the loud prolonged strains of "The Union, forever, hurrah boys, hurrah! Down with the traitor, up with the star, and we'll rally round the flag boys, rally once again, shouting the battle cry of freedom."

It was worth all the toil and suffering of the campaign to hear these patriotic notes echoing along the streets of the boasted citadel of the rebellion. After passing through the main portion of the city and reaching the eastern extremity of Peachtree Street, our troops were put in position behind some works built for us by the enemy. Almost the entire corps is now here and occupies the various works around the city. It is to be hoped that the star of the brave old 20th Corps may be the guiding star that shall lead this erring people into the safe way of loyalty to the flag they have so causelessly torn down and insulted.

The city of Atlanta is beautifully located. Its site is commanding and overlooks a vast scope of the country in almost every direction, but particularly to the northward and westward. Standing near the southern extremity of Peachtree Street, one beholds a view which is truly magnificent. For a distance of 25-30 miles the country unfolds itself like a map to the beholder. Far away toward sunset the dark shadow of Lost Mountain looms up like that of a lonely giant, while a few miles to the right of it the twin peaks of Kennesaw lift their proud and now classic summits toward heaven. Still farther to the right a nameless peak adorns the deep blue grandeur of the landscape, which far to the southwestward Stone Mountain rears its graceful outline in beauteous majesty and gives the finishing touch to a picture almost too fair for painter's pencil or poet's dream. The city itself is handsome for a Southern city. The loftiness of its situation and the rolling character of the surface in and around it, gives it the advantage of pure air and clean streets. There are many large and handsomely constructed edifices, including several churches, academies, and other public buildings. There are, besides these, many large hotels, warehouses, and stores, all of which are invaluable to our army. The hospital accommodations for our sick and wounded promise to be superior to those of Nashville or any city south of that. The streets are mostly well shaded, particularly in the suburbs, which adds much to the comfort and beauty of the place. The railroad buildings and depot are well built and commodious, and remain almost intact. They are already being rapidly filled with stores brought here by our locomotives which, it must be understood, follow the advance of our skirmish lines. They were here almost as soon as our soldiers, shrieking exultation over the new home found for them in the land of cotton.

The effects of our bombardment are visible in every part of the city. There is scarcely a building that has not been more or less shattered by shot and shell. The missiles have usually gone clear through the buildings struck, and must have infused terror as they spread desolation everywhere. There is no place in the city where anyone could find perfect security from their uninvited intrusions. The people of this war-scourged city were as likely to make the acquaintance of these impolite messengers from Yankeedom at their morning meal or midnight repose as in the open street at noonday. The first intimation of their coming would be the ferocious whistling which would just precede their mad crashing through fragile roofs and walls. Think of this you who from day to day enjoy the undisturbed quiet of your Northern homes, yet are thankless to the God who has given peace to your borders, and unappreciative of the government which remains the only barrier between your loved homes and war's desolation. Think of our peaceful Delaware, our beautiful Dayton, and our Queen and Forest City, being ravaged and desolated as has been the once prosperous and happy city of Atlanta. Yet such, O, ye Copperheads and sympathizers with treason, is the fate ye fain would bring upon our fair and peaceful Buckeye State. If you desire peace, permanent and lasting peace, you must sustain the government of the United States. If you desire war, war for yourselves and children's children, tear it down. God has given you the blessed heritage of free government and expects you to maintain it. If you do not, woe be unto you.

The house in which I write, for I have been so far reclaimed to civilization as to dwell in a house once more, is located near one of the enemy's works on Peachtree Street. It is a neat and pleasant cottage, but for weeks it has had no other occupants than some Rebel officers, probably a portion of Gen. Hood's staff, as his headquarters were in an adjoining building. Even this humble, I might almost say, innocent little cottage ranks among the victimized. A cannon shot has plunged through the outside wall tearing a hole nearly a foot in diameter. Passing straight through the room it has left daylight shining through a large aperture in the wall opposite. Crossing a hall it penetrated a third wall and finally dodged in a room on the farther side of the building. This huge iron monster seems to have had a contemporary in mischief named Minie- a delicate name to be sure for a thing so fraught with death. This interesting young member of the saltpeter fraternity struck the building near the same spot as its granddad of weightier caliber, but seems to have been content with less ambitious progress, for after passing through one wall and leaving its "handwriting" on another it seems to have dropped harmlessly on the floor. Citizens say that most of the casualties which occurred in the city during the siege were caused by bullets. The statement is confirmed by the marks left on trees, fences, and houses by those far flying messengers.

Notwithstanding the fall of Atlanta there is but little bitterness of feeling manifested openly by its inhabitants. Many of them profess to be loyal and there is no doubt but some of them are. Even those who claim to be secessionists are not very ardent in asserting it, and all classes seem to be more approachable than the irreconcilable traitors of Kentucky and Tennessee. But I have written enough as Artemus Ward would say "for onct." Therefore with my tender regards to the "peace brethren" and to the mourning friends of the late Major General McClellan, for all of whom I shall probably have a word of consolation in my next note, I remain yours for the Union.

The Confederate entrenchments on the north side of Atlanta in the summer of 1864. Such extensive field fortifications would have made any assault on the citadel a costly one; Sherman chose to lay siege and eventually flanked John Bell Hood's army out of the city and defeated him at the Battle of Jonesboro on August 31-September 1, 1864. Hood retreated from the city on the night of September 1st and on September 4th, the 20th Corps marched into the city for occupation duty. Captain Lee remembered "The column halted for a breathing spell in the shade of the pine trees that grow in comfortable profusion all about the suburbs of Atlanta. This gave us an opportunity to observe something of the execution done by our artillery. Along this portion of the line were many handsome suburban residences, once models of comfort and the abodes of wealth and fashion. Those that had stood between the hostile entrenchments were completely demolished. Others that stood behind the enemy's line were ruined monuments of the waste and devastation of war. Near one of the Rebel forts, on a commanding site just opposite the position occupied during the siege by the Third Brigade, was the wreck of what had been a beautiful edifice."
(Library of Congress)

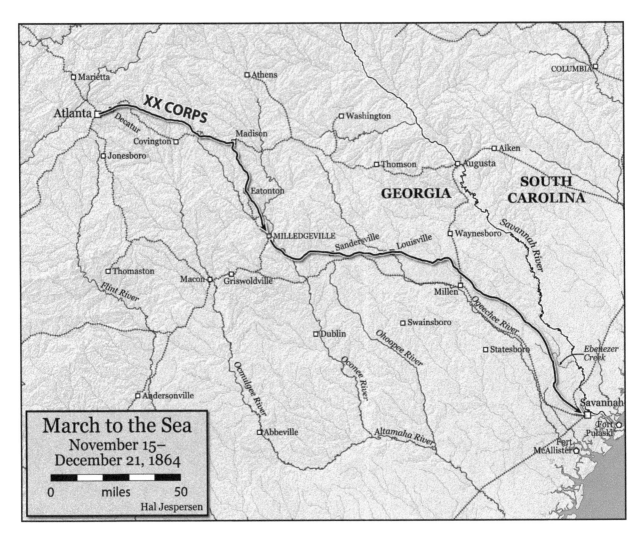

March to the Sea
November 15–
December 21, 1864

0   miles   50

Hal Jespersen

Captain Lee was awe struck by the audacity of the Sherman's March to the Sea, and wrote feelingly of it at the first opportunity. "One month ago I closed my portfolio hoping to reopen it among the seaside oaks that overhang the wide reedy Savannah River. This expectation has been fully realized. Since this pen traced the twentieth number of these notes one month has elapsed, and how eventful! What changes have been wrought, what thrilling episodes in the chaotic tragedy of war! From Atlanta to the Atlantic! What a march, what a journey, what a campaign! Enough to fill a volume, enough to employ a pen infinitely abler than mine." It was a long march without a battle for the 20th Corps; a foraging expedition without equal, and one of the primary events that broke the back of the Confederacy. (Hal Jespersen, www.cwmaps.com)

CHAPTER NINE

Marching Through Georgia

Notes in Dixie Vol. XVII

Atlanta, Georgia
September 15, 1864

"Aye! Failure, freedom's work is done.
Falter before the Southron's rod.
Betray the victory we won,
And compromise the truth of God!
Drag freedom's banner in the dust,
To endless scorn consign her name;
For transient peace and hallow trust,
Barter the future's hope and fame."

The first mail received after the fall of Atlanta brings us intelligence of the doings of the Chicago junta of peacemakers. The first message that comes from this philanthropic assemblage of power-seeking patriots to Sherman's triumphant host as it returns from pursuing the routed and flying legions of rebellion proclaims that the experiment of war to restore the Union is a failure. It declares that the constitution has been disregarded, that public property and private rights have been trodden down, and that the material prosperity of the country has been impaired, not by Jeff Davis and his Rebel crew, not by the treacherous conspirators against the public peace who instigated this war for disunion and slavery, not by those who have torn down and insulted the flag of the country, not by those who without just cause have turned the fairest, freest, and happiest portion of man's heritage into an abode of woe and wailing, but by the government of the United States! There is not one word of reproach for the enemies of the Republic, not one word of congratulation for the glorious victories of our armies, not one word of encouragement to sustain the flag and the government of our fathers. On the contrary, at the close of one of the most brilliant campaigns ever recorded in which not a single reverse has occurred to our army- that which the enemy has been driven from half a score of lines of defense among the most formidable on the continent- in which he has been compelled to surrender nearly half of the keystone state of the South including many of its valuable mines, manufactures, and the larger portion of the railroad system of the cotton states- in which he has lost all of his boasted strongholds from the Tennessee to the Etowah, from the Etowah to the Chattahoochee, and from the Chattahoochee to the Ocmulgee- in which he has been compelled to fly terror-stricken from his own Gate City and seek in hasty retreat that safety necessary for him to collect his scattered legions- after all this we are invited to humbly sue for an armistice and for conditions of peace! We are asked to lower the flag which now proudly floats over Atlanta, Fort Morgan, and Mobile Bay, and make it do reverence to the piratical emblem of treason. What an absurd proposition! What a strange misconception of the spirit and temper of the men who throughout 125 days campaign have borne steadily southward through storm and flame the banner of the Union![171]

---

[171] Captain Lee is referencing the Democratic National Convention held in Chicago on August 29-31, 1864. Former Army of the Potomac commander George B. McClellan received a unanimous nomination as candidate for the presidency. The convention adopted a peace platform which candidate McClellan rejected.

Colonel Horace Boughton of the 143rd New York Infantry commanded the Third Brigade while Colonel James S. Robinson was home on sick leave in the late summer of 1864. Colonel Boughton had the honor of leading the brigade into Atlanta on September 4, 1864 and was given a brevet promotion to brigadier general in March 1865, having rendered prior service with the 13th New York Infantry. He is buried at Arlington National Cemetery.
(Library of Congress)

Do I mistake the purport of this message from the would-be president makers at Chicago to the army and the people? Is it not clearly and distinctly a proposition to stop the war for the Union? Is it not plainly a proposal to compromise with the traitors in arms? If such is its meaning- and upon this point there can be no question- then it is perfectly clear that the basis of peace proposed (a Federal Union of the States) is only a union of those states which do not choose to join in the slaveholding Confederacy. Have not the authorized leaders and exponents of the rebellion claimed time and time again that they will hearken to no other terms of peace and compromise than those which admit as a primary and essential principle the right of secession and the independence of the seceded states? Upon what other terms then can peace be obtained, by a cessation of hostilities? The dissolution of the Union is therefore just as plainly embodied in this so-called Democratic Platform as if it were expressed in words.

How absurd to stop the advance of our armies and loosen their iron grasp from the throat of the rebellion unless it be for some clearly attainable object. But the object proposed being peace, and the only peace clearly attainable being peace which it is expected by this means to secure. No other can, with the most generous construction, come within the purview of the platform which the peace fraternity at Chicago have prescribed as the political faith of their party. If the war be stopped it cannot be resumed after a long and fruitless peace negotiation except at a vast disadvantage. To negotiate the seceded states back into the Union is simply out of the question. The Northern states may perhaps obtain a subordinate place in the so-called Confederacy, but that the insurgent states can be brought to submission to the constitution and government of the United States only by force of arms, is a fact patent to the most superficial mind. The peace party must therefore have one of these two objects in view; either a delay in our military operations and a consequent prolongation of the war, or a dissolution of the Union by recognition of the independence of the South.

Such is the interpretation which we soldiers, far away from strong partisan influences, are prone to give to the medley of inconsistencies known as the McClellan platform. And with this interpretation it seems to us a piece of the most insane folly. It is worse than folly. It is so far as it goes a humiliating confession of our inability to maintain our republican constitution and enforce the laws. It is a shameful attempt to degrade a great and free people in the estimation of all civilized nations. It is a base betrayal of all the blood which has been poured out to preserve the integrity of this county and thereby perpetuate its free institutions. It is a criminal acknowledgement of the justice of a causeless rebellion against the freest and best government ever vouchsafed to man.

Of the nominee of this peace party we soldiers have also our opinion. However, much of the fabulous stories told by interested political newspapers of his popularity in the army may have been true, it is certain that his nomination as a pro-slavery peace candidate for the presidency has not increased that popularity in the least. Even those who have been the blindest admirers and have stoutly held out for him as a military man, are now generally willing to confess that politically he is a blundering humbug. The gross inconsistencies between the platform upon which he was nominated and the letter in which he accepts that nomination, marks him in the minds of all fair thinking men as a hypocritical demagogue, willing to obtain his ambitious ends at any and all sacrifices of principle. In politics, as in religion, the truth is undeniable that no man can at the same time service God and Mammon. Besides, the great crisis now upon us is too plain and positive in its developments to permit of a shuffling and prevaricating course in regard to the great issues of the day. The object and tendencies of this war are as plain and unalterable as the sun in its course. No human agency can change them. He who attempts to do so arrays himself against the war and the principles for which it is waged.

This is a war for free institutions. Freedom is its animating soul. All who sustain it are friends of freedom, all who oppose, enemies. There can be no middle ground, neither can any man lend his influence to more than one side of the great question. McClellan is either for the war as announced in his letter of acceptance, or is opposed to it as proclaimed in the platform of his party. To declare he is both is an outrage to common sense. He cannot at the same time fully and heartily endorse war and peace sentiments, and to attempt such a thing is the lowest grade of political charlatanism. Its net results cannot be otherwise than opposition to the war and moral comfort to the Rebels in arms. He that is not for us is against us. McClellan is not for us except as he is also for peace measures utterly inconsistent with a hearty support of the war. That the soldiers of this or any other army are made in their admiration for McClellan is a great mistake. On the contrary, there is hardly a single prominent major general now in the field for whom they do not manifest a far more decided regard. To compare him to Grant or Sherman in point of either ability or popularity would be to provoke a smile in nine cases out of ten. The general impression is that McClellan is a man elevated by the singular chances and exigencies of a great crisis to a position far above his proper level, while the heroes of Vicksburg and Atlanta have slowly and steadily won their way upward by the unobtrusive and genuine merit which seldom gets above and cannot sink below its proper equilibrium. Let the people but endorse the verdict of the soldiers upon the peace party, platform, and nominee in November, and they will receive such an overwhelming defeat as will consign them to a lasting and merited oblivion.

The army has returned to the vicinity of Atlanta and is now enjoying a season of rest. The 20th Army Corps still occupies the city and suburbs. General Sherman has required all the citizens to leave the place, and they are rapidly emigrating either North or South. This measure is a hard military necessity, for which the Rebels themselves are responsible. Those helpless people have been stripped of the means of subsistence by the Rebel army and are left upon General Sherman's hands simply that he may have that many more mouths to feed. At the same time their friends are doing all in their power to destroy our communications and thus diminish our ability to subsist both them and ourselves. They would applaud the guerilla who shoots our guards and burns our railroad bridges and at the same time cry out against the inhumanity of denying bread to starving women and children. For some of the families residing here this is the second or third emigration they have been compelled to make by the advance of our armies. Many of them came here (firmly believing as they naively acknowledge) that this point never could be reached by our forces. I now write from a neat comfortable dwelling of a Mr. Marsh who formerly lived in Chattanooga where he acquired a large fortune. Being a leading and influential rebel, he thought it prudent to abandon to its fate a large portion of his property and with the residue fly from our approaching army and hunt a more permanent and congenial home in the far South. He came here and established himself, thinking that the uneven tenor of rebellious ways would certainly meet with no interruption at so remote a point. But 'the best laid schemes of mice and men oft go astray,' and particularly the schemes of traitors. Tomorrow he goes to hunt another asylum within the Rebel lines and a good deal nearer the Gulf. This time he leaves behind him the remnant of his fortune and goes almost a pensioner upon the charity of his friends. He confesses too that he has now no assurance that he will not be shortly again overtaken by our audacious columns and be made a homeless and dependent captive. Such is the punishment overtaking those who have dared to lift unholy hands against our just, free, and equitable government under the constitution and the Union.

Central Atlanta under Union occupation- Peachtree St. at the railroad. (Library of Congress)

Though there are many professedly and doubtless truly loyal people among the citizens of Atlanta, yet the secession element is strong and bitter. It manifests itself more noticeably among the female than the male population. Among this portion of the community contorted faces, upturned noses, and scornful glances are so common as to have become chronic. It is fearful to witness the painful distortions of countenance which these secession ladies undergo in order to indicate their aversion for the 'vandals.' Yet they are not unwilling to display the latest Southern fashions and most revolting Southern toilet in many a daily promenade in full view of Yankee optics. On the other hand they seem rather fond of improving every opportunity for an exhibition of their precious selves to the vulgar gaze of the thronging blue coats; imagining no doubt that our nerves are unaccustomed to being impressed by such transcendent female loveliness. And yet nine cases out of ten these gentle creatures are indebted for what little culture or refinement they may have to Northern books, teachers, or schools, and have done little during their natural lives except thumping upon Northern pianos a smattering of music taught them by Northern governesses. Apropos of pianos, permit me to say that while I am writing this a soldier of our brigade, one whose home is in the prairie west and who has passed through the privations of the long campaign, is improving the Boston piano in an adjoining room about as skillfully as could probably be done by any lily-fingered lady in Atlanta. The hands that draw lanyards and pull triggers in behalf of the Union are by no means strangers to the fine arts of life. On the contrary the amount of culture and intelligence which a careful observation discovers in the ranks of this army is truly surprising. Our soldiers reflect immense credit upon the free institutions under which they have been nurtured and which have extended the priceless boon of moral and intellectual improvement.

The recent raid made upon the communications of this army by the Rebel General Joseph Wheeler caused a temporary suspension of mails but otherwise occasioned no serious embarrassment. It is a remarkable fact that through the campaign the army has operated in a wild and destitute county and has frequently abandoned its communications in order to execute flanking movements, yet it has not been short of supplies for a single day. The enemy in all his efforts to destroy our railroad has accomplished little except to wear out his horses and weaken his force in our front. Vast quantities of supplies of every kind are now being brought here by rail and are being stored away for future use in the depots and warehouses of the city.

A clear calm September night made radiant by the full-orbed moon tempts me from this profitless writing. It is one of those glorious Southern evenings the inspiration of which it is easy to feel but impossible to describe. It is a time when earth seemed touched with too much of heaven's beauty to be the corrupt and sinful world that it is. Alas for the delusion!

Notes in Dixie Vol. XVIII

Atlanta, Georgia
October 13, 1864

Mail, mail, once more! Heaven be thanked for the mail, the soldiers' most treasured boon and blessing. After a long, dreary, letterless period of nearly three weeks, the joyful announcement of the arrival of a train bringing a score or more of plethoric mailbags flies from camp to camp on wildfire wings. Immediately the anxiety to solve the chances of the letter lottery becomes universal and irrepressible. By common consent postmasters are outlawed as the slowest creatures which breathe, and by those who make indiscriminate use of language, are unmercifully consigned to a climate somewhat warmer than this, and to the keeping of him whom 'the old painters lined with hoof and horn, a beak, and a scorpion tail.' Finally after anxious hours of waiting, the epistolary treasures are sorted and distributed to the different divisions, brigades, and regiments. Almost everyone draws a prize of some kind and all vexations are forgotten in thinking over the latest information from that most sacred and most cherished of earthly places-home. For none can realize more deeply than soldiers that 'there is a magic in that little word, it is a mystic circle that surrounds, comforts and virtues never known beyond, the hallowed limit.' [172]

The acrobatic performances of the Rebel General Hood and his shabby followers have of late become quite interesting. As early as the 25th, it became known to General Sherman that the enemy was moving in considerable force towards the Alabama line. It was soon afterwards ascertained that the main portion of the Rebel army had reached the Chattahoochee River at a point about 20 miles south of this place. It does not seem to have been anticipated, however, that these movements meant anything very serious, certainly not the wild, desperate enterprise in which they have since culminated. The consequence was that the simple movements which would have easily thwarted the enemy's designs were not made until after he had partially accomplished his purposes. Hood seeing our inertness, suddenly crossed the Chattahoochee and moving northward precipitated his entire force upon our railroad at a point above Marietta and far in our rear. He immediately tore up a large portion of the track and sent a strong detachment to assault our works at Allatoona Pass and if possible carry that important stronghold. The brave garrison at Allatoona held out until the arrival of reinforcements from Rome under Brigadier General Corse. The enemy made several fierce assaults upon the position, all of which he was handsomely repulsed. Sherman was by this time close upon Hood's gang of raiders with the armies of the Ohio, Tennessee, and Cumberland excepting the 20th Army Corps under Major General Slocum which was left in Atlanta. Hood, not wishing to risk any engagement with a force anything near equal to his own, at once fled from the railroad and from Allatoona leaving his dead, wounded, and several hundred prisoners in our hands. The Rebel army now moved westward beyond Dallas, pursued by our cavalry. Hood, still bent upon his foolhardy undertakings against our communications, again shaped his course northward. Crossing the Coosa River a few miles below Rome, he hastened to reach the railroad at a point far remote from Sherman's troublesome columns. Moving up the valley of the Oostenaula, he managed to again place himself upon our line of communications at a point near Dalton. He is said to be somewhere in that vicinity at this time with Sherman close on his heels.

What the next and final results of all these desperate adventures of the enemy will be it is difficult yet to foretell. The rapidity and hazardous nature of his movements prevent his transporting more than very limited quantities of ammunition and supplies, and he doubtless finds himself already compelled to subsist entirely upon a country in which the ravages of war have left scarcely enough to sustain a meager population. He dare not risk a

---

[172] From the poem "Hymn to the Penates" by 18th/19th century English Romantic poet Robert Southey.

battle with Sherman's intrepid army. All that he can accomplish must be done by swift and unexpected movements. By this means he may for a time interrupt our communications and succeed in destroying a few carloads of supplies. But such results are a poor compensation for the fearful hazard and inevitable loss which must be incurred to secure them. If the Rebel general expects by this species of strategy to compel us to evacuate Atlanta, he will be grievously disappointed. The veteran 20th Corps feels fully competent to hold the place against all the traitors that can be mustered in this part of rebeldom. Our supplies are sufficient for all present or prospective contingencies. A new line of works completely encircling the main portion of the city is being rapidly constructed, that built by the enemy being too extensive to be held by a single corps. This new line passes through some of the principal streets and will occasion the destruction of a large number of buildings. Where have been quiet homes and happy hearthstones, lunettes, and redans are rapidly looming up and being prepared for their grim occupants.

No considerable force of the enemy has yet appeared in our front, almost the entire Rebel army having gone off with Hood. It is not improbable, however, that ere the close of the campaign which has been so suddenly sprung upon us, some attempt will be made to reclaim by force this important point to the rebellion. If such be the case, the enemy will find that the "Old Star Corps" has lost none of its valor or prestige. He will find it is the 20th Corps of Resaca, New Hope Church, and Peach Tree Creek. The Red, White, and Blue Stars will gleam upon him as defiantly as they did amid the Wilderness at Chancellorsville, through the sulfurous canopy of Gettysburg, or from the rocky steeps of Lookout.

A few evenings since a pleasant incident occurred at the headquarters of the Third Brigade. I have spoken of the Third Brigade so often in these notes that I presume it will be understood that I always mean the Third Brigade of the First, or Red Star, Division. The incident I refer to was the raising of a magnificent garrison flag. The brigade was formed in front of Colonel Robinson's headquarters for the purpose of saluting the flag when hoisted. At the appointed time, the halyards were drawn and the brave old stars and stripes went up to receive the amorous kisses of the gentle evening breeze. No sooner did the flag begin to ascend than there went up from the entire brigade a spontaneous and deafening cheer such as it probably never received before in Atlanta. The devotion of the soldiers to the flag of the Union is beyond all painter's dreams or poet's rhapsodies. They love it as they love their lives, aye, far more. They love it as they love freedom, as the love right, as they love their homes and native land.

"Land of the forest and the rock,
Of dark blue lake and mighty river,
Of mountains reared aloft on high to mock,
The storm's career, the lightning's shock,
My own green land forever!" [173]

The Third Brigade has just been ordered upon a foraging expedition to be sent out tomorrow. The busy note of preparation breaks in upon my reflections and I must therefore divert my attention from arts to arms. Au revoir.

Notes in Dixie Vol. XIX

Atlanta, Georgia
October 22, 1864

Blessings on Ohio! Blessings on her great, noble, loyal heart! The first intelligence that flashes to us over the reopened telegraph line announces that Ohio's ballot, more effective than her bullets, have won a glorious victory for freedom. Once more she has pledged herself unmistakably and irrevocably to the Union. Again she has sealed her devotion to our flag and the government of our fathers and to that cause for which tens of thousands of her soldier-sons have made a free will offering of their blood. Again she has proved that those who cast her votes are not unworthy of those who fight her battles. Again she has lifted her voice in thunder tones against that giant treason that would cleave this land asunder. Again she has given assurance to the world of unalterable purpose never to yield the rich heritage of freedom to the rebellious advocates of human bondage, and contemptuously spurned the weak, cowardly language that the war for the Union is a failure. Blessings on Ohio! Blessings too on her worthy compeers, Pennsylvania and Indiana, for these have joined hands with our western queen. They, too, have turned

---

[173] From a poem "Moll Pitcher" by 19th century American poet John Greenleaf Whittier.

away from the loud cajoling and serpent charm of the traitor, and have given themselves to the good cause. From the vales and mountains of old Pennsylvania, and from the prairies of the west, the song of freedom goes up and meets glorious responses from the camps beside the Mississippi, the Chattahoochee, and the James. The soldiers, too, have spoken and their voice gives no uncertain sound. It is the language of patriots, or freemen: Union and Liberty, now and forever, one and inseparable.[174]

Ere this appears in the columns of the *Gazette* it will probably have been announced to the public that the Ohio regiments of this army have given large majorities for the Union ticket. They have given an earnest of what may be expected from them in November. Strange that they should thus turn their back upon him who was so zealously affirmed to be their idol. But the truth is that they love liberty and their country more than they can possibly love any man, and there is good reason to hope that no individual, however brilliant his qualities, shall ever be able to seduce them from these first idols of their affections.

It is well for our army that it is so far separated from the turbid channels of political influence. It thus becomes a conservatory for the purest and best patriotism of the country. Demagogues cannot tamper with or corrupt it, while all its interests and feelings become thoroughly identified with those of the government. A genuine soldier knows no such thing as party or politics. His only party is his country, his only politics the preservation of its integrity and glory. For these his services and life are sacredly pledged. He can no more sympathize with the selfish passions and differences of the crowd than they can appreciate the disinterested earnestness of his patriotism. While they, through interest or prejudice, may grow disaffected, he becomes more and more devoted to the flag of the country with each new peril and privation endured on its behalf. In view of these facts, it may be questioned whether a great standing army is after all an institution dangerous to the welfare of the state as has been represented.

Atlanta, Georgia
October 22, 1864

Of the isolation of army life the soldiers of the 20th Corps have for a month past the full benefit. The enemy, desperately beat upon the mission of starving us out of Atlanta, has concentrated his energies in one grand effort to destroy our communications. He succeeded in badly tearing up the railroad first near Marietta then at Dalton. He was rapidly pursued by General Sherman's forces with which he could not be induced to give battle, as it was not his intention to fight, but only by rapid marches to obtain possession of and destroy railroads. He is now driven entirely off of it and the communication with Chattanooga is expected to be reopened by tomorrow. The troops here are abundantly supplied with rations and there is scarcity of nothing except forage, of which large amounts have been obtained from the country.

The main portion of our forces having pursued Hood's nomadic army and the railroad being severed, city life in Atlanta has been rather monotonous. The citizens, male and female, black and white, have almost all decamped, leaving the town in exclusive possession of the soldiery. There remains scarcely a house unoccupied by the troops that is not vacant, while scores of buildings of all kinds are being demolished to make room for the new defenses being built. This place is doomed to the rough uses of war and in the end there can be but little left of it.

Apropos of foraging, I might relate some of my experiences while accompanying an expedition for that purpose. On the 16th inst., a detachment consisting of three brigades of infantry, a division of cavalry, and two four-gun batteries marched from this point with a train of 730 empty wagons. The expedition was commanded by Colonel James S. Robinson of the Third Brigade. At the close of the first day's march it arrived at Flat Shoals, a point on the south of Ocmulgee River 18 miles southeast of Atlanta. Here it became necessary to choose a strong defensive position and park a portion of the immense train while the remainder collected the forage. The country was found to be a half-cultured region with unfruitful soil and inhabited by a few squalid people of whom the able-bodied male population had long since gone to fight for the rebellion. Their chief means of subsistence seemed to be corn and sweet potatoes, of which there was a comparative abundance.

---

[174] In the 1864 Presidential election, Ohio gave 56% of its vote to Abraham Lincoln with the soldiers' vote coming in at 4 to 1 in favor of Lincoln.

Arriving at the localities where these were found, detachments of troops with wagons were sent into the fields and the products gathered with as much sangfroid as if they had been planted and raised expressly for Uncle Sam. The wagons as fast as they were loaded were hurried back to the general rendezvous of the train. While this process was going on, armed parties rummaged the country in search of articles of diet more savory than those usually found in army cuisine. It was amazing to behold with what nonchalance that crime so abhorrent to industrious housewifery (robbing hen roosts), was perpetrated even by those somewhat above the rank of private. I have in my mind a very ridiculous picture of a certain dignified staff officer galloping into camp with a number of choice selections from the feathered tribe lashed to his saddle in such a way that each one made most extravagant gyrations in the air at every leap of the horse. And such shams were very common. They extended even to the forcible abduction of certain quadrupeds whose external coverings are similar to the hirsute appendages of the Negro, and which it is not considered very honorable to take without the consent of the owner. Violent raids were made upon the peaceful dominions of unwary swine and one might have imagined from the panic created among them that they were possessed by a set of those wicked spirits of which a legion entered into the herd that fed by the seaside of old. Each porker was sure to find his man and if he failed to heave-to at the first shot fired across his bows he might calculate upon receiving a full broadside at once. If he still managed through some lucky chance to save his bacon, he was sure to be run down immediately by a gallant charge by a bevy of soldiers evidently not of Jewish extraction.

The wagons all being loaded, the soldiers went their way back to camp, the bright fires of which are seen in the distance glistening merrily through the dusky air of evening. Impaled upon bayonets, slung upon mules, or hauled in rickety farm wagons drawn by badly-matched steers, the various fruits of the days' plundering are brought in. The soldiers' culinary genius is at once set to work upon the new acquisitions to his larder, and is aided by a voracious appetite with many time saving suggestions. We will leave him snugly sandwiched between his blankets, forgetful of his anxieties, privations and perils, and perchance, wandering in his thoughts amid the peaceful scenes of his distant home and over 'the pleasant fields traversed so oft, in life's morning march when his bosom was young.'[175]

At headquarters there is a sound of revelry which arrests the sober ear. Capt. Snooks, the ornithologist of the expedition, is being made the butt of some rather uncharitable jokes. But Snooks is withal a good-natured soul and takes it patiently. His fondness for fowl, however, led him into some little mishaps which do not commonly befall the more professional disciples of Agassiz and Audubon. Among these may be mentioned the loss of his sword and revolver, which were mysteriously spirited away while he was intently engaged in providing for certain contraband gratifications of his palate. The 'topog' (topographical engineer), a sedate bachelor if dirty, is roundly accused with having devoted much more of his time to studying the features of certain handsome widows of the neighborhood than the features of the country. 'Topog' incontinently blushes a confession while his lips make a denial. Ah! Topog! I charge thee in the language of one who knew, or seemed to know, whereof he spoke, 'beware of the widders!'[176]

On the following day an adventurous band of Rebel cavalry attempted to interfere with our corn-gathering operations. Posting themselves behind some houses on an eminence they fired upon our advance guard without the preliminary inquiry of 'who comes there.' The bullets had that wicked rebellious whiz which told all too plainly of their origin, while the nearness of their flight indicated very certainly that they were meant for us. A detachment of 100 infantry was quickly dispatched by a circuitous route to take the enemy in flank, while a few cavalry were held in readiness to charge him at the opportune moment in front. The infantry succeeded in almost turning the Rebel position, when it became manifest that the enemy had chosen the better part of valor and made good his escape.

---

[175] Lee is quoting from Thomas Campbell's poem "The Soldier's Dream" from 1804.

[176] The 'topog' in question is Captain Frederick Stephen Wallace of Company A, 61st Ohio Volunteer Infantry. Like Captain Lee, Captain Wallace has been wounded at Gettysburg and has been selected to serve on General Tyndale's staff, continuing on as topographical engineer for the Third Brigade into the Carolinas campaign. Wallace led company B of the combined 61st/82nd Ohio then was promoted to major just before mustering out in July 1865. After the war, Major Wallace would write a regimental history of the 61st O.V.I.

Thereupon the infantry at once sent up a defiant shout and charged his position. The cavalry simultaneously dashed up the road and joined in the brilliant charge which resulted in carrying the hill just vacated by the Rebels without loss to either side. The force of the enemy was variously estimated from three to 50. Thus closed the brilliant fight at the crossroads, one of the most successful affairs of the war.

On the 19th inst., the expedition returned to Atlanta. Its grotesque appearance as it slowly wended its way into this city would have been a fit theme for a painter. Miss Davidson's procession of 'forty old bachelors, some younger some older, each carrying a maiden home on his shoulder' could not have been more amusing.[177] But unfortunately all the special artists have suddenly disappeared since the Rebel raid, and therefore the interesting scene remains unrecorded.

Notes in Dixie Vol. XX

Atlanta, Georgia
November 3, 1864

Number twenty! These humble papers, begun amid the April bloom of the mountainous valley of the bright-rolling Tennessee and continued from time to time through the long, eventful campaign terminating in the capture of the Gate City of the South have finally grown in numerical repetition at least in the modest pretensions of a score. Whether or not they have been trained in the way they should go the readers of the *Gazette* must decide. It is hoped, however, that if anyone chooses to do them the honor of a criticism, we will not only 'be to their faults a little blind, and to their merits very kind,' but charitably remember that they are the roughly-bred rantings of the march, the bivouac, and the battlefield. Written amidst the distractions of an office that permits no certain respite from the interruptions of business and grants no lease upon leisure; composed often amid the excitement of actual conflict, and upon the gory field still strewn with the wreck and debris of battle, it is, perhaps, unfair to expect in these hastily written sketches the continuity of matter and the garnished smoothness and fluorescence of style which are expected to adorn a newspaper article.

It is unfortunate that those who inform the public press of army affairs are not always as reliable and accurate as they should be. Usually depending upon others as sources of information and rarely being eyewitnesses and still more rarely participants of those sanguinary events which give shape and character to the campaign, they are prone to give partial, defective, or too highly colored descriptions of them. Some favorite general, brigade, or corps is lauded to the skies for doing that of which the credit belongs entirely to others. I do not mean to say that these persons are always untruthful in their statements, but I do assert that they are frequently so. Glowing accounts are published of 'brilliant' military operations, which to those conversant with the facts are simply ridiculous. Mr. Adolphus Scribble, who enjoys a wide circle of acquaintance among the 'reliable gentlemen' who accompany the rear of an army, eagerly snatches up the story of some excited straggler who tells him that his regiment is 'all cut to pieces,' that the artillery was all captured by the enemy, but was immediately recaptured by the gallant Brigadier General so-and-so's brigade who led his men sword in hand against the confident foe, that the enemy was finally driven back utterly demoralized and vast numbers of arms and prisoners taken. All this and a thousand things more which Mr. Scribble gathers from his own fertile brain and he well knows will amaze the gullible public, he hastily transmits by the first courier for publication in the Gossipville Journal. Perchance, too, Scribble overtakes an 'intelligent contraband' just from Rebeldom who, with wide stretched optics, relates to him wonderful stories of the starvation and demoralization prevailing in the enemy's camps, of his distressing desire to desert en masse and come over to our lines, and of the marvelous mysteries of a recently bereaved master's household. All these things together with the manifold little additions which Scribble's suggestive mind would make, duly embellish with glaring headlines, the columns of the above named valuable journal. Thus the public is deceived, the army is misrepresented, and newspapers are disparaged.

If there be any merit in these papers, it lies chiefly in the fact that I have written of that which I do know. It has been my humble fortune to be an eyewitness of the patriotic fortitude and gallantry of the soldiers of the Union both in the gloomy bivouac and on the weary march and on the bloody battlefield. I have seen them both when

---

[177] Lee is quoting from Lucretia Maria Davidson's poem "Auction Extraordinary" from 1824.

overwhelmed with disaster and when exultant with the flush of glorious victory. I have heard their wail of anguish at defeat, and listened also to their shout of triumph springing from distant hilltops and swelling along the vales and up the mountainsides in one sublime echoing peon of rejoicing. I have marked the unconquerable patriot toiling on his painful march with pale face and bleeding feet, I have hearkened to the faint echoes of his failing breath when gushing wounds have taken that heroic soul and made its last, greatest sacrifice for freedom. I have caught from feverish lips the story of long, reliefless suffering under the slow conquest of disease that could subdue the manly frame, but never provoke complaint that all was born and suffered in our country's holy cause. These are not matters of hearsay; I have seen them. And if having seen them I have been able to convey a truthful idea of the inside of army life, and of the unquenchable patriotism and devotion of our soldiers, I am content.

I am aware that I am speaking as if with the twentieth number I am about to close this series of articles. And yet I would not have the readers of the *Gazette* understand that it is my intention to bid them a final farewell or that I have adopted the mournful peroration of Walter Wilie: 'And here I send the long ballad, The which you have just read, I wish that it may stay on earth, long after I am dead.'[178] I only wish to notify them that our interviews (if such is the proper term) are, for an indefinite time, about to be suspended. This vast army will soon launch forth into the enemy's country without regard to lines of communication or bases of supply, and the dark scathing gulf of rebellion will close in between me and those who care to peruse these lines. Great ventures are about to be made in behalf of the Union and this army is soon to stake its existence upon the success of one of the boldest military enterprises ever undertaken. Until its final accomplishment our friends must be content to watch and wait, not, however, without assurance that when our columns emerge from the cloud that shall temporarily hide them from view, they will come dazzling in the light of victory and the dawn of new and glorious hopes for our beloved country.

In the meantime the great civil conflict for our nation's life draws apace. The people are about to determine at the ballot box whether freedom or slavery, union or disunion, shall prevail. And shall it be that when this army comes from its long, perilous march through the dominions of rebellion, bearing the starry flag all garlanded with victorious wreaths, it shall be greeted by the unwelcome intelligence that the people of the great loyal North have decided that the war for the Union is a failure? I trust not. I trust the song of our triumph shall be marred by no such unpleasant discord, but that its highest accents shall be inspired by news of glorious victory at the polls over the treason we fight in the field. Fail? Not while the God of battles is upon our side. This army is strong not only in its mere physical prowess but in the strength of that truth which is resistless and imperishable. It is strong in the justice and rectitude of its cause and in its confidence that that cause will be befriended by Him who overrules the destinies of men and nations. Armed with such strength it cannot fail. Let the people stand by this army assured that to the last it will stand by them. Its watchword is union and with nothing less than the union, divided and unconditional, can it be satisfied.

> "We want the brave old flag to wave,
> From Texas up to Maine,
> From Delaware to Golden Gate,
> Around and back again;
> Over each blade of grass that grows.
> And every grain of sand.
> The Stars and Stripes and Union,
> Thank God, for these we stand."

And for these we fall, if fall we must. But even though our friends fail us and we perish, and this great nation proves untrue to its sacred and immeasurable trust, yet from our ashes, enriching this slave-cursed soil, the spirit of freedom shall spring up with ten-fold vigor to bloom and bless the countless millions yet to be.

---

[178] Walter Wilie was a 17th century poet from New York.

Atlanta, Georgia
November 5, 1864

The weather, which for the past few days has been exceedingly rough and unpleasant, has now brightened up and augurs favorably for the great expedition. That fine dreamy season has arrived 'when first the frost, turns into beauty all October's charms; when the dreadful fever quits us, when the storm of the wild equinox with all its wet, has left the land as the first deluge left it, with a bright bow of many colors hung upon the forest tops.'[179] Field and grove and glen are clad in russet robes of beauty softly unfolded by the gentle touches of the Southern autumn. Nature looks forth from half closed eye-lids in a sadly cheerful, bewitching smile, as if her frame were inspired by the sweet uncertainty between reluctant loss of pleasure past and hopeful gain of richer joy to come. The mellow days glide by but rarely roughened by gloom or storm, or ought presageful of the bursting of the dark clouds gathering in the military horizon. But the calm is about to be broken for the marching orders have come. For union and liberty, evermore yours.

Report of Colonel James S. Robinson, 82nd Ohio Infantry, commanding Third Brigade.

HDQRS. THIRD BRIG.. FIRST DIV., TWENTIETH CORPS,
Near Savannah, Ga., December 28, 1864.

LIEUTENANT: I have the honor to submit the following report of the services and operations of this brigade from the occupation of the city of Atlanta down to the capture and occupation of Savannah:

On the 5th of September the entire brigade was encamped near Atlanta, Ga., having marched to that place from Montgomery's Ferry, on the Chattahoochee River, on the day previous. At this time and up to the 27th, at which date I rejoined the brigade from sick leave, it was commanded by Col. Horace Boughton, of the 143rd New York Volunteers. From this officer I have received no report, and shall, therefore, limit myself to the time of actual command. On the 28th, by order of Brig. Gen. Alpheus S. Williams, commanding division, I formally resumed command of the brigade. I found the troops at this time in good health, with tidy, well-policed camps, and well supplied with clothing, arms, and food. Daily drills in company and battalion tactics had been established, under which exercise the troops seemed to be rapidly improving in discipline and efficiency.

On the 4th of October the 20th Corps having been charged with the sole occupation and defense of Atlanta, a new chain of defenses around the city was commenced. A detail of 7 officers and 350 men to work upon these fortifications was now required from and daily furnished by my brigade. This work was continued, with but little interruption, on the part of my command down to the 15th. On that date the brigade was designated to accompany a foraging expedition consisting of three brigades of infantry, a division of cavalry, a battery of artillery, and 733 wagons sent out on the following day and to the command of which I had the honor to be appointed. The infantry, the Third Brigade, First Division, the Second Brigade, Second Division, and the Second Brigade, Third Division; the artillery, Captain Sloan's battery, and the train under charge of Capt. E. P. Graves, assistant quartermaster, rendezvoused on the Decatur road at 6 A.M. The expedition marched at 6:30 A.M. and was joined at 1 P.M. by Colonel Kenner Garrard's division of cavalry at Avery's Crossroads. The head of the column encamped at Flat Shoals at 7 P.M., and by 10 P.M. was joined by all the troops and trains. On the 17th, leaving the Third Brigade of the First Division and two sections of artillery in Charge of about 400 wagons at Flat Shoals, I took the remainder of the troops and wagons and marched down the left bank of the South River in quest of forage. Though the country was poor and unproductive, I succeeded in loading most of the train by night-fall.

On the following day, the 18th, leaving the Second Brigade, Third Division, and two sections of artillery at Flat Shoals in charge of the loaded wagons, with the remainder of the troops and wagons I crossed South River. Here I found a country more fertile than that foraged the day previous, and succeeded without difficulty in obtaining

---

[179] Lee is quoting from "Autumnal Musings" by 19th century American poet William Howe Cuyler Hosmer.

enough corn to load the entire train. A slight resistance offered by the enemy's cavalry was easily overcome without loss. The expedition at night-fall rejoined in safety the detachment left at Flat Shoals, and on the next day, the 19th, returned to Atlanta. The quantity of corn brought in amounted to about 11,000 bushels. The troops obtained besides this a considerable quantity of fresh beef, fresh pork, poultry, sweet potatoes, and other species of provisions. The immediate command of my brigade during this expedition was entrusted to Lieut. Col. Edward S. Salomon, of the 82nd Illinois Volunteers, who was the senior officer present. I take pleasure in acknowledging the efficiency and zeal with which Lieutenant Colonel Salomon discharged the duty thus devolving upon him.

On the 21st the work on the fortifications was resumed by my brigade, which furnished a detail of 200 men for that purpose. On the 24th this detail was reduced to 100 men. On the 25th I received an order to join with my brigade a foraging expedition to be sent out on the following day under the command of Brigadier General Geary. According to directions, my command reported to General Geary on the Decatur road at 6 a.m. on the 26th, and was assigned, in connection with a battery of artillery, to the duty of covering the rear of the column. Passing through Decatur at 11 A.M., my command reached Stone Mountain at 9:30 P.M. Early on the 27th, by General Geary's direction, I sent out two regiments, the 101st Illinois and 82nd Ohio Veteran Volunteers, to assist in loading wagons with corn. They returned to camp at 6:30 P.M., having succeeded, in spite of the very inclement weather and prowling detachments of hostile cavalry, in loading 196 wagons.

On the 28th, by direction of General Geary, I proceeded with my brigade, a section of artillery, a battalion of cavalry, and about 300 wagons, across Yellow River in the direction of Lawrenceville. I found here a productive country and had no difficulty in loading the entire train. My command returned toward Berkshire at 3 P.M., crossing Yellow River upon a bridge which, though partly burned by the enemy the day previous, was nevertheless easily rendered passable for the train. The column reached Berkshire at sundown and pushed forward, following the remainder of the expedition, which had already preceded us on its return march. Reached Stone Mountain at 10:30 P.M., and encamped three miles beyond Stone Mountain Station at about midnight. On the following day my brigade formed the vanguard of the expedition and returned without accident to its encampment at Atlanta. During this expedition my brigade secured about 6,000 bushels of corn, besides the usual amount of provisions and other promiscuous articles. On the 30th orders were issued to send all surplus baggage to the rear, and such preparations began to be made as clearly indicated the approach of a great movement. No further work was done on the fortifications, and all attention was given to putting the command in the best possible condition to march.

On the 5th of November, at 1 P.M., I received an unexpected order to move my brigade immediately. In a very short space of time the column was moving out the McDonough road, every one supposing this to be the initial step of the campaign, but the sequel proved otherwise. Proceeding about three miles the troops bivouacked for the night, and on the following day marched back to their camps near the city. The payment of my command, which had been but partially completed, was now continued. On the 8th the Presidential election was held in those regiments entitled by law to vote. On the 9th, at daybreak, a violent cannonade suddenly broke out on the southeastern side of the city. The cause of this was hardly comprehended, but it soon became apparent that a hostile force, either great or small, had appeared in front of our works. The firing soon shifted to our right, in front of General Geary's division, and began to be mingled with musketry; my brigade was soon afterward ordered to move to the support of General Geary, whose lines were reported as being dangerously threatened. In a few minutes my column was in motion down White Hall Street, the troops keeping step to the martial bands, and the colors floating in the breeze. I had hardly reached the suburbs of the town, however, when I was informed by Major General Slocum, that the enemy, about ---- in number, under the Rebel General Alfred Iverson,[180] had been driven off, and that my brigade would not be needed, and might return to its camp. I thereupon counter marched my column and moved it back to its old

---

[180] Brigadier General Alfred Iverson had led a North Carolina infantry brigade during the Chancellorsville and Gettysburg campaigns. Iverson had been reassigned away from the Army of Northern Virginia following a disastrous charge on the first day of Gettysburg in which his North Carolina brigade was ambushed northwest of town, suffering very heavy casualties. It appears that General Robert E. Lee held Iverson responsible for that disaster. Iverson helped organize troops in Georgia and led a cavalry brigade until the end of the war.

position. Excepting the changes incident to the reorganization of the army, no further event of importance transpired until the 14th, when the final marching orders were received.

Notes in Dixie Vol. XXI

Tweeside, near Savannah, Georgia
December 19, 1864

One month ago I closed my portfolio hoping to reopen it among the seaside oaks that overhang the wide reedy Savannah River. This expectation has been fully realized. Since this pen traced the twentieth number of these notes one month has elapsed, and how eventful! What changes have been wrought, what thrilling episodes in the chaotic tragedy of war! From Atlanta to the Atlantic! What a march, what a journey, what a campaign! Enough to fill a volume, enough to employ a pen infinitely abler than mine.

On the 15th of November, the Army of Georgia, under the leadership of its own tried and trusted Tecumseh, moved out of Atlanta in four columns. Each column consisted of an army corps, including its artillery and trains. The army was divided in two wings; the right wing consisted of the 15th and 17th Corps under Major General Howard and the left wing composed of the 14th and 20th Corps under Major General Slocum. These two wings diverged from each other at the outset, the right moving on the McDonough Road towards Macon and the left on the Decatur Road toward Augusta. The morning of the 15th was cold, hazy, and dull. The troops, however, were cheerful, their hearts buoyant, and their step elastic. The prospect of a long adventurous campaign stirred their blood and awakened that romantic love of hazardous exploit which glows in the bosom of every veteran soldier. Behind them lay a terribly thrilling scene. The war-scourged city of Atlanta was enveloped in a fiery shroud of smoke and flame. All the railroad buildings, depots, warehouses, manufactories, shops, and public property of every sort that might be of value to the enemy, had been fired. The seething flames communicated themselves to many of the private dwellings, mostly unoccupied, and the greater portion of the town thus became prey to the devouring element. A vast column of smoke ascended into the air signifying to the inhabitants more than a score of miles away that the former citadel of treason in northern Georgia was being purified by fire. And when the evening fell and night stretched her dusky mantle around our camps, a fiery, flickering glare overspread the western sky, pointing out with vengeful finger the desolate locality of the once proud Gate City of the South.

Our army had swung entirely loose from its moorings, and was now adrift upon the turbulent sea of rebellion. It had nothing to rely upon but its own inherent strength and the help of that God who smiles upon the right and frowns upon the wrong. All the railroads for many miles in our rear were utterly destroyed, leaving not a spark of hope for succor or retreat. In our wagons were 30 days' supply of bread and coffee. What was needed beyond this must be obtained from the country. Whether these small resources our vast enterprise should succeed or fail depended solely upon the prowess of the army and the genius of its leader.

The enemy soon became perplexed beyond measure by our movements. He had suddenly found himself powerless at our feet. His cavalry hung about our flanks and rear like groups of spiteful whippets impatiently watching the movements of an elephant. The Rebel state governor ordered an immediate levy en masse of the able-bodied population of the state. The Rebel Legislature, just convened at Milledgeville, whisked about its cushioned seats, not knowing what to do. Rebel Governor Joseph E. Brown directed his militia to rendezvous at Macon which seemed to him to be our objective point. He repaired thither himself, just in time to find that our movement towards Macon was only a feint to cover was appeared to him to be a descent upon Augusta, by far the more important city. The lieutenant governor countermanded the order of Governor Brown and directed the militia to assemble at that point. Thus the slender forces of the enemy became divided and Sherman, with his magnificent army, moved grandly on between the two cities, threatening both and hopelessly severing all communication between them.

The 20th Corps moved rapidly out on the Georgia Railroad, destroying the track as it proceeded. The magnitude of the army may be comprehended when I say that this single corps occupied by troops fully 12 miles of road when on the march. Calculating that each of the other corps occupied quite as much space, the aggregate length of our vast column, while marching, was not less than 48 miles. It often occurred that the vanguard of the 20th Corps marching at 6 o'clock in the morning would get into camp before the rear guard had vacated the camp of the night before. This caused a great deal of night marching for the troops that happened to be in the rear. These night marches have a weird grotesqueness which can scarcely be adequately described. In the early part of the evening, the troops wile away the tedious hours by shouting, singing, and merry talk. The old woods and mountains are made to echo with roistering melody from loyal throats. But the men soon grow tired and sleepy and the merriment subsides. The column then moved on in moody silence, which is broken only by the rumbling of the wagons and the rattling paraphernalia of the men. If the night is cold, fires are kindled along the line of march and its course for miles is marked by the blazing gleam. Finally glittering through the distant forests, the cheerful camp fires are descried lighting up hill and valley and overhung by a smoky canopy. The sight is not unwelcomed by the weary soldiers, grown restive for their coffee and their sleep.

Arrived at Madison, a beautiful village in Morgan County, the left wing filed off from the railroad and moved toward Milledgeville. Great numbers of Negroes of all shades, sizes, and ages now began to accompany the column. The appearance of these poor creatures as they wended solemnly along on either side of the troops would have adorned the canvas of a Hogarth or Vernet.[181] Their method of carrying their luggage and babies is peculiarly their own. The former is usually transported on the head and the latter on the back of the owner. Sometimes a combination of these two methods would be seen in the same individual. To the often propounded query, 'Where are you going?', they would invariably answer, 'Don't know massa, gwine wid you all.' There was a deep philosophy to this, for it indicated a calm, simple confidence in us and the cause we represented. It was not artificial trust either, but dictated by that childlike instinct of nature which cannot be mistaken. 'We knowed we's free when you'uns come,' said they. How did they know it? Why should they at the first sight trust us as friends and accept us as emancipators? Because the God of Nature told them to. A strange indefinable something which they could neither comprehend or describe beckoned them on and they followed us. Tying up their little parcels, and gathering together the children left them by the mercies of the mercenary master, they gladly abandoned that which left along of earth possessed for them the attractions of home, trudged along through sun and rain, accepted the meager hospitalities of an army, gladly entrusted themselves to the care of utter strangers, and left the rest to that God who made all men free and equal.

The column now emerged into a rich and productive country furnishing all kinds of subsistence. A great number of excellent horses and mules were speedily collected and made to take the place of the exhausted animals in the trains. The white inhabitants mostly fled precipitately before us, taking with them such of their effects as could be gotten away. Trunks and boxes containing valuable goods and ware were unearthed from gardens and confiscated by the finders. Had these people stayed at home and kept their property by them, they would have fared much better. Their fleeing from us and hiding their goods was prima facie evidence of guilty distrust which furnished a license for our soldiers. It was amusing to witness the nonchalance with which they appropriated what they wanted. A lady laughed as she told me of a soldier who came into her house by night and politely requested a

Confederate View

A lesson in emancipation

As Sherman's army marched through Georgia, they were met by thousands of slaves who cautiously met their liberators. Reception by the Union soldiers was mixed; some relishing the role of liberation while others treated the slaves with shocking cruelty. Thousands of freedmen followed the army, while others preferred to stay on their home plantations. One man refused to help the Yankees, stating that he was "too old to go with you and too young to stay here and be murdered."

Martha Colquitt, then a young slave upon a plantation in Georgia left the following account of the emancipation of her family by Sherman's army:

"They busted down the smokehouse door and told my mother she was free now to help herself to anything she wanted because everything on the plantation was to belong to the slaves that worked there. They took grandma to the kitchen and told me to give her some of the white folks' dinner. Ma said 'But the white folks ain't eat yet.'

'Go right on,' the Yankee said 'and give her the best in the pot.'

[181] Lee is referencing 18th century painters William Hogarth of England and Claude Joseph Vernet of France.

candle with which to search her poultry yard. The same lady spoke of the merriment she experienced in witnessing some of the troops carrying off barrels of lime which they supposed to be flour. Emphatically soldiers are sui generis.

All cotton, cotton gins, and cotton presses along the line of march were burned. The route taken by each corps could easily be traced by the columns of smoke by day and fiery gleam by night from these burning buildings. Millions upon millions of dollars' worth of Confederate credit basis were thus disposed of. During the cold, cloudy night of November 22, the dusky columns of the 20th Corps filed through the silent and gloomy streets of Milledgeville. The town had fallen without resistance, the Rebel state authorities and many of the citizens having abandoned it to its fate. The Rebel Legislature, after having voted a wholesale conscription, precipitately fled to the woods, some of them paying $1,000 to be conveyed out of the way of the Yankee Colussus. Crossing the Oconee on a fine wooden bridge, the troops encamped on its left bank and rested until the 24th.

On the 23rd about 200 of us convened in the State House and organized a loyal legislature. Colonel Robinson commanding our brigade was chosen chairman. A clerk was then appointed and a committee on Federal Relations announced. This committee retired and prepared a report. In the meantime there was considerable noisy debate and bunkum speech making. An ardent secessionist, Colonel Henry A. Barnum[182], made several blood-thirsty speeches in which he played well the part of Southern orator. The worthy colonel was well provided with pistols, bowie knives, and something in a little zinc flask with wickerwork on the outside. It was observable that the zinc flask went quite frequently to the colonel's lips, at which times he took occasion to make sly winks at the sundry knowing conferees. What all this meant the writer does not pretend to know, but leaves the matter to the sophisticated.

During the interval of debate certain verdant looking members from distant counties were duly sworn in as loyal sardines. The swearing was done in genuine Southern style with a cocked pistol at the head of the swearer. In due time the committee reported. The resolutions offered chiefly related to the Ordinance of Secession, of which a genuine copy was read. It was proposed that said Ordinance be forever repealed, abolished, and utterly abrogated. It was recommended that Governor Brown and his Rebel legislature 'scratch gravel' to a 'considerable extent.' These with other resolutions of similar import and containing certain emphatic expletives which is not proper to repeat were offered for adoption. The secession corner, always garrulous, objected and moved that the committee and their resolutions be pitched out of the window. After considerable noisy debate, the question was put upon the adoption of the resolutions and was carried by an 'aye' so thunderous as to leave no doubt of their adoption. Here, General Hugh Judson Kilpatrick made his appearance in the lobby and was welcomed to the Speaker's desk amid uproarious applause. [183]

Taking advantage of this episode, the writer withdrew from the assemblage and ascended the cupola of the building in order to get a good view of the capital of Georgia. It is a dingy, sleepy, Rip Van Winkle sort of an old town, with grass-grown streets and fairly represents the spirit of Southern civilization. The most prominent buildings are the State House and prison, the latter of which is now in ruins. The principal dwellings are of that pompous style of architecture which consists in making the greatest possible amount of show at the least possible expense. Around the town (for it is not a city) extends a range of hills too soon lost in dense groves of pines to be picturesque or beautiful. The whole landscape is tame and would require an erratic pencil to make an attractive picture. I came down from my lofty station thinking of the magnificent view from the capitol dome at Columbus and reflecting upon the suggestive contrast between that and my present surroundings.

---

[182] Colonel Henry Alanson Barnum of the 149th New York was then leading the Third Brigade of John Geary's Second Division, XX Corps.

[183] The "rump session" of the Georgia Legislature continued with General Kilpatrick's drunken speech, followed by a lengthy and lively debate on Georgia's secession ordinance. A resolution was passed repealing the ordinance, and the meeting broke up in bedlam when other soldiers rushed in to inform the body that the Yankee army was on its way. Soldiers then looted the statehouse, throwing priceless law volumes into the streets to be trampled and taking worthless Georgia currency to be used in poker games. Davis, Burke. Sherman's March. New York: Vintage Books, 1988, pgs. 63-65

On the 24th of November the march was resumed. The right wing reached the Georgia Central Railroad at Gordon and was now moving eastward, destroying the road on its route. General Slocum directed his columns towards Sandersville, the county seat of Washington County. In this way the two wings began to rapidly concentrate as they neared the Ogeechee River. At the crossing of the Oconee, General Howard discovered a detachment of Rebels entrenched and ready to dispute his passage. The enemy made a bold show of resistance for a few hours, but being in imminent danger of being cut off he hastily withdrew towards Millen. The train carrying the flying chivalry passed down the road on the morning of November 26. The 20th Corps struck the line at Tennille Station during the afternoon of the same day. The work of destroying the finest railroad in Georgia immediately commenced. The brigades being deployed along the track, the different regiments took hold of the ties and overturned mile after mile in a jiffy. The ties were then gathered in piles, the iron rails laid across them, and the match applied. In a few minutes the whole would be ablaze, the iron would bend of its own weight, and tens of thousands of dollars' worth of Rebel railroad stock would be blotted out of existence.

On the 28th the Red Star Division crossed the plantation of Herschel V. Johnson, once a candidate for vice president of the United States. His mansion was abandoned and naturally fell prey to the rummaging propensities of the soldiers. As the Governor happened to be in the Rebel Senate assisting in devising ways and means for the success of the rebellion, not much mercy was shown to his premises. Much valuable correspondence was discovered including the original letter from Brown, Stephens, and other Rebel worthies. The general purport of these letters illustrated admirably in the case of these men the truth of Pope's stanza: 'Vice is a monster of such frightful mein, That to be hated needs but to be seen; But seen too oft, familiar with her face, We first endure, then pity, then embrace.' These men seem not to have been at first willing disciples of treason. They hesitated, reasoned, demurred. But they were too selfish, too much in love with the praises of the multitude to resist the popular torrent. Gradually they were drawn nearer and nearer to the current and finally swept along with it. Soon the vortex they foresaw, but would not heed, will dash them to pieces. Let us throw over their deeds the mantle of charity and kindly say 'tis human.[184]

On the 30th the First and Second Divisions crossed the Ogeechee and arrived at Louisville. This was an important era in the campaign. To obtain possession of the peninsula between the Savannah and Ogeechee Rivers was naturally one of our most coveted designs. Once across the Ogeechee and our army possesses itself of a splendid

Rump Session of Georgia Legislature

General H. Judson Kilpatrick entered the chamber to the uproars of the crowd and proceeded to speak about his success in raiding plantation cellars. It goes without saying that General Kilpatrick had been imbibing heavily. "Though I am very modest man that never blows his own horn, like other gentlemen whom I could name, I must honestly tell you that I am Old Harry on raids. My men, too, have strongly imbibed the spirit. I must confess that my fellows are very inquisitive. If perchance they discover a deserted cellar, believing it was kindly left for their use by the considerate owner, they take charge of it. It sometimes happens, too, that they take after the plate and other little matters. Coming to my own particular raid, it was one of the handsomest and most brilliant affairs of the war."

~ *Major General Hugh Judson Kilpatrick*

---

[184] Herschel Vespasian Johnson (1812-1880) served briefly as a senator then was Georgia's 41st governor before running with Stephen Douglas on the Democratic ticket in 1860. Johnson initially opposed secession but later served as a senator in the Confederate Congress. The 1860 census shows that Johnson had 115 slaves on the plantation Lee describes in his letter.

highway to Savannah with a river covering each flank. It will be seen by a glance at the map of the country what a vast advantage was thus gained. It no longer became necessary to employ the whole army in guarding the immense trains. Not more than one-third of it was now needed for that purpose; the rest could be disengaged for fighting. On the 3rd of December the column struck the Waynesboro Railroad near Millen. Here the indignation of our soldiers was fully aroused by the sight of the den in which the inhuman foe had confined the Andersonville prisoners. It consisted of a high stockade enclosed a space of ten acres, in the midst of dismal swamps and forests which make up the greater part of the wretched country. Our men evidently had no shelter except such as they obtained by burrowing in the earth or constructing booths from pine branches. The prisoners had all been removed previous to our arrival and naught remained to tell their sad story save the unburied remains of one of their number, scraps of letters and clothing, and the usual debris of a deserted camp.[185] The miserable pen was burned as was also the dwelling of the Rebel General Winder who had charge of it.[186]

On the 10th of December the 20th Corps struck the Charleston and Savannah Railroad at Montieth Station ten miles from Savannah. This important line, coveted by our forces since the beginning of the war, was finally broken. It is hardly necessary to say that its demolition was accomplished with a right good will. The rails were not only bent but twisted and the bridges and trestle works reduced to ashes. The army with its flanks resting on the two rivers now swept grandly down toward Savannah. The road pursued by the 20th Corps, though leading through tangled and intractable swamps and over sluggish streams, was nevertheless excellent and betokened the influences surrounding a city. Looking at the somber cypress trees, their branches hung with long gray moss that seemed like a mournful drapery, their trunks beclambered with a profuse network of vines and their roots embedded in the brown, brackish water of the swamps, one's mind readily took a romantic turn and conjured up many a weird old story beside the youthful fireside far away in the rugged North. But there was not much time to think of these things. The column pushed rapidly forward and soon reached the sixth milepost from Savannah. Cannonading now began to be heard in front. The vanguard had found the enemy. The old Third Brigade came up the fifth milepost and were directed to file off into the woods. Half a mile further sat the Rebel works. In a moment the question was solved- the enemy had determined to defend Savannah. The troops were deployed, the line of battle formed, and the enemy's position developed. The serried line stretched from the Savannah to the Ogeechee and thus it still remains.

On the 13th Fort McAllister was gallantly carried by the Second Division, 15th Corps and water communications was opened to Ossabaw Sound. The fleet was signaled and straightaway Admiral Somebody sends off a dispatch that he had opened communications with Sherman's army. But when asked to send a few ironclads up the Ogeechee, he declined, alleging that the river was infested with torpedoes. Thereupon Tecumseh embarked upon a dugout and went down to pay his respects to the doughty admiral. Such is the dispatch which has been circulating upon the grapevine telegraph for several days. 'I know not how the truth may be, I tell the story as 'twas told to me.' It is also alleged that Tecumseh told the admiral that if he would provide his men with a little hardtack and keep out of his way, it would be all he would ask of him. Be this as it may, it is certain that a small supply of hard bread reached us today and the fleet has kept out of our way admirably so far. So much for the fleet, to which I propose the following toast: the Army and Navy forever, particularly the Army.

Soon the communication was reopened, and a rumor became current that an indefinite number of tons of mail awaited us on shipboard. 'Corn male?' inquired an Irish soldier. 'No, no, letters. 'Bedad, and that's it?' That was it, as the sequel proved, though the Irishman's appetite had evidently become stronger than his love of home, which I am happy to say is not the case with all of us. Thank heaven for home, the dearest, best of all places. A few hundred miles of blue ocean are all that seems to intervene now, and no Rebel can sever that line. No burning bridges or tearing up tracks now. A regular daily mail from New York! The very thought is a thrill of joy. Savannah

---

[185] The prisoner of war camp, just recently built, was also known as Camp Lawton. A Union chaplain commented that the prisoners' quarters at the camp were "hardly fit for swine to live in." Davis, op. cit., pg. 88
[186] John Henry Winder, a Maryland-born 1820 graduate of West Point and lifelong army officer, gained a notorious if perhaps undeserved reputation in the Northern press as the commander of Libby Prison, Andersonville, and Millen. General Winder died of a heart attack while on duty in February 1865 at age 64.

must fall in due time. Great obstacles must be overcome but the army is strong and confident. Lett all its friends be patient, assured that success will ultimately come.

Notes in Dixie Vol. XXII

Near Savannah, Georgia
December 24, 1864

      Savannah is ours! Another citadel of the rebellion has fallen! None will thank me for the announcement for the cheering intelligence has already flown on lightning wings to every Northern household. But there is something interesting in the story of every witness of great events, for besides each one's special experience each has his own method of relating it. Please listen, then, while I tell my story. As the swift runner steps backward before starting upon his race, so those who tell of wonderful occurrences always go back and review the preliminary events which lead to them. Permit me, therefore, to revert to those matters which were sequent to Tecumseh's famous voyage in the dugout down the muddy waters of the Ogeechee.

      After Neptune and Mars had concluded their consultation and the former had duly stipulated to the latter the required contributions to his larder, all attention was at once given to devising the best ways and means for capturing the rebellious city of Savannah. It was soon discovered that the enemy's works were not only strongly built, but were almost inaccessible by reason of the swamps, canals, abatis, etc. in front of them. The position, too, was one which could not be easily turned, inasmuch as the right flank was covered by a wide and almost impassable river and the left by the ocean. There seemed no alternative, therefore, but to assault the works. Preparations for this began as early as the 17th. A considerable number of heavy guns were brought up and quietly gotten into position close to the Rebel entrenchments but screened from view by the dense entanglements of the swamps. A large number of fascines were constructed of rice straw bound together with telegraph wire. With these it was designed to hastily fill up or bridge the canal under fire and during the assault. A number of barges had been captured and were turned to good account in transporting a brigade of infantry and a section of artillery over the first arm of the Savannah to Argyle Island. This movement gave us partial possession of the river and made the enemy uneasy lest we might make a sudden descent upon the South Carolina shore and get possession of his precarious line of communication. Thus matters progressed up the 19th, when the forces on Argyle Island succeeded in crossing to the left bank and after a slight opposition affected a lodgment. This was too much for our nervous foe, and he at once began to send away his trains and baggage preparatory to evacuating the city. He had but one line of retreat and that was by means of a rickety pontoon bridge stretched across the two arms or branches of the Savannah. It was, therefore, slow work and occupied most of day and night of the 20th.

      Intimations of the enemy's retreat were received coincident with its commencement but were not considered wholly reliable. The preparations for the assault were continued with unabated vigor and the afternoon of the 21st was designated for the ground attack to be made all along the line. The night of the 20th was dark and gloomy. Under its cover the rebel gunboat *Macon* ventured far above its lair at the lower extremity of Argyle Island and commenced shelling with unusual persistence the lines of the First and Second divisions. She continued her practice until about midnight when, her ammunition apparently exhausted, the vengeful flashes of her guns no longer gleamed upon the dark welkin. Thus the gloomy silence of the night was restored to be disturbed only by an occasional shot on the picket line.

      Just as the first gray streaks of dawn were struggling up through night's loosened curtain our slumbers were dispelled by the jingling of an orderly's saber. 'Get your brigade ready to move at a moment's notice. Gen. Geary reports the enemy evacuating,' read the order. No further incentive was needed; everyone was immediately astir. The half blown blushes of the coming morn had just began to be reflected from the gauzy clouds in gorgeous tints of green, gold, and crimson when a second messenger from General Geary announced that the Second Division occupied a portion of the enemy's works. There could be no mistake then; the birds had flown. The sun came up grandly from behind the horizon and looked down with a pleasing eye upon the long serpentine line of Rebel defenses stretching from Savannah to Ossabaw and all vacant. No, not vacant. Here and there, crouched in a lonely embrasure, some truculent iron monster in grim silence expected our advancing line. And soon it came. Above the Cerberean throats that so savagely had echoed Rebel vengeance a ringing cheer burst from the throats of loyal soldiers, and the redoubts that might have cost us so many precious lives were ours. General Geary at once pressed his line forward toward the city. He was soon met by the mayor and other civil authorities of Savannah who made a formal surrender of the place. Thus the great campaign closed and the 21st day of December 1864 made forever memorable.

The glorious tidings of the occupation of the city soon spread like wildfire throughout the army. The impatience to get a glimpse of our prize was tormenting. The Third Brigade had been entrusted with the duty of protecting our vast trains from the Rebel cavalry, which continually hung about our rear. 'And now we must wait until all these wretched wagons move to the city before we can go?' It was but too true. Prurient curiosity would no longer brook such a restraint, so mounting our war steeds we galloped with impetuous haste down the straight sandy road leading directly to Savannah. Be assured we left the mileposts behind us as rapidly as the bone and sinew of our straw-fed chargers would admit of. Soon we near the Rebel works and found two clumsy old 32 pounders staring at us with a sort of ghastly sneaking grin, as much as to say 'we are spiked.' Yes, but you are the wretches who pitched such nasty nuggets of iron down the road at us, thought I as I gazed at the unlovely duo.

Passing the entrenchments we galloped on past the old camping places and haunts of the foe. The road has scarcely a curve and looked like some long stately avenue with its narrowing vista and its fine overshadowing of moss-hung pines. At length we reached a sort of framework supporting above our path a board on which some verbose Southern corporation had inscribed 'Look out for the engine when the whistle blows.' Not caring for the injunction or the engine either, we dashed across the track and emerged into full view of the ancient and once respectable but lately rebellious city of Savannah. A hasty ride about town demonstrated to our minds that it neither a city of magnificent distances or very great expectations. It wears the air of having been finished several years ago. Its suburbs are the swamps and its confines are the limits of dry land. Yet it is withal pleasantly situated. Being about 30 feet above tidewater, it commands a fine view of the Savannah River and its various windings to the ocean. The country all around is flat and marshy and does not afford that beauty of landscape which belongs only to a broken or undulating surface. Three miles below the city Fort Jackson could be distinctly seen. Its staunch walls and bristling armament are now beneath the starry folds which traitorous hands tore down from those battlements nearly four years ago. On the further side of the river beyond Hutchinson's Island, the Rebel gunboat *Savannah* yet lay moored awaiting her chance to break through our fleet and make her way to Charleston. The opportunity did not arrive and the Rebel monster was blown up on the night of the 21st. Two or three of her compeers had previously been sunk or otherwise destroyed.

The city is compactly built, regularly laid out and finely shaded by live oak trees. Many of the buildings exhibit touches of the antique style of architecture common in Colonial times. Others wear the air of culture and taste, and suggest wealthy and luxurious occupants. A large proportion of the inhabitants remain and are not slow to cast themselves upon the good will of conquerors. Many profess loyalty to the national government and show good evidence of sincerity. It was the pleasure of the writer to receive the welcoming benediction of one white handkerchief, which uncommon event indeed, almost set him mad. The troops are now all encamped in the immediate vicinity of the city. The 20th Corps being the first to enter it is honored with its military occupation and government. This duty belongs more especially to the Second Division, the First and Third being encamped on the bank of the Savannah one mile above the city.

Great effort is now being made to clear the channel of the river of the torpedoes and other obstructions. This promised to be accomplished in a few days, when we can expect an abundance of supplies now greatly needed. Indeed, so long have we been living on rice and beef that many a soldier's mind will revert with unusual zest to the old-time Christmas dinners at his home on the coming morrow. In fact I am not sure but I might confess such a weakness myself, for I already discover my mind wandering back to its old and cherished memories of Christmas Eve. It is time, therefore, for me to drop this profitless writing by wishing with a soldier's earnestness to every reader of these lines a merry Christmas and happy New Year.

Sherman's March to the Sea

Itinerary of the Third Brigade, First Division, 20th Corps

Nightly camps of the march

November 15th	Stone Mountain
November 16th	Rock Bridge
November 17th	Flat Creek
November 18th	5 miles west of Madison
November 19th	3 miles east of Madison
November 20th	4 miles east of Eatonton
November 21st	6 miles west of Eatonton
November 22nd	Milledgeville
November 23rd	Milledgeville
November 24th	Gum Creek
November 25th	Gardner
November 26th	Tennille Station
November 27th	Davisboro
November 28th	Spiers Turnout
November 29th	2 miles west of Ogeechee River
November 30th	Louisville
December 1st	4 miles west of Birdville
December 2nd	Buck Head Church
December 3rd	Horse Creek
December 4th	1 mile east of Little Ogeechee Creek
December 5th	4 miles east of Little Ogeechee Creek
December 6th	6 miles east of Ogeechee River
December 7th	1 mile north of Springfield
December 8th	8 miles north of Savannah
December 9th	Montieth Swamp
December 10th	4 miles north of Savannah
December 11th	4 miles north of Savannah
December 12th	4 miles north of Savannah
December 13-22nd	Savannah River
December 23rd	McAlpin's Plantation on Savannah River

Report of Colonel James S. Robinson, 82nd Ohio Infantry, commanding Third Brigade

HDQRS. THIRD BRIG., FIRST DIV., TWENTIETH CORPS,
Near Savannah, Ga., December 28, 1864.

On the 15th November, at 7 A.M., my brigade filed out of its encampments and made its final exit from the city of Atlanta. Behind us all means of communication and supply had been utterly destroyed, and the town itself was a blazing ruin, abandoned alike by citizens and soldiers to the harsh fortunes of war. Before us lay a vast stretch of country, containing no organized army, yet thoroughly infested with enemies clear to its natural boundary, the ocean. There was nothing left for us to rely upon but ourselves, our leader, and the God of battles. Moving out on the Decatur road, my brigade passed the village of Decatur at 2 P.M. Our first day's march terminated near Stone Mountain, about 15 miles from Atlanta. Early on the morning of the 16th, I was directed by General Jackson, commanding division, to take my brigade and commence destroying the Georgia Railroad at a point about half a mile beyond my encampment.[187] Extending my brigade along the track, I succeeded in thoroughly destroying about two miles of it by the A.M. After this was accomplished, having been assigned as rear guard of the corps, my command awaited the passage of the troops and trains. This was not completed until 5 P.M., at which hour my brigade marched from Stone Mountain. My column crossed Stone Mountain Creek at 10 and Yellow River at 11:30 P.M. It encamped on the left bank of Yellow River, near Rock Bridge Post Office, about midnight, having marched about seven miles.

My brigade, still the rear guard of the corps, marched from its camp near Rock Bridge at noon on the 17th. It crossed No Business Creek at 1, Big Haynes Creek at 5, and Little Haynes Creek, at Summers' Mills, at 7 P.M. My column was greatly detained by the trains, which moved very slowly, owing to the heavy loads carried in the wagons and the difficult places in the road. My command did not get into camp until one hour after midnight, when it reached a point near Flat Creek. The distance marched on this day was about 13 miles. My brigade marched, following the Second Brigade of the First Division, and charged with the protection of about 100 wagons, at 8 A.M. on the 18th; it passed Alcovy Mountain at 11, and crossed Alcovy or Ulcofauhachee River at 11:30 A.M. At 1:30 P.M. it reached Social Circle, on the Georgia Railroad. Here it emerged into a fine, level, open country with a good road which enabled us to move along briskly. At 8 P.M. my command passed through Rutledge Station, and at 10 P.M. encamped five miles west of Madison.

My brigade marched at 7:45 A.M. on the ensuing morning, November 19th, leading the division and corps, and unencumbered with wagons. At 10 A.M. it passed through the village of Madison and marched in a southward course on the Eatonton road. At 12 noon it encamped three miles south of Madison. The aggregate distance marched on this and the preceding day was about 25 miles. On the 20th my command resumed its march at 7:15 A.M. It moved in rear of the division and was charged with the protection of about 300 wagons, including the pontoon and a large portion of the Second Division train. Considerable rain had fallen, which rendered the road heavy and retarded the movement of the column. It crossed Sugar Creek at 11:30 A.M., and Clark's Fork at 1 P.M. The country now being traversed was quite fertile, and afforded an abundance of all kinds of supplies. A considerable number of fine horses and mules were also brought in. By this means the transportation of my brigade was greatly improved. At 7 P.M. my command reached a point about four miles and a half from Eatonton and encamped. The distance marched this day was about 12 miles.

On the 21st the morning dawned dark and lowering, with occasional gusts of rain. My brigade was again assigned to duty as rear guard of the corps. A battery of artillery accompanied my command, which was unencumbered with wagons. Our march commenced at 11 A.M. At 1 P.M., the column being temporarily delayed by the breaking of a tongue in an artillery carriage, the rebel cavalry appeared in our rear and made a slight demonstration. It was driven off precipitately by the 61st Ohio Veteran Volunteers, which constituted my rear guard.

---

[187] General Sherman elevated General Slocum to wing command, which gave General Alpheus S. Williams command of the 20th Corps. Brigadier General Nathaniel J. Jackson had been serving on light duty in New York when he was ordered West and assumed command of the First Division in November 1864. Jackson would lead the division through the Carolinas campaign.

At 4 P.M. my command marched through the village of Eatonton. At 9 P.M., the column having been tediously delayed, I discovered, upon investigation, that about 60 wagons had become almost hopelessly stalled in a sort of quagmire. My troops were at once put to work lightening out these wagons and were thus employed for about two hours, when the march was resumed. My brigade encamped six miles from Eatonton at midnight, having marched ten miles and a half.

At 7:15 A.M. on the 22nd my march was continued. My command moved in the rear of the division and was charged with the protection of about 400 wagons. The weather had now cleared up, but the column still moved slowly. My brigade did not cross Little River until 12:30 P.M. From that point the march was resumed again at 3 P.M. on the direct road to Milledgeville. My brigade marched into Milledgeville at 7:30 P.M. Passing through the town, and crossing the Oconee River on a wooden bridge, it encamped on the left bank at 9 P.M., having marched seventeen miles. On the 23rd my brigade remained in camp near the Oconee bridge. This day's rest enabled the foraging parties to collect a considerable quantity of provisions and a number of horses and mules.

At 6 A.M. on the 24th my brigade resumed its march, leading the division and corps. Being charged with the duty of advance guard it was unencumbered by the trains. Our line of march pursued the Oconee through a sparsely settled, broken, piney country. My column crossed Beaver Dam at 11 A.M., and at 12:15 P.M. crossed Town Creek. At 3 P.M. my brigade crossed Gum Creek and at 4:30 P.M. encamped on the ridge beyond. The distance marched on this day was about 15 miles. On the 25th, at 6 A.M., my brigade continued its march, again being the vanguard of the division and corps. Bluff Creek was passed at 7, and the column reached Hebron Post-Office at 8 and Buffalo Creek at 9 A.M.

Over Buffalo Creek, a wide, swampy stream, was a series of bridges, nine in number, all of which had been destroyed by the enemy. According to directions, I detailed a regiment, the 101st Illinois Volunteers, to assist in their reconstruction. While this work was going on, the rebel cavalry made a demonstration on the pickets on the left bank of the stream. At the instance of the general commanding division, I at once dispatched five companies of the 101st Illinois Volunteers to re-enforce the picket-line. The enemy at once withdrew, and the bridges were completed without further annoyance. The remainder of my brigade crossed Buffalo Creek at 3:30 P.M., and the entire command, excepting the five companies of the 101st Illinois Volunteers left to cover a side road, pursued its march toward Sandersville. Having ascended a plateau three miles from the creek lively skirmishing was overheard toward the front, which proved to be the cavalry advance engaging the rebel forces under Wheeler. As the enemy appeared to be charging down the road I was directed by the general commanding division to throw my command immediately forward into line, extending across and covering the road. My troops came up promptly on the double-quick, and were in a very short space of time advancing in a steady line of battle. Contemporaneously with this movement a line of skirmishers, consisting of two companies from the 31st Wisconsin Volunteers and two from the 82nd Ohio Veteran Volunteers, had been thrown forward, covering the front of the brigade. My line of battle had not advanced but a short distance when, it not being deemed necessary to push it any farther, it was, by direction of the general commanding division, halted and the troops put in camp. My skirmish line, however, under direction of two officers of my staff, Capt. Alfred E. Lee, acting assistant adjutant-general, and Capt. Cyrus Hearrick, acting aide-de-camp, steadily advanced, and without hesitation and without loss drove the enemy from a commanding position from which he had charged our cavalry half an hour previously. Not content with this my skirmish line pursued the enemy and drove him through woods and open fields one mile farther, when it was, by my order, halted and withdrawn.[188]

On the ensuing day, the 26th, my brigade resumed the march at 6:15 A.M., following the Second Brigade, which was in advance of the division and corps. This brigade at 7 A.M. commenced skirmishing with the enemy's cavalry at the point where it had been left by my skirmishers on the evening previous. Soon afterward a detachment of rebels having been discovered observing our movements on a side road leading to our right, I was directed to send a regiment to drive them off. I immediately dispatched the 101st Illinois Volunteers, Lieutenant-Colonel Le Sage. This regiment charged the enemy and drove him precipitately to the woods, capturing one prisoner, and discovering about 100 bales of cotton, which were burned, including the cotton gin. The regiment then rejoined the brigade,

---

[188] This particular action took place near the present day town of Gardner, Georgia.

which had by this time resumed its march toward Sandersville. My column reached that village without any further opposition at 11 A.M. Here the trains being left in charge of the Third Division, the troops of the First Division, including my brigade, marched unencumbered toward the Georgia Central Railroad, three miles distant. My command struck the road at Tennille Station at 3:30 P.M. and immediately began the destruction of the track. About one mile was thoroughly destroyed by my brigade by sundown. My troops were then encamped near the station. The entire distance marched on this day was nine miles.

On the 27th my brigade marched in the center of the division at 7 A.M. The route from Tennille pursued a secluded, untraveled road on the south side of the railroad. The troops being unencumbered, marched rapidly and made Jackson's Church by 11 A.M. At 4:30 P.M. my command crossed Williamson's Swamp Creek and arrived at Davisboro. Here the troops were encamped for the night, having marched about seventeen miles. At daylight the next morning, November 28th, my brigade marched down the railroad track three miles and commenced its destruction. Inasmuch as the track bed for the most part ran through a difficult swamp much of it was composed of trestle-work and bridges, all of which were effectually destroyed. When the track was laid upon a road bed the rail upon one side, with the stringer attached, was unfastened by means of levers and lifted over against the rail on the other side. Rails and dry wood were then piled on top and the whole set on fire. The heat would soon spring the rails, still attached to the wooden stringers, into a variety of contortions, and the work of destruction was completed. Thus my brigade, in connection with the other brigades of the division and alternating with them, proceeded down the track, destroying mile after mile. At night-fall my command reached Spiers Turnout, and there encamped, having marched eleven miles and destroyed four miles of track during the day.

At 7 A.M. on the 29th my brigade returned about two miles up the track and completed its destruction down as far as Spiers. The station house and other railroad fixtures were then burned or otherwise effectually destroyed. At 11 A.M. my command marched singly on the wagon road from Spiers. The corps and division headquarters trains were placed in its charge, but it was otherwise unencumbered. My column crossed Great Coat Creek at 12:30, and arrived at Bethany at 1:30 P.M. At 3:30 P.M. it crossed Boggy Girt Creek, and at nightfall encamped two miles and a half from the Ogeechee River. By direction of the general commanding division, I sent forward a regiment (the 82nd Ohio Veteran Volunteers) with orders to proceed as far as the Ogeechee, and there encamp for the night, picketing well the bank of the river. On the morning of the 30th the regiment sent forward to the river was withdrawn and rejoined the brigade, which marched up the right bank at 8:30 A.M. At 1 P.M. the column crossed Mill Creek and halted for dinner on Blake's plantation. At 4:30 P.M. my command crossed the Ogeechee River, at a point two miles below Louisville. The bridge here had been ineffectually destroyed by the enemy, and was repaired by my pioneer corps. My brigade pushed forward and encamped two miles beyond the river at nightfall. It marched on this day about fifteen miles.

On the morning of December 1st, the march was resumed in the direction of Birdville. My brigade moved in the center of the division and in charge of the division train. However, it did not leave its encampment near Louisville until noon. During the afternoon it crossed Big, Dry, Spring, and Bark Camp Creeks, all small, swampy streams of clear water. The march was very much retarded by the boggy places in the road. My command did not get into camp until half an hour after midnight, when it reached a point about four miles from Birdville, having marched thirteen miles. On the 2nd my brigade resumed its march at 9:45 A.M. leading its division and following the Second Division, which was in advance. At noon it reached Birdville, and at 8 P.M. crossed Buck Head Creek at Buck Head Church, and there encamped. The distance marched on this day was about 15 miles. Shortly after passing Birdville, having received reliable information that a planter named Bullard, living in that neighborhood, had made himself conspicuous for his zeal in recapturing and securing prisoners from our army escaped from the rebel authorities, I dispatched an officer with authority to destroy his outbuildings and cotton. He accordingly set fire to the corn cribs, cotton gin, cotton presses, and a warehouse containing $50,000 worth of cotton. These were all consumed, and the owner admonished that a repetition of his offense would bring a similar fate upon his dwelling at the next visitation of our army.

On the 3rd my brigade marched at 7 A.M. on the Sylvania road; my command occupied the center of the division, and was unencumbered with wagons. My brigade crossed the Augusta branch of the Central Railroad at noon. The Michigan Engineers[189] having been charged with the destruction of this road, my command pressed forward and encamped near Horse Creek at 4:45 P.M. The distance marched on this day was about 15 miles. On the 4th my brigade, having in charge the entire division train, the pontoon trains, the corps supply train, and the artillery ammunition train, marched at 9 A.M. The column crossed a number of small, swampy streams, and passed through a sterile, sandy country, bountifully timbered with groves of pine. At 12:30 P.M. it crossed Little Horse Creek, and at 5 P.M. Little Ogeechee Creek. At 6 P.M. my troops encamped one mile beyond the Little Ogeechee, having marched thirteen miles. On the 5th the First Division, which had previously been in advance, dropped to the rear, allowing the other two divisions to go ahead; this consumed most of the day. My brigade marched at 5 P.M.; the road was very sloughy, greatly detaining the trains. The column advanced only about three miles and a half, when it encamped at 10:30 P.M.

On the 6th my brigade, with a battery of artillery, was detailed as a rear guard for the corps. It marched at 9.30 A.M. unencumbered with wagons. The line of march pursued the Springfield road through a moderately fertile country. My foraging parties, which were now kept out dally, were enabled to obtain a considerable quantity of sweet potatoes and fresh meat. Ample supplies of forage were also obtained along the road. My command marched on this day about 12 miles, and encamped at a point about six miles from the Ogeechee River, six from the Savannah, and 16 from Springfield. On the 7th our march was resumed at 8 A.M. My brigade had charge of about 300 wagons, consisting of the division and the cavalry trains. The road soon entered the Cowpens Branch Swamp, a low, flat, boggy surface, about three miles in width. The wagons easily cut through the surface and many of them became completely mired. In the meantime a drizzling rain set in, which had no tendency to improve the roads. In many instances the animals had to be entirely removed from the wagons and the vehicles drawn out of the slough by the troops. By 1:30 P.M. the trains were all gotten safely through the swamp and the column moved slowly on. At 8 P.M. it reached Turkey Creek and Swamp, and at 10 P.M. encamped one mile above Springfield. The distance marched on this day was fifteen miles. At 8 A.M. on the morning of the 8th my brigade crossed Jack's Creek and arrived at Springfield. My command was now unencumbered and marched in advance of the division, following the Second Division. Our course followed the Monteith road about nine miles, then turned to the right and pursued a southwesterly direction for a distance of six miles, which brought us to our encampment, having marched in the aggregate 15 miles.

The march was resumed at 8:30 A.M. on the 9th. My brigade followed the Second, the First being in the advance. At 10 A.M. the column struck the main road leading to Savannah. Cannonading and musketry were now occasionally heard in the advance. It began to be evident that a considerable force of the enemy had gathered in our front and meant to oppose our onward march to Savannah. At 3 P.M. my brigade reached Monteith Swamp, where the First and Second Brigades had already encountered a considerable force of the enemy. The rebel forces were so disposed as to completely command the only practicable passage of the swamp, which was by the main road. Their artillery, which they were disposed to use freely, was so posted as to completely sweep the road, and was covered by earth-works. The advance of the First Brigade against the enemy's front, together with that of the Second Brigade against his left flank, having failed to dislodge him, I was instructed by the general commanding division to send two regiments around the left, with directions to push through the swamp if possible and turn the enemy's right. I immediately dispatched the 31st Wisconsin and 61st Ohio Veteran Volunteers, the whole commanded by Colonel Francis H. West, of the 31st Wisconsin Volunteers, to whom I gave the instructions above repeated. Making a detour of about one mile to the left Colonel West formed his command in line of battle and plunged into the almost impenetrable swamp. It was found impossible to get a horse over the miry surface, and officers and men were alike compelled to go on foot. The swamp, which was about 400 yards in width, was finally passed and the troops emerged into an open field skirted on the farther side by timber, in which the enemy lay concealed. The point at which he was struck was far in the rear of his main position, which was completely turned, yet he was not wholly unprepared to meet Colonel West's forces, upon whom he opened fire at their first appearance. The fire was returned with a good will, but only three volleys were needed to complete the overthrow and affect the precipitate retreat of the enemy.

---

[189] 1st Regiment, Michigan Volunteer Engineers and Mechanics

Colonel West now cautiously advanced his line, fearing an ambush. He soon discovered that the Rebel forces were all gone, and quietly occupied two fine redoubts, containing 80 abandoned knapsacks, well packed with clothing, &c. The remainder of my brigade except the 82nd Ohio Veteran Volunteer Infantry, which had been sent to the support of Colonel West, now crossed the swamp by the main road, and the whole encamped near the Rebel redoubts. This little affair, in my judgment, reflects great credit upon those concerned in it, and I take this occasion to express my appreciation of the skill and promptitude with which Colonel West handled his troops. I regret to say, however, that this affair cost us one man killed and four wounded.

My brigade marched again at 7 A.M. on the 10th, in the center of the division, the Second Brigade leading. The road was excellent, and devoid of all obstructions. My brigade struck the Charleston and Savannah Railroad at Monteith Station at 10 A.M., and soon afterward commenced destroying the track. By 11:30 A.M. half a mile of the track was thoroughly destroyed by the brigade, and the column resumed its march, now on the direct road to the city of Savannah. By 2:30 P.M. my command reached the fifth mile-post from the city. About one mile in advance of this the enemy had already been encountered, strongly entrenched, with artillery in position. It was evident that this was the main line of the defenses of the city. My brigade immediately went into position on the left of the Second Brigade, which had already formed in the dense forest on the left of the road. My left flank joined the right of the First Brigade. Pickets covering the line were at once thrown forward, but no demonstration was made upon the enemy. My troops encamped in the position thus taken. On the 11th my command was thrown forward and to the left about 400 yards, and the troops again encamped in their position. At 11 P.M., by direction of the general commanding division, I detached the 101st and 82nd Illinois and 61st Ohio Veteran Volunteers, the whole under the command of Lieutenant-Colonel John B. Le Sage, of the 101st Illinois Volunteers, and sent them to the rear, to be used in guarding the trains of the corps.

On the 13th I was directed to move the remainder of my brigade to the rear, to cover the approaches to the trains. At 3 P.M. my entire command was posted, covering the different roads coming from the rear. My line was about three miles in extent, joining the pickets of the 22nd Wisconsin Volunteers[190] on the right, near the Savannah River, and those of the 14th Army Corps on the left. The 143rd New York Volunteers was placed near the junction of the Tweedside, the Potter's plantation, and the Savannah roads. The 82nd Ohio Veteran Volunteers was placed about three-quarters of a mile farther to the right, on the Potter's plantation road. The 101st Illinois Volunteers and 61st Ohio Veteran Volunteers covered the Savannah road, near Cherokee Hill. The 82nd Illinois Volunteers covered the line of the Charleston and Savannah Railroad. The 31st Wisconsin Volunteers was placed three-quarters of a mile south of Cherokee Hill, on a road leading in that direction. The positions thus chosen, excepting those of the two regiments first named, were covered by substantial breast-works. A section of artillery, which reported to me on the 14th, was posted on the Savannah road and was covered by a redoubt. My brigade remained in the position just described without incident worthy of note until the 19th. On that date, by permission of the general commanding division, I sent out a foraging expedition, consisting of twelve companies of infantry, two from each regiment, and eight wagons. My instructions to Lieutenant-Colonel Le Sage, commanding the detachment, were to proceed about four miles north of Monteith Station, to obtain all the forage and supplies he could, and to develop the strength and position of a hostile force reported to be in that neighborhood. The party returned at 3 P.M. without having obtained either provisions or forage. It had encountered the enemy's outposts and driven them back to within one mile and a half of his main camp, capturing one prisoner. During the night of the 20th, according to direction, I detailed a regiment, the 143rd New York Volunteers, to cross to Argyle Island and there go into position, covering the flank of the Second Brigade, which had crossed to the South Carolina shore. On the morning of the 21st it was discovered that the enemy had evacuated the city and defenses of Savannah. The 143rd New York Volunteers therefore rejoined the brigade on the morning of the 22nd. On the 23rd my command moved back toward the city and encamped on McAlpin's plantation, on the right bank of the Savannah River. The position assigned me was on the right of the Second Brigade and one mile above the city of Savannah. Here my troops erected comfortable quarters, in which they still remain.

---

[190] The 22nd Wisconsin was part of Colonel Daniel Dustin's Second Brigade, General William T. Ward's Third Division, XX Corps.

During the extraordinary campaign which has terminated, my command marched over 350 miles, completely destroyed 9 miles of railroad track, burned a station-house, several water-tanks, and a large quantity of wood and railroad lumber; burned 12 cotton-gins and presses, and 250 bales of cotton; captured 5 serviceable horses, 42 serviceable mules, 460 head of cattle, 200 sheep, 500 hogs, 12 barrels of molasses, one barrel of whiskey, 50,000 pounds of sweet potatoes, 10,800 pounds of rice, besides a vast quantity of flour, meal, bacon, poultry, and other promiscuous kinds of provisions. The quantity of forage captured it is difficult to estimate, but it is safe to say that it amounted to not less than 130,000 pounds. Excepting the articles of bread, coffee, and sugar, my troops subsisted almost entirely from the country. The animals also were fed almost exclusively upon what was obtained from the same source.

I take pleasure in expressing my hearty commendation of the soldierly behavior of the officers and men of my command during this long and arduous campaign. The fatigues and privations of the march were borne with cheerfulness. The heavy labor of assisting trains, destroying railroads, building bridges, repairing roads, &c., was performed with alacrity, and when the voice of danger summoned, every soldier sprang to his post with enthusiasm. The commanders of my regiments and the officers of my staff deserve and are tendered my sincere thanks for their ready co-operation in every laudable undertaking, and their earnest zeal in carrying out my orders. But the soldiers and officers of my command need no praise from me. Their own achievements are their highest encomium, and the united admiration of their countrymen their best reward. These are already theirs, and neither my pen nor voice can add anything to them.

In conclusion I have the honor to add the following list of the regiments composing my brigade and the officers commanding them during the campaign: 31st Wisconsin Volunteers, Col Francis H. West, 82nd Ohio Veteran Volunteers, Lieut. Col. David Thomson; 143rd New York Volunteers, Lieut. Col. Hezekiah Watkins; 101st Illinois Volunteers, Lieut. Col. John B. Le Sage; 82nd Illinois Volunteers, Maj. Ferdinand H. Rolshanson; 61st Ohio Veteran Volunteers, Capt. John Garrett.

The officers of my staff were as follows: Capt. Alfred E. Lee, acting assistant adjutant-general; Capt. Benjamin Reynolds, acting assistant inspector general; Capt. Frederick S. Wallace, topographical engineer; Capt. Charles Saalmann, acting commissary of subsistence; Capt. W. T. George, acting assistant quartermaster; Surg. Henry K. Spooner, surgeon-in-chief; Capt. Cyrus Hearrick, acting aide-de-camp; Capt. Myron H. Lamb, acting aide-de-camp; Lieut. Charles M. Lockwood, acting assistant provost-marshal.

The following casualties and losses occurred in my brigade during the campaign: One enlisted man killed in action, 4 deserted, 1 missing in action, 4 injured in destroying railroad, 2 captured while foraging, making an aggregate loss of 12 enlisted men.

Respectfully, your obedient servant,

J. S. ROBINSON, Colonel, Commanding

CHAPTER TEN

Carolinas

Notes in Dixie Vol. XXIII

Near Savannah, Georgia
January 5, 1865

Immediately after the fall of Savannah and its occupation by the "white stars," the Red Star Division also moved in and encamped in the precincts of the city. One brigade, the Second, had crossed the Savannah River and affected a lodgment on the rebellious soil of South Carolina. This movement, threatening as it did the enemy's only chance of escape, probably did more than anything else to hasten his evacuation of the city of Savannah. Indeed, had the entire division been precipitated across the river at the beginning, this loophole might have been easily closed and Hardee's forces all captured. But the adventure was thought too hazardous and was consequently delayed until too late to be effective. This incident illustrates how much easier it is, in military affairs particularly, to see how a thing ought to be done after it has been accomplished than before.

Our new encampment was allotted to us on McAlpin's plantation, one mile from the city. Our flank rested on the Savannah River, our line circling about among the venerable live oaks, whose huge spreading tops completely embowered the camps and seemed in their gnarled and mossy stateliness like the bending forms of so many fostering patriarchs. The troops, well pleased with this delightful locality, immediately fell to work gathering boards and building quarters. The continual clack of their hatchets resounded merrily through the forest, making it vocal with busy life. The triangular star color of the Third Brigade was unfurled from McAlpin mansion, signifying it as headquarters. And now amid the spacious richly painted walls let me moralize and speculate a little about their former occupants.[191]

Were I a writer of a romance I would revel in the materials here afforded for a story rivalling the most thrilling productions of Bulwer or Charlotte Bronte. The mansion rests on the bank of the Savannah, of which its reverse front commands a fine view. It is a fine two story building, displaying a style of architecture which indicates abundant means and cultivated taste, bordering on the aristocratic order. It wears a sort of selfish independent aspect, standing as it does widely separated from all other buildings except the multitude of outhouses and the colony of Negro quarters that surround the mansion of every rice planter. In front a magnificent avenue canopied by a stately colonnade of live oaks stretches away in an enchanting vista as far as the moss-hung leafy bower will permit the eye to wander. Around the columned verandas the hand of taste has trained rich vines to climb their arching trellises and planted the rarest shrubs and flowers. Such are some of the outside adornments of the beautiful home of the McAlpins. Let us go inside the uncarpeted, untapestried parlors and hollow sounding halls and see what we can learn of the domestic life of the inhabitants.

Here lies a chaotic pile of books and manuscripts, doubtless from the library and private papers of the McAlpin family. Here are old thumb worn French and Latin lexicons and scientific works of ancient print, bearing the rampant English lion on the title page indicated that the McAlpins were leisurely educated people of foreign extraction,[192] and possessing something of a taste for antique literature. There is a jumbled mess of newspapers and

---

[191] The plantation Lee is referring to was known as "The Hermitage," a 400 acre property that belonged to Henry McAlpin (sometimes spelled McAlpine), one of the wealthiest citizens of the area. McAlpin made his fortune in a variety of ways, including cultivating rice, making bricks, cast iron products, and rice barrels.

[192] Henry McAlpin was born in 1804 in Sterlinshire, Scotland and married Ellen McInnis in 1819. The couple had eight children before Mrs. McAlpin died at age 31. Mr. McAlpin sent his daughters to be raised by his family in Charleston, South Carolina while the boys were raised at The Hermitage. See: http://library.armstrong.edu/McAlpin%20James%20Wallace.pdf

pamphlets among which we discover frequent copies of *The Albion, The Gentleman's Sporting Magazine, Porter's Spirit of the Times, Journal of the Turf*, etc. It is plain therefore that the McAlpines were given to amusements as well as study. They evidently delighted in hunting, angling, and horse racing. I am told that a number of fine race boats were destroyed in a building close by indicated that the fine manly exercise of boating was also part of their sporting creed.

Methinks I see them too in glossy broadcloths and flaunting silks enjoying a moon light sail on the rippling Savannah. Dulcet notes of music and silvery song wafted from the water, tell the grave old oaks, who stoop to bathe their tops in the flood of harmony that the McAlpins are happy tonight. A gentle sea breeze whispers something to the long reeds that grow by the river

"The Hermitage" served briefly as headquarters for the Third Brigade, First Division, XX Corps in January 1865. "The mansion rests on the bank of the Savannah, of which its reverse front commands a fine view," wrote Captain Lee. "It is a fine two story building, displaying a style of architecture which indicates abundant means and cultivated taste, bordering on the aristocratic order."

side, and they in turn like a myriad of gossips, betray the secret with 10,000 clattering tongues. Far away through the dazzling moonlight a blue veil flutters in the breeze and reveals- but for the conclusion of this interesting story, see the *New York Ledger*.

Here is a bundle of old letters, real domestic tell-tales and containing within themselves a whole volume of romance and family history. Here is one postmarked Berlin, Havre, America; it relates to business matters, connections abroad, and were widely known in the commercial world. Here is another from a dutiful heir in England who manifests most anxious concern about the health of his aged progenitors. Here is a filial missive from the delicate jeweled hand of a daughter in South Carolina. All these documents are old, being mostly written a score of years ago. They are, therefore, suggestive relics of an aristocratic, very respectable, wealthy, traveled, and ancient family, proud of its family name and genealogy. They created in my mind an anxious desire to know more of their authors.

I moused about the old corridors and sideboards in pursuit of something that would gratify a curiosity that became every day more prurient and insatiable. My nervous condition became very similar to that which Irving so admirably describes in his 'Stout Gentleman.' Indeed I fancied that this might be the time-honored habitation of a real prototype of the Bracebridge family. I pictured in my mind the gallant captain and his gentle Julia coursing up and down the long avenue on their nimble chargers, the blue veil fluttering in the wind. I fancied I saw them in loving moonlight conference slowly perambulating among the deep shadows of the live oaks and discoursing love's sweet sorrow while seated by the gnarled roots of some confidential giant of the forest. My mind had just been well filled with these whims and like a sail swelled with empty air was rapidly drifting me among those romantic shoals so dangerous to bachelorhood when my reverie was broken and my dream dispelled by one of those most unromantic and matter of fact things in the world, an order to march. It was cruel to thus tear my mind from the soft meshes of the blue veil but was nevertheless probably for my good. Who knows but I might have perpetrated some yellow-covered indiscretion or fallen into some melancholy and mystical mood which would have upset the philosophy of my brotherhood, and brought reproach upon the time honored adage, 'The bachelor most joyfully in pleasant plight does pass his dales, good fellowship and company he doth maintain and keep always.'

Our march was only a change of camp, but it took me away from the mysterious mansion of the McAlpins. It brought me to a dwelling of more humble pretensions and not quite so suggestive of romantic ideas or of the elegance and luxury attending Southern aristocracy and wealth. If the materials I have collected may be considered valuable to any of the contributors of the *New York Ledger* or *Mercury*, I announce myself ready to dispose of them cheap.

The rice culture in America was first initiated at Savannah. The lands within a circuit of 30 miles radius from here are probably the best adapted for the cultivation of this cereal of any on our continent. The nature of the grain is such as to require that the ground be frequently overflowed by water during its growth. For this reason only the very low flat lands can be used. The numerous islands of the Savannah are admirably adapted for this purpose, being always accessible to tide water. The process of growing rice is not more curious than the method of hulling it. Each grain is enclosed in a strong, raspy husk, which clings firmly and is difficult to remove. After the grain is separated from the straw by threshing, the husk still remains upon it and is taken off by a special process. This is simply pounding and may be done by manual labor or by machinery. In the first instance the rice is merely placed in a stone or wooden trough and pounded with a pestle until the hulls are loosened. This method is only used by the Negroes or on minor plantations.

The large and well-organized establishments use machinery driven by horsepower or steam. In this case a series of immense wooden pestles are arranged in such a way as to be raised alternatively by a toothed cylinder and let fall in the stone basins filled with rice. In this way and effectual hammering it kept up which rapidly separates the husk from the grain. But the process does not end here. The grain after being hulled must be winnowed and cleaned, the broken grains separated from the whole ones, the good from the bad. This requires additional machinery which is not necessary to describe. Apparatus for grinding the rice into flour is also frequently attached to the hulling mills, the whole being conjoined in the same building. The rice mills are mostly worked by Negroes, mostly females. It is surprising to observe how much of the labor which properly belongs to the steam engine is performed by the slaves, simply for want of the ingenuity or the enterprise necessary for making some trifling additions to the machinery. For instance, a train of Negro workmen is kept constantly employed in carrying rice in baskets from the first to the second floor when the whole of this labor might be done by a pair of elevators. Such a thing in the North would be laughed at. But such is Southern enterprise.

Men who would surreptitiously deprive a New England man of the benefits of his patent of the cotton gin would not be likely to have the enterprise to inventory anything which would render the great Southern principle of slave labor any less necessary. The truth is that so thoroughly are the wealthy people of this country imbued with the idea that labor is degrading and that Negroes are designed by nature to perform the drudgery of white men for nothing, that their minds are rarely awakened by the necessity of encouraging labor. Nor is there anything which these Negro drivers hate with more hearty hatred than that very inventive genius of the Northern people to which their social principle that it is right and honorable to labor has given life and animation. Said a buxom she-traitor in my presence during a conversation about the destruction of the Georgia railroads, 'Well we'll have some Northern Yankees detailed to come down here after the war and repair our railroads.' A friend of mine remarked to a lady in Savannah the other day that in the North the people all labored, considering it honorable to sustain themselves in this way. 'Do you think,' she said unfolding a pair of jeweled hands which would scorn the stain of industrious toil, but which for long, long years have kept back from the laborer his hire, 'do you think I could earn a living with those hands?' Ah, people of the North, did you but realize how strong and unreasonable this contempt not only for labor but for you as laborers has grown here, you would say it is time this lazy, worthless Southern aristocracy were overthrown.

I have often remarked and it has given me infinite pleasure to do so, the frank manly appearance of our soldiers. There is scarcely a man among them whose countenance does not beam with intelligence and whose whole physique does not denote a well-developed manhood. On the other hand, the Rebel soldiers are spare, sallow, and cadaverous, as though life had been stinted in its growth and development. Why this difference? It is because Northern boys are taught to labor and to study, to work with hand and brain, while Southern boys are taught to despise labor, to love dissipation, and to cultivate passion rather than intellect. God bless our noble, rugged, healthy, manly, intelligent Northern soldiers. Theirs' is the true nobility with the stamp of nature upon it. The splendid Army of Georgia is already preparing for a new campaign. The weather continues mild and pleasant. Much of the time it is hardly cold enough to be comfortable. Now is the time to strike for the Union, 'for our altars and our fires, for the green graves of our sires, God, and our native land.'

Notes in Dixie Vol. XXIV

Savannah, Georgia
January 13, 1865

One of the most prominent features of this country is its live oak groves. I have made frequent reference to them in previous numbers of these notes and I trust I shall be pardoned for again recurring to the same subject. Keats says 'A thing of beauty is a joy forever.' It is in the soul-coined philosophy of these words that I seek my apology for never being weary of talking of these beautiful trees, writing from the very midst of their embowering branches while the bright sunbeams glance merrily from their glossy green leaves and curtain my window with a changing drapery of light and shade. I cannot but feel, even while wintry vapors still hang over the wide Savannah and the ground still wears its January brown, that these giant evergreens possess a perennial charm, and ever-enduring every-fascinating glory. Nor is it difficult while gazing upon their stately forms to wander in one's mind back to that imaginative period when each had its tutelany faun or dryael and the fairy folk nightly held their airy revels in every grove. Indeed so venerable, so patriarchical do these forest monoliths appear with their great cloud-like tops, their rugged storm-defying steams, their immense sinewy branches and their flowering drapery of gray moss appearing amid the green like sprinkled frost upon the head of age, that one's mind involuntarily seizes upon the pleasing fantasy that these are beings informed with a species of intelligence, holding in their oaken hearts the mysteries of ages past and gifted by nature with a sort of superiority of race which makes them kingly of their kind. I confess each tree commands my profound respect and I cannot but cry shame upon the vandal axe that fain would subvert their ancient solitary reign. Their beauty and their age would seem to be enough to defend them from sacrilegious hands, but alas, these are their only defense. Even the rose has its armor of thorns and almost everything in nature has some sort of defensive arrangement. But not so the emerald-crowned Titanus of the forest. They are helpless victims of the cupidity and caprice of man.

There are many historical reminiscences which cluster around these live oaks like the rich fruitage of the centuries, and which entitle them still more to my profound veneration. Here around the gnarled trunks the swarthy Indians gathered in grave council and joined in savage dance and song before these shores were visited by white man from beyond the sea. Beneath these umbrageous boughs the pioneers of the New World planned their infant states and fastened upon American soil the foothold of empire. Screened by the same leafy canopy the scarlet-coated Britons marshaled in pompous array against the brave patriots who fought our young republic into birth. Here, too, the proud invader quailed and grew pale as he heard far off in the deep forest the echoing call of Marion's troopers or saw the distant waving of Pulaski's plume. And here in 1865 we come from the far Northland to replant among these majestic oaks the same starry banner which our fathers so gallantly fought and died for on this soil in 1779. Verily these grand old evergreens have a history. Where the undergrowth has been so cleared out as to afford a prolonged view through the midst of these trees the vista is most enchanting. Overhead is a thick interlacement of enormous boughs, making a leafy canopy so dense that it casts upon the ground an almost unbroken shade. From this emerald roof long beautifully-netted tufts of gray Spanish moss profusely hang like stalactites from the roof of a cavern. The whole picture is indescribably beautiful. Too beautiful, seemingly, for earth that it lifts one's mind to the visionary bowers of the blessed.

But it is by moonlight that this forest pageantry seems most fascinating to me. The great green tops then stand out in such bold relief against the spangled sky and the deep shade is so strongly contrasted with the radiant patches of open space, the spreading boughs stretch upward in such vast, indefinite reach toward heaven, the long colonades of stems loom forth in such stately majesty from their dark royal vesture, the whole scene is animated by a beauty so pure, so serene, so grand, so charming, that one seems to have been carried in fancy to some lovely dreamland, some moonlit abode of the poets.

It is difficult for me to wander among these stately solemn groves at any time without catching a tinge of sentimentalism from their speaking silence. They call to mind sylvan associations of boyhood and awaken fond regretful memories of a rougher clime far away. With the buried associations come up the dead associates of other days, and they pass in shadowy review down the long dim vista of time. One comes from the dread wilderness of Virginia where his unnoted clay rests hard by the Rappahannock. His was a brave and noble spirit, 'Mild to obey, generous to command, tempered by forming heaven with kindest, firmest hand,' and all aglow with patriotic fever. He gave his life an offering to freedom at Chancellorsville. Another comes whose mangled form as it lay upon the bloody turf at Gettysburg haunts me still. Another who yielded up his brave young life in the midnight assault at Wauhatchie, and another who fell in the fruitless attack at Kennesaw- but why enumerate? They have given all to their country and are dead upon the field of honor. Dead? No! 'Strew his ashes to the wind, whose sword or voice has served mankind, and is he dead whose glorious mind, lifts thine on high? To live in hearts we leave behind is not to die.'

My object in these notes is not to communicate news. On the contrary I endeavor to deviate from the usual channels pursued by newspaper correspondents. I write from the camps of our soldiers and representing them I desire to communicate their feelings and views upon those matters which newspaper men are least likely to take notice of. With puffing or criticizing generals, planning campaigns, or shocking the sensitive public with lists of killed and wounded, I have nothing to do. I leave this to the professional Bohemian, who is very wise upon these matters but knows about as much of the real thoughts and feelings of the rank and file of the army as he does the thoughts of the gentleman who inhabits the moon. As I have wandered about over this sunny Southern land, coming in contact occasionally with its rebellious people, sometimes on terms of social intercourse, at others in the exciting issue of battle. I shall look at things with a soldier's eyes, and describe them, as well as I can, with a soldier's pen. If there are any who upon these terms desire to follow me in my wanderings, they will always be welcome to such hospitalities as we afford by the knapsack of A.T. Sechand.[193]

Notes in Dixie Vol. XXV

Purrysburg, South Carolina
January 21, 1865

The army is in South Carolina. The red star division of the 20th Corps crossed the Savannah opposite the city on the 17th inst. The 17th Corps had several days previously embarked on transports and gone to Pocataligo via Hilton Head. The 15th Corps crossed the river at Savannah on the 18th and marched in the direction of Grahamsville. The 14th Corps on the same date marched up the right bank of the Savannah designing to cross the river at Sister's Ferry. The First and Third divisions of the 20th Corps moved up the left bank of the river and on the 19th the former reached Purrysburg. Thus the main portion of the army has gained a footing on South Carolina soil and the initial movements of a new campaign have been made.

Yet this grand movement, whatever it may be destined to be, is at present at a dead lock. It is as true of individuals in military as any other kind of life that 'man proposes and God disposes.' The puny belligerents of this world are as nothing when opposed by that immeasurable power which rules and sways the universe. The armies of earth move forth in proud, triumphal array often to be taught by the simplest laws of nature their utter dependence and helplessness. Cambyses under the withering sun of a tropical desert, and Napoleon in the midst of the stinging blasts of a Russian winter were thus made to know that the most splendid armies are not proof against those inevitable laws which sway the elements and are themselves controlled by a higher power than that of man.

---

[193] While camped near Savannah, newly minted Brigadier General James S. Robinson wrote a letter to the War Department seeking a regular appointment for Captain Lee as assistant adjutant general. Citing his 14 months of service in the role as acting assistant adjutant general, General Robinson recommended that Captain Lee was "well qualified for the position. He is a young officer of experience, education, and impeachable private character. At the Battle of Gettysburg, he was so severely wounded as to disable him from his duty as a line officer." Robinson's letter received approval at divisional, corps, and wing levels, General Alpheus Williams "strongly recommending" the appointment. No action being taken, Robinson sent another letter at the end of March but to no avail.

It may be that this army, hitherto so highly favored in all respects, may also be about to be taught a lesson of this kind. For the last 36 hours rain has been almost incessantly falling. This low, flat country is being flooded with water and the roads are already impassable. Even in dry weather the surface is boggy and treacherous but a few hours rain render it terribly so. The passage of a few army trains will at any time cut through the thin crust that overlies what seems to be a fathomless bog commensurate with the country. But now, after this long continued storm, the stability of the soil is almost gone. The swamps have swelled to vast lakes enveloping the roads and creating unusual currents which carry off the bridges and float the corduroy. The trains and artillery are immovable and the troops can perambulate their camps only by wading shoe-deep in mud.

Thus the army is water-bound at the very outset of the campaign. It is fortunate for the Red Star Division that it happens to be at Purrysburg, a landing on the Savannah 17 miles above the city. Here there is no difficulty in obtaining an abundance of supplies by means of transports sent up from below. Mountains of barreled pork and pyramids of pilot bread are already beginning to adorn the primitive wharf of this rustic entrepot. The U.S. gunboat *Pontiac* lies anchored in the channel opposite, ready to salute with thunderous and fiery welcome the first insolent foe that dares molest this newly established line of communication. Thus situated we are prepared to 'let it rain' unless, perchance the storm continues, long enough to drown, though it cannot starve us, out of our camps.

This locality (for I cannot call it a town) has been named with an alarming license of terms. The 'burg' consists, in all, of three buildings, at least one of which has been demolished by the vandals. The excuse for this vast destruction of property lies in the inclemency of the season, rendering necessary the use of boards and bricks in the construction of quarters. Purrysburg, whatever may have been its past grandeur and glory, is likely hereafter to be numbered among the forgotten landmarks of an obsolete era. When the busy camps that are now pitched around it shall have been removed, desolation and ruin will mark its site. The garrulous waterfowl shall here meet in unbroken conclave and the moping owl hoot his complaining notes undisturbed save by Plutonian contraband who come to rummage the army debris, *sic transit Gloria Confederacy.*

There is some consolation for the ennui of our mud-environed camps in the current report that Gen. Lincoln and his army were similarly detained at this point in the Indian Wars. There is also, perhaps, some honor to be found in being the humble successors of this patriot general even in misfortune. To pursue the same difficult paths as those whose valiant swords framed our infant republic ought to be an encouraging coincidence for those who fight to save our nation's life. Carrying the same flag that they carried we differ from them only in bearing it up against a more dangerous and violent opposition. But let us not disparage their triumphs or detract one iota from their glorious and self-sacrificing patriotism. Rather let us gather hence that inspiration which is our proper incentive and without which this war would be merely wholesale murder. Noble patriots, worthy progenitors, immortal founders of our freedom, may we, heirs of a priceless heritage, following the same weary way they trod and for the same lofty ends, never cease to honor them in heart and deed, or prove to be unworthy descendants of

"The sages who in days of yore,
In combat met the foeman.
And drove them from the shore,
Who flung our banner's starry field,
In triumph to the breeze.
And spread broad maps of cities where,
Once waved the forest trees."[194]

My tent is pitched hard by a cemetery which contains graves over a century old. Here I doubt not some of the Revolutionary patriots lie buried. The inscriptions are so much worn and defaced that it is difficult to ascertain the names of those who sleep in these ancient vaults. It is pleasant, however, and not unnatural for a soldier of this second revolution to entertain the fancy that here are entombed some of those noble spirits who fell gloriously fighting despotism and barbarism from this continent nearly 100 years ago. Imbued with this idea it is pleasant for

---

[194] Lee is quoting from "The Land of Washington" by 19th century writer George Pope Morris.

him to bend in solemn reverence upon this turf and here renew his vows to be true to those great principles which first took root among these ashes, and which have since sprung up into a magnificent growth of freedom which showers its rich fruitage upon every hearthstone of this western world.

Writing from the rebellious soil of South Carolina, I might wish that I could speak with tongues of flame against the accursed heresy that was here nurtured and cradled, and which has grown to a lusty life, has since struck its poisoned fangs into the vitals of my country. I fain would dip my pen in that ocean of brave young blood which during the past four years has flowed from the nation's heart and write a curse upon this soil ten-fold more withering than that graven by the unseen hand upon the walls of the Mother of Harlots. Methinks almost a half million tongues forever silenced by this unholy war would, if they could, join with shrieking emphasis in the dreadful malediction. South Carolina, violator of a nation's peace! Fermenter of a gigantic war! Home of the slave hunter and the duelist! Accursed of the states, ruin is thy doom, and this shall be thy epitaph: "The birthplace of the slaveholder's rebellion."

But let me not speak the language of vengeance for that becomes not mortal lips. Let me be content that the God-given banner of the Union once more, through the blessings of Providence, floats proudly and triumphantly over the soil of that state, which four years ago tore it down from the battlements of Sumter. It has come hither baptized by flame and blood, but it is here, and that is glory enough. May its thrice hallowed folds soon float over the slave pens of Charleston and the prisons which confine our starving fellow soldiers at Columbia. The rain will cease, the floods will disappear, and the smile of heaven will again in due time rest upon this army. Then its two mighty wings will be again outstretched and portentous as the pinions of the death-angel, will be seen moving in resistless flight over the bulwarks of Southern rebellion and despotism.

Notes in Dixie Vol. XXVI

Robertsville, South Carolina
February 1, 1865

The campaign in South Carolina has been fairly commenced. The right wing of the army has succeeded in penetrating the interior about seventy miles from the coast while the left wing has meanwhile reached this point. Tomorrow the 20th Corps will push forward to Lawtonville, at which place, when reached it will again be abreast with the most advanced column of the army. The 14th Corps, now crossing the Savannah at Sister's Ferry, will follow, the line of communication will once more be abandoned and army of Atlanta and Savannah will again have disappeared amid the dark, dreary confines of the rebellion. When and where it will next emerge from the wrathful cloud that for a time will conceal it from the fondly searching gaze of its friends remains yet unknown and indeed almost beyond the reach of conjecture. A great blow in behalf of the Union and liberty is about to be struck but how and where it will be delivered probably no one except the commander-in-chief fully comprehends.

The movement of the troops has thus far been greatly retarded by the difficult nature of the roads, resulting in part from the bad weather but chiefly from the peculiar character of the country. The territory of the Carolinas for the first hundred miles from the sea coasts consists of a low, flat surface almost unbroken by a single hill or valley and clothed with an interminable growth of pines and others evergreens. This soil is a loose vegetable mold or else a sandy loam of moderate fertility but destitute of consistency and stability necessary for making substantial roads. For this reason the travelled highways are usually banked up so as to be much above the ordinary level or else corduroyed with pine logs. Being constructed with a view to the exigencies of country travel, they are incapable, particularly in wet weather, of bearing the heavy tramp of any army. Hence a strong pioneer force is kept constantly employed in repairing the road as the army advances.

The column has now reached the border of this tract and begins to emerge upon higher and more substantial ground. The surface is still level but is more redeemed from swamps which though still numerous and difficult to penetrate are more local and confined. Perhaps I can best describe the country by using the language of a Colonial historian which I shall transcribe verbatim. "The soil near the sea of a mold sandy, farther distant, more clay or sand and clay mixed; the land lies upon a level in 50 or 60 miles round having scarce the least hill or eminence. It's clothed with odoriferous and fragrant woods, flourishing in perpetual and constant verdure; the loft pine, the sweet smelling cedar, and cypress trees. There are many other fragrant smelling trees including the Myrtle,

Bay, and Laurel. Fruit trees there are an abundance of various and excellent kinds, the Orange, Lemon, Pomegranate, Fig, and Almond. Sponges grow on the sandy shores for which Samos in times past was famous. Ambergris is often found upon the shoals, a precious commodity to him who finds it if native and pure in worth and value it surpasses gold."

Of the peculiarities of the country as seen by an early immigrant named T.A. Gent, a clerk on board His Majesty's ship *Richmond* which was sent out in the year 1680, it may be profitable to speaker further using his own language. "Of birds the country yields of differing kinds and colors; for prey, the pelican, hawk, and eagle, etc. For pleasure the red, copped, and blue bird, which wantonly imitates the various notes and sounds of such birds and beasts which it hears, wherefore, by way of allusion, it's called the mocking bird. Birds for food and pleasure of game are the swan, goose, duck, mallard, wigeon, teal, curlew, plover, partridge, pigeons, and parakeets. They have a bird named the humming bird in magnitude not exceeding the humble bee. They are a deep green shadowed with a murry, not much unlike the color of some dove's necks; they take their food humming or flying by feeding on the exuberant moistures of sweet odoriferous leaves and flowers. I have frequently seen them in many parts of the West Indies, but never observed them to have any musical air but a loud note of admiration crying chur, chur, chur which at a distance of half a mile is plainly heard."

"There are in Carolina great numbers of fire flies who carry their lanterns in their tails in dark nights flying through the air shining like sparks of fire enlightening it with their golden spangles. Amongst large orange trees in the night, I have seen many of those flies whose lights have appeared like hanging candles or pendant flambeaus which amidst the leaves and ripe fruit yielded a light truly glorious to behold; with three of these included in a glass bottle in a very dark night I have read small characters. There is in the mouth of their rivers or in the lakes near the sea a creature well known in the West Indies called the alligator or crocodile whose scaly back is impenetrable refusing a musket ball to pierce it, but under the belly an arrow finds an easy place to destroy it. This country was first discovered by Sir Sebastian Cabott by the order and at the expense of King Henry VII. The principal place where the English are now settled lies situated on a point of land about two leagues from the sea between the Ashley and Cooper Rivers so named in honor of the right honorable Earl of Shaftsbury, a great patron to the affairs of Carolina, the place called Charles Town by an express order from the Lord Proprietors in the year 1680." Thus speaks the erudite incognito historian T.A. Gent. Let us not do him the discourtesy to cast a shade of doubt over his learned and accurate statements even though in this modern age the fact be so notorious that no humming bird hums loud enough to be heard half a mile, and no lightning bug lights bright enough to make very small characters legible in a very dark night.

Concerning this valuable and charming portion of Dixie other very ancient and voracious historians have written and from their works it may be well to glean a few choice and characteristic statements wherewith to adorn these notes. In reference to the climate, it is said that "Negroes by reason of the mildness of the winter thrive much better than in any of the Northern colonies, and require less clothes which is a great charge saved." Again with another author "Nor is winter here cloudy, overcast, or foggy. The summer is not near so hot as in Virginia which may hardly gain belief with those who have not considered the reason; which it its nearness to the tropics which makes it in a greater measure than those parts more northward, partake of those breezes which almost constantly rise about 8 or 9 o'clock from the tropics and blow fresh from the east till about four in the afternoon; and a little after the sea breeze dies away, there arising a north wind which blowing all night keeps its fresh and cool." Still another historian says on the climate of this favored country. "The summers are generally dry, clear, calm, and excessively hot; the autumn is moist, warm, and unequal; one minute serene the next cloudy and tempestuous; the winter is near the same length as in England, and pretty cool though the midday sun is always warm; the spring is the most delightful season. The boundless forests are then clothed with leaves and enameled with aromatic flowers and blossoms of the most lively colors, perfuming the ambient air; the winged songbirds chirping on every bough with enchanting melodies. This province is subject to frequent and dreadful tempests of thunder and lightning in May, June, July, and August. We have suffered little from lightning since the erecting the sharp points in many public buildings and some private houses of this town, recommended by the ingenious Mr. Franklin of Philadelphia to draw the electrical fluid (or fire or by whatever name I ought to call it) from the clouds that are charged with it and thereby prevent an explosion." [195]

Such was South Carolina as seen in primeval beauty and described by the Colonial chroniclers. I might multiply extracts from the writings of these sage and ancient historians, but I have quoted enough to show how the country appeared to the pioneers of the New World and before it became the home of a turbulent and dissatisfied people and the birthplace of treason. The natural features of the country have not so greatly changed since then as to render these descriptions inappropriate to its present condition. But in its political affairs what vast changes have been wrought! And how strange, how mighty, how grand, is that which is now transpiring! A vast republican army is on South Carolina soil and marching on her capital. The foremost is a gigantic conspiracy against the rights of man, she is one of the last to reap the bitter and legitimate fruits of her conduct, but she will not be least. The somber-winged war-angel is already sweeping in destructive flight across her once happy domain leaving a blazing blackened ruin behind. Whatever tenderness may have been shown to traitors of other states, but little will be exhibited to those of South Carolina. Indeed they expect none. Fleeing precipitately before our advancing columns, they are already abandoning their rich plantations to the ravaging soldiery and their fine mansions to the inevitable torch. Scarcely a building now stands between this point and Savannah- all have been laid to ashes. And yet this is done in spite of every precaution that can be taken to prevent it. The destroyer can never be found and brought to punishment, though he seems to be everywhere present, in front, or on the flanks, and in the rear. It is as if the unseen hand of vengeance lingered about our army executing long deferred punishment upon those whose rash treasonable conduct initiated this dreadful war.

The country affords an abundance of supplies and there is a fair prospect that the troops will live well. They are now in excellent health and spirits and anticipate a prosperous march through the territory now most vital to the Confederacy. The weather has again cleared up and skies wear a genial smile. The nights are frosty, but the days are usually warm and pleasant indicating the speedy approach of the warm fragrant breath of spring. For the first time this army is making a campaign northward. May the march in that direction not cease until it terminates at our home firesides, which happy consummation I devoutly pray may soon be attained.

---

[195] This is a reference to Benjamin Franklin and his lightning rod invented in 1749.

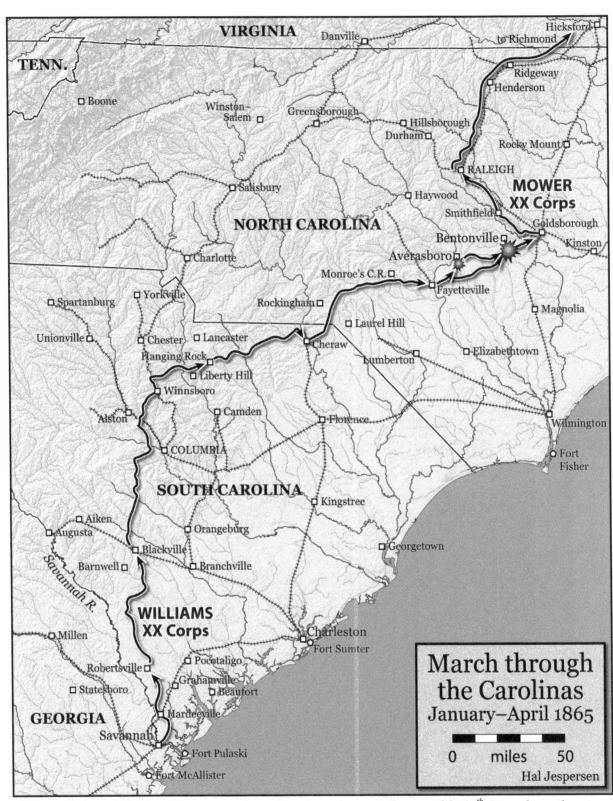

VIRGINIA

TENN.

NORTH CAROLINA

MOWER
XX Corps

SOUTH CAROLINA

WILLIAMS
XX Corps

GEORGIA

Danville
Hicksford
to Richmond
Ridgeway
Henderson
Boone
Winston-Salem
Greensborough
Hillsborough
Durham
Rocky Mount
RALEIGH
Salisbury
Haywood
Smithfield
Goldsborough
Bentonville
Kinston
Averasboro
Charlotte
Monroe's C.R.
Fayetteville
Magnolia
Yorkville
Rockingham
Spartanburg
Laurel Hill
Chester
Lancaster
Cheraw
Lumberton
Elizabethtown
Unionville
Hanging Rock
Liberty Hill
Winnsboro
Alston
Camden
Florence
Wilmington
COLUMBIA
Fort Fisher
Kingstree
Aiken
Orangeburg
Augusta
Blackville
Georgetown
Barnwell
Branchville
Savannah R.
Millen
Charleston
Fort Sumter
Robertsville
Pocotaligo
Grahamville
Statesboro
Beaufort
Hardeeville
Savannah
Fort Pulaski
Fort McAllister

March through
the Carolinas
January–April 1865

0   miles   50

Hal Jespersen

The march through the Carolinas presented a variety of experiences to the men of the 20th Corps; heavy foraging and depredations marked their path in South Carolina followed by a time of "poverty" in the pine forests of North Carolina. Two pitched battles (Averasboro and Bentonville) proved to be Union victories but showed that the Confederates could still put up a fight.
(Hal Jespersen, www.cwmaps.com)

Near Goldsboro, North Carolina

March 25, 1865

Sixty-seven days ago we of the "Red Stars" tramped across the two long arms of the Savannah River opposite Savannah, Georgia. The January sun of the South shone forth clear and mild, as if smiling auspiciously upon the new and marvelous adventure we were just inaugurating. A deep yet cheerful silence reigned over the smooth brown rice fields, once the domains of cruel task-masters and the scenes of unrequited toil. Twittering bevies of rice birds whirled in merry excursion around the moving column while groups of ungainly water fowl, scared from their lurking places among the reeds, spread their crooked pinions and sailed away over the long level marshes. The blackened chimneys of burned buildings showed where the rough hand of war had already given its gloomy touches to the landscape while, grouped around them in strange contrast, beautiful magnolias, spreading palmettos, and scores of other varieties of rich Southern plants indicated by their careful training and tasteful arrangement what the hand of culture, aided by this genial clime, had done to adorn the beauteous but unappreciated homes of luxury, wealth, and pride.

The column defiled rapidly along the high level dikes thrown up to regulate the flooding of the rice marshes of Hutchinson's Island. Then another pontoon bridge was passed and our vandal feet for the first time pressed the rebellious soil of South Carolina. A feeling of manly exultation swelled every heart as we realized that our bustling column was indeed threading the live oaks and pines of that state which boasts of having inaugurated a bloody war for slavery. Yes, we were indeed at the threshold of the homes of the Rhetts, the Keits, the Hammonds, the Pickens, and the Haynes, who for 20 years or more have been plotting that abominable treason which in 1861 tore down the starry flag from the battlements of Sumter. My mind roamed back to Big Bethel, Manassas, Chancellorsville, Chickamauga, and a score of other bloody fields and bethought itself of the river upon rivers of the bravest and best blood which have been poured out by this unholy crusade against human rights, and then returned to fasten the deepest and most damning of the guilt upon the men whom these dark swamps have nurtured, the so-called chivalry of South Carolina. 'Now we'll repay them for the reason and avenge all this blood,' was the inward thought of every mind, and most terribly has that purpose been executed.

I have already in previous papers traced the march of the left wing as far as Robertsville, South Carolina. Here this portion of the army abandoned all its communications and moved directly into the interior of the Rebel dominions. The 20th Corps marched from Robertsville on February 2, 1865. The 14th Corps, not having yet succeeded in crossing the Savannah, did not follow until several days later. The column shaped its course toward Barnwell Courthouse as if about to move on Augusta. The right wing was in the meantime coming up from Pocotaligo and moving toward the same point. Thus the enemy was led to believe that General Sherman designed to concentrate his forces near Branchville and consequently sent most of his available troops to that important railroad center. But our skillful leader saw that he could take Branchville then go by, leaving Hardee and his chivalry to patiently guard their carefully built breastworks far in our rear. The 20th Corps crossed the Big Salkahatchie River on the 6th and were joined to the right wing of the army. The enemy now seemed to suppose that our entire army would move upon Augusta and prepared himself to surrender a place which it did not seem likely he could defend against such odds. A portion of Hood's army had reached the city but what could they avail against Sherman's well-appointed legions? While the Rebel leaders still meditated upon this troublesome question General Sherman wheeled his splendid army to the right and moved directly toward the South Carolina Railroad. The 20th Corps struck the road near Graham's Station on February 7th. Our old occupation of ripping up rails, piling up ties and bending iron was immediately resumed. In a few hours, almost the whole army including the cavalry was strung along the track and vast volumes of dense black smoke rolled upward along a line of 15 miles or more which indicated the total ruin of the railroad which for so long a time had furnished immense supplies to the armies of the rebellion. A portion of the track was badly worn but most of it was laid with new English iron of excellent quality. Care was taken to make thorough work of heating and twisting the rails. By the 11th, all destructible railroad property from the Edisto bridge to Williston, a distance of 35 miles, was either utterly destroyed or rendered unserviceable. Thus the last line of communication between Richmond and the Gulf States was disposed of.

Up to this time no serious opposition had been encountered by our forces. The Rebel cavalry hung about our flanks, now capturing a forager or two, and then burning a bridge. But the pontoon trains were always on hand and streams afforded no considerable barrier to our progress. The army moved leisurely along, going where it wished and gathering its subsistence from the rich plantations of the treason loving Rebels of South Carolina.

Columbia now lay before us, Augusta on our left, and Charleston on our right. The enemy seemed uncertain in his opinions as to which of these three points we would now move on. But General Sherman exhibited no hesitation in the execution of his plans. The work of destroying the railroad was no sooner completed than the entire army resumed its march. The four corps moved on different roads keeping nearly abreast with each other. The right wing diverged far enough toward that flank to strike the railroad leading from Branchville to Columbia to Orangeburg. The place first named had already been evacuated by the enemy and our army without delay continued its march to Columbia.

On the 13th the 20th Corps crossed the North Fork of the Edisto. On the 15th its advance entered the town of Lexington. Thus without scarcely the shadow of resistance our army reached the environs of Columbia. Yet it was known that the enemy had considerable force there and very few seemed to think that the place would fall without some sort of blow struck in its defense. On the morning of the 16th the advance resumed at an early hour. The trains were left in the rear and the column was stripped for action. Every preparation was made for a vigorous assault upon any force that might have the temerity to attempt to withstand our progress toward the Rebel capital. The troops marched rapidly for each corps was endeavoring to be the first to enter the city. At 11 A.M., cannonading was heard at the front. The 15th Corps had reached the banks of the Congaree and was shelling the city across that stream. The enemy appeared but made no serious resistance. He seemed to be preparing to abandon the place to its fate. He withdrew during the ensuing night and the glorious banner of the Union was hoisted on the capital building early on the following morning. Thus the birthplace of the first Ordinance of Secession was at length brought back to the authority and dominion of the United States government.

Previous to our occupation of the city the Rebel governor had issued the most urgent appeals to his subjects to immediately rally to the defense of the state and promised the utter overthrow of our army. He recommended his people to destroy all provisions that might fall into our hands, to block up the roads, burn the bridges, and in every possible way harass and annoy our column. But these appeals availed no more than would in incoherent ravings of the pinioned mad man. General Joseph Wheeler, commanding the Rebel cavalry, when asked to report how much force he had with which to hold the South Carolina Railroad is said to have sarcastically replied that he had three brigades and five proclamations.

The Rebel newspapers also made the most frantic appeals to the people to come out in response to the call of their governor. They boasted that if Charleston might be called the cradle of secession, Columbia was the very couch of its birth. They therefore called most vehemently upon every able-bodied man to come quickly to the defense of the city which was so intimately associated with the history of the rebellion. But the valorous chivalry could not see it in that light. In fact, they considered their blood of too royal a tincture to have it poured out by such a set of varlets as Sherman's thieves. They had rather fight 'gentlemen' or men of 'honor.' Then, too, there was a vast difference between fighting 60,000 such scape-graces as Sherman commanded and bombarding with mortar, paixhan, and petard, a helpless garrison of 60 patriots shut up in an isolated fort a mile or two away. Duelists and negro-whippers are inclined to be somewhat choice in their method of dispatching live Yankees. In the first place, they would rather not have too many of them collected together in the same locality. Secondly the shrewd methods of ambuscade, torpedoes, and poisoned wells are better adapted to their ideas of refined and effective warfare. Thirdly, the code of honor prescribes that combatants shall have an equal amount of choice in the time and place of fighting, the weapons to be used, the distance from each other, etc. But in our rough and tumble style of warfare one party often arrogates to himself the exclusive regulation of all these matters. Consequently chivalry of the first water are often compelled to deny themselves the pleasure of fighting us on account of scruples about these points of honor. So, I fancy, it was in this case. Consequently Sherman captured Columbia and did with it what he pleased.

And what did he please to do? Not probably, to destroy it, yet nevertheless, it was destroyed. A large quantity of spirituous liquors was found in the city and a great many of our soldiers became intoxicated. Then began a scene which beggars description. House after house was fired and soon the whole town was in flames. The fire engines were ordered out but the men made of a mockery of working them. When, perchance, a few willing hands attempted to use them in stopping the conflagration, others unseen cut the hose and rendered the whole machinery useless. Officers appealed to the men to stop the pillaging and destruction, but their words fell on deaf ears or else provoked only maudlin replies. Yet I would not have anyone believe that the discipline of our army is so lax that it could not have been enforced under almost any other circumstances. The troops fully realized that they were in Columbia, the birthplace of nullification and treason. They thought of the dangers they had passed, the sufferings endured on account of the unholy war here originated. The taunting epithets of 'cowardly Yankees,' 'mudsills,' and 'greasy mechanics' crossed their minds and inflamed them with rage. The dark treachery of Sumter loomed up before them-long gloomy processions of bony forms, the starved victims of Southern dungeons, passed in review before their mental vision. What wonder then that Columbia was destroyed? Rather it is not a wonder that one stone of their traitorous city was left lying upon another.

Notes in Dixie Vol. XXVIII

Near Goldsboro, North Carolina
March 28, 1865

The fall of Charleston was nearly coincident with that of Columbia. If the enemy evacuated the one to save the other, he made a most egregious and ridiculous blunder. Yet we might, perhaps, find more excuse for the awkwardness of his strategy could we observe it from a different standpoint. The Rebel leaders had not calculated upon this unexampled winter campaign. After Sherman's splendid success in capturing Savannah they supposed that, a la McClellan, he would quietly sit down, enjoy the glory he had won, and wait for the weather. In the meantime they proposed to collect their scattered forces, fortify their defensible points, and prepare themselves generally for our spring campaign. But they miscalculated their man. In trusting in the interminable bogs and swamps of South Carolina and in the watery atmosphere of a Southern winter as obstacles against the genius and energy which carried our army from Atlanta to Savannah, they were decidedly victims of misplaced confidence. The world was about to be taught a lesson in strategic movements as it had not received since the days of Napoleon. In spite of winter, mud, rain, swamps, and bogs, the two wings of the grand Army of Georgia swept northward in resistless flight, until their ominous twin shadows rested over the doomed capital of South Carolina. So sudden and unexpected was the blow that our enemies moved hither and thither in confused haste, apparently not knowing what to do. In spite of all their desperate threatening and truculent bravado, they abandoned one after another of their strongholds and the old flag waved in triumph over the proudest citadels of the rebellion.

The enemy had no sooner fled in dismay from Columbia than our great leader prepared to improve the opportunity now afforded him to work still more alarming mischief to the Confederacy. On February 17th, the left wing moved to the Saluda River and immediately began crossing that stream eight miles above Columbia. Inexperienced persons have but little idea of the tedium accompanying the crossing of so large a force by a single bridge. Here, for once, the whole command is concentrated and compelled to pass in slow procession by a given point. An immense train of nearly 2,000 wagons drags its slow length along at a most wearisome pace. All day and night the sluggish wheels keep moving, save when they are interrupted as they are every half hour or so by some disarrangement of the bridge. In addition to the trains are the cavalry and thousands of mounted men, all of whom must pass over the single boat bridge, the safety of which requires the animals to move in single file. The cattle droves, too, must have their turn when the water happens to be too deep for fording. Thus the motley procession of men, horses, wagons, mules, and cattle moves in slow irregular current until all are over.

The passage of the Saluda was concluded on the 18th. The column then shaped its course northwestward, thus making a detour to the left. This gave the army larger scope for foraging purposes which had become by this time an important item. One-fourth rations of bread, sugar, and coffee was all the subsistence the troops now received from the trains. The deficiency had to be made up by foraging. For this purpose each regiment mounted a party of men upon captured mules and horses. These soon became a notorious class in the army and were characteristically styled 'bummers,' 'smokehouse cavalry,' etc. General Sherman is said to have called them his 'subsistence department.' But the truth is there is no term in the English language which does the subject justice. Even Falstaff's ragamuffin files would have been completely eclipsed by one of these parties just returned from an expedition. Even Don Quixote mounted upon his fiery Rosinante or illustrious Ichabod Crane astride Van Ripper's redoubtable Gunpowder might have been eclipsed by one of these improvised cavaliers.

Mounted upon all kinds of steeds, from the broken down hybrid of the train, the discarded jade of the corral, the whinnying colt from the stable yard, and the long-eared discordant scion of ancient Balaam's monitor, up to the well-fed prancing favorite of the stall; clad in all the grotesque costumes which are a soldier's whim aided by the contents of trunks and boxes exhumed from almost every swamp and graveyard could devise; equipped with a gun and knapsack they soon became the terror of all poultry and piggery, the plague of all housewives, the scare crows of the Rebels, the abused of all honest men, the ridicule of all proper men, the scape goat of all mean men, the jest of everybody. The terrified citizens vainly endeavored to conceal their goods and provisions, but no ingenuity of secretion could thwart the ferreting instinct of these men. They became so adept in their art as to be looked upon as professional men of their kind. Thus the chivalry of South Carolina were suddenly confronted with a new style of cavaliers, not so gallant or romantic, it is true, as those of fictitious fame, yet more dangerous and insidious foes than ever tilted lance or leaped a castle's moat. No hen roost was so obscure as to escape their notice; no pig sty so remote or smokehouse so unpretentious as to escape their scrutiny. Sometimes trunks containing clothing and valuables were carefully interred in suspicious graves, and their place of sepulture marked with boards solemnly inscribed with the names and years of pretended dead. It is needless to say that these shrines were almost universally violated. Neither was the sacredness of the cemetery always respected when it had been previously desecrated by the concealment of plate, money, jewels, and firearms among the confined bones of family ancestry. To this extent at least our foragers were acknowledged vandals.

The extent of country which was permeated and stripped by these men was perfectly surprising. It was a common thing for them to go 20 or 30 miles in advance or on the flanks of the column. They thus kept the Rebel cavalry at a distance and the enemy was very rarely permitted to get a glimpse of the main body of the army. Did he attempt to resist them in their excursions, our bummers would immediately concentrate from all points and help each other out of a scrape of which Johnny Reb almost invariably got the worst. In affairs of this kind, prisoners, horses, mules, and large quantities of plunder were often captured by our men. On one occasion, twelve Rebel cavalrymen leaped from their horses and fled to a swamp in order to escape being captured by five bummers, two of whom were unarmed. Thus twelve fine horses with complete equipment became the reward of a little shrewdness and daring.

The amount of subsistence stores obtained by the foragers was immense. In our single Third Brigade it is estimated that during the campaign, 1,000 bushels of sweet potatoes, 100,000 pounds of bacon, 15,000 pounds of flour, 20,000 pounds of meal, 500 beef cattle, and 2,000 live hogs were obtained. In addition to this the same brigade gathered 125,000 pounds of corn and 77,000 pounds of fodder. Besides all this, the brigade captured 200 horses, 350 mules, burned 50 cotton gins and presses, two saw mills, three flouring mills, 1,800 bales of cotton, and destroyed five miles of railroad track. Multiply these estimates by the number of brigades in the army and some idea may be formed of the extent to which the Confederacy has been paying the expenses of a war against itself.

On the 19th, the left wing reached the Broad River at Freshley's Ferry. Our next objective point being Winnsboro, it will be seen by a glance at the map that our army was now executing a grand right wheel around Columbia. The enemy interpreted this movement as an advance upon Charlotte, but how sorely he was deceived in this is already known. His scattered forces still unable to concentrate, Hardee's army which was now increased by the Charleston garrison, moved northward toward Cheraw, hoping probably to intercept us during our eastward march from Charlotte. But as we did not go to Charlotte, Hardee soon found it necessary to pick himself up and get out of our way.

On the 21st of February the 20th Corps marched into Winnsboro. This is a handsome village situated on the railroad from Columbia to Charlotte and in the midst of one of the most wealthy, aristocratic, and rebellious portions of South Carolina. Our foragers were now 'in clover' and right well did they improve their opportunities. I remember seeing the following equipage pass through the principal street of Winnsboro: it was a splendid barouche, to which were attached a fine span of matched horses with silver mounted harness. The top of the vehicle had been summarily torn off for convenience sake and the following was an inventory of its freight as nearly as I can recollect: six soldiers with stove pipe hats a la Uncle Abe. One barrel of sorghum molasses, several bushes of sweet potatoes, some fresh pork, a big haul of nice hams, several bunches of chickens and geese hung out on the sides of the carriage by way of ornament. I have mentioned this pageant only as a specimen. I have often witnessed others of the same sort.

Having a curiosity to know something of the people of Winnsboro we called on one of the first families. The mansion presented a rather ordinary appearance on the outside but we had no sooner entered than we bowed ourselves, rather were ushered, into a gorgeously furnished parlor. The furniture and trappings were of that high style of art which suggests great wealth and very poor taste. In fact there was as much display as might have been seen on a country muster day before the present war. 'Evidently we've struck oil,' we thought as we glanced around the department. The mistress of the house, a brusque keen-eyed old lady dressed in black soon appeared. She was accosted with 'This is a fine day, madam.' 'Well I don't know,' said she. 'Perhaps you may think it a fine day but to us it does not seem very fine.' 'These Northern blasts are not considered very wholesome down this way,' suggested someone inquiringly. The old lady replied by a sort of sarcastic leer and gentle upturning of the nasal organ. She evidently considered herself assailed by a set of abolition mudsills and made herself as unsociable as possible. It is needless to say that the interview did not last much longer, and that we soon turned our backs upon Southern hospitality in Winnsboro.

There is another class of people pervading this country to whom it may be proper to speak a word here. They usually constitute the great majority of the population and are generally styled by the wealthy classes as 'common people' or 'white trash.' The distinctions of caste are recognized in South Carolina almost as distinctly as in the aristocracies of the Old World. The rich and the poor have but little affiliation. The latter in all political and social relations are hardly more that servitors of the former. Being deprived in a great measure of the rights of freemen and the amenities of a truly republican society, they are usually very ignorant. Some of their expressions in regard to our army were very amusing. A widow woman told me that her husband died at Hanover Conjunction in Virginia. Another, in describing a skirmish near her house, said that our folks had 'two strings of fight' meaning two lines of battle. These people commonly spoke of the cavalry as the 'critter company' and of the artillery as the 'gun company.' In conversation they called themselves 'we'uns' and us, 'you'uns.' A captured Rebel soldier when asked what he preferred to do, replied that if he had his 'rather' he would rather go home and stay there. These and many other droll expressions have become of the current brogue among our soldiers who fully appreciated a good thing and never permit it to 'waste its sweetness.'

The entire army concentrated at Winnsboro. It then shaped its course in a northeasterly direction and moved to the Wataree. This stream was the Rubicon on this campaign. Upon its high and precipitous banks General Sherman evidently expected the enemy to make a decided resistance. But in this he was agreeably disappointed. Without any difficulty, the left wing secured a crossing near Rocky Mount post office on the 22nd of February. Thus the birthday of Washington was signalized by another strategic triumph. While our far-off friends were celebrating this gala day, we were climbing the difficult banks of the Wataree. The passage of this stream was not fully accomplished until the 26th. The army then moved slowly on towards Chesterfield Courthouse. Heavy rains had now set in which added to the treacherous nature of the soil made our march very difficult. Frequently the troops had to work en masse in corduroying the road. The whole surface of the country seemed to be a bed of clay and sand. Sometimes the sand so far predominates as to destroy all firmness of the soil. A single horse cannot pass in such places without getting mired. In the localities almost the entire road must be corduroyed, that is embedded with rails and poles. Even then the trains and artillery are gotten along with great difficulty.

Thus we floundered along through Lancaster and Chesterfield districts. On the 14th of March the army reached the Great Pedee near Cheraw. The Rebels had collected immense quantities of ordnance stores at this point. These fell into our hands and were destroyed. Among other articles captured was a splendid brass field piece which had been presented to the State of South Carolina about the commencement of the war. This piece was fired a goodly number of times in honor of the re-inauguration of Honest Old Abe. So it will be seen that our illustrious President was not forgotten by his nephews on this great triumph day of the Republic. The 20th Corps crossed the Great Pedee at Cheraw during the night of March 6th. Thus the ninth river of the campaign was left behind us. Hardee withdrew his forces from our front and the march was continued without impediment except from the bogs and swamps. At 12 o'clock on March 7th the old Third Brigade crossed the line separating South from North

Carolina. We had now fairly entered the pitch pine region. The eye wearied of the piney pitchy monotony which everywhere presented itself. In vain it wandered in search of some object to change the scene. 'Where to the North, pines trees in prospect rise; Where to the East, pine trees assail the skies; Where to the West, pine trees obstruct the view; Where in the South, pine trees forever grow.'

The country now became wretchedly poor and the occupation of our bummers was gone. Now and then a squalid cabin would be found which was the home of some distiller of turpentine. To me it was a mystery how the few inhabitants of the country lived. I tried to conjure their daily bill of fare and finally made it out as follows: breakfast of pitch muffins, rosin biscuit, fried tar. Dinner of turpentine soup, pitch pudding, and tar pie. Supper of chewing gum. This information is not obtained from the oldest settler but is simply deduced from observations of the country. When the troops are on the march they usually kindle fire at every halt. A soldier can hardly stop ten minutes without setting fire to something. It matters not what comes in his way, whether it be a fence, a log heap, or a corn crib; if it will make a fire suitable for warming his hands or cooking a tinful of coffee he will apply the match to it. Thus these combustible turpentine forests all along the line of march became fired. The gum which gathers on the outside of each tree that has been tapped for turpentine is very flammable. Consequently when the fire begins to spread itself among the dry debris of the forest it soon communicates itself to this gum and the trunk of each tree becomes enveloped in a shroud of rigid flame. This will continue until the gum is all consumed which requires about 20 minutes. The appearance of a pine forest burning in this way is at night especially very beautiful. It resembles very much the myriad fires of the camp.

The effect upon our soldiers of being constantly exposed to the dense black smoke caused by the burning of pitch pine was remarkable. They become transformed in spite of themselves into 'colored troops.' Indeed there is no exaggeration in saying that an enemy might easily have mistaken them for Negro soldiers. I have seen many a man in the fineaments of whose countenance was so disguised by the all-pervading pitchy soot that I doubt if his best friends could have recognized him. As might be inferred, much of the country, particularly that in the vicinity of the Lumber River, is very wild. During the march of 18 miles I observed only three dwellings and these were rude cabins. Wild deer were seen skipping about in the woods as the column moved along. The road was little more than a mere opening through the interminable pine forests.

On the 9th of March the 20th Corps crossed Drowning Creek on the Lumber River at McFarland's Bridge. The old Third Brigade had the honor of being assigned to work the reconstructing of this bridge which had been destroyed by the enemy. Emerging from the gloomy pine forests which border the deep narrow channel of the Lumber we came into a more fertile district and our foragers soon added some other articles of diet to the parched corn which had begun to be nearly our only means of subsistence. On the 11th the Left Wing arrived at Fayetteville. The troops had hardly gotten possession of the town when the whistle of a steamer was heard far down the Cape Fear River. It was a Union gunboat coming up from Wilmington. Such is the vast energy with which our government prosecutes this war! How amazing! A Union steamer from Wilmington arriving at Fayetteville almost coincident with the Grand Army from Savannah! Could such splendid episodes and coincidences occur in a war waged for a cause less great, less just than ours? Methinks not. God watches over the destinies of this nation and guides its armies and fleets. He prospers our cause for the reason that it is just and in this sign we shall conquer.

Notes in Dixie Vol. XXIX

Near Goldsboro, North Carolina
March 31, 1865

When the Army of Georgia reached Savannah, its great leader announced in General Orders that he was satisfied with its success so far, but that the campaign was not yet completed. Accordingly, as soon as the ammunition and subsistence trains were reloaded and the troops well clothed, the army continued to prosecute the task proposed for it. I have, in previous numbers of these papers, traced its operations as far as to Fayetteville, North Carolina. Here again the troops received a congratulatory order from the chief, setting forth the splendor of their achievements and announcing that the campaign was not yet over, but would be continued as soon as some of the most necessary supplies were received from Wilmington. To use General Sherman's own language, we had "one more march to make."

Accordingly, we had hardly finished perusing the meager contents of our mail which, like wine, were none the less relished on account of being old, until we again slung our knapsacks and resumed out peregrinations among the pines. On March 14th, the 20th Corps crossed the Cape Fear River opposite Fayetteville. But ere I bid adieu to this ancient town of the Old North State, let me briefly discuss its merits. Like most other towns and cities in the Southern states, it wears the air of being finished. The most ingenious Yankee could hardly add anything that would make its completeness more complete. In short, it is one of that conservative sort of old towns which seem to know what they are about, and ask no odds of anybody. Belonging to the great independent Confederacy, of course it feels independent. To be sure, during the short occupation by Sherman's hordes, its lofty spirit was brought down to the ashes of humiliation. But when these decamped, that is, evacuated the place and retreated from its limits, its wonted highmindedness doubtless was resumed.

Yet it is fair to acknowledge that Fayetteville has some agreeable qualities even for a migratory Yankee. I must confess that I found more true hospitality here than in almost any other Southern town. The secret of this is found in a vein of genuine Unionism which underlies the turbid current secession feeling. Here, almost for the first time, I observed unmistakable evidences that there is a truly loyal party in this section of the country. Here for the very first time I heard the declaration from a representative from the higher circle of Southern society that he 'loved the Union.' The words made me feel more hopeful for my country and humanity. A man of wealth, education and culture, born and bred in the very center of Rebeldom loved the Union! The fact pleasantly surprised me and yet it was not surprising for how can any good and sensible man help but loving the Union?

Directly after crossing the Cape Fear River, the two wings of the army again diverged from each other. The right moved by the most direct roads leading to Goldsboro. The left, having sent most of its trains with the right, moved up the left bank of the river toward Raleigh. General Slocum's command being thus stripped for action, it was apparent that in the execution of its share of the program a fight was at least possible. Indeed, when it was considered that Hardee's forces had withdrawn from Fayetteville by the very route we were now taking and were but one day's march removed from us, the probabilities of battle became very strong. It was known to us, too, that Johnston, our old antagonist in Georgia, had assumed the chief command of the Rebel forces and our knowledge of his military character was such as to lead us to the belief that he would give us trouble if such a thing were possible.

On the 15th the left wing reached Kyle's Landing, a point on Cape Fear 16 miles above Fayetteville. The weather had now grown very wet and the mud fathomless. The country was low and flat with very little undulation and thickly timbered with the inevitable pines. Early on the morning of the 16th the column began to drag itself along the wretched road. We had not proceeded far before the old significant booming of artillery announced the presence of an enemy. A drizzling rain filled the air and the dull reverberations resounded gloomily among the pines. If there was a man among us who ever had a relish for a battle he could scarcely have experienced it on that dreary March morning. There was that customary silence in the column which precedes an expected conflict. Each soldier carefully examined his firelock and, as it seemed to me, thought of home. In many a serious countenance I thought I could read the sentiment of the popular army song: 'Just before the battle mother, I am thinking most of you. While upon the field we're watching with the enemy in view; Comrades brave around me lying, filled with thoughts of home and God, for well they know that on the morrow some must sleep beneath the sod.'

Yet there was but little gloominess in the countenances of the men. They seemed to possess their usual calm confidence. Many were barefoot, for they had now marched over 450 miles. All were ragged as might be expected after 60 days of continuous campaigning. Some were clad in nearly complete Rebel uniform, having exchanged their torn and filthy garments for others of gray color but of more sound and cleanly material. But the difference between a blue blouse and a Confederate jacket amounts to but very little if beneath there beats a heart loyal to our country's starry emblem. By 11 A.M., our old Third Brigade had gotten into position and planted its triangular star color within close musket range of the enemy. The line of battle extended through a pine forest, the level surface of which was so swampy and boggy that it required great caution to move about on horseback without becoming mired. The firing had already grown severe, particularly on our left where the Third Division of the 20th Corps had become engaged. It was evident that the enemy was bent on making a determined stand.

Our line had just gotten well into position when it was ordered to advance. Grandly it moved on, bearing the tattered ensigns which had floated in the stormy blasts of a dozen battles. Some had seen the bloody sunset of

Chancellorsville and the three sanguinary days at Gettysburg. All had received fiery baptisms at Wauhatchie, Missionary Ridge, Resaca, New Hope Church, and Peachtree Creek. All had been carried in triumph over the defiant walls of Atlanta and Savannah. Need I say that they now swept all before them? The firing along our front began at nearly the same time as the advance. As the line moved forward the enemy sullenly withdrew firing as opportunity served him. Thus a running fight was kept up for about half a mile. Our line had now swept around the Rebel left flank and compelled the enemy to hastily withdraw from our front. In doing so, he left behind him three pieces of artillery and a considerable number of prisoners. All of these fell into the hands of the Third Division. Our own losses were thus far numerically small though the affair cost us some valuable officers and men.

The new phase that affairs had now taken required that new dispositions be made of the troops. A new line was formed which by 2 P.M. resumed the advance. The Rebels again steadily but stubbornly fell back. They at one time made a desperate effort to turn our right flank. Massing a division (McLaws') they precipitated it upon the cavalry, which was driven back in some confusion. The onset was checked, however, by a brigade of infantry which came up just at the right time and which poured a few volleys so sweeping and destructive into the Rebel columns as to cause them to fall back in great confusion. The fight continued thus desultorily until nightfall by which time the enemy had been driven about two miles. The night closed in dark and stormy and our soldiers slept by their arms within speaking distance of the foe. The wind moaned sadly among the pines as if chanting nature's requiem for the fallen brave. The firing ceased the deep shadows of night gathered over the forest. The enemy took advantage of the darkness and betook himself to hasty flight.

Thus terminated the Battle of Smith's Farm, an affair that cost our brigade 39 officers and men.[196] The march was resumed on the 17th. The column now moved toward Cox's Bridge on the Neuse River, a point ten miles above Goldsboro. Hardee's forces were no longer in our front but upon our left flank. No further trouble was therefore apprehended but in this we were greatly mistaken. Before we reached our destination we were destined to meet the enemy in an encounter as compared to which the firing at Smith's Farm was but a skirmish.

On the 18th the 20th Corps crossed the Black River. The weather had now cleared up but the road continued miserable. The effect upon our wounded of being hauled over such a track was most distressing, yet they bore their suffering bravely and there was very little complaint. At noon on the 19th we were again within hearing of the enemy's cannon. Johnston had succeeded in concentrating his forces near Bentonville. Seeing the two wings of the army separated, he thought himself to crush the left before the right could come to its assistance. He had Hardee's army and the greater portion of Hood's old command, constituting a force of nearly 40,000 men. To fight these we had hardly 25,000 effectives. Johnston therefore felt sanguine of success, and accordingly sent couriers along his lines to announce that the time to strike a decisive blow had at length arrived and the designed to "whip Sherman today."

In each of the two corps (14th and 20th) there were but two divisions available for the fight. Each corps had sent one division to take care of its trains. The two divisions of the 14th Corps being in advance became engaged first. By noon the fighting became severe, though it was as yet nothing more than a mutual development of position by the hostile parties. The First Division of the 20th Corps arrived at the scene of the hostilities at 2 P.M. It was the fortune of the old Third Brigade to be, as usual, sent immediately to the front. The other brigades were placed in position covering the flanks. A vacancy existed at this time in the line of Carlin's Division of the 14th Corps. The 31st Wisconsin, 61st and 82nd Ohio veteran Volunteers were assigned the duty of filling this gap. They were supported by the 143rd New York and 82nd Illinois. Such was the disposition of the five regiments of our brigade. The position was well chosen and the arrangement of the troops was all that could be desired, but we were unfortunate in having no connection on our right or left. There is nothing about which a soldier feels more concern during a fight than his flanks. If he feels that these are secure, and that there is no danger that the enemy will get in his rear, he can meet with redoubled confidence the danger which comes from the front. But in the present instance this assurance was wanting. On either side of us there were wide gaps in the line which, to say the least, offered a great temptation to try and break through. I shall not attempt to fix responsibility of this unfortunate arrangement

---

[196] This engagement is also known as the Battle of Averysboro. The official report shows 3 men killed and 39 wounded in this action.

which, as the sequel will show, jeopardized the safety of the whole army. Suffice it to say that none of it belonged to our brigade commander.

As soon as the line was formed, our men commenced building a breastwork. With no other entrenching tools than hatchets, they built with amazing quickness a respectable shelter from the fire of the Rebel sharpshooters. The instinct of some great and immediate danger seemed to animate them and it was well that it was so. The enemy had already massed his forces for a grand desperate effort to break our line. Our skirmishers had been thrown forward but had gained their position only by gallantly charging across an open field under a sweeping fire. I cannot soon forget the manly heroism of Lieutenant Lyman and his noble comrades in this affair. The word 'forward' was given and well they knew that for some of them it was a death summons. The lieutenant shouted 'Forward! Forward!' and his men obeyed like soldiers. They were following their brave young officer for the last time for he now sleeps his last sleep among the gloomy pines of the field on Bentonville. Alas, how many of the bravest, noblest and best this war costs us! Of such was Lieutenant George Lyman of the 31st Wisconsin Volunteers.[197]

The skirmish line advanced about 200 yards when it encountered the enemy sweeping down upon us in full force. Our skirmishers drew a heavy fire from the Rebels and were compelled to fall back with a severe loss in killed, wounded, and captured. The firing immediately rolled to the left and became very heavy in front of Carlin's line which was considerably advanced instead of it being reformed as it should have been. In five minutes more the enemy struck the line of the Third Brigade which immediately opened fire. We had now but three regiments with which to hold our position, all the others having been previously sent a half mile to the rear to cover the trains. But our brave men were not daunted by their numerical weakness. They proposed to hold their line in spite of all the force that could be brought against them in front.

The fighting had but fairly commenced along our front when it was discovered that the troops on our left were being driven back in great disorder.[198] The enemy followed in close pursuit and in a few minutes emerged from the woods and began closing in upon our rear. There was not a single regiment at hand to check him, for there were no reserves. There was but one alternative left, and that was to fall back and form a new line. This was a bitter dose for our brave old brigade, which had been accustomed to never yield an inch under any circumstances. But every soldier saw what the exigencies of the occasion required and the command to fall back was executed in good order. The line was withdrawn a quarter of a mile when it reformed. This was no sooner done than the enemy again assailed us both in front and flank. There was again a large vacancy in the line on our left and through this Rhett's South Carolina brigade endeavored to force its way. But the gap was fortunately commanded by the artillery and by the 82nd Illinois which had been put in position on the farther side of the vacancy. This gallant regiment joined so galling a fire to that of the artillery that the enemy soon suspended his attempt at a flank movement and

---

[197] Lieutenant Lyman survived his injuries and was discharged in May 1865.

[198] These two brigades of Carlin's division under George Buell and Harrison Hobart were struck in front and on their left flank by Confederate troops of Bates' and D.H. Hill's divisions.

confined his efforts to a front attack.[199] The firing therefore rolled to the right where we now had four regiments in position. The line was still without connection on the right or left and the men were destitute of breastworks. The ground being level afforded no shelter from the enemy's fire. The situation could scarcely have been more trying to our troops. But with the firm determination of heroes they maintained their ground. The first onset of the enemy was gallantly repulsed in 20 minutes. The men took advantage of the temporary lull in the firing to gather rails and build a temporary breastwork. This was not finished before the enemy renewed his attack. The battle now raged with great fury and became fearfully sublime. It was a fight worthy of our old times on the Potomac and the Chattahoochee. Our lines were shrouded with a sulphurous canopy and the incessant roar of the musketry mingled with the deep thunderous bellowing of artillery added an awful and terrible solemnity to the scene. The murderous bullets whistled madly through the air, and their bleeding victims were being continually borne to the rear or stretched lifeless upon the cold earth.

The second attack of the enemy continued about 30 minutes when it was also repulsed. The Rebels withdrew into the woods, leaving behind them numbers of deserters who now sought admission to our line. I need not say that they were warmly welcomed to Union hospitality. The appearance of these poor fellows as they came running over our breastworks with pale faces and fluttering bosoms was most singular. It was a pleasing episode amid the fearful tragedy, a glance of sunlight in the storm. At each cessation of the firing the breastworks were strengthened by the collection of additional materials. It was well that this was done for the after a short breathing spell the enemy advanced a third and still more desperate attack. This met with no better success than those which preceded it. A fourth and fifth were in like manner repulsed. By this time the sun was setting and an evening gloom gathered over the field. The enemy withdrew to the cover of the woods, the musketry dwindled down to silence, and the cannons' lips grew cold. After a desperate struggle victory had perched upon our banners and a wild hurrah rang out amid the solemn pines. Our weary soldiers were relieved by fresh troops and sought their nightly bivouac.

The 20th was marked by no important event except the occupation by our forces of the ground lost on the previous day. On the 21st the 15th Corps came up from Cox's Bridge and striking the enemy on his left flank and rear, compelled him to abandon his position. On the morning of the 22nd the whole field was ours and our march toward the Neuse was continued without interruption. During the afternoon of the 23rd the 20th Corps crossed at Neuse at Cox's Bridge and on the 24th arrived at Goldsboro. Thus on the 66th day after leaving Savannah our great campaign terminated. The army had accomplished a march of 494 miles during which it crossed 12 deep and difficult rivers, captured eight important towns including the capital of South Carolina, destroying the whole railroad system of the Southern Atlantic states excepting North Carolina, defeated the enemy in two pitched battles and compelled the evacuation of Charleston, Georgetown, Wilmington, and Kingston. Who will not say that this is the severest blow the rebellion has ever yet received?[200]

For the special comfort of all Rebel sympathizers let me say that the campaign inaugurated at Atlanta, Georgia on the 15th day of November 1864 is not yet ended. In due time this army will resume its onward march. Where that march will end is not yet definitely known, but for one, I could heartily wish that its terminus might be at a certain cozy little town in central Ohio.

---

[199] This attack on the left flank of Robinson's brigade was made by two small brigades (Elliott's and Rhett's) belonging to Brigadier General William B. Taliaferro's division, which included some former artillerists who had been converted into infantrymen.

[200] The 31st Wisconsin suffered the most heavily of the six regiments of the brigade at Bentonville, losing a total of 70 of the brigade's 107 casualties. Seventeen year old Corporal Peter Anderson of Co. B, 31st Wisconsin was awarded the Medal of Honor for his heroism on March 19, 1865 when, during the retreat from the first line, he dragged an abandoned field piece from the field unassisted.

March Through the Carolinas

Itinerary of the Third Brigade, First Division, 20th Corps

Nightly camps of the march

January 28th	Bradham's, S.C.
January 29-February 1st	Robertsville, S.C.
February 2nd	Lawtonville, S.C.
February 3rd	Duck Branch, S.C.
February 4th	Smyrna, S.C.
February 5th	Buford's Bridge, Big Salkehatchie River, S.C.
February 6th	Little Salkehatchie River, S.C.
February 7-8th	Graham's Station, S.C.
February 9-10th	96-Mile Turnout, S.C.
February 11th	1 mile north of South Fork of Edisto River, S.C.
February 12th	Jeffcoat's Bridge, North Fork of Edisto River, S.C.
February 13th	8 miles north of North Fork of Edisto River, S.C.
February 14th	Columbia Crossroads, S.C.
February 15th	Red Branch Creek, S.C.
February 16th	4 miles south of Columbia, S.C.
February 17th	Zion Church, S.C.
February 18th	Crooked Branch, S.C.
February 19th	Alston Depot, S.C.
February 20th	Myrtle Hill, S.C.
February 21st	Winnsboro, S.C.
February 22nd	Rocky Mount, S.C.
February 23rd	4 miles north of Wateree River, S.C.
February 24-25th	Patterson's Plantation, S.C.
February 26th	Hanging Rock, S.C.
February 27th	3 miles north of Hanging Rock Creek, S.C.
February 28th	Little Lynch's Creek, S.C.
March 1st	Johnson's Plantation, S.C.
March 2nd	Chesterfield, S.C.
March 3rd	Potter's Plantation, S.C.
March 4-5th	4 miles south of Great Pedee River, S.C.
March 6th	Cheraw, S.C.
March 7th	Wilmington & Rutherford Railroad, N.C.
March 8th	McFarland's Bridge, Lumber River, N.C.
March 9th	2 miles north of McFarland's Bridge, N.C.
March 10th	Rockfish Creek, N.C.
March 11-12th	2 miles south of Fayetteville, N.C.
March 13th	Fayetteville, N.C.
March 14th	3 miles north of Cape Fear River, N.C.
March 15th	Silver Run, N.C.
March 16th	Averysboro, N.C.
March 17th	Black River, N.C.
March 18-21st	Bentonville, N.C.
March 23rd	Falling Creek, N.C.
March 24th	Cox's Bridge, Neuse River, N.C.
March 25th	Goldsboro, N.C.

Report of Brigadier General James S. Robinson, U.S. Army, commanding Third Brigade, of operations January 17-March 24, 1865

Headquarters, Third Brigade, First Division, 20th Army Corps
Near Goldsborough, North Carolina, March 27, 1865

I have the honor to submit the following report of the services of this brigade during the late campaign:

On the 17th of January last my command crossed the Savannah River opposite Savannah, Georgia. The brigade consisted at this time of six regiments as follows: 31st Wisconsin Volunteers, Col. F.H. West, 82nd Ohio Veteran Volunteers, Lt. Col. D. Thomson, 143rd New York Volunteers, Lt. Col. H. Watkins, 101st Illinois Volunteers, Lt. Col. J.B. LeSage, 82nd Illinois Volunteers, Maj. F.H. Rolshausen, and 61st Ohio Veteran Volunteers, Capt. John Barrett. The regiment last named was at this time detached for special duty in the quartermaster's department at the headquarters of the Military Division of the Mississippi. It did not rejoin the command until the 10th of February. My brigade encamped during the night of the 17th about four miles from Screven's Ferry. Here it remained until 2 P.M. of the 18th when its march was resumed. At 5 P.M. my command encamped on Garrett's plantation, four miles below Hardeeville. On the 19th the march was continued as far as Purrysburg, which point was reached about noon that day. My brigade remained at Purrysburg until the 28th of January. The weather had become so inclement as to preclude operations until that date. In the meantime, communication with Savannah was kept open and my command was provided with some much needed supplies. On the 28th the march was resumed. My command camped the following night at Bradham's. On the 29th it pushed forward toward Robertsville at which point it arrived at 1:30 P.M. The enemy's cavalry was driven back to this point by the 143rd New York, which had preceded the rest of my command, having gone forward to assist in repairing the road. When on the point of entering Robertsville the regiment was relieved by the Second Brigade.

My command remained at Robertsville until the 2nd of February. The march was resumed on that date, the column moving in the direction of Lawtonville. The Third Division, which led the advance, encountered the enemy's cavalry near this place during the afternoon. My brigade came up at 3:30 P.M. and was so disposed as to cover the left flank and a portion of the train. The enemy was driven off by the Third Division, and my command encamped near Lawtonville at 6 P.M. Lt. Col. E.S. Salomon of the 82nd Illinois, who had been absent on leave, here rejoined and assumed command of his regiment. The march was continued on the 3rd at 7 A.M. At 1:30 P.M., the column reached Beech Branch Post Office. Shortly afterward my brigade was ordered to reconnoiter the road leading to Matthews' Bluff. My command moved out this road about four miles when it was discovered that the enemy's cavalry had abandoned their camp in that vicinity on the night previous. After obtaining a considerable quantity of provisions and burning one cotton gin containing 30 bales of cotton, my command returned to the division and encamped near Duck Branch Post Office. On the 4th my brigade recommenced its march, leading the division, at 8 A.M. My regiments were distributed through the trains of the First and Third Divisions. The road being extremely bad, my pioneer corps was kept almost constantly employed repairing it. The troops assisted as often as necessary. At 7 P.M. the command reached Smyrna where it encamped for the night. On the 5th my brigade marched, via Allendale and Hay's Crossroads, to Buford's bridge on the Big Salkehatchie River. This river was crossed about noon of the 6th. The troops then moved in the direction of Barnwell, but the trains were sent by a different road, accompanying those of the 15th Corps. The 82nd Illinois was detached to assist in guarding them. At 6:30 P.M., my brigade encamped near the Little Salkehatchie River, where it was rejoined by the 82nd Illinois. My command crossed the Little Salkehatchie at 10 A.M. on the 7th. At 4:15 P.M. it struck the South Carolina Railroad near Graham's Station. Early on the morning of the 8th my troops moved two miles above Graham's and commenced destroying the railroad. They ripped up the rails and after having heated them by means of fires built of ties, bent them so thoroughly as to render them useless. During the day, my men effectually destroyed two miles of the track. They also burned one sawmill, four cotton gins and presses, and 140 bales of cotton. My command encamped near Graham's during the ensuing night. On the 9th my brigade marched to Blackville, which point it reached about noon, having guarded a portion of the train on the route. From Blackville it moved up the railroad as far as 96-Mile Turnout, where it encamped for the night. Early on the morning of the 10th my regiments resumed the work of destroying the railroad. Commencing at 96-Mile Turnout, they worked westward and destroyed over two miles and a half of the track. They were assisted by the Michigan Engineers, who twisted the rails. My foragers on this day captured a considerable number of fine horses and mules and burned one cotton mill.

At 8 A.M. on the 11th my brigade marched from 96-Mile Turnout, moving in the direction of New Bridge on the South Fork of the Edisto River. The brigade crossed the Edisto at this point at 5 P.M. and encamped one mile beyond. My foragers on this day obtained a considerable number of horses and mules and large quantities of provisions. My troops also burned two cotton gins, one cotton press, and 25 bales of cotton. On the 12th my brigade was entrusted with the care of the cavalry train, consisting of 250 wagons. During the march, my troops were distributed through the train and charged with its protection. At 6 P.M., the command reached a point near Jeffcoat's Bridge near the North Fork of the Edisto River, and there encamped. My foragers brought in a number of horses and mules and burned considerable cotton. My brigade crossed the North Fork of the Edisto at 2 P.M. on the 13th. It then moved eight miles in a northerly direction and encamped. The march was continued at 7 A.M. on the 14th. My brigade moved on this day in advance of the corps. The 82nd Illinois, being my leading regiment, was sent forward as advance guard. The enemy's cavalry hovered around the front and flanks, and occasionally made a dash upon the foraging parties and stragglers. In one of these bold adventures, he captured Capt. Benjamin Reynolds of the 143rd New York Volunteers, acting assistant inspector general upon my staff. Capt. Reynolds was at the time of his capture near the road and between the corps escort and the vanguard. A detachment of hostile cavalry unexpectedly dashed upon him and carried him off before he could be rescued. At 11 A.M. my brigade reached Columbia Crossroads. The 82nd Illinois handsomely drove the enemy's cavalry back about three miles beyond this point. The regiment then rejoined the brigade, which had been encamped for the night. Later in the day, a foraging party, under Lt. Col. Salomon, was sent up the Columbia Road about five miles, but owing to the barrenness of the country was unsuccessful and returned at nightfall. On the 15th, 148 wagons of the train were assigned to the care of my brigade. The regiments were distributed through the train and directed to be unusually watchful against attacks from the enemy's cavalry. The column moved on the Lexington road. At 2 P.M. seven prisoners were brought in by foragers from the 82nd Ohio. At 3 P.M., the brigade reached Congaree Creek, the bridge over which had been burned by the enemy. While the column awaited the repair of the bridge, a squad of five foragers from the 82nd Ohio brought in eleven good horses with complete equipments, all of which they had captured from a detachment of Rebel cavalry. Twelves horses were taken, but one being severely wounded had to be abandoned. My brigade crossed Congaree Creek at 6 P.M. The road beyond contained many boggy places which retarded the march very much. My advance regiment did not get into camp until 10 P.M. At that hour the head of the column reached the crossroads near Red Branch Creek.

At 7:30 on the morning of the 16th, my brigade moved in the direction of Columbia. The troops marched unencumbered by wagons, the trains being left in charge of the Second Division and the column being stripped for action. At noon cannonading was heard toward the right, supposed to be caused by the advance of the 15th Corps. At 9:30 my brigade crossed the unfinished line of railroad constructed between Columbia and Augusta. At 10:45 it arrived within five miles of Columbia without having met any opposition. It was now ascertained that the 15th Corps had reached the Congaree opposite the city. At 3 P.M. my brigade crossed a small creek and encamped. On the 17th my command marched to Zion Church, a point on the right bank of the Saluda. My troops encamped at nightfall near the pontoon bridge which had been laid at that point. On the following morning they crossed the Saluda. My brigade, being in the rear of the corps, moved three miles beyond the bridge and halted to await the passing of the troops and trains. The 101st Illinois was stationed on the left bank near the bridge to cover its removal. At 4:30 P.M., the rest of corps having all passed, my entire command resumed its march. The troops continued to move until 10 o'clock at night when they encamped at Crooked Branch. On the following day (February 19th) my brigade was placed in charge of the entire division train. The column moved at 10 A.M. and in an hour afterward reached Rockville Post Office. At 2 P.M. it left the road and pursued the crest of a ridge directly through the woods and fields. The soil was soft and gravelly, rendering it very difficult for the trains to get through. At 5:30 P.M. my brigade encamped near the Broad River about one mile below Alston Depot. Foragers from the 31st Wisconsin captured on this day two horses and fifteen mules. The party from the 82nd Ohio captured eight mules and burned one cotton gin with 23 bales of cotton. At 9 A.M. on the 20th, my brigade crossed Broad River. The column then moved northeastward and at 11 A.M. crossed Little River at Gibson's. The country now became quite undulating and we seemed to have gotten fairly out of the swamps. There were many well-stocked plantations and our foragers brought us a plentiful supply of provisions. At 3 P.M. the column struck the direct road to Winnsboro. At 4 P.M. the troops encamped at Myrtle Hill. The march was resumed at 9 A.M. on the 21st. My brigade was put in charge of 420 wagons. The column moved through a fine, undulating country toward Winnsboro. My command arrived at this place at 4 P.M. At 6 P.M. it encamped three miles beyond. At 10 A.M. of the 22nd it resumed its march, having been put in charge of 540 wagons. At 2 P.M. it passed Wateree Church and at 4 reached Wateree Creek. Only three of my regiments, together with the wagons assigned them, succeeded in getting over this stream until the bridge broke down. These regiments, excepting the 101st Illinois which was detached by the division commander to cover a side road, moved on toward Rocky Mount Post Office, near which point they encamped at midnight. The regiments which had been cut off by the breaking of the bridge over Wateree Creek did not get into camp until toward morning.

My brigade crossed the Wateree River on a pontoon bridge at 10 A.M. on the 23rd. After crossing it was directed to assist the trains in getting up the high and difficult hill on the left bank. My command was thus kept employed until 3:30 P.M. when it continued on its march four miles further and encamped. On the 24th my brigade marched at 7:30 A.M. in the advance of the corps. The rain which had commenced falling during the previous night continued throughout most of this day. The soil of this region, any time soft and boggy, now became doubly so, and the trains moved with great difficulty. At 10 A.M. the head of the column encountered the 17th Corps moving on the only road that could be taken by the 20th Corps. The troops encamped on Patterson's plantation and here remained until 2 P.M. on the 26th when the march was resumed. My brigade had charge of 112 wagons. The road was extremely bad and had to be corduroyed almost entire. At nightfall, my command encamped at a crossroads two miles from Hanging Rock Post Office. Early on the following morning, it moved forward to that point. Then crossing a stream of the same name it advanced three miles further and encamped. On this day some foragers of my command brought in a handsome silk banner inscribed on one side thus: 'Presented by the ladies to the Lancaster Invincibles.' My brigade marched again at 7 A.M. on the 28th in charge of the train of the Second Division. A drizzling rain had kept falling during the previous night and continued through the day. The road consequently became very bad. The first two miles of the road had to be corduroyed almost entire. At 11 A.M. the brigade passed Horton's. After this the road became much better and the train moved along rapidly. At 2 P.M. the brigade crossed Little Lynch's Creek on a substantial wooden bridge which the enemy had left standing. The troops encamped one mile from the bridge at 4 P.M. The 82nd Illinois was, by order of the corps commander, sent forward twelve miles to seize and hold the bridge over Lynch's Creek. The regiment pushed rapidly forward and succeeded in obtaining possession of the bridge by 10 P.M. The enemy made no resistance.

Our march was resumed at 6 A.M. on March 1st. At 11:30 A.M. my brigade crossed Lynch's Creek on the bridge seized by the 82nd Illinois at Ferrily's Ford. It then moved four miles farther and encamped on Johnson's plantation. Early on the following morning the march was continued in the direction of Chesterfield Courthouse. My troops guarded the train of the division as far as Big Black Creek, where they were relieved by troops from the Third Division, and my brigade moved forward unencumbered. The First Brigade, in my advance, began skirmishing with the enemy about 2 P.M. At one time my command was ordered up to its support but did not happen to be needed. Afterward it moved rapidly forward and arrived at Chesterfield at 4:30 P.M. After marching through the town my troops went into position and finally encamped just beyond it. At 9 A.M. on the 3rd my brigade marched to the upper bridge over Thompson's Creek, which stream it crossed by fording. It then moved down the creek to the lower bridge and went into position covering an important crossroads. It was at this time expected that the entire command would push forward to Cheraw and attack the enemy there, but before the movement was commenced intelligence was received that the Right Wing had succeeded in gaining possession of the town. No farther advance was therefore made and my brigade encamped for the night on Potter's plantation. Next day (March 4th) my brigade marched again at 4 P.M. having in charge 180 wagons of the train. At 5 P.M. it crossed Little Westfield and at midnight Big Westfield Creek. Shortly after crossing the latter stream my troops encamped at a point about four miles from the Great Pedee River. My brigade remained in this position until 9 A.M. on the 6th when it marched again in charge of 180 wagons of the division train. The road being good, the column moved along rapidly and at 3 P.M. arrived at Cheraw. Here my brigade remained until 11 o'clock at night when it crossed the Great Pedee on a pontoon bridge. The troops continued to march until they reached a point four miles beyond the bridge where they encamped three hours after midnight. The march was resumed again at 7:30 on the following morning (March 7th). The column moved in a northeasterly course toward Fayetteville, N.C. My brigade crossed the North Carolina line at noon. The route lay through a sandy, rolling country abounding in pitch pines. Its barrenness stinted the customary success of our foragers. At 4 P.M. my brigade encamped near the unfinished railroad known as the Wilmington & Rutherford Railroad.

At 7 A.M. of the following day (March 8th) my brigade marched again in the advance of the corps. The general direction of the march was toward McFarland's Bridge on the Lumber River. At 9 A.M. the column encountered the 14th Corps which was moving on the road designed for the 20th. After some delay the brigade again pursued on its way, moving through woods and fields about two miles when a new road was found leading to the Lumber. At noon my command crossed Gum Creek Swamp. Soon afterward, in obedience to orders from the corps commander, it pressed forward with the design of getting possession of and, if possible, saving the bridge over the Lumber. The line of the march led through a wild and almost uninhabited country thickly timbered with pines. It afforded nothing whatever to our foragers. During a march of some 15 miles two or three wretched cabins were about the only observable signs of civilized life. Just before nightfall my command reached McFarland's Bridge which was found to be already destroyed. The enemy had burned it during the night of the 7th. The Lumber is a deep, narrow, and difficult stream, rarely fordable at this season of the year. It was therefore necessary that the bridge be reconstructed. I put almost my entire command, including the pioneer corps, at work upon it early on the morning of the 9th. The work was prosecuted with great energy and by 3 P.M. the bridge was ready for the crossing of the troops and trains. This bridge was, when completed, about 125 feet in length. The celerity with which it was constructed, considering the meagerness of the tools and materials, reflects great credit upon the officers and men who had the work in charge. My brigade crossed the Lumber in advance of the corps. It then moved two miles beyond the bridge and at 5:30 P.M. encamped. My command marched again at 6 A.M. on the 10th in the advance of the corps. It moved on the Fayetteville road, much of which it repaired as it proceeded. At 10 A.M. it crossed Beaver Dam and at 11 Toney's Creek. Soon after crossing the stream last named I was directed to push my brigade forward to Rockfish Creek which was reached by 2 P.M. This stream was found to be much swollen by the recent rains and required a long bridge. My pioneer corps under Lt. Charles H. Tinkler, was put to work constructing an approach. This work was completed by nightfall and my command encamped near the crossing. My brigade remained in this encampment until 11:30 A.M. on the 11th, when, unexpectedly, an order was received to push forward to Fayetteville unencumbered with trains. My troops moved immediately and were all over Rockfish Creek by noon. The column moved very rapidly and at 3 P.M. crossed Puppy Creek at Lamont's Mill. At 7 P.M. my brigade crossed Little Rockfish Creek and soon afterward struck a plank road leading directly to Fayetteville. The road, which had previously been extremely troublesome, was now as good as could be desired. At 11 P.M. my command encamped near the plank road two miles from Fayetteville.

There was no further movement of my command until the 13th when it marched in review down the principal street of Fayetteville and encamped on the farther side of town. On the following day it crossed the Cape Fear River about noon and moving about three miles from the bridge, encamped. On the 15th my brigade marched again at 8 A.M. pursuing the road to Kyle's Landing. Only the ammunition and headquarters wagons accompanied the troops. The remainder of the train was put in charge of the Second Division. The road being good, the column moved rapidly and at 4 P.M. my brigade reached Silver Run where it encamped. It was again on the march by 7 A.M. on the 16th. Much rain had fallen and the weather was damp and cloudy. The road was very troublesome yet the troops withal moved rapidly. At 9 A.M. cannonading was heard at the front, indicating that the enemy had been encountered. By 10 o'clock my commanded reached the locality where the Second Brigade, sent forward the evening previous, had already been engaged with the enemy. I immediately put my troops into position, as directed, on the right of the Second Brigade. I formed my regiments in two lines, three being in front, and three in reserve. About 10:30 I was ordered to advance my line which was done immediately. My skirmishers handsomely drove in those of the enemy and the entire command moved forward about half a mile, changing front while doing so. A new position was thus assumed and my brigade awaited the advance of the troops on its left. Meanwhile the First Brigade moved up on my right and while doing so encountered a strong force of the enemy in the act of turning my flank. Fortunately this design was thwarted and the enemy seemed to withdraw a considerable distance from my front. A new line was formed and the advance recommenced at 2 P.M. My formation was the same as before- three regiments in front and three in reserve. My regiments moved forward in excellent order about one mile. The enemy was steadily driven back until he sought refuge behind a breastwork which was covered in front by a marsh. Here I was directed to halt my command for the night. My men threw up a temporary breastwork to cover their line from the fire of the enemy's artillery. The firing mostly ceased at dark and the enemy withdrew during the night. I regret the loss of two enlisted men killed and 32 wounded in this engagement. It is also with much sorrow that I mentioned of the loss by wounding of seven commissioned officers of my command. They all deserve the highest praise for their gallant conduct and it affords me pleasure to report their names which are as follows: Lt. Col. David Thomson, 82nd Ohio, severely wounded; Lt. Col. Hezekiah Watkins, 143rd New York, contusion in right leg; Major John Higgins, 143rd New York, severely wounded; Captain John Heinzmann, 82nd Illinois, severely wounded; First Lt. R.M.J. Hardenbaugh, 143rd New York, mortally wounded, since dead; Lt. Edwin E. Cummings, 31st Wisconsin, thumb shot off; Second Lt. William Brant, 82nd Ohio, severely wounded in arm.

To my entire brigade, including both officers and men, I must reward the credit of having behaved with great gallantry throughout this affair. Though the fighting was all done on the level field and without breastworks or fortifications of any kind, yet there was no discoverable straggling and each officer and man seemed to desire above all things to acquit himself well and nobly.

My brigade marched again at 3 P.M. on the 17th and reached Black River at nightfall. On the following morning its march was resumed at 6 o'clock. The Black River was crossed by fording and my brigade pushed forward toward Bentonville. The troops corduroyed the bad places in the roads and assisted the trains when necessary. At 3 P.M. I was directed to move my brigade out a side road and cover the left flank. My regiments were placed in position and remained until 5 o'clock, when my brigade was relieved by troops from the Third Division and its march resumed. My command kept moving until 11 o'clock at night when it encamped. The march was continued at 6 o'clock the following morning. The road was very bad and had to be corduroyed. My command alternated in this work with the Second Brigade. At noon I crossed Mingo Creek and halted my brigade for dinner at the crossing of the Smithfield and Goldsborough roads. At this point lively cannonading was heard, apparently about five miles to the front. I was directed to leave a regiment to relieve the 150th New York in covering the Smithfield road. Detailing the 101st Illinois for this purpose, I pushed forward with the remainder of my command at 2 P.M. In about an hour my brigade arrived at the scene of the fighting. The 14th Corps had become considerably engaged. I was directed to move my command immediately to the front and fill up a gap in the line of Carlin's Division. I complied with this order at once and formed my regiments in two lines, three being in the front and two in reserve. The former were the 61st and 82nd Ohio and 31st Wisconsin, and the latter were the 82nd Illinois and 143rd New York. As soon as my line was formed it began the construction of a breastwork covering its front. This work was just fairly commenced when I was directed to send my two rear regiments, the 82nd Illinois and 143rd New York, back about a half a mile to go into position supporting Colonel Hawley's brigade, which was covering the left flank. Thus I had but three regiments remaining which have been mentioned as being on the front line. My line as thus situated was between a portion of Carlin's Division, 14th Corps on its right and another portion of the same division on its left, but formed no connection on either flank, as I had not troops enough to fill the vacancy. Neither did I find any skirmish line in front of that portion of Carlin's line occupied by my command. Furthermore, Carlin's line on my left, instead of being refused, was thrown forward which seems to me was a most dangerous and unfortunate arrangement, as it rendered it much more easy to be flanked than it ought to have been. In my front was a small ravine easily crossed and beyond an open field, containing on its farther side a group of buildings. In my rear was a dense pine forest along the outer edge of which my line extended.

Having no entrenching tools, my men were compelled to build their breastworks by means of their hatchets. They had, nevertheless, succeeded in erecting a respectable shelter from the fire of the enemy's sharpshooters, when it was reliably reported to me that the enemy was advancing his skirmish line, apparently with the intention of obtaining possession of the buildings in the field and from thence the elevated ground extending to the left and covering my position. I ordered a strong skirmish line to be pushed forward immediately to forestall the enemy in this purpose if possible. No sooner had my skirmishers begun to deploy that they seemed to be discovered and were fired upon. They were, however, gallantly pushed forward by Lt. George Lyman of the 31st Wisconsin, who was at this time in command of the line. Lt. Lyman quickly led his men across the open field and obtained possession of the buildings before mentioned. By this time the firing became very lively and the fact was developed that the enemy was advancing in force. The firing rolled to the left and soon grew heavy in Carlin's front. My skirmishers now began to fall back, losing many of their number in killed, wounded, and captured. The enemy now appeared in strong force in my front, and as soon as my skirmishers had come in my main line opened fire. Up to this time no other idea pervaded my command than that of holding their position; but in a few minutes it became apparent that the troops on my left were being driven back in great disorder. This permitted the enemy to come directly in upon my left flank and rear, and left me no alternative but to withdraw my regiments or have them captured. The line was held until to have remained upon it longer would have been madness. I therefore reluctantly gave the command to fall back, which was done in good order. My three regiments withdrew under cover of the thick woods and reformed their line about a quarter of a mile farther to the rear. The 143rd New York having now returned to me I ordered it to form on the left of the new line. The left of this regiment rested in an open field and had no connection with any other command. About 400 yards farther to the left was the 82nd Illinois on the right of Colonel Hawley's line, thus leaving a vacancy of that distance between those two regiments. The right of the line rested in the woods on the Cox's Bridge road, and afterward connected with the left of Fearing's Brigade of the 14th Corps.

My new line had hardly been formed until it was assaulted by the enemy. He again attempted to turn my left and to force his way through the gap between the 143rd New York and the 82nd Illinois. He managed to obtain a crossfire upon my four right regiments, which were at this time almost destitute of breastworks and without a connection right or left; but not an inch of ground was yielded. My four right regiments held their ground most gallantly, while the 82nd Illinois, aided by the artillery which commanded the gap and behaved very gallantly, poured so galling a fire into the enemy's flanking column as to compel it to hastily withdraw. My men now collected rails and quickly built themselves a breastwork. This work had to be suspended several times owing to the repeated attacks of the enemy. It was finally completed as far as to render it a respectable covering from the enemy's fire. But this was not accomplished a moment too soon. The enemy made at least five furious assaults upon the line, but was in each instance handsomely repulsed. He was not permitted to maintain a line of battle five minutes at one time within a hundred yards of my line. At each successive repulse numbers of his men came in and surrendered themselves as prisoners of war.

Thus the tide of battle ebbed and flowed along my front until nightfall when the firing ceased and my four right regiments were relieved by Col. Selfridge's brigade, and withdrawn to a line of works about 300 yards to the rear. The 101st Illinois, having rejoined the brigade late in the afternoon, had already formed in this second line of works but had not been seriously engaged. Thus terminated an action which cost my brigade 107 officers and men, killed, wounded, and captured. Among the number were many of the bravest and best of my entire command, but where all did so well I cannot find it in my heart to make invidious distinctions. I sincerely regret the loss in this affair of Capt. William Ballentine of the 82nd Ohio who was mortally wounded and has since died. He was a young officer of great promise and his loss cannot be easily repaired. The same statements are true of Lt. George Lyman of the 31st Wisconsin, who was wounded and captured by the enemy while gallantly leading the skirmish line at the beginning of the engagement and who also afterward died. (Lt. Lyman survived, and was mustered out May 16, 1865). I cannot bestow too much praise upon these two young officers who have fallen at the post of duty and given their lives for their country. The following additional officers were wounded in the engagement: Capt. Robert Patterson, 61st Ohio, slightly; Lt. William H. Thomson, 82nd Ohio, severely.

On the 20th and 21st my brigade remained in the same position it occupied on the night of the 19th except that it advanced about noon of the 21st and held for a short time nearly the same ground occupied by it at the commencement of the battle of the 19th. The enemy had withdrawn to his original position. Several wounded men of my command who had been left upon the field were brought in during this temporary advance. My troops did not engage the enemy and I was soon directed to move them back to their old position which I did. During the night of the 21st the enemy retreated. My brigade marched at 9:30 A.M. toward Troublefield's Store en route for Cox's Bridge. The trains preceded the troops early in the morning. At 8 P.M. my command encamped near Falling Creek. It crossed Falling Creek at 7:30 the ensuing morning. At noon it reached a point near Cox's Bridge over the Neuse River. My command crossed the Neuse River at 2 P.M. and having moved one mile beyond, encamped for the night. At 2 o'clock in the morning of the 24th all pack animals and headquarters wagons were sent forward to Goldsborough in obedience to an order from Major General Slocum. The troops were notified that they would be expected to pass in review through the town upon their arrival there. My brigade marched at 7 and crossed Little River at 9:30 A.M. At 10:30 it reached Goldsboro and moved three miles beyond the town, where it went into permanent camp near its present situation, in the vicinity of the Weldon Railroad.

During the campaign which thus terminated, my brigade marched 494 miles. It captured from the enemy 60 prisoners, of whom two were commissioned officers and 52 enlisted men were well, and one commissioned officer and five enlisted men wounded. It destroyed five miles of railroad track and two cases of new Enfield and Springfield rifle muskets, containing 60 in all. The troops of my command subsisted mostly upon the country. They captured 500 beef cattle, 200 sheep, 2,000 live hogs, 15,000 pounds of flour, 20,000 pounds of meal, 1,000 bushels of sweet potatoes, and 100,000 pounds of bacon, besides vast quantities of poultry and miscellaneous provisions. The command burned 50 cotton gins and presses, 1,800 bales of cotton, two sawmills, and three flouring mills. It captured 200 horses and 350 mules. The animals of my command were also chiefly subsisted upon forage obtained from the country. The quantity gathered for and consumed by them was, as nearly as it can be estimated, 125,098 pounds of corn and 77,340 pounds of fodder. Besides these there were vast number of miscellaneous captures of articles valuable to the enemy.

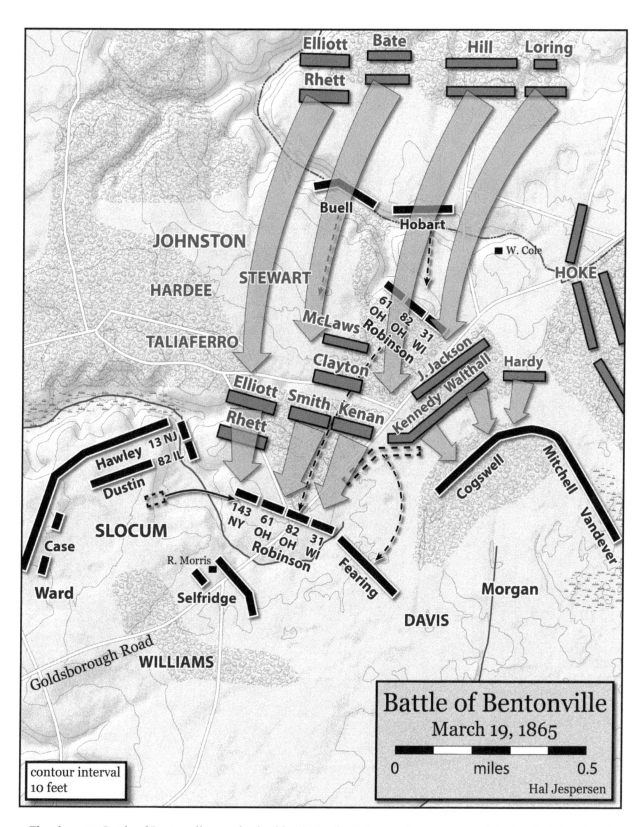

Elliott
Bate
Hill
Loring
Rhett

Buell
Hobart
W. Cole

JOHNSTON
HOKE

HARDEE
STEWART

TALIAFERRO
McLaws
61 OH
82 OH
31 WI
Robinson
J. Jackson
Hardy

Clayton
Kennedy
Walthall

Elliott
Smith
Kenan

Rhett

Cogswell
Mitchell
Vandever

13 NJ
Hawley
82 IL
Dustin

143 NY
61 OH
82 OH
31 WI
Robinson

Case
Fearing
Morgan

SLOCUM

R. Morris

Ward
Selfridge
DAVIS

Goldsborough Road
WILLIAMS

Battle of Bentonville
March 19, 1865

0   miles   0.5

Hal Jespersen

contour interval
10 feet

The climactic Battle of Bentonville was the final battle in which Captain Lee participated during the Civil War. It was a surprisingly hard-fought battle, and one that nearly ended in disaster for Robinson's brigade. A quick retreat and frantic construction of breastworks staved off multiple Confederate assaults.
(Hal Jespersen, www.cwmaps.com)

Equestrian statue of Major General Alpheus S. Williams in Detroit, Michigan.

CHAPTER ELEVEN

One More March

Notes in Dixie Vol. XXX

Near Goldsboro, North Carolina

April 6, 1865

    Probably no army that ever existed experienced such a time of unbounded rejoicing as this one has today. From early forenoon to sunset the tide of enthusiasm swept from camp to camp and kept rolling upward in one unceasing flood of cheers. From Major Generals to Privates, the entire army seems rapt in a transport of joy. I need hardly say that the occasion of all this has been the announcement of the fall of Petersburg and Richmond. The glorious news reached Goldsboro about 9 A.M. and soon afterward began to sweep like wildfire through the army. Everywhere the bands began to play and from myriads of voices the joyous 'Hurrah' swelled in a deafening storm upon the breeze. 'Richmond is taken' was the rapturous utterance of every lip, the thrilling inspiration of every heart. Battalions, brigades, divisions, and corps vied with each other in vociferous expression of an ecstasy of delight, while at least one among them all said to himself in silent yet unutterable thankfulness, 'God be praised.'

    Then Richmond is indeed ours! After four years of stupendous war, the capital of the Confederacy has succumbed. After the expenditure of millions of treasure and oceans of blood this noble government, this glorious Union, has vindicated itself against the greatest rebellion, the most gigantic treason of modern times. After a terrific four years' struggle, freedom has gained the earnest of speedy and complete triumph over slavery, and this magnificent land of ours is free throughout all of its borders. GOD BE PRAISED!

    The heart sickens as it contemplates what infinite blood and suffering this consummation has cost. The living can rejoice only when they forget that our triumphant flag waves over unnumbered graves of patriots slain. Yet the achievement is fully worth the sacrifice, ay, more than worth it. Principles are of as much more value than lives as the hopes and destinies of individuals are outweighed by those of all mankind. Whatever the struggle may cost, truth must triumph over error and right over wrong.

    Richmond has fallen! The great Babylon of American slavery is no more. Let us rejoice that the power of the tyrants is broken and that his chosen citadel cowers beneath the starry folds of the banner of freedom. Let humanity rejoice, let earth rejoice, for this conquest is the world's. None can regret now that to our generation and our people belongs the praise for having achieved it. It is a matter for congratulation that the capital of the Confederacy is the exclusive trophy of that noble army which has so long, so patiently, and so heroically struggled for its capture. The Army of the Potomac has on many a hard-fought bloody field earned the glory of taking Richmond. To that gallant army all the praise of its capture belongs. Let it be ascribed without stint and the army of Atlanta, Savannah, and Columbia will say amen.

    Despite this glorious triumph, let no one be sanguine that the war is over. There may be much hard fighting yet, for the enemy is desperate and means to die game. The armies under Sherman are already preparing to intercept his retreat into the Gulf States, but the wary foe may elude their vigilance, surpass their activity, or with the bold energy of despair, cut his way through their lines. Yet with careful and energetic handling of the armies of the Union, the speedy and utter overthrow of the rebellion is now certain. Then for the last crowning struggle of the war, let us 'rally round the flag boys, rally once again, shouting the battle cry of freedom; We'll rally from the hillside, we'll gather from the plain, shouting the battle cry of freedom, down with the traitor, up with the star, while we rally round the flag boys, rally once again, shouting the battle cry of freedom!'

Notes in Dixie Vol. XXXI

Raleigh, North Carolina
April 17, 1865

This bright spring morning the flag of the Union floats serenely from the dome of the capital of the old North State. It was planted there by Ohio's braves on Thursday last. "The 5th Ohio Cavalry was the first troops that showed the Stars and Stripes on the streets of this city and to hoist the old flag from the State House," says the *Raleigh Progress*. And there it proudly waves in this morning's gleaming sunlight, kissed by the blossom-scented air, hallowed by a thousand glorious memories. 'Washed in the blood of the brave and the blooming, snatched from the altars of the insolent foes, burning with star fires but never consuming, flashes its broad ribands of lily and rose.'[201]

And yet, immortal as it is, a new glory seems to await it that shall mark even this as one of its most splendid triumph days. Before sunset, 30,000 Rebels are expected to lay down their arms and pay it homage. At 10 o'clock last night a messenger arrived within our lines bringing Johnston's agreement to a proposal for conference upon the subject of surrender of his (Johnston's) forces. This news easily leaked through the meshes of official red tape and created the wildest enthusiasm throughout the army. Until long after midnight the air was made vocal with the strains of martial music and the enthusiastic cheers of the troops. Next to the fall of Richmond and the surrender of Lee's forces, no event has ever occasioned such rejoicing in this army.

But alas! Alas! For all earthly joy and all mere human triumphs! Almost while the above lines were being penned, the sad intelligence reached this brigade that President Lincoln was, during the night of the 14th inst., assassinated at a theater in Washington. And is it indeed true that our brave, noble, heroic President is no more? Murdered by an assassin! Can it be? Murdered in the very capital of the nation and in the flush of the glorious triumph of that cause which he has long been the embodiment and the faithful able champion! Abraham Lincoln, the soldier's friend, the people's representative, the nation's hope, stricken down in the zenith of his fame and usefulness by the traitorous hand of a Southern villain! Oh, it is too much for loyal hearts to bear or tongue to utter! It is a wrong which calls to heaven for vengeance and which 'Stirs a fever in the blood of age, and makes the infant's cries as strong as steel.' It is an injustice and an outrage which brands a withering curse, not only upon the treacherous perpetrator, but upon the worse than barbarous people and institutions of which he is the exponent. 'Virginia avenged forsooth!' The curse of Cain is upon her henceforth and forever. And not upon her alone, but upon all who sympathize with and exult in her cowardly dastardly vengeance.

The announcement of the death of the President created the profoundest grief throughout this army. Never before was it realized how much affection the army entertained for its honest and patriotic commander-in-chief. Upon the repeated assurance that he had really fallen a victim to cowardly Southern hate, 'scarred and war torn soldiers, like girls, flushed through their tan, and down the thousand wrinkles of the battles, a thousand tear drops ran.' And then there was a low, ominous murmur of vengeance. Hearts unwont to be stirred, glowed with the red heat of passion and flashed baleful fire through eyes that had witnessed the carnage of a score of battles for the Union. 'Let not Johnston surrender-let us have another campaign- let us avenge our murdered President.' This was the almost universal sentiment. 'Oh, for another march through North and South Carolina and through Georgia and Alabama. One more chance and we'll annihilate the vile Rebel crew and scatter fire and sword and sweeping devastation throughout the length and breadth of the dark lurking places of treason.'

I am confident that in thus giving language to the natural impulses of my own heart, I but express the almost universal sentiment of this army. Ah, let Southern traitors beware how they provoke the ardor of Northern blood. Though it boasts no chivalrous tincture and bears in its warm current the generous flow of human sympathy, yet when stirred by gigantic wrongs, it glows with a fiery spirit, quick, remorseless, and destructive as the oak-rending lightning.

---

[201] Lee is quoting from the poem "God Save the Flag" by Oliver Wendell Holmes.

Abraham Lincoln is not dead. The assassin's stiletto failed to accomplish its purpose. It might hurt, but it could not destroy him whose name and fame are as immortal as the principles for which he lived and died. He still lives. He lives in the hearts of thousands of soldiers who long since learned to love him and call him, with unfeigned affection, Father Abraham. He lives in the memories of all who admire honesty and firmness of purpose and clear, strong, and vigorous intellect. He lives in the hearts of all who love liberty, justice, and law. He lives in the brightest and most glorious pages of the history of this nation. He lives the defender of free government, and the foremost champion of human rights. He lives the shining exponent of republican institutions, the glorious self-made pioneer of a new age and destiny for mankind. He lives the beautiful and marvelous illustration of the justice and righteousness of that free constitution which opens the way for honest, manly merit to attain even from the humblest walks of life the loftiest stations known among men.

In Abraham Lincoln, the South has killed her best and truest friend. Humane, honest, manly, and enlightened, he was the man above all others best adapted to reconcile the Southern people to the authority and power of the central government. Magnanimous to a fault, he has ever throughout his official career exhibited the kindliest spirit toward those who were his most bitter and unscrupulous foes. Though maligned by Southern blackguards, misrepresented by Northern doughfaces, sneered at by the proud men-stealers and their sympathizers, scoffed by the haters of human equality, ridiculed by the ignorant and unappreciative, abused by all enemies of free institutions, yet he never seemed to permit any feeling of political persecution or personal revenge to control in the least his official conduct. None know how to appreciate this better than the soldiers who of all others best understand how bitter and uncharitable has been the enmity of those who have endeavored to make the President the chief object of political hate and prejudice and the excuse for armed treason and rebellion.

In the army, President Lincoln has been not only honored and admired, but beloved. During three and a half years of service I have never witnessed such universal and deeply-felt sorrow as that which prevailed in our camps subsequent to the announcement of his assassination. Each soldier seemed to have found himself suddenly bereft of a dear friend. Not even the gloom and despondency that followed the great disaster at Chancellorsville or the bloody repulse at Fredericksburg was equal to that yesterday. The dreadful news came like a clap of thunder in a clear sky and overcast the noonday of our rejoicing with midnight darkness. Abraham Lincoln- he who through four long years of bloody war has so faithfully and ably borne our standard is no more! Fallen upon the ramparts of the last citadel of this accursed rebellion, his legions of faithful war-worn followers mourn him with an irreconcilable sorrow. In his honesty, integrity, and ability, they reposed the most unreserved and childlike confidence. While Abraham Lincoln was their chief magistrate and commander, they felt all was well. 'Honest Old Abe will do what is best' was their proverbial and favorite sentiment. His name was their rallying cry, and to them and their cause was a tower of strength. Throughout the borders of our loyal land the bravest and best rallied around their glorious republican chief as they would have rallied around no other living man. The hardy self-made pioneer of the West suddenly found himself raised up by Providence to be the leader of a great people through a gigantic national trial. The vast responsibility would have confounded an intellect less clear, appalled a will less determined, crushed a spirit less strong and manly than his. God gave us Abraham Lincoln and the same infinite giver has taken him away.

Never can I forget the occasion when I first saw our dead and now immortal President. It was at that time of universal gloom and despondency- when an American citizen could scarcely say he had a country and a government. Mr. Lincoln was then on his way to Washington to assume the functions and responsibilities of his office.[202] Upon him were the eyes of the whole nation and the civilized world. The conspirators of the South were having things all their own way, having scarcely met a rebuke or the shadow of resistance in their treason. Discouragement was seizing upon every Northern heart and the wisest and best lovers of our liberty were preparing their minds to give up the Union. Not so Abraham Lincoln. While all were despondent, he was cheerful and hopeful. 'Politicians say that a crisis has come upon the country but I think it altogether an artificial crisis,' said he. In these brave, manly, hopeful words patriots found their cue. The gloomy incubus of Southern treachery and Northern imbecility began to be lifted from their hearts and they felt that they had even yet a President, a Constitution, and a

---

[202] Lee likely saw Lincoln when he passed through Cleveland February 15-16, 1861 as Lee was in law school in Cleveland at the time.

country. Abraham Lincoln, with his own strong right arm lifted this great people from the pit of despondency and made them feel their manhood, their patriotism, and their power. That they are not today humiliated before a proud Southern aristocracy is, under God, owing to Abraham Lincoln and him alone. Washington established our free institutions; Lincoln preserved them. The one is the father, the other the savior of his country.

When I next saw the President, it was at a review of one of the bravest and best appointed armies of the world and he was the reviewing officer. It was my privilege to stand in the ranks of the nation's defenders and to admire from that standpoint the simple honesty, uprightness, yet greatness of character marked in the manner and bearing of our illustrious chief. On that glorious gala day hardly a soldier's bosom did not swell with pride at the thought that it was part of the living bulwark of defense of that Constitution which permits a great and free people to call to the highest place in their gift a man so humble in birth and fortune, but yet so great in all of the glorious qualities of manhood as Abraham Lincoln of Illinois.[203]

When I next saw Mr. Lincoln, he was an attendant at an entertainment for the benefit of sick and wounded soldiers. His humane heart had not forgotten even in the midst of his vast cares and responsibilities to do an act of charity in behalf of the suffering ones who had sacrificed health or limb in behalf of the great cause of which he was the chief representative. This was the last time I saw him, nor shall I see him again until the grand rally of victor souls on the plains of immortal light. I shall expect to see him there, crowned by unfading wreaths and greeted from the four quarters of the world by the hosts of those who have perished in behalf of human rights, singing, as of old, the rejoicing song 'We are coming Father Abraham, three hundred thousand more!'

It is not yet determined whether the last of the Rebel armies this side of the Mississippi will voluntarily surrender to our forces. Johnston has asked time for consult with the arch-Rebel of Rebeldom. What the result of this consultation will be cannot be well conjectured. Nor is there now much anxiety upon the subject. Another campaign will afford the opportunity, much coveted, to retaliate upon the scoundrels whose villainy has culminated in the cowardly assassination of the President of the United States. God pity the country where this army moves if it is once more let loose upon the wicked and dastardly sustainers of the rebellion. The dread word subjugation will have a mild and acceptable meaning for this iniquitous people. Hereafter devastation, extermination, and annihilation will be the watchwords.

There is no style of warfare which can be too severe against a people so barbarous, so lost to all sense of honor as to employ the fiendish torpedo, insidious poison, inhuman starvation of helpless captives, and the bloody treacherous knife of the assassin as a means for the destruction of their antagonists. Let them beware how they give one more opportunity to hundreds of thousands of veteran soldiers exasperated almost to madness. These whipped, conquered traders in human flesh will be made to woefully rue the day when they introduced the bloody barbarism of the French Revolution and the stealthy unmanly treachery of the Mexican guerilla into American warfare.

But enough. Let us leave all vengeful feeling to Him to whom it rightfully belongs. The events of this war and the destiny of this nation are controlled by an abler wiser hand than that of man. Whatever else may happen, the right must ultimately triumph. 'For right is right, since God is God, and right the day must win; To doubt would be disloyalty, to falter would be sin.' There is yet hope for our country and humanity. Let us not despair. Following the example of our illustrious martyred President, let us stand firmly by truth and justice, never doubting that their final triumph will be sure and complete.

Notes in Dixie Vol. XXXII

Raleigh, North Carolina
April 29, 1865

It is with inexpressible joy that I chronicle the fact that the long-looked-for and longed-for 'Home campaign' of this army is about to commence. Today for the first time, on account of the close of hostilities, the veteran Star Corps about-faced and marched toward what was formerly the rear. The Corps has marched out from Raleigh expecting to pursue the uttermost parts of Dixie the shattered remnants of the once proud and defiant Confederate armies. But lo! After one day's sweaty march through dust and sun, the last faint shadows of armed

---

[203] This would have been the review held in April 10, 1863 at Brooke Station, Virginia.

resistance to our glorious Union disappeared and Peace, Heaven's own blessed messenger, unfolded her dove-like wings over our bristling columns and bade the march be stayed. The Rebel General Johnston, accepting the terms offered him, had surrendered the remaining forces of the Confederacy, thus rendering unnecessary our anticipated campaign and crowning with complete and glorious triumph the Union armies.[204]

So suddenly and almost unexpectedly has this long hoped-for and prayed-for consummation come that it is difficult to comprehend its reality. Yet there is a buoyant and cheerful satisfaction manifested throughout the army which indicates that a great load has been removed from the hearts of all and that this long and bloody struggle for the unity of the Republic and the rights of man has indeed closed in glorious and complete triumph. Each man's mind possessed with home ideas and anticipations leads him already in thought to his beloved fireside in the good old Northland where, in fancy, he already received the greeting of the dear ones whose hands he clasped years ago in more bitter and painful parting. The bloody experiences, the toils, the sufferings, and dangers of the past four years are, for the time being, dropped from memory and the mind leaps forward to the blessed reunion with home and friends, the gladsome fruition of which surpasses romance and outshines the brightest dreams of the past.

It is expected that the Army of Georgia will set out on its northward journey by Monday next. It is proposed to march via Petersburg and Richmond to Fredericksburg and to encamp the army between Aquia Landing and Alexandria along the right bank of the Potomac. Thus the Twentieth Corps which was transferred from Virginia to the Department of the Cumberland in the autumn of 1863 and which has successively marched and fought its way from Bridgeport, Alabama to Chattanooga, Tennessee, from Chattanooga to Atlanta, from Atlanta to Savannah, from Savannah to Columbia, and from Columbia via Fayetteville and Goldsboro to Raleigh, will have completed its grand circuit through the very heart and center of the most powerful and rebellious states of the would-be Southern Confederacy. This brave old corps poured out its blood like water upon many a sanguinary field in Virginia, Maryland, and Pennsylvania, and its dead are strewn from the Susquehannah to the Rappahannock. For nearly two years it persistently and hopefully struggled for access to the Rebel capital from the North, no one ever dreaming meanwhile that its final entrance would be made via Atlanta, Savannah, Columbia, and Raleigh. Such have been the marvelous vicissitudes of this greatest and most glorious war ever waged.

It is needless to say that the dastardly assassination of President Lincoln has caused throughout this army and deep and lasting bitterness of feeling toward the wicked and treacherous originators of this war for slavery, of whose diabolical treason and rebellion this vile act is the exponent. Nothing less than the extreme penalty of the law executed upon these men can now satisfy the public sentiment of the army. No set of men every more richly deserved the halter than Jefferson Davis and his co-conspirators. In being the authors and abbetters of a causeless and unprovoked rebellion they have become not only traitors to their country but the murderers of hundreds of thousands of brave men. No more red-handed or guilty set of criminals were ever pursued by the sword of avenging justice. Let them receive the punishment due for their crimes. Not only our army but all civilized armies and civilized people will exclaim amen when the gibbet feels the weight of these guilty misanthropes, these enemies of law and good government, these advocates of barbarism, these willful destroyers of a nation's peace. It is for the interest of the whole world that a great and notable example should be made of these most treacherous and dangerous of all modern conspirators against our common humanity.

Let no one be deceived by the glossy and polished manner of these Southern gentlemen. It is the charm of the serpent and only proves that 'a man may smile, and smile, and prove a villain still.' Men who received in the Northern states the culture and education which smooths and refines the native coarseness and vulgarity of the Southern character and who have used all the influence and power thus acquired by them in an insane endeavor to ruin their country, need not seek to palm themselves off upon an intelligent people as men of honor deserving the charity and consideration of their countrymen. This ruse may succeeded among the ignorant and prejudiced people who have for so long a time been the dupes of men gifted with great minds but devil-inspired with the wickedest and basest natures. But among a free people accustomed to think for themselves and vote without restraint, thee

---

[204] General Joseph E. Johnston surrendered the remnants of the Army of the Tennessee and coastal forces on April 26, 1865 at Bennett Place, North Carolina, ending most active conflict east of the Mississippi River. Scattered forces across the South surrendered through the following month.

traitorous hypocrites can never appear respectable. Dyed in the innocent blood of slaughtered thousands and bathed with tears unnumbered save by Him who notes all human sorrow, their hands may never meet again in friendly grasp those of loyal freemen. Hence, foul murderers, vile assassins, go and enjoy your immortality of infamy! 'Hence and trouble us not, for you have made the happy earth your hell, filled it with cursing cries and deep exclaims, if you delight to view your heinous deeds, behold this pattern of your butcheries, O'gentlemen, see. See! Dead Lincoln's wounds!'

These men having once so foully betrayed their county can never be trusted again. They must never be restored to political authority or influence upon any conditions whatever. Those who have been most prominent in the rebellion and most responsible for it must be utterly disenfranchised, provided their proper punishment on the gallows is commuted. Having endeavored by every means in their power to destroy the government they should never be permitted to enjoy any of the rights and privileges which it guarantees or protects. In short, if I had my way (I speak as a soldier), I would hang every man of whatsoever name or station who by proper judicial authority may be convicted of having joined and setting on foot and in subsequently aiding and abetting the execution of a gigantic plot against our liberties. I would forever disenfranchise and expatriate all officials of the Confederate government, including the most prominent and influential leaders of the insurgent armies. I would disenfranchise all members of Rebel state governments who have given active aid and influence to the cause of secession. I would further disenfranchise and forever prohibit from holding property or enjoying any right or privilege under the government of the United States all men who have in any way given aid or support to the rebellion, and who do not within a specified time subscribe to an oath of allegiance so strong and terrible as to render its violator and his posterity subject to the severest penalties known to human law. Let these things be done, and slavery utterly abolished, and the rebellion of the South will never be repeated.

I hope it may not be supposed that these sentiments are dictated by mere bitterness of feeling. Though I have not escaped suffering some of the bitter depths of sorrow and misery occasioned by this war, I am not incapable of exercising charity toward the worst rebels provided that such kindness was not cruelty to my country. Strong maladies require severe remedies and our body politic, possessed with the fell disease of treason, can be restored to perfect health and safety only by the purifying treatment of stern, inflexible justice. Such is the only process by which the peace and unity of the Republic, purchased by such great sacrifices, can be rendered permanent and enduring.

Notes in Dixie Vol. XXXIII

Near Washington City,
May 27, 1865

With strange reflections and amid wonderful reminiscences I enter upon this, the last of these erratic pen excursions. The vast march is ended, the grand review is over, and all thoughts are now turned homeward. The great campaign which began at Atlanta, Georgia on November 15, 1864 and which General Sherman declared to be unfinished at Savannah and Fayetteville is not even yet fully concluded. 'We have one more march to make.' It is not to go out and receive the shock of battle and grapple with deadly foes in bloody conflict. Vastly different from that. It is to go and grasp the warm and friendly hands of those we love by our own home firesides in the good old Northland. The toils, the sufferings and the dangers of the tremendous war for the Union are among the things of the past. Leaving them behind us, we turn our faces toward a future which, as compared with desolate track over which we have come, seems like a flower-strewn path leading through the peaceful abodes of the ever-blessed. Oh what compensation for countless toils and pains- for nameless hardships and privations. Thank God that he has reserved it for our age and generation-even for us.

It is hardly necessary to say that we of the Red Stars never felt so proud or so happy as when our feet felt the sublime cadence of martial tread up Pennsylvania Avenue on our last grand gala day. One hour of that was worth an age of common life. For him whose score of campaigns and battles in behalf of his country's flag had seamed his cheek and scarred his frame, and who now followed that flag all torn to shreds yet garlanded with wreaths of victory, one hour, one moment of that day possessed more happiness than a whole eternity of the tame plodding life which never knows such sacrifices, such sufferings, such triumphs.

Those who gazed upon us in our holiday costume amid the fascinating ceremonies of parade could little know or feel the full import of this grand episode. None could appreciate as we that in this day were centered the baffled hopes and reserved joys of four long years of untold danger, labor, and privation. For them and to them who bore the stains and scars of battle, who with shoeless feet on many a long and painful march had marked the rebellious soil with bloody tracks, who shelterless and foodless had endured upon the outposts of liberty the pitiless peltings of the storm through dreary days and darker nights, who had toiled and fought through the scorching sun of summer and the chilling wintry blast, who breasted again and again the leaden rain of battle and felt the awful solemnity and feverish terror of bloody conflict, who had buried scores of comrades in obscure and sunken graves amid gloomy Southern pines, who for months and years had carried life at their finger ends ready to be snatched by 'The fire angel in the front of death' or by 'The death angel lurking in the rear,' who had sat face to face with death through seeming ages of confinement in loathsome Southern prison pens, who had heard upon the disastrous field the bitter taunt of the victorious Rebel, who amid flame and smoke and death had carried the 'banner of beauty and glory' over the defiant strongholds of traitors and unfurled it from the proudest citadels of rebellion; for these and to these were reserved the most exquisite depths of joy, the most glorious heights of the exultation of this triumph day of our Republic and our age.

But this splendid pageant is now over and the sorrowful parting of those whom mutual perils and pains have so long bound together is about to take place. Corps, divisions, and brigades that have so often withstood the furious tide of battle will soon melt away, and the sun-browned companions of so many trials and hardships will disperse to their quiet homes scattered throughout the length and breadth of this great free land. The separation brings sorrow and joy- sorrow for the death of old associations and joy, inexpressible joy, for the glad and friendly greeting awaiting the returning soldier at his own home threshold. Years ago, shouting Freedom's battle cry, we rallied around her starry banner to save it from the infuriate clutches of traitors. Singing their stirring songs the thousands hastened forth to fight the boastful Rebel foe. How changed the scene now, and how different, how diviner the refrain that will soon be caught up the armed legions. 'We are marching home at last, now the cruel war is past, and the time of peace draws near. We are marching home at last, now the cruel war is past, to the home our hearts hold dear. With our banners stained and torn, that through many a fight were born, where death rained thick and fast, now our glorious work is done, now the Union cause is won, we are marching home at last.'

The joy of our coming has but one tinge of sadness. It is our grief for those who went gaily forth with us but who, alas, can never return. We are the victors, they are the martyrs. With their blood they helped to purchase our laurels and we owe them the lasting debt of kindest and most honorable remembrance. In our hearts and in the great heart of their country their names must be wreathed with chaplets of immortal honor. Their noble forms are not ours. They lie enshrouded in cold neglected clay and are found scattered wherever armed foes struck their dastard steel at the nation's life. Their sunken graves are the footprints of freedom, the way marks of civilization. This country, this generation, this age can never pay them too much honor. Praise may be lavished upon the living and it is some slight compensation for risk, toil, and suffering. But how can we repay the glorious dead- they who not only risked but have given all for their liberties and ours? 'Can honor's voice provoke the silent dust, or flattery sooth the dull, cold ear of death?' It cannot. But these are not dead. The perishable part has vanished, but the brave and noble soul, the immortal example, still walks among us a living presence. Let us bestow upon it our highest admiration, or most profound respect. Let us enshrine it in our memories and affections, hallow it with our tears, and honor it in every possible way, and thus transmit it to the grateful generations to come. It will be their richest best legacy.

And now, though it may seem a little presumptuous, let me say to those who have cared to accompany me in these pen wanderings, farewell. In one sense at least my notes are noted. This old portfolio, greasy with the sweat of long marches and blackened with the soot of camps, has served out its time and must be discharged. This stub of a pen, which has so long perplexed the printer, and which protests against being responsible for his mental ejaculations will disturb his waking thoughts no more. Nor will it trouble his dreams provided he repents of the manifold typographical injuries he has done it. If he will not do this he is respectfully consigned to the hoofed and horned individual who is said to lurk about every printing office.

Dixie being, to use an army phrase, 'played out' and the great independent Confederacy having taken itself to petticoats, I feel that my occupation is gone. King Cotton is not only crownless but badly out at the elbows. There is no longer a ditch left for the Confederacy to die in, not a Confederacy to die for even if there was a ditch. The chivalry have all disappeared like the dew of early morning- it has become too hot for them- and there is no longer a true born Southron left who can whip ten Yankees. The great Christian President of the Confederacy has gone over to the female persuasion.[205] I think I shall do so, too. I am satisfied that it is the only safe course for an unmarried soldier just mustered out. I shall therefore shut up this shop. No more notes to dispose of here. 'Done sold out.' The war is over.

Finis.

Brevet Major General James Sidney Robinson

---

[205] Lee is referencing the widely circulated reports that Confederate President Jefferson Davis was captured wearing petticoats as a disguise.

CHAPTER TWELVE

One More Letter

Captain Alfred E. Lee traveled home with the 82nd Ohio and went into camp at Louisville, Kentucky in June, obtaining a short furlough to travel to Delaware, Ohio for a visit connected with the class of 1865 graduation ceremonies at Ohio Wesleyan. On July 24, 1865, the 82nd Ohio Volunteer Infantry was mustered out of service at Columbus, Ohio and the regiment's members returned to their homes. The *Delaware Gazette* noted Lee's return. "None stand more conspicuous than Capt. Lee who bears on his person an honorable wound received in the front ranks at the Battle of Gettysburg," the editor noted. "We wish him abundant success in whatever pursuit he may engage."[206]

The Battle of Gettysburg and the dramatic circumstances of his "honorable wound" suffered there remained on Captain Lee's mind, and he felt a great debt to the kindly Confederate soldier who had tended to him and to Adjutant Burnham while upon the battlefield. With the war at a close, Captain Lee addressed the following letter to James O. Marks in Lynchburg, Virginia. That letter, embedded in an article Lee wrote under his wartime no-de-plume of A.T. Sechand which contains Private Marks' reply, give some insight into how our Civil War veterans started to heal the wounds engendered by that bloody conflict.

After the Storm

Not seven score days ago more than a million armed men stood embattled in behalf of the existence of this great Republic. The dark, thunderous battle cloud stretched its gloomy folds throughout the borders of the land, while beneath it mighty hosts grappled with each other in a gigantic life and death struggle. The gales that swept the rough bosom of the Mother of States carried with them the unceasing din of battle; the soft breezes of the South wafted the feverish, sulfurous breath of war, and the clangor of arms rolled westward in fierce echoes until lost in savage wilds far beyond the Father of Waters. Little was it realized that in a few brief and glorious days, all this violence and bloodshed, this darkness and terror, this gloom and doubt, would cease and that from our lurid horizon the bright and glorious dawn of peace would break in almost unclouded splendor. Yet even so it was to be. In the dim gray of early morning, a heroic band, bearing as their symbol the sign of human hope in which martyrs to truth have always conquered, were seen gathering softly to their places under frowning battlements which were the last dread bulwarks of oppression and rebellion. Suddenly the fierce engines of slaughter open their dread voices and blue lines of men, raising freedom's battle cry, sweep forward toward the parapet crowned with the bristling steel of treason. Amid a pitiless storm of death those lines surge forward like an ocean tide and soon sweep over the ramparts, driving from his lair in hopeless rout the angry foe. The fort is won, the enemy's line irrecoverably broken, and his army and his capital are gone forever. The decisive blow has been struck, and the Republic respires easily for the first time in four years.

Thus the brightest sun of victory burst almost full-orbed upon us. It gleamed upon our regenerated nation holding aloft the sword of justice dripping with the blood of its enemies, and lifting on high its laurelled brow all begrimed with bloody sweat. But that hand soon exchanged the sword for the olive branch, and that brow soon irradiated with the smile of peace. The storm of war rolled away in solemn mutterings and the long dismal night was suddenly illumined by almost unlooked-for dawn.

---

[206] "Personal," *Delaware Gazette*, August 4, 1865, pg. 3

But ah! What splendors fire the sky!
What glories greet the morn!
The storm-tossed banner streams on high,
Its heavenly hues new burn!
Its red fresh dyed in heroes' blood,
Its peaceful white more pure,
To float unstained o'er field and flood,
While earth and seas endure.[207]

And now that morning has come, the historian's pen will be busy in tracing the bloody pages of the night. Volume upon volume will be written, and yet it will be only as a drop compared with that which remains unsaid and unsung. To the angels it must be left to record the vast unwritten history of the war. Romance, with her light-winged fancy, may endeavor to compass it, but her most fabulous flights must ever droop far short of the reality, and the truth remain infinitely stranger than her fiction. Poetry, with all her witching charm, can never reclaim it from the buried past. Painting, even with her boundless reach of fancy can never reproduce it. It consists of thoughts, feelings, and events which have passed away with those who experienced or enacted them. It consists of a height of sublimity, a depth of pathos, a volume of thrilling reality, which can never be painted, sung, or described.

Of the hundreds of thousands of soldiers who have participated in the war, each has had his individual experience, different from that of all others. It is a volume written upon his soul, and which can never be fully unfolded to others gaze than his own. Adequately impart it to others he never can until he receives the untrammeled speech of an immortal and disembodied spirit. Until then, it must ever remain a vivid and enduring consciousness which he can only imperfectly communicate. These personal experiences the historian can never reach, nor would he if he could. He deals with great armies, great leaders, great campaigns, great battles, great defeats, great triumphs. All that is not so great, or so regarded by the public, he dismisses, for he writes for the great future. But they who desire to know the inner and hidden history of those great affairs will turn from his page and seek it in a humble source. Perchance by such the following correspondence would not be despised as leading to a clearer view of individual experiences within the lines of two great hostile armies:

Headquarters, First Brigade, Provisional Division, 14th Army Corps
June 19, 1865

Mr. James Marks, Lynchburg, Va.:
It is with great pleasure that I attempt in this way to find out and open communication with you, whom I consider my friend and benefactor. Your name is associated with a chapter in my life which combines at once more pain and pleasure than any other, I refer to my experiences at the Battle of Gettysburg. In that battle I was severely wounded during the afternoon of the 1st of July. I shortly after fell into the hands of the Confederate forces and became their prisoner. Some artillerymen carried me out of the way of their guns and laid me, together with a wounded comrade and friend, in the corner of a fence. Here we were visited by a number of persons, most of whom came, or seemed to come, out of mere curiosity. At length a cavalryman rode up to where we lay and inquired about our injuries. He stooped over my dying friend and offered him all the means of relief in his power. He proposed to get an ambulance to convey us from the field and a surgeon to dress our wounds. He ministered with his own hands to our comfort, and ordered those who stood idly by to do the same. He wore the Confederate gray, but beneath it beat a heart as manly and humane as ever throbbed.

He revisited us again and again, and after the sun had set upon the bloody field and my poor comrade, with the damp upon his brow, had fallen into that sleep "which knows no waking," he brought a surgeon to attend me and a carriage to bear me to a place of comfort and safety. The carriage was drawn by some citizens whom he, the cavalryman, had induced to volunteer for that kind of office. He saw me lifted to the seat, and then spoke these

---

[207] A poem by Oliver Wendell Holmes written in tribute to Admiral David Farragut in 1865.

words. "Sir, I have done for you what I would expect you to do for me under like circumstances. I may someday fall into your hands as you have fallen into mine." Surprised at such noble kindness, I asked, "What is your rank?" "A private," was the reply. "I thought you were an officer, but that makes no difference. I shall remember you to the latest day of my life." "Thank you," said he, "and if you wish to know my name, it is James Marks, of Lynchburg, Virginia. Farewell." That name and address I have not forgotten. They will remain in my memory forever. Around them clusters a brightness which sheds luster over all the dark and bloody pages of the past.

The great war is now over, and I trust that you have been no less fortunate than I in escaping its perils. The authority of the general government is everywhere restored and the starry flag for which we fought now floats in its wonted splendor wherever Americans have rights to be protected or wrongs to be redressed. Cannot you unite with me under that flag, and as you are my friend and benefactor, become my fellow citizen also? Let the bitterness and passion of the past sink under the sway of uprising reason, and let all Americans North, South, everywhere, strike hands as friends under the flag and government of their fathers.

With feelings of most grateful regard, I am most truly yours,
A.E. Lee

Lynchburg, Virginia
July 3, 1865

Dear Sir:

Your letter of the 19th of June has just reached me and it occasioned me no little thought as to who the writer was. Going from the post office to my room, I began to think who there could be in that far off country who was likely to write to me after four years of silence and suffering. I could recall no one, and therefore opened your letter, never believing for one moment that it was from one who had been battling against me for so long. But after reading it and seeing so much sympathy expressed therein, I am inclined to think that perhaps our fate as Rebels will not be so unjust if left to those who have been fighting against us.

The incident referred to by you at the bloody battle of Gettysburg and for which you thank me, is scarcely remembered by me. It was ever my custom through the whole of the bloody war which had just closed so disastrously for us, to render any assistance I could to a fellow man though he were an enemy. For this I claim no thanks. A common humanity, which is supposed to exist in the breasts of all men, dictates such a course and he is indeed a brute who would not do as I have done.

You, dear friend, entirely over-estimate the kindness I was privileged to do for you. If, on the battlefield, I gave you one moment's cheer or comfort, by one kind word or look, or relieved you of suffering in any manner, I am happy for it. It is indeed pleasant to know that a deed of the past is remembered by a stranger with pleasant reflections, yet it will have accomplished more if it shall have taught one who, no doubt, regarded us as Negro drivers and savages, that feelings of the tenderest humanity exist in Southern hearts.

The war, as you say, is now over- that is, the fighting part of it- and the stars and stripes, that proud emblem of American liberty which has always floated so triumphantly, is again hoisted on Southern soil and floats by Southern breezes, while our once proud and defiant stars and bars is now trailing in the dust, never to be reclaimed I hope, for as long as we are back under the old flag there let us remain until driven away by meanness and cruelty.

Although this war ended very differently from what I desired, yet I can join you, since there is no longer any hope of Southern independence and nothing left me but the noble steed which bore me to your rescue. I escaped uninjured. It is sad indeed to think of the thousands who are lying yet in misery all over our land. A great many homes have been desolated and ruined by the ruthless hands of war.

Well my friend, there is nothing else to write but to say, with all my heart, God bless you. I shall always be ready to reply to any communication from you, and although we have fought each other with a right good will for four long, bloody years, there is no reason why we should not now shake hands, and with the Constitution and the laws begin anew the battle for freedom.
I am very respectfully,
James O. Marks

"And why may not, now that the war clouds have rolled away, join each other as freemen under the banner of the Republic? Why may not all, sharing equally the privileges of our free Constitution, unite in a common brotherhood and fight together against the world the "great battle for freedom?" The fighting part of the war being over, let the war of prejudice cease also. Let the bitter feelings and passions of the past be buried, let all men be elevated to the same broad platform of equal rights, let all earnestly renew their devotion to the great cause of liberty and justice, and the time will soon come when the great magnanimous North will not receive the unjust accusation of meanness and when the valorous South will not provoke such epithets as Negro drivers and savages.

On last year's blossoming graves, with summer calm,
Loud in his happy tangle hums the bee;
Nature forgets her hurt and finds her balm,
Alas, and why not we?[208]

---

[208] From a poem entitled "Peace" by Massachusetts poet and writer Harriett Prescott Spofford.

History of the 82nd Ohio Volunteer Infantry
By Whitelaw Reid

The 82nd was composed of men from the counties of Logan, Richland, Ashland, Union, and Marion. Recruiting began on the November 5, 1861. The regiment rendezvoused at Kenton, Ohio and was mustered into service on the December 31, 1861 with an aggregate of 986 men.

On January 25, 1862, the regiment moved for western Virginia. It crossed the Ohio River at Benwood and on the 27th arrived at Grafton. On the 28th it went into camp near the village of Fetterman where a regular system of instruction was instituted. On March 16, 1862, the 82nd was assigned to General Schenk's command. It was transported by railroad from Grafton to New Creek and from there it marched to Moorefield, arriving on March 23rd. The regiment was ordered by General Schenk to explore the Lost River region and to capture, if possible, a noted guerilla named Harness; but Harness made his escape. The 82nd moved with Schenk's brigade up the South Branch Valley and on May 3, 1862 crossed the Potomac at Petersburg. Franklin was reached on the 5th. Here the troops halted two days and then moved in the direction of Monterey. On the 6th, a courier arrived with information that Stonewall Jackson was threatening the force under Milroy. Schenk hastened to his relief and by noon the next day joined the troops under Milroy near McDowell. The Rebels were posted on Bull Pasture Mountain and were well sheltered by natural obstacles. At 3 P.M., the National troops moved to the assault and the fight continued until dark. During the night, the troops under Schenk and Milroy withdrew and arrived at Franklin on the 10th. The Rebel army followed but did not molest the retreat. On the 12th the enemy moved apparently to attack the lines at Franklin. He threw out his skirmishers but these were repulsed and on the night of the 13th the Rebels retired.

Schenk's brigade left Franklin with the army under Fremont on May 25, 1862. On the 26th it passed through Petersburg where knapsacks and all other baggage which could not be carried on the person were left. On the 29th the Potomac was crossed near Moorefield and the next day the troops entered the defiles of Branch Mountain. On June 1, the advance of the army became engaged near Strasburg. Schenk's brigade hastened forward and deployed, but a tremendous storm put an end to the battle. During the night the Rebels under Jackson withdrew. The pursuit commenced at early dawn and many Rebels who had given out on the march were captured. The column passed through Woodstock and Harrisonburg and on the 8th fought the Battle of Cross Keys. Schenk's brigade, though in season and participating but little in the actual fighting, was exposed throughout the battle to the enemy's artillery and musketry. The next day the Rebels were in retreat and the National army in pursuit; but the destruction of the bridge over the Shenandoah stopped the chase. The troops moved back through New Market, Mount Jackson, and Strasburg to Middletown where General Sigel took command of the army.

In the organization of the Army of Virginia under General Pope, Sigel's command was denominated the First Corps and the 82nd was assigned to an independent brigade under Milroy. Severe campaigning had fearfully thinned the regiment's ranks and it now mustered only about 300 men and additions to the sick list were made daily. On the night of August 7, Sigel's corps moved toward Culpeper and on the following morning halted in the woods south of the village. At 7 P.M., the corps moved toward Cedar Mountain where fighting has been going on nearly all day. It arrived in the field at 10 P.M. and Milroy's brigade moved to the front and relieved a portion of the exhausted forces. The troops remained under arms all night. On the 9th there was some skirmishing but no general engagement and on the night of the 10th the Rebels retreated. In the pursuit, Milroy's brigade led the advance of Sigel's corps. On the 11th the brigade crossed Robertson's River and went into camp on the south bank.

On August 15, the Army of Virginia began to withdraw from Robertson's River. Milroy's brigade covered the movement. On the 16th Sigel's corps arrived at Warrenton Sulphur Springs; but on the next day it reversed its course and marched southward along the left bank of the Rappahannock River to Rappahannock Station. Here the two armies met on opposite banks of the river. Sigel's corps was at the front constantly and on the 18th participated in a sharp skirmish at Freeman's Ford. For ten successive days, Milroy's brigade was within hearing and most of the time under fire of the enemy's guns. On the 21st, Sigel's corps moved northward, hugging closely to the river.

Milroy's brigade was charged with the defense of Waterloo Bridge. The Rebels made a persistent effort to gain the bridge but with no avail. The destruction of the bridge was ordered finally and the work was entrusted to the 82nd. A select party dashed forward under a brisk fire, ignited the timbers, and in a few moments the work of destruction was complete.

On the evening of the 27th, McDowell engaged the enemy in a short but severe conflict five miles east of Gainesville. Sigel's corps hastened to his assistance but darkness prevented a general engagement. At early dawn the next morning, the battle opened and Milroy's brigade was pushed forward to reconnoiter the enemy's line. At 9 A.M., Sigel's corps began a general advance. Milroy's brigade proceeded the main body in battle order. The 82nd and 3rd West Virginia were deployed and supported by the other regiments of the brigade in column. The Rebel skirmishers were driven back through a dense timber to their main force which was posted behind a railroad embankment. When within a few yards of the embankment some of the troops sprang from behind it and crying 'Don't fire on your friends,' threw down their arms and while at the same time the remainder of the force opened a heavy volley. The ruse did not have its expected effect. The firing was returned vigorously. The 82nd pressed forward and commenced scaling the embankment, a portion of the regiment passing it through an opening for a culvert. Just at this moment a large force of Rebels appeared on the regiment's right flank. The 82nd was now unsupported and it was necessary to change front in order to repel the new attack. The movement was executed successfully, under a galling crossfire, but during the evolution Colonel Cantwell fell from his horse dead with the words of command and encouragement upon his lips. The brigade had already retired and the regiment under orders from Milroy now withdrew. Under the personal direction of General Milroy, the 82nd (now consisting of only a handful of men) was reformed and assigned to the support of a battery. The advancing Rebels were met resolutely and repulsed and an opportunity afforded for the regiment and battery to retire to a safe position. In this engagement the 82nd lost heavily. At dawn on the 30th it was in line and by 2 P.M. it had advanced to the position so fiercely contested the day before. At 4 P.M., the Rebels massed in front of McDowell's corps and a portion of Sigel's corps, including Milroy's brigade, was sent to his assistance. The brigade was in position in time to receive the enemy's advance. The formation was slightly concave with the 82nd being in the center. The Rebels advanced repeatedly but were driven back and Milroy's brigade maintained its position. The fighting ceased when night came on, and under cover of darkness, the National army withdrew to Centreville.

On September 3, 1862, Sigel's corps arrived at Fairfax Courthouse. Here the 82nd was detailed as provost guard for the corps and was attached to General Sigel's headquarters. On September 9, Sigel moved his headquarters to Fort De Kalb. The corps about this time, by orders from the War Department, was denominated the XI Corps and assigned to the Army of the Potomac. On the 25th the corps advanced back to Fairfax Courthouse and on November 4th it moved to Gainesville; but on the 18th it was again withdrawn to Fairfax. Here the corps remained until General Burnside's advance on Fredericksburg, when it marched to join the Army of the Potomac at that point. On December 17, General Sigel established his headquarters at Stafford Courthouse and the corps went into winter quarters, the campaign having closed with the attempted capture of the heights of Fredericksburg. General Howard succeeded General Sigel in commanding of the XI Corps and at the request of Colonel Robinson, the 82nd was relieved from duty at headquarters and was ordered to report to its division commander General Schurz. By him it was designated as a battalion of sharpshooters for the division and was not assigned to any brigade but was held subject to his personal direction.

The XI Corps broke camp at Stafford on April 27, 1863 and moved in the Chancellorsville campaign. It crossed the Rappahannock at Kelly's Ford and the Rapidan at Ely's Mills; and on the evening of the 30th it halted within three miles of Chancellorsville. At 9 A.M. on the following day, the corps took up a defensive position and began to entrench. When the battle opened on the afternoon of the 2nd, the regiment stood to arms and awaited the orders of General Schurz. By his direction it was deployed with fixed bayonets to repel the attack. It was ordered very soon to fall back to the rifle pits. The movement was executed in good order. The men moved steadily into the entrenchments and opened a rapid fire upon the advancing foe. Disorganized bodies of troops were falling back though the 82nd and the regiment was left unsupported. The enemy swept around the flanks of the 82nd but the regiment stood to its post until retreat or capture became inevitable. The order was reluctantly given and the regiment fell back in good order; and when the new position was reached 134 men were with the colors. It remained in this position until ordered by General Howard to retire to Chancellorsville. On the morning of May 3, the XI Corps was transferred to the extreme left of the army and was charged with the defense of the approaches to the river and the pontoons. The regiment was on duty in the trenches of the picket line until the morning of the 7th when the army commenced to retire; and at 7 P.M. the 82nd reached its old camp near Stafford.

The regiment was assigned to the Second Brigade of the Third Division and was engaged in ordinary camp duties until June 10, when it moved on the Gettysburg campaign. The XI corps marched by way of Catlett's, Manassas Junction, Centreville, Goose Creek, Edward's Ferry, Middletown, and Frederick to Emmettsburg where it arrived on the 29th. On July 1, the march was resumed and at 12 noon the corps came in sight of Gettysburg. Without any halt, the troops were formed in order of battle and the 82nd was placed in support of a battery. In about an hour, the battery was withdrawn and the regiment prepared to join in a general advance. It moved over an open plain swept by the Rebel artillery and before the regiment fired a shot it lost 20 men killed and wounded. The gaps were filled promptly and the 82nd advanced to within 75 yards of the Rebel lines. The Rebels were in force in overwhelming numbers and the 82nd was compelled to retire. It was assigned a position near the entrance of the now famous Gettysburg cemetery. It went into this action with 22 commissioned officers and 236 men; and of these 19 officers and 147 men were killed, wounded, and captured, leaving only three officers and 89 men. This little band brought off the colors safely. It was not engaged during the remainder of the battle.

On the evening of July 5, the XI Corps in pursuit of the rebels, passing through Emmettsburg, Middletown, Boonsboro, and Sharpsburg to within a few miles of Hagerstown where it arrived on the 11th. At this point the 82nd was assigned to a new brigade which was denominated the First Brigade of the Third Division. The brigade was commanded by General Tyndale. The XI Corps continued the pursuit as far as Warrenton Junction and soon after arriving there the Third Division was assigned to the duty of guarding the Orange and Alexandria Railroad. The 82nd was ordered to Catlett's Station and there it performed very arduous guard and patrol duty until September 25, when the XI Corps left Catlett's Station to join the Army of the Cumberland.

On October 1, 1863, Tyndale's brigade arrived at Bridgeport, Alabama. On the 3rd it crossed the Tennessee River and was engaged in patrolling the adjacent country. On the 27th the XI Corps under Hooker moved up the left bank of the Tennessee and on afternoon of the next day, as the column emerged from the defiles of Raccoon Mountain, it drew the fire from a Rebel battery on Lookout Mountain. After a lively skirmish the Rebel outposts were driven in and by 5 o'clock the troops were encamped quietly in Lookout Valley. About 10 P.M. firing was heard in the rear and it was found that Longstreet had occupied Wauhatchie Heights and descended into the valley. Detachments were at once sent out from the XI Corps and Tyndale's brigade was directed to recaptured Wauhatchie Heights. The brigade moved out on the double quick and upon reaching the point where the assault was to be made, the 82nd deployed two companies as skirmishers and the remainder of the regiment supporting them, led the advance up the steep and rugged slope and drove the Rebels from the summit without difficulty. The position thus gained was held by the 11th Corps until November 22 when the corps moved down the valley, crossed the Tennessee twice, passed through Chattanooga and bivouacked under the guns of Battery Wood. The corps was held in reserve during the engagement at Orchard Knob but it moved up under a heavy fire from the batteries on Mission Ridge to the left of the XVI Corps and assisted in the skirmishing which followed the engagement and in building the entrenchments. On the 25th the XI Corps marched to join Sherman's forces. The movement was completed by 10 P.M. Sherman was still engaged on Mission Ridge and the XI Corps was ordered to support the assaulting column. The Third Division took position on the southern face of the ridge and there proceeded to entrench. A party from the different regiments of the First Brigade reconnoitered the front and drove in the enemy's flankers. By night, the entrenchments were complete and the position secure. The XI Corps moved in pursuit of Bragg's army as it fell back from Chattanooga to within seven miles of Ringgold. From this point an expedition was sent from the corps to destroy the railroad connecting Cleveland and Dalton. The enterprise was entirely successful.

On November 28, the corps moved to the relief of Knoxville. When it arrived near the town of Louisville only 18 miles from Knoxville, a courier arrived from General Burnside with the information that Longstreet had raised the siege. Then commenced the return march; and after many hardships the troops half-naked and half-starved arrived at their old encampments in Lookout Valley on December 17th. The 82nd had scarcely recovered from the effects of the Knoxville campaign when it declared anew its devotion to the country by veteranizing. Out of 349 enlisted men present, 321 were mustered into the service as veteran volunteers on January 1, 1864. On the 10th of the same month the regiment started to Ohio on veteran furlough. It arrived at Columbus on the 21st and was furloughed for 30 days from the 24th. I rendezvoused on the 23rd of February with 200 recruits. It started for the front on the 26th and on March 3, 1864 joined its brigade at Bridgeport, Alabama.

The XI and XII Corps were consolidated forming the XX and the 82nd was assigned to the Third Brigade of the First Division of this corps. On the 30th of April marching orders were received and the regiment entered upon the Atlanta campaign. It marched by way of Whitesides, Lookout Valley, Gordon's Mills, Grove Church, Nickajack Gap and Snake Creek Gap to Resaca. Toward evening on May 14th, the XX Corps under Hooker was shifted to the left in order to envelop the enemy's right. Robinson's brigade (the Third) of Williams' division (the First) reached the Dalton Road just as a division of the Fourth Corps was being forced back in great confusion. Robinson's brigade at once charged and drove back the Rebels in gallant style. The 82nd participated in the charge but sustained little loss as the enemy was too much surprised and embarrassed to fire effectively. On the next day Butterfield's and Geary's divisions advanced and captured the enemy's first line. Williams' division was then thrown forward and took position on the left with Robinson's brigade on the left of the division, constituting the extreme left of the army. The flank 'hung in the air' and being without breastworks was much exposed. The enemy seeing this, moved two divisions into position for an attack. Robinson's brigade was posted behind a low rise of ground with an open field in front. The enemy charged gallantly across the open space and advanced within 50 yards of Robinson's position, but a terrible fire forced him to retire. In 20 minutes the enemy renewed the attack but with the same result; he again advanced and again was forced back with fearful slaughter. Throughout the engagement, the 82nd held an important position but had a slight advantage in being protected by a breastwork. It lost one officer killed. Darkness ended the conflict and during the night parties were employed caring for the Rebel wounded.

The Rebels withdrew by night and in the morning the National army started in pursuit and on the evening of the 19th the enemy was found in position near Cassville. The enemy evacuated without a battle and the National army was allowed a few days to rest. One the 23rd the march was resumed. Hooker's Corps crossed the Etowah River and marched by way of Stilesboro to Burnt Hickory. On the 25th while the three divisions of the XX Corps were advancing by different roads, General Geary encountered the enemy on a high wooded ridge four miles northeast of Dallas. Williams' division, which had arrived within three miles of Dallas by another road, at once about-faced and marched to the support of Geary. Upon arriving it was determined to attack the Rebels and Williams' division was formed in column of brigade with Robinson's in front. At the sound of the bugle the column advanced and fire was opened immediately. The troops moved with great steadiness and in almost perfect order, sometimes, even in the midst of firing, halting for a moment and dressing the line. General Hooker accompanied the column and turning to Colonel Robinson said, 'Your movement is splendid, Colonel-splendid.' The 82nd held the center of the line and behaved with conspicuous gallantry. After advancing about half a mile, Robinson's brigade was relieved and Ruger's brigade took the lead. General Ruger advanced within 200 yards of the Rebel parapet and maintained his position until the ammunition failed, and then Robinson's brigade again moved to the front. The brigade was exposed to a severe canister fire and by sunset almost every cartridge was gone. The cartridge boxes of the dead and wounded were searched and a straggling fire was kept up until night when Robinson's brigade was relieved.

During the 26th and 27th Williams' division was in reserve. About midnight on the 27th, Robinson's brigade was detailed to escort a supply train for ammunition to Kingston and back. This duty was performed successfully. On June 1st the army began to move toward the left. On 6th Robinson's brigade arrived at a position near Pine Knob where it remained until the 15th when the line was advanced about two miles and to within a stone's throw of the Rebel parapet. The enemy was forced back upon Kennesaw and in the operations around that place Robinson's brigade was held in reserve and only engaged the enemy in skirmishes. After the evacuation of Kennesaw the XX Corps went into position near Nickajack Gap. The corps crossed the Chattahoochee River at Pace's Ferry on July 17 and pressed forward towards Atlanta. On the 20th it crossed Peachtree Creek and found the Rebels in their works four miles from Atlanta. About 10 A.M. the Rebels made a determined attack. Williams hurried his brigades into position. While Robinson's brigade was forming, it received a volley which would have disconcerted any but veteran troops. The 82nd was the second regiment in position and it was hardly formed before the Rebels were upon it. The combatants became mingled with each other and for some time the issue seemed doubtful; but at last the Rebels were forced to yield. In this engagement the 82nd lost not less than 75 killed and wounded. Lieutenant Colonel Thomson was struck by a bullet but it was turned aside by a pen knife in his pocket and inflicted only a slight wound.

During the siege of Atlanta the 82nd held an important and exposed position on a hill adjoining Marietta Street. It was within range of both artillery and musketry and on one occasion a cannon shot carried away the regimental colors and tore them to shreds. On the night of August 25th the XX Corps withdrew from the entrenchments and before daylight it was fortifying a new position along the Chattahoochee. At this point General Slocum assumed command of the corps. The rest of the army in the meantime moved southward. During the night of September 1st loud explosions and a bright light were seen in the direction of Atlanta. Early on the next morning a reconnoitering party was sent toward Atlanta. About noon the 82nd joined another party moving in the same direction. The city was found evacuated. The entire corps moved up and the regiment went into camp in the suburbs near Peachtree Street.

The regiment remained in camp at Atlanta engaged in work on the fortifications and occasionally moving on a foraging expedition until November 15 when it started with Sherman's army for Savannah. The 82nd met with nothing worthy of particular note until the 25th when Wheeler's cavalry was encountered at Buffalo Creek. One company from the 82nd Ohio with one company from the 31st Wisconsin was sent forward to dislodge the enemy. The work was well done. Wheeler was forced from his position and driven back about a mile. Robinson's brigade was on the front line about Savannah for a time, but it was moved to the rear and was formed facing outward in order to cover the trains. Here it remained until the city was occupied by the National army.

On January 17, 1865, the Third Division, commanded since leaving Atlanta by General Nathaniel J. Jackson, crossed the Savannah and on the 19th arrived at Purrysburg, South Carolina. Here the command was detained by high water until the 27th when the march was resumed and on the 29th Robertsville was reached. Here again the column was delayed until the 2nd of February when communications were abandoned and the march through the Carolinas commenced. The 82nd performed its full share of marching, foraging, and corduroying. Upon one occasion three 'bummers' from the 82nd with only a carbine unexpectedly encountered a Rebel patrol of twelve cavalry fully equipped; the bummers put on a bold front calling out "Forward boys, here they are," started for the rebels who betook themselves to flight. A swamp impeded their progress and accordingly they dismounted and fled on foot, leaving their horses and equipment to the bummers.

On February 18 the XX Corps crossed the Saluda four miles above Columbia; Broad River was crossed near Alston on the 20th and one the 21st Winnsboro' was reached. One the 23rd Wateree River was crossed near Rocky Mount post office and on the 27th some foragers from the 82nd captured at Lancaster a beautiful silk banner inscribed on one side 'Our cause is just; We will defend it with our lives;' and upon the other 'Presented by the ladies to the Lancaster Invincibles.' The march was continued by way of Chesterfield and Cheraw and on March 11th the XX Corps reached Fayetteville. On the 14th the march was resumed up the left bank of the Cape Fear River and on the 16th the enemy was encountered three miles below Averysboro. Robinson's brigade arrived on the field about 10 A.M. The Rebels were gradually forced back and toward evening they occupied a fortified line at the junction of the roads leading to Averysboro and Bentonville. Here they made an obstinate stand and held position until nightfall when they withdrew. In this affair the 82nd lost two officers and eight men wounded.

On the 18th the column crossed Black River and advanced 12 miles toward Cox's Bridge. At 10 A.M. on the 19th cannonading was heard in front and at 1 P.M. orders were received for the troops in the rear to hasten to the front. As soon as Robinson's brigade arrived it was thrown forward to fill the vacancy in Carlin's division of the XIV Corps. The men were without entrenching tools but with their hatchets they at once commenced building a breastwork. Skirmishers were thrown out and an effort made to gain possession of some buildings, but the skirmishers were driven back by a murderous fire and the enemy moved forward to the attack. The assault was made on Carlin's left and in five minutes all the troops to the left of Robinson's brigade were swept away, and the enemy was coming down upon the flank in irresistible masses. The brigade immediately changed front but it was now enveloped both on front and flank and orders were given to withdraw. The line was reformed and again Robinson's brigade was enveloped on front and flank but with the aid of the artillery, the Rebels were repulsed. No less than six assaults were made on this line during the afternoon and every time the enemy was repulsed handsomely. The firing ceased shortly after nightfall and Robinson's brigade was relieved and permitted to drop to the rear. The next day the enemy was content to assume the defensive and on the 21st he retired. In the Battle of Bentonville, the 82nd lost two officers and nine men wounded and 14 missing.

The whole army now turned towards Goldsboro where it arrived on March 24, 1865. On April 9th and while still at Goldsboro, the 82nd and 61st Ohio were consolidated. The new regiment was denominated the 82nd and a few surplus officers were mustered out. On the 10th the troops were moved to Raleigh where they remained until after the surrender of Johnston's army. On April 30th, the corps marched for Washington City by way of Richmond and on May 19th arrived at Alexandria. The regiment participated in the Grand Review in Washington on May 24th and then went into camp near Fort Lincoln. When the XX Corps was dissolved, the 82nd was assigned to a provisional division which was attached to the XIV Corps. On June 15th the corps moved to Louisville, Kentucky. At Parkersburg the troops embarked on transports. Upon reaching Cincinnati the boats carrying Robinson's brigade, of which the 82nd was still a part, stopped a short time and General Hooker came down to the wharf. He was greeted enthusiastically by his old soldiers and in return made a brief speech. On arriving at Louisville the regiment went into camp on Speed's plantation five miles south of the city. Here it remained until July 25th when it proceeded to Columbus, Ohio where it was paid and discharged on the 29th.

A SAD CODA

Alfred Emory Lee lived through extraordinary times, and left an extraordinary record of his experiences to enlighten future generations of the sublimity and pathos of the Civil War. One would hope that after the traumatic experience of four years of war, Lee's final years would be pleasurable ones, but the final twist of his story ends with a somber note. Captain Lee remained active in Ohio politics into the 1890s and in 1894 married Ada M. (Mitchell) Granbery of Piqua, Ohio, settling into semi-retired life having achieved significant financial success during his busy career in newspapers and politics. In 1901, Captain Lee moved to California and began life as a gentleman orange grower, moving into a Queen Anne style home on Clifton Avenue in Redlands, California, joining many other wealthy Easterners who moved to Redlands to enjoy the fine climate. Lee joined the Fortnightly Club, a literary society, and presented a paper in 1903 detailing his experiences at Gettysburg.

It was at this time, however, that the signs of general paresis started to strongly manifest themselves. The following article from the *San Bernadino County Sun* of April 2, 1903 tells the sad story:

Alfred E. Lee, formerly a United States consul-general in Germany, and a man of prominence in Redlands, was adjudged insane yesterday and today will be taken to the State Hospital in Highland. His case is one that calls for compassion. The cause of his mania is not apparent, but his mental faculties are wrecked, probably beyond repair. Even now, with disordered brain, he discusses with ease subjects of the day, giving rational opinions on National politics and affairs of state. But while in the midst of some clever argument, his mind will wander and his mania come into evidence. His mania of wealth, for he believes that he is possessed of a fortune that would rival that of any millionaire in the country. And yet, he tells all the weird tales of his vast fortune in a realistic and commonplace manner. Previous to being taken into custody he walked into a newspaper office in Redlands and after shaking hands with the city editor, informed the scribe that he had a "nice little story," though he preferred that it should not be published until the end of the week. The story was that he had purchased Smiley Heights, that he intended to erect in Redlands an Opera House to cost $200,000, and that on the crest of the Heights he would establish the most magnificent hostlery in southern California. He discussed the plans of the proposed buildings, even going into details, but it was all the weird wanderings of a diseased mind.

Another one of his weird fancies was that he would purchase all the property and buildings in San Bernardino county, and later in southern California, that he would run a string of colored lights across the valley from the top of the highest mountain peak on the north to the to the highest peak in the mountains on the south; that from Smiley Heights he would run a string of lights to the top of Old Baldy and have various streamers running from these two main lines, so as to illuminate the whole valley.

One other evidence of his mania was to destroy books and papers in his possession. Many of these he had burned and many of the documents thus destroyed were of immense value. He had collected them while in diplomatic circles and they embraced a library that money alone could not buy.

The charge of insanity was placed against Lee by his aged wife, Mrs. Ada M. Lee. She sat in court yesterday while the examination of her husband was being held, and she told of his irrationalities, but it was a painful ordeal for her, and one not craved. The husband, with his mind as it is, cannot realize that the action taken by his wife is the best thing that could be done for him and he threatens to sue her for a divorce, thus making the burden for her even harder than it otherwise would be.

The examination of Lee was the first to be held in this county under the new insanity law, passed by the last Legislature. Lee was represented in court by counsel, but his dementia was so apparent that the attorney made no attempt to secure the release of the unfortunate man. The examination was conducted by Drs. Huff and Dickey. Judge Oster presided. After the examination Lee was taken to the County Hospital, where he will be held until taken to the State Hospital this morning.

Alfred Emory Lee in 1892

The historic Alfred E. Lee home in Redlands, California; at the time the home was built it was surrounded by orange groves. While living in the home, Captain Lee began to suffer from hallucinations including seeing dragons inhabiting his orange groves. The state judged him to be insane, and he spent the last two years of his life in the state mental hospital. Captain Lee is buried at Hillsides Cemetery in Redlands but no stone marks the gravesite.

11th Corps Headquarters Flag

SOURCES

Articles:

"Our First Battle: Bull Pasture Mountain," *Magazine of American History*, Vol. XV, January-June 1886, pgs. 391-396

"The Battle of Cross Keys," *Magazine of American History*, Vol. XV, January-June 1886, pgs. 483-491

"Battles of Port Republic and Lewiston," *Magazine of American History*, Vol. XV, January-June 1886, pgs. 590-595

"Cedar Mountain I," *Magazine of American History*, Vol. XVI, July 1886, pgs. 81-88

"Cedar Mountain II," *Magazine of American History*, Vol. XVI, August 1886, pgs. 159-167

""From Cedar Mountain to Chantilly I," *Magazine of American History*, Vol. XVI, September 1886, pgs. 266-282

"From Cedar Mountain to Chantilly II," *Magazine of American History*, Vol. XVI, October 1886, pgs. 370-386

"From Cedar Mountain to Chantilly III," *Magazine of American History*, Vol. XVI, November 1886, pgs. 467-482

"From Cedar Mountain to Chantilly IV," *Magazine of American History*, Vol. XVI, December 1886, pgs. 574-585

Alfred E. Lee Letters: (*some are listed under his proper name, the majority under nom-de-plume A.T. Sechand*)
Delaware Gazette (42 letters): November 28, 1862, pg. 2; December 19, 1862, pg. 2; January 2, 1863, pg. 1; March 6, 1863, pg. 1; May 22, 1863, pg. 2; November 27, 1863, pg. 1; January 15, 1864, pg. 1; February 26, 1864, pg. 1; March 25, 1864, pg. 1; April 22, 1864, pg. 1; May 13, 1864, pg. 1; June 10, 1864, pg. 1; July 8, 1864, pgs. 1-2; July 15, 1864, pg. 1; July 29, 1864 pg. 1; August 5, 1864, pg. 1; August 12, 1864, pg. 1; August 19, 1864, pg. 1; September 2, 1864, pg. 1; September 16, 1864, pg. 1; September 23, 1864, pg. 1; September 30, 1864, pg. 1; November 4, 1864, pgs. 1-2; November 11, 1864, pg. 1; November 18, 1864, pg. 2; January 13, 1865, pg. 1, January 20, 1865, pg. 1; January 27, 1865, pg. 1; February 3, 1865, pg. 1; February 10, 1865, pg. 1; February 24, 1865, pg. 1; April 14, 1865, pg. 1; April 21, 1865, pg. 1; April 28, 1865, pg. 1; May 19, 1865, pg. 1; May 26, 1865, pg. 1; June 9, 1865, pg. 1, August 18, 1865, pg. 1

Books:

Becker, Carl M. and Ritchie Thomas, editors. <u>Hearth and Knapsack: The Ladley Letters, 1857-1880</u>. Athens: Ohio University Press, 1988

Davis, Burke. <u>Sherman's March</u>. New York: Vintage Books, 1988

Castel, Albert. <u>Decision in the West: The Atlanta Campaign of 1864</u>. Lawrence: University of Kansas Press, 1992

Catton, Bruce. <u>Glory Road: The Army of the Potomac</u>. Garden City: Doubleday & Co., 1952

Century Co. <u>Battles and Leaders of the Civil War, Vol. 3</u>. New York: The Century Co., 1888

Cox, Jacob D. <u>Sherman's Battle for Atlanta</u>. New York: Da Capo Press, 1994

Cozzens, Peter, editor. <u>Battle and Leaders of the Civil War, Vol. 6</u>. Urbana: University of Illinois Press, 2004

Cozzens, Peter. <u>General John Pope: A Life for the Nation</u>. Urbana: University of Illinois Press, 2000

Cozzens, Peter. <u>Shenandoah 1862: Stonewall Jackson's Valley Campaign</u>. Chapel Hill: University of North Carolina Press, 2008

Engle, Stephen D. <u>Yankee Dutchman: The Life of Franz Sigel</u>. Baton Rouge: University of Louisiana Press, 1993

Hennessey, John J. <u>Return to Bull Run: The Campaign and Battle of Second Manassas</u>. New York: Touchstone Books, 1993

Hebert, Walter H. <u>Fighting Joe Hooker</u>. Lincoln: University of Nebraska Press, 1999

Howard, Oliver Otis. <u>Autobiography of Oliver Otis Howard, Major General United States Army</u>. New York: The Baker & Taylor Company, 1907

Lamers, William M. <u>The Edge of Glory: A Biography of General William S. Rosecrans</u>. Baton Rouge: Louisiana State University Press, 1961

Lee, Alfred Emory. <u>The Battle of Gettysburg</u>. Columbus: A.H. Smythe, 1888

Lee, Alfred Emory. <u>The History of the City of Columbus. Volumes I and II</u>. New York: Munsell & Company, 1892

McLaughlin, John. <u>A Memoir of Hector Tyndale.</u> Philadelphia: Collins Printer, 1882

Reid, Whitelaw. <u>Ohio In the War: Her Statesmen, Generals, and Soldiers, Volumes I and II</u>. Cincinnati: Robert Clarke Company, 1895

Schurz, Carl. <u>Reminiscences of Carl Schurz</u>. Volumes 2 and 3. New York: Doubleday, Page, and Company, 1917

Swinton, William. <u>Campaigns of the Army of the Potomac</u>. Secaucus: Blue & Grey Press, 1988

United States. War Department. Department of the Army Department of the Interior Navy Department War Office. <u>The War Of the Rebellion: A Compilation of the Official Records of the Union and Confederate Armies</u>. Washington :[s.n.], 1894.

Newspapers:
Ashland Union (Ohio)
Clearfield Republican (Pennsylvania)
Confederate Veteran
Delaware Gazette (Ohio)
Hardin County Republican (Ohio)
Highland Recorder (Ohio)
Jeffersonian Democrat (Chardon, Ohio)
National Tribune
New York Daily Tribune
New York Herald
Portage County Democrat (Ohio)
Richmond Dispatch (Virginia)
St. Clairsville Gazette (Ohio)
Sandusky Commercial Register (Ohio)
Stark County Republican (Ohio)
Tiffin Tribune (Ohio)
Tuscarawas Advocate (Ohio)
Wooster Republican (Ohio)

Manuscripts and Other Materials:
Biography of James McAlpin. http://library.armstrong.edu/McAlpin%20James%20Wallace.pdf

Military Service Record of Alfred E. Lee, Form 86, National Archives and Records Administration.

Newspaper articles of the 154th New York Volunteer Infantry, New York State Military Museum and Veterans' Center

Index

31st Wisconsin Volunteer Infantry (168, 207, 209-210, 229-230, 233, 237)

Confederate Military Units:
18th Alabama Infantry (140)
38th Alabama Infantry (140, 142)
46th Alabama Infantry (119, 172)
4th Georgia Infantry (93)
12th Georgia Infantry (10)
44th Georgia Infantry (108)
28th Georgia Artillery Battalion (230)
4th Texas Infantry (72)
23rd Virginia Infantry (10)
25th Virginia Infantry (10)
44th Virginia Infantry (10)
48th Virginia Infantry (19)
Charlottesville (VA) Artillery (110)